CW00430317

The Origin and Evolution of China's Names I

This is the first volume of a two-volume set on the names of China, focusing on the country's official titles throughout history.

Using interdisciplinary approaches from fields such as history, geography, ethnic studies, linguistics, psychology and toponymy, this two-volume set examines the origin and evolution of China's names over more than 4,000 years of history. The first volume examines the official names of the country given by the rulers or government, including the names of the imperial dynasties, from the earliest Xia to the last Qing, and the title of the Republic of China, which symbolises a new era in national naming. The author examines the common features as well as the cultural contexts and historical traditions that underlie these diverse titles. The origins and meanings of national titles, their secondary connotations, evolving understandings and related implications are explored. The book also analyses the lifespan and spatial references of these national titles.

This book will appeal to both academic and general readers interested in Chinese history, Chinese historical geography and Chinese toponymy.

HU A-Xiang is Professor and Ph.D. supervisor at the School of History, Nanjing University, China. His primary research interests lie in Chinese history, Chinese historical geography, and Chinese toponomy.

China Perspectives

The *China Perspectives* series focuses on translating and publishing works by leading Chinese scholars, writing about both global topics and China-related themes. It covers Humanities & Social Sciences, Education, Media and Psychology, as well as many interdisciplinary themes.

This is the first time any of these books have been published in English for international readers. The series aims to put forward a Chinese perspective, give insights into cutting-edge academic thinking in China, and inspire researchers globally.

To submit proposals, please contact the Taylor & Francis Publisher for China Publishing Programme, Lian Sun (Lian.Sun@informa.com).

Titles in history currently include:

Sino-Foreign Cultural Exchange
A Historical Perspective
Cai Hongsheng

A Study of Chinese Characters
Wang Guiyuan

A Study of Excavated Documents in China
Wang Guiyuan

The Origin and Evolution of China's Names I
The Reigning Dynasties
HU A-Xiang

The Origin and Evolution of China's Names II
Domestic and Foreign Appellations
HU A-Xiang

For more information, please visit www.routledge.com/China-Perspectives/book-series/CPH

The Origin and Evolution of China's Names I

The Reigning Dynasties

HU A-Xiang

Routledge
Taylor & Francis Group

LONDON AND NEW YORK

First published in English 2025
by Routledge
4 Park Square, Milton Park, Abingdon, Oxon OX14 4RN

and by Routledge
605 Third Avenue, New York, NY 10158

Routledge is an imprint of the Taylor & Francis Group, an informa business

© 2025 HU A-Xiang

Translated by Ye Danmin

The right of HU A-Xiang to be identified as author of this work has been asserted in accordance with sections 77 and 78 of the Copyright, Designs and Patents Act 1988.

All rights reserved. No part of this book may be reprinted or reproduced or utilised in any form or by any electronic, mechanical, or other means, now known or hereafter invented, including photocopying and recording, or in any information storage or retrieval system, without permission in writing from the publishers.

Trademark notice: Product or corporate names may be trademarks or registered trademarks, and are used only for identification and explanation without intent to infringe.

English version by permission of Jiangsu People's Publishing House.

British Library Cataloguing-in-Publication Data
A catalogue record for this book is available from the British Library

Library of Congress Cataloging-in-Publication Data
Names: Hu, Axiang, 1963– author.
Title: The origin and evolution of China's names / HU A-Xiang ; translated by Ye Danmin.
Other titles: Wu guo yu wu ming. English.
Description: Abingdon, Oxon ; New York, NY : Routledge, 2025. |
Series: China perspectives | Includes bibliographical references and index. |
Contents: v. 1. The Reigning Dynasties – v. 2. Domestic and Foreign Appellations. |
Identifiers: LCCN 2024023948 (print) | LCCN 2024023949 (ebook) |
ISBN 9781032815817 (v. 1 ; hardback) | ISBN 9781032836416 (v. 1 ; paperback) |
ISBN 9781032834801 (v. 2 ; hardback) | ISBN 9781032836454 (v. 2 ; paperback) |
ISBN 9781032834795 (hardback) | ISBN 9781032836409 (paperback) |
ISBN 9781003510390 (v. 1 ; ebook) | ISBN 9781003510413 (v. 2 ; ebook) |
Subjects: LCSH: China–Name–History. | Names, Chinese–History. |
Names, Personal–Chinese. | Royal houses–China. | Clans–China.
Classification: LCC DS706 .H796413 2025 (print) | LCC DS706 (ebook)
DDC 929.9/7–dc23/eng/20240621
LC record available at https://lccn.loc.gov/2024023948
LC ebook record available at https://lccn.loc.gov/2024023949

ISBN: 978-1-032-81581-7 (hbk)
ISBN: 978-1-032-83641-6 (pbk)
ISBN: 978-1-003-51039-0 (ebk)

DOI: 10.4324/9781003510390

Typeset in Times New Roman
by Newgen Publishing UK

This book is published with support from the Jiangsu Scholars Translation Program.

Contents

List of Figures   *vii*

Introduction: Titles of the Reigning Dynasties since
Ancient Times   1

1 Xia: "Residing High and Drinking Dew"   4

2 Shang: "The Heavenly Commissioned Dark Bird Descends
   and Gives Birth to Shang"   19

3 Zhou: Emphasizing Agriculture   32

4 Qin: The Cattail (Forage Grass) for Raising Horses   44

5 Han: "The Name 'Tianhan' (Milky Way) is Magnificent"   58

6 Xin: "Complying with the Heavenly Mandate"   76

7 Wei, Han and Wu: The Three Divisions of the Country   91

8 Jin: The "Well-known Ambition" of Sima Zhao   102

9 The Sixteen Kingdoms and the Southern and Northern
   Dynasties: Turmoil, Rise and Fall   110

10 Sui: Auspicious or Ominous?   114

11 Tang: Emperor Shen Yao's Aspirations and Self-Assessment   123

12 Zhou: The "Ancient Ancestor Ji Zhou" of the "Empress
     of the Holy Mother"   141

13 Five Dynasties and Ten Kingdoms: Inheritance and Division   154

14 Song: Moments of Serendipity   165

15 The Great Yuan: How Grand is the Primal Beginning
     of Creativity   178

16 The Great Ming: "In the Radiant Light of the Buddhas"   189

17 The Great Qing: Turning the Tide   205

18 The Republic of China: A New Era of National Titles   221

     References   *230*
     Index   *250*

Figures

1.1	Cicada	10
1.2	A jade cicada unearthed from the tomb of the King of Chu in the Western Han Dynasty in Xuzhou, Jiangsu Province.	12
2.1	On July 13, 2006, the Yin ruins in Anyang was inscribed on the World Heritage List	28
3.1	Millet (grass grain)	37
3.2	Ji Wang Temple in Jishan, Shanxi Province	38
4.1	Specimen of high-quality forage grass Phleum pratense in the Poaceae family	48
4.2	High-quality forage grass Phleum pratense in the Poaceae family	49
5.1	A blue and white porcelain plum vase depicting Xiao He's pursuit of Han Xin under the moon, unearthed from the tomb of the Mu family in the Ming Dynasty in Nanjing.	65
5.2	Scenery of the Upper Han River	69
5.3	Ancient Chinese star map mural, with the Milky Way in the middle	70
7.1	The author of this book is in front of the tomb of Emperor Zhao of Han (Liu Bei) in Chengdu	97
8.1	Statue of Shu Yu at the Jin Shrine in Taiyuan, Shanxi	105
11.1	The tomb of the couple Chen Yinke and Tang Yun in Lushan Botanical Garden	126
11.2	Image of Emperor Yao	131
11.3	Portrait of Li Yuan	135
11.4	The stone tiger at the Mausoleum Xian of Li Yuan, Emperor Gaozu of the Tang Dynasty	136
12.1	The Temple of the Holy Mother of Empress Wu in Wenshui, Shanxi	144
12.2	The Luohan Buddha in the Fengxian Temple of the Longmen Grottoes in Luoyang, believed to be the incarnate form of Emperor Wu Zhao	150
14.1	The place where Zhao Kuangyin donned the yellow robe at Chenqiao Relay Station	168

14.2   Yanbo Terrace in Shangqiu   172
15.1   The statue of Mongolian cavalry at the Mausoleum of Genghis
       Khan in Inner Mongolia   179
16.1   Thangka of Amitayus Buddha   196
17.1   The city wall of the earth-based fortress on the Ming Great Wall
       in Huailai, Hebei in 1907   209
18.1   Sun Yat-sen's Former Residence in Zhongshan, Guangdong   224

Introduction

Titles of the Reigning Dynasties since Ancient Times

National titles, as the name suggests, refer to the titles of countries. Throughout China's long and ancient history, every ruler who possessed territory and established political power, whether they founded a small state in a corner of land or a unified country dominating all directions with control over the Central Plains, established a national title at the beginning of their reign.

National titles have always been symbols of sovereignty over the entire nation, gradually becoming representations of the Mandate of Heaven, numerical signifiers, and symbols revered by the people. They even became symbols of the country's political and cultural identity.

The concept of national titles emerged with the formation of nation-states. The "Records of the Grand Historian–Annals of the Five Emperors" states, "From the Yellow Emperor to Shun and Yu, they shared the same surname but had different national titles to highlight their virtues." According to the research of many modern scholars, it was in the lower and middle reaches of the Yellow River, in the 21st century BC, that Yu, the leader of a tribal alliance, eventually passed his position to his son Qi. Thus, the tradition of tribal leaders electing the leader of tribal alliances transformed into a hereditary monarchy, where the position was passed down to descendants following the death of their fathers and brothers. This marked the transition from a society "governing everything under heaven" to an era of a "peaceful and prosperous" world, a concept akin to "our country as our home." The state established by Qi, which used "Xia" as its national title, was the first in Chinese history to integrate the roles of ruler, family, and country, marking the first credible national title in Chinese history.

The system of hereditary kingship (Xia, Shang, Zhou) or imperial sovereignty (Qin, Han, Yuan, Ming, Qing, and so forth.) persisted and then gradually declined over more than 4,000 years of Chinese history. During this period, numerous national titles appeared. According to the continuity of a specific imperial clan, traditional Chinese historiography refers to a period as a dynasty or generation. Each dynasty or generation usually shared the same national title. A change in national title generally signified the transfer of state ruling power, commonly known as a "dynastic transition." These transitions took various forms, including external military conquests, peaceful abdications within the ruling family, or division and

DOI: 10.4324/9781003510390-1

contention, eventually leading to the establishment of a single ruler. Therefore, a national title represents a family's ruling power over the nation. The succession of different national titles reflects the succession of different imperial clans. The rise of a new national title while the previous one remains in use indicates the establishment of a new state and the emergence of a new imperial clan within or beyond the boundaries of the existing nation.

The imperial family in China came to an end in 1912 with the establishment of the Republic of China, symbolized by the "Last Emperor," Puyi of the Aisin Gioro clan. Both the Republic of China and its successor, the People's Republic of China, are distinct nations in their own right. However, whether it is the Republic of China or the People's Republic of China, the governmental structure of class rule retains its national title. The eventual disappearance of national titles will coincide with the demise of the state. The obsolescence of the state and its national title, however, remains as unpredictable as the distant history of the state's formation and the emergence of national titles.

In this vast historical expanse—from the emergence of the "Xia" title in the 21st century BC to the prosperous and formidable "People's Republic of China" in the 21st century AD—within the territorial confines of the Qing Dynasty from 1759 to 1840, an expanse that spans modern-day China, areas east of Lake Balkhash, and the Pamir Plateau as well as regions south of the Greater Khingan and encompassing the Mongolian Plateau, various states were formed. These entities were established by the Han Chinese—who are predecessors of today's majority Han ethnic group—and by non-Han and non-Huaxia ethnic groups. National titles employed across these regions were diverse and numerous. It's an incontrovertible historical reality that these states differed notably in terms of territorial ambit, duration, status, and impact. Correspondingly, the national titles, their spatial designation, and the period of their utilization displayed significant variation. As for their status and influence, this also varied widely.

These national titles, despite each possessing unique characteristics, exhibit several commonalities. The origins and significances of national titles stem from particular rationales, cultural contexts, and historical traditions. Even national titles that are inherited or bear similarities possess distinct meanings and specific underpinnings. Hence, this volume underscores the importance of delving into the origins and significations of national titles, addressing their principal meanings, secondary connotations, evolving interpretations, and related implications. Additionally, it offers analyses on the lifespan and spatial references of the national titles under discussion.

This volume's research centers on national titles, considering their status and impact. While some topics receive a detailed examination, others are mentioned in passing. The basis for thorough scrutiny versus cursory mention is as follows:

Firstly, there is a detailed analysis of national titles that pertains to the so-called "Central Plains Dynasties" as these are acknowledged in traditional Chinese historiography. In the annals of Chinese history, dynasties established by the Han Chinese are termed "Central Plains Dynasties" or "Central Empires." Even when a non-Han ethnic group founds a dynasty that becomes highly Sinicized, and is chiefly located in traditional Han areas or governs predominantly Han populations, it is similarly designated as a "Central Plains Dynasty." The Yuan Dynasty, established by the Mongolians, and the Qing Dynasty, founded by the Manchus, are examples of this.

Secondly, the national titles that receive less extensive attention generally encompass regional or autonomous governments formed by border ethnic groups, regional regimes or separatist governments from eras of political fragmentation or pre-national unification, and local regimes that did not align with the "Central Plains Dynasties" or evolve from them. This also includes puppet states and various subordinate or vassal entities under the sway of the "Central Plains Dynasties."

Thirdly, we discuss in detail the following 14 national titles, listed from the oldest to the most recent: Xia, Shang, Zhou, Qin, Han, Xin, Jin, Sui, Tang, later Zhou, Song, Yuan, Ming, and Qing. These titles are recognized as encompassing the entire nation. They represent not just the Central Plains dynasties but also central empires—that is, empires with extensive unification and territory, that attained a dominant national stature in their time. These unified dynasties, despite their eventual decline, are considered to be the orthodox ruling entities and continued to use their respective national titles. They hold a more prestigious position and exert a more lasting influence than other titles. They are quintessential and emblematic of China's national titles, forming the chronological backbone of traditional Chinese historiography and serving as denominations for China during their respective eras.

Fourthly, we touch upon national titles that were prominent during epochs characterized by fragmented rule, wherein no single entity controlled the entire nation. These national titles, invariably, did not reach the level of governing the entire country as a unified power. They are not indicative of an undivided nation. This includes the titles from periods like the Three Kingdoms, the Sixteen Kingdoms, the Southern and Northern Dynasties, the Five Dynasties, and the Ten Kingdoms. While these titles, which total over 40 different names, are significant and influential, they do not fall into the category of titles representing the entire country, such as those of the Liao, Xia, and Jin. For these titles, the volume primarily presents essential historical information and summarily details their origins, including the primary perspectives about their sources and meanings.

Based on these four criteria, this part covers two categories: the extensively discussed and the briefly discussed, together comprising approximately 60 national titles that span the entire historical territory of China over more than 4,000 years. The national titles associated with the Central Plains dynasties represent the most frequently used and well-known national titles in China.

Lastly, it is worth mentioning that though the Republic of China does not belong to the traditional imperial era, it still bears the nature of national titles. Consequently, it is discussed separately in this part as the appendix. The purpose is to bridge the historical trajectory from the past to the present, enabling readers to consider this section as supplementary to the main body of the first part.

1 Xia

"Residing High and Drinking Dew"

In the traditional chronological records of Chinese history, the first reliable dynasty of the Central Plains is the Xia Dynasty. Prior to the Xia Dynasty, it was considered the prehistoric era, with Pangu being the mythical figure responsible for creating the world. There are seven variations of the "Three Sovereigns" and four variations of the "Five Emperors," representing legendary ancient and prehistoric rulers. Regarding these myths and legends, explanations can be sought from historical cultural anthropology, such as the belief that the Five Emperors were leaders of tribal alliances in late primitive society. However, the deeds related to Pangu, the Three Sovereigns, and the Five Emperors in mythological legends cannot be taken as factual accounts. The era of Chinese history entering the period of recorded history can be traced back to the Xia Dynasty.

To this day, we have not come across any written records from the Xia Dynasty, which means the history of the Xia Dynasty is only known through later writings. Nonetheless, various aspects provide evidence that the Xia Dynasty existed before the Shang Dynasty. According to the research findings of the Xia-Shang-Zhou Chronology Project under the "Ninth Five-Year Scientific and Technological Key Project" of the State, the estimated framework of the Xia Dynasty's era is as follows:

> The estimated framework of the Xia Dynasty includes two points: the separation between the Xia and Shang Dynasties and the starting year of the Xia Dynasty. The separation between the Xia and Shang Dynasties has been estimated to be around 1600 BCE. As for the starting year of the Xia Dynasty, it is mainly determined based on the study of historical records related to the annual chronicles of the Xia Dynasty and by considering the results of astronomical calculations and relevant carbon-14 dating data.
>
> Regarding the upper limit of Xia culture, there are mainly two opinions in the academic field: the first phase of the Erlitou culture and the late period of the Longshan culture in Henan province. The confirmation of the remains from the second phase of Xinzhai has closely connected the first phase of the Erlitou culture with the late period of the Longshan culture in Henan. If we trace back 471 years from the starting year of the Shang Dynasty in 1600 BCE, the starting

DOI: 10.4324/9781003510390-2

year of the Xia Dynasty would be approximately 2071 BCE, falling within the second phase of the late period of the Longshan culture in Henan (2132 BCE to 2030 BCE). For now, the starting year of the Xia Dynasty is tentatively set at around 2070 BCE.[1]

The excerpt above reflects the best research achievements of the 20th century. In summary, archaeological evidence has proven the existence of the Xia Dynasty, and the combination of archaeological and literary evidence indicates that the Xia Dynasty existed from approximately 2070 BC to 1600 BC. According to the chronological table provided by the Xia-Shang-Zhou Chronology Project, the Xia Dynasty spanned 17 rulers, starting with Yu (commonly known as Da Yu or Yu the Great) and ending with Jie (commonly known as Xia Jie).[2]

If we consider the Xia Dynasty as the first integrated state that established the triad of ruler, family, and country, it actually began with Qi, the son of Yu. The character "Qi" itself implies the meaning of a founding ancestor.[3] Therefore, the Xia Dynasty should include 13 generations and 16 rulers. And the title used by these 16 rulers, who were the first group of highest rulers in Chinese history, was "Xia."

Since Xia is the first reliable dynasty in Chinese history, the significance of the name "Xia" is evident. However, the origin and meaning of the name "Xia" have been subjects of speculation and debate among historians and commentators throughout history. Various theories have been proposed, including the interpretation of "Xia" as a dynasty of dance (proposed by Xu Hao), waters of Xia (Zhang Binglin), land of Xia (Li Dexian), strange creatures in water (Jiang Liangfu), stone chamber (proposed by Xu Tongxin), frog (Lu Sixian), animals such as female monkeys (Li Xuanbo), wild people (He Guangyue), the bird species "Zhainiao" (Zheng Jiexiang), or the Altai language term Ɣa (which originally means tall and big).[4] This is just a partial list, and the theories are diverse and numerous. Based on previous research, this chapter also attempts to present a hypothesis that "Xia" originally meant cicada, and the name was adopted as the national title because of the positive qualities associated with the cicada.

1.1 Xia Represents Cicada

The name "Xia" is generally believed to have been in use since the time of Yu the Great. According to the annotated edition of 'Annals of Xia' in the *Records of the Grand Historian*, published by Zhonghua Book Company: "All the feudal lords in the world abandoned the Shang Dynasty and pledged allegiance to Yu. Yu then ascended to the throne, facing south and ruling over the whole country. The national name was Xia Hou, and the surname was Si." Zhang Shoujie of the Tang Dynasty, in his *Annotations on the Records of the Grand Historian*, stated that "Xia" was the country name conferred by Emperor Yu. However, there are two issues with the interpretation of the *Annals of Xia* in the original text and the annotated edition by Zhonghua Book Company, as well as Zhang Shoujie's *Annotations*:

Firstly, although Yu came to be known as Xia Yu or King Xia Yu in later times, in the pre-Spring and Autumn Period texts, he was only referred to as Yu without the "Xia" title. The use of "Xia" as the country name began with Qi, which means that it was only after Qi's reign that "Xia" became the national title.[5]

Secondly, saying that "the national name was Xia Hou" is not entirely accurate. Based on the records in classical texts, "Hou" was the earliest royal title in China. In oracle bone inscriptions and bronze inscriptions, the character for Hou (后) initially depicted a woman, and its original meaning referred to the respected mother of the entire clan. In the ancient society where the mother's identity was known but not the father's, the authoritative and leadership role of the matriarch who gave birth to all descendants of the clan was natural, and her title became "Hou." After the matriarchal system transitioned to the patriarchal system, "Hou" became a male title and retained this usage for a considerable period of time until it was replaced by titles such as Emperor and King, used exclusively for male rulers. The character "Hou" also evolved into an honorary title for the female consort of a ruler.[6] In the case of Xia, the highest ruler was called "Hou," while the national name was "Xia." Thus, it is more accurate to interpret the sentence as "the national name was Xia, and the surname of Hou was Si." Here "the surname of Hou" refers to the ruling surname of the royal family.[7]

Then what does "Xia" mean? *Shuo Wen Jie Zi* by Xu Shen of the Eastern Han Dynasty proposed: "Xia (夏) refers to the Chinese people. It consists of the radicals 夂 (suī), 页 (yè), and 臼 (jiu). It represents two hands and two feet, which everyone possesses." In reality, having two hands and two feet is not a unique characteristic of the Chinese people, so Xu Shen's interpretation is based on a superficial analysis and cannot be fully endorsed. However, many scholars have loosely followed Xu's explanation and directly equated "Xia" with China. For example, in the 'Geographical Records' of the *Book of Han*, Yan Shigu of the Tang Dynasty commented: "Xia means China," and this view was also echoed by Li Xian of the same period in his annotations to the 'Biography of Ban Biao' of the *Book of Later Han*, and by Bao Biao of the Southern Song Dynasty in his annotations to the *Strategies of the Warring States*. Xu Hao of the Qing Dynasty stated in his annotations to the *Shuo Wen Jie Zi*: "During the Xia Dynasty, when the barbarians first entered China, they referred to the Chinese people as 'Xia'." This explanation suggests that the name of "Zhong Guo" (China) as a later development but not an original concept since the notion of "Zhong Guo" did not exist during the Xia Dynasty. The name Zhong Guo first appeared during the reign of King Wu of the Western Zhou Dynasty and might have been traced back to the Shang Dynasty.

Furthermore, Lin Huixiang's interpretation in his book *History of the Chinese Nation* suggests that in the *Shuo Wen Jie Zi*, "the primitive ethnic groups often referred to themselves as 'people' ... Therefore, the character 'Xia' in the *Shuo Wen* is without error and is the language used by our clan to refer to ourselves, meaning people."[8] However, this interpretation by Lin is not entirely suitable. In the *Shuo Wen Jie Zi*, the character for "Yi" (夷) is also explained as the people of the east, using the radicals 大 (dà) and 弓 (gōng). Following this logic, "Xia, referring to the Chinese people," should be understood as "people residing in China who are called the people of Xia." The meaning of "China" will not be elaborated on here, but it can be concluded that the original meaning of the character 'Xia' (夏) is definitely not 'people,' which can be reasonably inferred.

So, what was the original meaning of the character Xia (夏)? To clarify the original meaning of Xia, it is better to refer to the earliest form of the character.

In the late 19th and early 20th centuries, a substantial number of oracle bone inscriptions from the Shang Dynasty were discovered in Xiaotun, Anyang, Henan Province. These unprecedented historical materials laid the foundation for new developments in the research of ancient history.

Among these oracle bone inscriptions, a group of characters was found as follows:

美蛾蛾蛾萬夢夢夢夢夢于

According to Ye Yusen's book *Yinxu Shuqi Qianbian Jishuo (Pre-Compilation and Explanation of Yinxu Inscriptions)*, he offers the following explanation for this group of characters:

> In the case of Xia (夏) ... its form is similar to a cicada, with a long body, wings, and legs. It closely resembles a cicada, and it is suspected that the divination term 蝉 (chán, cicada) was borrowed to represent 夏. The cicada is the most prominent summer insect, and hearing its sound is an indicator of the summer season.[9]

Ye Yusen, who passed away in 1934, was regarded as one of the most distinguished scholars in the study of oracle bone inscriptions after Luo Zhenyu and Wang Guowei. His explanation can also be found in Ye's book *Yin Qi Gouchen (Collection of the Lost Materials in Oracle-bone Writing)*, published in 1923. Not only Ye Yusen but also Dong Zuobin (in his *Yin Calendar in Oracle Inscriptions* published in 1931) and Zhu Fangpu (in his *Compilation of Characters in Oracle Bone Inscriptions* published in 1933) argued that the original form of the character '夏' is a cicada (now commonly known as '知了' in Chinese). However, there are scholars who believe these characters represent a cricket, locust, beetle or a turtle with two horns, opposing the cicada theory. It is not surprising to find various interpretations within the field of oracle bone inscriptions.

Personally, I tend to support the cicada theory proposed by Ye, Dong, and Zhu. Compared to the theories suggesting representations of a dance pose, aquatic creatures, stone chambers, frogs, female monkeys, wild humans, and thrush birds, as well as the cricket, locust, beetle, and horned turtle theories, the cicada theory seems more reasonable in both form and meaning.

Firstly, let's discuss the resemblance in form. Many characters in the oracle bone inscriptions of the Shang Dynasty are pictographic. Pictographic characters do not depict the entire object but rather highlight specific parts that signify the object. For instance, the character for "牛" (niú, cow) portrays only the head of a cow, and the character for "羊" (yáng, sheep) depicts just the two horns. By applying this principle, the twelve zodiac animal characters in oracle bone inscriptions can generally be recognized. The cicada is known for its broad head with antennae and its thin, web-like wings. These features are present in the early forms of the character 夏, resembling the side profile of a cicada.[10]

Secondly, the association in meaning. Cicadas are associated with the summer season as they are commonly seen and heard during this time. In the *Liji*, it is stated that "in the fifth month, the cicadas begin chirping." This fifth month refers to midsummer in the lunar calendar. As an emblem of summer, linking the cicada to the concept of summer is logical. Similarly, many scholars contend that in oracle bone inscriptions, the character for "春" (chūn, spring) illustrates young grass, "秋" (qiū, autumn) symbolizes mature crops, and "冬" (dōng, winter) portrays fallen branches and fruits. These characters convey their respective seasons through the depiction of specific phenomena. In this vein, the early form of "夏" in oracle bone inscriptions, with its side profile reminiscent of a cicada, encapsulates the idea of cicadas chirping in summer. This is consistent with the meaning of the character.

Further speculation might lead us to imagine that the formation of the character '夏' predating the Shang Dynasty oracle bone inscriptions would have been even more closely akin to a cicada, as suggested by Tang Lan in *An Introduction to Ancient Chinese Characters*.

During the Shang Dynasty, written characters began to simplify in form. A process that transformed four legs into two and also thick brush strokes into double hooks or thin lines. Objects started being depicted in profile rather than front view to facilitate the continuous writing of texts. These evolutions indicate progress in script development. Additionally, the use of pictographic and ideographic characters decreased, giving way to phonetic characters, a transition likely starting early in the Shang Dynasty, if not several hundred years prior. Before this shift, it is likely there was a period when pictographic characters evolved into ideographic characters.[11]

Tang Lan posits that during the early phases of the Xia Dynasty, there were historical records beyond rudimentary knot-tying or symbol-carving, implying the existence of a more developed written script. Thus, it can be inferred that in the early periods of the Xia Dynasty, the character "夏" (Xia), as the name of the dynasty, would have been frequently used, and its pictographic essence would have been more pronounced, resembling the shape of a cicada. Hopefully, the future discovery of the Xia Dynasty script will confirm this hypothesis.

1.2 Why Qi Chose the Title of Xia

Why did Qi (Emperor Qi) select the character 夏 (Xia), which resembles a cicada, as the national emblem? This decision is thought to be related to the totem worship of Emperor Qi, as suggested by Tian Qianjun in his research on the origins of the terms "Zhong Guo" and "Huaxia."[12] The concept of totem, which originates from the vernacular language of North American Indians meaning "his kindred," denotes religious beliefs among primitive ethnic groups. Cen Jiawu, in *History of Totem Art*, outlines several totemic characteristics:

Firstly, primitive ethnic groups adopt certain animals or plants as their emblems, believing these to be their ancestors or that share a kinship with them. Secondly, there is a reverence for these totemic symbols; members of the group are prohibited from harming or killing their totemic ancestors, with violators facing punishments. Thirdly, members of the same totemic group are viewed as a unified entity, bonded by their common belief in the totem.[13]

An important observation is that primitive ethnic group names often stem from their totems. For instance, Native American tribes exhibit names such as Wolf Tribe, Bear Tribe, and Snake Tribe, based on animals, and others like Corn Tribe or Tobacco Tribe, based on plants. Primitive Chinese ethnic groups followed a similar pattern.

According to the *Shuowen Jiezi*, the Four Branches of Chinese minorities were Qiang, Man, Rong, and Di, all derivatives from different animal totems. The radicals of 羌 (qiang) and 戎 (rong) are both 羊 (sheep); the radical of 蛮 (man) is虫 (worm); the radical of 狄 (di) is 犬 (dog). Another illustration from Lin Huixiang states in this way: "Man, barbarous tribes in the south, worship snakes," while "Min, in the south east of Yue, also worships snake," illustrating their totemic origins.[14]

The ethnic group led by Emperor Qi, the founder of the Xia Dynasty, also revered a totem. The annals of Xia in the *Records of the Grand Historian* recounts that Yu, the Dynasty's founder, was born after his mother, of a snake totemic origin, swallowed a divine pearl and Yiyi seeds. Yu's name, in oracle bone script and bronze inscriptions, features a serpentine form, indicating its derivation from the snake totem. The Yellow Emperor in *Liezi* even describes the Xia's progeny as having snake-like bodies with human faces, underscoring the snake totem's significance.

Yu managed the Great Flood and delineated the Nine Provinces, and during this period, his wife Tushan bore Qi. Qi, Yu's successor and son, was born to a woman of the Tushan clan.[15] The exact site of Tushan elicits various theories: it may lie in Henan, Sichuan, Anhui, Zhejiang, or east of Chongqing. The first theory, placing Tushan south west of Song County, Henan, aligns with the Xia state's initial territory and influence, thus is considered most reasonable.[16] Yu's marriage and alliance with the Tushan clan implies an intimate connection.

Li Zongtang in "*Ancient Chinese Social History*,"[17] concurs with Tian Qianjun that the Tushan clan's totem was the toad, citing linguistic links between 'tu' and 'chú,' indicated in classics such as "*Classic of Mountains and Seas–Classic of the Northern Mountains*" and "*Book of Poetry*–Xiao Ming." The toad, also symbolically associated with the cicada, led to using 蝉 (cicada) as the Xia Dynasty's name, which persisted in later generations.[18]

According to the statement made by Tian Qianjun, there are actually some fatal flaws. Although the characters "蟾" and "蝉" might be confused due to their similar pronunciation,[19] they are fundamentally different animals. Based on today's understanding, "蟾蜍" belongs to the class of amphibians, and the most common type is commonly known as the "toad." Its skin and glands behind the ears secrete toxic substances that can be used in medicine. It has an exceptionally strong resistance to bacteria and a powerful stimulating effect on the cardiovascular system. It is also speculated that the ugly appearance of the toad and its medicinal value may have a certain relationship with Tushan, who regarded the toad as a totem. As for "蝉," it belongs to the class of insects and is commonly known as the "cicada." Its eggs are laid in trees, and the hatched larvae (cicada nymphs) reside in the soil, extracting sap from tree roots. After several years of molting, they finally emerge from the soil, climb onto trees, and shed their final layer of dry, pale-yellow shell. This shed shell is used in medicine to treat conditions such as cold and fever, cough with hoarseness, measles in children, rubella, and epilepsy. Adult cicadas also rely on sap for survival. Cicadas are divided into male and female, with female cicadas laying eggs in trees, which then hatch into nymphs, become cicadas, and lay eggs again. Male cicadas are known for their characteristic chirping. In conclusion, "蟾蜍" refers to the toad and "蝉" refers to the cicada. The two cannot be equated. Tian Qianjun may also be aware of this flaw and tries to make up for it by stating, "In the Xia Dynasty, the '蝉' was taken as a totem," and "using a totem as a dynastic name is a natural evolution." As a result, there are contradictions and inconsistencies in the statement (see Figure 1.1).

In fact, the clan name and the name of a nation are not the same thing. Although in the history of ancient societies, clan names related to totems are frequently seen, and there are also examples in modern ethnographic materials, in higher stages of social development, the name of a nation does not necessarily have to come from a clan name.[20] The choice of a nation's name can be made through various methods. As mentioned earlier, the character "夏" in the oracle bones of the Shang Dynasty originally represented a summer cicada, and in ancient China, scholars held a high regard for cicadas. For example, Cao Zhi's "Ode to Cicadas" includes the following lines:

Figure 1.1 Cicada

The exclusively cleanness and simplicity of cicada are like the moon,
In the midsummer of the blazing sun, it begins to wander in the fragrant forest.
Truly content and low in desires,
Alone filled with joy and continuous singing.
Its sound is clear and resounding, resembling the steadfast heart of a
    virtuous man.
Internally contained and not consuming food,
It is harmonious with all things and seeks nothing.
It perches on tall branches and looks up,
Gently rinsing in the clear flow of morning dew ... [21]

Furthermore, Yu Shinan of the Tang Dynasty wrote in the poem "Cicada:"

Hanging on branches, drinking clear dew,
Flowing sound comes from sparse Paulownia trees.
Residing high, its sound reaches far,
Not relying on autumn wind as a pretext.[22]

Shen Deqian of the Qing Dynasty commented in Volume 19 of his book *A Selection of Tang Poetry*: "Those who praise the cicada always praise its sound, but this poem praises its character alone." In ancient China, there were numerous literary works that featured the cicada as a theme. Scholars liked to compare themselves to cicadas and wore jade cicadas, highlighting the noble character of the cicada. They believed that cicadas "dined on wind and drank dew," and thus remained unaffected by the impurities and deceit of the world, maintaining purity and integrity. Observing the cicada perched high on a tree, its voice carrying far, they aspired to possess such noble spirit and strength, hoping that their own convictions would reach far and be heeded by rulers. These symbolic meanings and aspirations led to the enduring presence of the cicada as an image in ancient Chinese literary works.

Of course, the works and ideas cited above are from a later period. So, what did the cicada symbolize during and around the Xia Dynasty? If we trace back further, we naturally turn our attention to archaeological findings of jade cicadas and cicada patterns. In earlier periods, such as the Hongshan culture in western Liaoning and the Liangzhu culture in southern Jiangnan, jade cicadas had already appeared. This may be related to the people of that time already realizing the mysterious phenomenon of the cicada's continual cycle of transformation from pupa to cicada and back, symbolizing the eternal continuity and resurrection of life. Similarly, during the Shang and Zhou periods, especially among the Zhou people who claimed to be the inheritors of the Xia culture, there were frequent discoveries of jade cicadas, and cicada motifs were widely engraved on ritual bronze vessels such as tripods. The *Jin Shi Suo*, a book by Feng Yunpeng and Feng Yunchuan, explains that the cicada symbolizes "residing in the heights and drinking the pure." In the Han Dynasty, it was common to find jade cicadas in the mouths of the deceased during funeral rituals, which explicitly symbolized the hope of life like the cicada, obtaining rebirth (see Figure 1.2).

Figure 1.2 A jade cicada unearthed from the tomb of the King of Chu in the Western Han
Dynasty in Xuzhou, Jiangsu Province

To sum up, from ancient times, the symbolic meanings of the cicada, such as its ability to transform and be reborn, its transformation from impurity to purity, its habitation in lofty heights and its far-reaching voice, and its preference for drinking dew to maintain purity, gradually became apparent and enriched. Therefore, we can infer that by adopting the shape of a cicada as the national emblem, the Xia Dynasty likely recognized and valued these mysterious and beautiful meanings associated with the cicada. These hidden and beautiful meanings not only reflected the aspirations of Emperor Qi, who hoped for the eternal existence of his country, reminiscent of Emperor Qin Shi Huang's desire for his empire to last for "generations upon generations without end," but also served to highlight the extraordinary political and cultural status of the Xia dynasty in a new sense. After all, which ruler would not desire their country to endure, resonate from great heights, and be heard from afar? Of course, by not using the totems of their own or maternal tribes as the national emblem, Emperor Qi also considered the psychological needs of other tribes belonging to his rule or influenced by it.

1.3 The Derivations of Xia as a National Title

It's interesting that after the character "Xia" became a national title, it progressively acquired various figurative meanings.

In the Eastern Han Dynasty, Wang Chong, in his book *Lunheng*, recorded a conversation between Fei Chang and Feng Yi, where Fei Chang asked, "What constitutes the Yin Dynasty? What constitutes the Xia Dynasty?" Feng Yi responded by saying, "The West represents Xia, and the East represents Yin."[23] In the Spring and Autumn period, the son of the Duke of Chen was named Xia, and the Grand Minister of the State of Zheng was named Xixi. It is known that ancient Chinese people generally followed the principle of "correspondence between name and character" when choosing names. This means that there should be a certain connection between the name and the character, either through synonymous meaning (such as Lu You, whose character Wu means "to observe," which has the same meaning as the name) or through contrasting meaning (such as Han Yu, whose character Tui means "to retreat," which has the opposite meaning to his name). Other principles include association through similar meanings (such as Qu Yuan, whose character Ping means "level," derived from his original surname) or association through similar categories (such as Bai Juyi, whose character Yue means "happy" and Tian means "heaven," implying that he is naturally happy). Sometimes, the name may change from the original name (for example, Du Mu, whose character Mu comes from his original surname). Additionally, some people have the same name as their character (for example, Sima Daozi, whose character Daozi is the same as his name). Hence, the names Xia and Xixi, corresponding to each other, comply with the principle of synonymous meaning or mutual training, indicating that Xia has the meaning of "west." Fan Wenlan also stated that "the western region of China is referred to as Xia." [24]

Why does Xia have the meaning of "west?" This is related to the geographical location of the Xia dynasty. According to historical records, Yu's father, Gun, was conferred the title in Chong (located north of Yi and Luo in present-day Henan). After Yu established his reign, he initially set his capital in Yangcheng (south east of Gaocheng Township, Dongfeng, present-day Dengfeng City, Henan Province). The chapter of "Yi Extension" in the book *Yi Zhou Shu* states, "From Luoruixu to Yirui, it is easy to live there, as there is a residence of Xia." This suggests that the early activities of the Xia dynasty were mainly in the Yi and Luo River valleys and the Song Mountain area in present-day Henan. By the end of the Xia dynasty, *Shi Ji* recorded: "Xia Jie's residence was to the left of the He River and the Ji River, and to the right of the Taihua Mountain. The Yi Pass is to the south, and the Yang Pass is to the north." This suggests that the late Xia dynasty extended east to Zhengzhou, west to Mount Hua, south to the Yi and Luo rivers, and north to Changzhi, roughly spanning the borders of today's Henan, Shanxi, and Shaanxi provinces. Furthermore, in the *Zuo Zhuan*, during Duke Ding's fourth year, it was mentioned that Tang Shu was conferred the title of "Xia Xu," and his fief was in the Fenshui River valley south west of present-day Shanxi. This place was called Xia Xu, indicating that it was the ancient residence of the Xia dynasty.[25] In the 16th century BC, Cheng Tang overthrew Xia Jie and established the Shang dynasty. Considering the Shang Dynasty's territory, the assimilated Xia territory belonged to the "Western Land" among the "Four Lands" mentioned in oracle bone inscriptions. Moreover, from a relative position perspective, the Shang dynasty was established by a people originating from the east, while the Xia dynasty was founded by a people originating from the west. This might explain the meaning of Xia as "west," which was attributed by other eastern ethnic groups, or it may be a clarification provided by the Shang dynasty and subsequent dynasties.

The traditional interpretation suggests that "Xia" has the meaning of elegance and greatness. Fan Wenlan pointed out, "Zongzhou poetry is called 'Ya' poems, while the 'Qin Wind' poems are called 'xia sheng,' which means 'elegant poetry,' singing with a western intonation."[26] At the time, "Xia" and "Ya" had similar pronunciations[27], and Qin was situated in the western region, which was earlier territory of the Zongzhou Dynasty. Therefore, the meaning of "Ya" should have originated from this. Additionally, the *Xunzi* states, "The people of Yue find their peace in Yue, the people of Chu find their peace in Chu, and the noble finds their peace in elegance." It also states, "Lives in Xia and becomes Xia," meaning the noble finds their peace in elegance. The character "Xia" clearly carries the meaning of elegance. However, the character "Ya" is also considered to be based on cultural hierarchy. For example, the Zongzhou poems are called elegant poems, and Liu Taigong in the Qing Dynasty's *Lunyu Pianzhi* believed that "the sound of the capital city is the most correct and elegant."[28] Furthermore, in the *Zuo Zhuan*, during the 29th year of Duke Xiang of Wu, Lord Ji Zha of Wu observed the music in Lu and sang the song "Qin," saying, "This is called 'xia sheng.' If one can embody the greatness of Xia, then greatness will extend to the old territory of Zhou!" Thus, "Xia" could also be interpreted as greatness, implying Xia as a grand and powerful country. In *Er Ya* it states, "Xia signifies greatness." In the Tang Dynasty, Kong Yingda's *Shang Shu Zheng Yi* explains, "Xia signifies greatness. In China, it represents the splendor of literature, etiquette, and righteousness." In the Western Han Dynasty, Yang Xiong's *Fangyan* states, "From Hangu Gate and further west, between Qin and Jin, anything magnificent and great is loved and referred to as 'Xia'." Even in ancient architecture, the character "Xia" (厦) was used to refer to grand and tall buildings. In fact, the character "Xia" in the *Shuowen Jiezi* has evolved to resemble a person with arms crossed and feet spread apart, which occupies a larger space than before. Therefore, in the Qing Dynasty's *Shuo Wen Jie Zi Zhu*, Duan Yucai explains, "Xia has the connotation of expansion and greatness." He Xin further elaborates, "The character 'Xia' has a broad semantic meaning in ancient Chinese and metaphorically signifies the leader. The use of the character 'Xia' to refer to the ruling class is, in my opinion, the origin of the name Xia."[29]

According to the transition from "Xia" to "Yda," it signifies the considerable stature and profound influence of the Xia culture. *Guoyu* mentions: "In ancient times, our former sovereigns succeeded Yu of Xia," illustrating that the Zhou Dynasty,[30] rooted in the ethnic group from the western region, saw themselves as successors of the Xia culture. In the *Book of Han*, a county named Daxia within Longxi Commandery is referenced, along with the Daxia River (originally called the Guangtong River, which flowed east into the Tao River, not to be confused with the present-day Daxia River). The names of the Fen and Hui River basins were also referred to as Daxia in ancient documents. Place names such as Xiakou and Xiayang also attest to the significant influence of Xia culture.

The distinct status and influence of Xia culture are derived from its grandeur. Indeed, as the China's first hereditary state that evolved from a tribal society, Xia was a formidable nation, especially when compared to the numerous regional states and tribes in its vicinity. The character 大 "da" (meaning big or great) has always been associated with majesty, symbolizing something remarkable, as reflected in phrases like "Great is Confucius" and "Only Heaven is great." Over time, owing to the refinement and potency of Xia's culture, the terms "elegance" and "greatness" became associated with Xia. To sum up, elegance and greatness are connotative meanings which evolved later; they were not the original designations of Xia.

Furthermore, with Xia's assimilation to "da" (great), and considering "da" is a pictogram representing a person in ancient Chinese characters, Xia took on a new connotation of "people." Its representation shifted to resemble a human figure with two arms and two legs. This can be seen in Xu Shen's *Shuowen Jiezi* and Lin Huixiang's explanation of "Xia as a person," indicating the evolution of character 夏. Nonetheless, as per research by scholars of ancient Chinese linguistics, such as Dong Zuobin, the character transformation of Xia began in the Zhou Dynasty's bronze inscriptions (like those on the Vessel Gui of Qin Gong), and during the Shang Dynasty's oracle bone script, Xia was depicted as a cicada. This reinforces the understanding that the original semantics of Xia pertained to "cicada," then changed its form to that of a "person" according to the connotation of "greatness."

1.4 National Titles: Reflections of the Era

The Xia Dynasty feels so distant today! As the cradle of Chinese civilization, almost everything concerning the Xia Dynasty is shrouded in vagueness and obscurity, including its national title, "Xia." Historical records do not provide a standardized answer regarding the process of establishing the national title and its underlying meaning. Even future archaeological excavations might fail to offer a definitive answer to this particular question.

This ambiguity is not exclusive to the ancient Xia Dynasty. Spanning from the Xia to more recent dynasties such as the Ming and Qing, the processes by which national titles were established and their significances are seldom documented. The genesis and importance of most national titles are enveloped in mystery and can seem baffling. However, does this uncertainty render the discussion of national titles a futile endeavor? Absolutely not!

Despite the obstacles of interpreting through the depths of time and space, the historical context, the society of the era, and the predominant ideology can serve as beacons, guiding an exploration of the genesis of national titles and uncovering their origins and meanings. Much like personal names, national titles generally mirror the zeitgeist. The *Debates of the White Tiger Hall* from the Eastern Han Dynasty articulates: "Upon receiving the mandate, a ruler should establish an auspicious national title to manifest their accomplishments. The Xia, Yin, and Zhou Dynasties all had majestic national titles. Since every emperor governed the realm, they sought a distinct national title to distinguish themselves from their predecessors and to broadcast their achievements and merits." This tradition of "manifesting accomplishments" and "broadcasting merits" offers us a pathway to examine national titles. In essence, through the lens of the period, we can deduce the establishment and nuances of national titles. Nonetheless, the "knowledge" acquired through such deductions can only aspire to approximate the "truth," never solidifying into an absolute "conclusion."

For instance, by inferring from the above the earliest verifiable national title in Chinese history, "Xia," we may glean an understanding that nears the "truth" without constituting an immutable "conclusion." Firstly, the selection of national titles is often complicated, and the origins and meanings of national titles must be carefully differentiated between their original implications and the later derived meanings. Secondly, the final choice of "Xia" as a national title is linked to the hidden depths and attractive connotations symbolized by cicadas, such as immortality, a lofty existence, far-reaching songs, and purity and grace. Therefore, embracing profound implications and appealing connotations as national titles became a conventional practice in successive eras of Chinese history.

Notes

1 The Xia-Shang-Zhou Chronology Project Expert Group, The Xia-Shang-Zhou Chronology Project, 1996–2000 Phase Achievements Report - Abridged Version, World Book Publishing Company, Beijing, 2000.
2 The Xia-Shang-Zhou Chronology Project Expert Group, "Summary" of the "Xia-Shang-Zhou Chronological Table" from the "Xia-Shang-Zhou Chronology Project, 1996–2000 Phase Achievements Report–Abridged Version."
3 In Fu Sinian's "The Eastern Yi and Western Xia Theory" (included in the Collected Papers of the Institute of Historical Linguistics, Volume I, an external compilation celebrating Mr. Cai Yuanpei's 65th birthday, 1933), it is mentioned, "The character 'Qi' (启) originally carried the meaning of 'founder', but during the Han Dynasty, to avoid the taboo of Emperor Jing's name, it was changed to 'Kai'(开), indicating the interpretation of the character 'Qi' ... We now establish a chronological order for the Xia period, and to exclude those related to Yu, we should use the character Qi as the cutoff point."
4 Zhang Binglin, "Interpretation to the Republic of China," Min Bao Magazine, 15th issue, July 1907; Li Dexian, "Speculative Claims about 'Huaxia'," Commentary Collections of Chinese Historical Geography, 2nd volume, 1985; He Guangyue, The Source of History of the Xia Dynasty, Chapter 1, Section 2, Jiangxi Education Publishing House, 1992; Zheng Jiexiang, A Preliminary Exploration to the History of the Xia Dynasty, Chapter 1, Section 2, Zhongzhou Ancient Books Publishing House, 1988; Tang Shanchun, The Mystery Culture of China, Chapter 1, Section 1, Hohai University Press, 1992.
5 Zhang Binglin, in his article "Interpretation to the Republic of China," states, "Regarding the phrase 'barbarians' invasion of the Central Plains, the 'Classics of Emperors' already contains such text, indicating that it did not originate in the Xia Dynasty." Although the character Xia appears in the "Classic of Emperor Shun" of the *Shang Shu*, it has been determined that the "Classics" is a pseudo-text of the "Ancient Texts of Shang Shu," and its composition occurred long after the Xia Dynasty.

6 He Xin, The Origins of Gods: Ancient Chinese Mythology and History, Chapter 7, Sanlian Bookstore, 1986.

7 In the 'Annals of Emperor Gong' of the *Book of Jin*, written by Fang Xuanling and other scholars of the Tang Dynasty, it is mentioned, "In his youth, the Emperor had quite an impatient temperament. When he was in the vassal state, he once ordered skilled archers to shoot horses for amusement. Later, someone said, 'Horses belong to the clan, and yet they are being killed. This is extremely ominous.' The Emperor understood and deeply regretted it." The surname of the royal family refers to the family name of the highest ruler of a country, such as Liu for the Han Dynasty and Zhu for the Ming Dynasty. During the Jin Dynasty, the surname of the royal family was Sima.

8 Lin Huixiang, in "A History of Chinese Ethnicities," Chapter 3, published by Commercial Press in 1936.

9 Ye Yusen, Pre-Compilation and Explanation of Yinxu Inscriptions, Volume 2, page 5, Shanghai Dadong Bookstore, 1934.

10 From the perspective of pictograms, although there are also interpretations for crickets, locusts, and beetles, their explanatory power is far inferior to that of cicadas. For a detailed discussion, please refer to the following section.

11 Tang Lan, An Introduction to Ancient Chinese Characters (Revised Edition), Volume 1, Part 2, Qilu Book Society, 1981.

12 Tian Qianjun, The Search for the Origins of the Terms 'Zhong Guo' and 'Huaxia', Continental Magazine, Volume 31, Issue 1, 1966.

13 Cen Jiawu, A History of Totem Art, Chapter 1, Xuelin Publishing House, 1986.

14 Lin Huixiang, A History of Chinese Ethnicities, Chapter 3.

15 Regarding the specific process of Yu passing the throne to Qi, various pre-Qin, Qin, and Han texts have conflicting records. However, one common point is that Yu's son Qi eventually succeeded him, marking a transformation from "governing the world publicly" to "governing the world as a family."

16 The claim that Tushan's current location is in Song County is discussed in detail in the works of Lu Simian, in Chapter 7 of Pre-Qin History, published by Kaiming Bookstore in 1941; Gu Jiegang, The Relationship Between Ancient Bashu and the Central Plains and Its Critique, Volume 1, Journal of Chinese Cultural Studies, September 1941; and Ma Shizhi, A Study and Identification of the View of Tushan Mountain, Journal of Historical Studies, March 1986.

17 Li Zongtong, A History of Ancient Chinese Society, Volume 1, the Committee of Chinese Culture Publishing Business, Taipei, 1954.

18 Tian Qianjun, The Search for the Origins of the Terms 'Zhongguo' and 'Huaxia.'

19 In poems such as "Ancient Bright Moonlight" by poet Li Bai of the Tang Dynasty, containing the line "The toad eats away the round shadow, the Great Ming night has already waned," and "Inscription on Xuwu Temple Pond" by Li Zhong of the Southern Tang Dynasty, with the lines "Night approaches, fond of cicadas and toads, steps light with an insatiable heart," the term "toad" refers to the moon. This usage relates to the legend of Chang'e, who fled to the moon and transformed into a toad. As recounted by Tang Dynasty writer Xu Jian in Volume 1 of "Records of Initial Learning" and as quoted from the ancient Western Han Dynasty text "Huainanzi": "Yi requested the elixir of immortality from the Queen Mother of the West. His wife, Chang'e, stole it and fled to the moon, taking the form of a toad and becoming a moon spirit." The "moon spirit" is thus associated with the toad. Additionally, the rabbit became symbolically linked to the moon during the Han Dynasty, but in the Jin Dynasty, the toad was omitted, and only the

rabbit was noted. Over time, the myth of the Jade Rabbit on the moon gained prominence and became the dominant lunar symbol.

20 Initially, "Xia" was not a clan name but came to be associated with a particular ethnic group after they established the Xia Dynasty. Consequently, this ethnic group was referred to as "Xia."

21 Yan Kejun cited and edited "Complete Works of Literature from the Three Ancient Dynasties to Qin, Han, Three Kingdoms, and Six Dynasties: Complete Works of the Three Kingdoms," Volume 14, Zhonghua Book Company, 1958. Individual articles cited in this work can also be found in the "Complete Works of Literature from the Three Ancient Dynasties to Qin, Han, Three Kingdoms, and Six Dynasties" and "Complete Tang Poems" (edited by Dong Gao et al., Zhonghua Book Company, 1983), usually without detailed footnotes to avoid cumbersomeness.

22 "Complete Tang Poems (Revised and Expanded Edition)," Volume 1, Volume 36, compiled by Peng Dingqiu and edited by the Editorial Department of Zhonghua Book Company, 1999 edition, features poems found in "Poetry from Pre-Qin, Han, Wei, Jin, and Northern and Southern Dynasties" (edited by Lu Qinli, Zhonghua Book Company, 1983), "Complete Tang Poems," and other well-known works, generally without detailed footnotes to maintain brevity.

23 Zheng Wen's "An Analysis and Explanation of Lunheng" includes Appendix 2, titled "Lost Texts of Lunheng," and was published by the Bashu Book Society in 1999.

24 Fan Wenlan, A Concise Compilation of Chinese General History (Revised Edition), Volume 1, Chapter 4, Section 5, People's Publishing House, 1955.

25 For further reference, see Chen Huaiquan's "Great Xia and Great Yuan," included in "Collected Works of Chinese Historical Geography," Volume 1, 1993.

26 Fan Wenlan, A Concise Compilation of Chinese General History (Revised Edition), Volume 1, Chapter 4, Section 5.

27 See Sun Zuoyun, Remarks on Elegance, Journal of Literature, History, and Philosophy, Volume 1, 1957.

28 "Selected Readings in Chinese Historical Linguistics" by Hong Cheng includes an appendix titled "Excerpts from Collated Branches of the Analects (Explanations of Elegant Language)," Jiangsu People's Publishing House, 1982 edition.

29 He Xin, The Origins of the Gods: Ancient Chinese Mythology and History, Chapter 10.

30 The origins and initial territorial roots of the Xia, Shang, and Zhou ethnic groups are exceedingly complex topics. Generally, the Xia originated in the west and gradually migrated eastward, the Shang emerged in the east and moved westward, and the Zhou, hailing from the west, shifted eastward. Throughout their migrations, these groups overlapped and influenced one another.

2 Shang

"The Heavenly Commissioned Dark Bird Descends and Gives Birth to Shang"

In the 16th century BC, King Tang defeated King Jie and brought an end to the Xia Dynasty, thereby establishing the second major dynasty in Chinese history–the Shang Dynasty. Prior to King Tang's reign, the Shang lineage traced back 13 generations, beginning with Qi, who is venerated as the founder of the Shang clan. According to legend, Qi supported Yu the Great in managing floodwaters. During the span from Qi to King Tang, the Shang lineage observed the Xia Dynasty rise and flourish, and ultimately became the power that terminated it. From King Tang to King Zhou, the Shang Dynasty was ruled by a total of 31 kings over 17 generations, covering roughly 500 years. The "Chronology Project of the Xia, Shang, and Zhou Dynasties" posits that the Shang period lasted from 1600 BC to 1046 BC.[1] However, these dates are based on traditional chronology and are subject to academic discussion but are not unanimously agreed upon.

Since 1899, the unearthing of numerous oracle bone inscriptions at the Yin ruins in Anyang, Henan, along with the discovery of bronze artifacts bearing inscriptions, and the remains of palaces, workshops, and tombs at various locations, has firmly placed the Shang Dynasty as an undeniable element of recorded Chinese history.

Yet, ambiguities still remain concerning the dynastic title of the Shang Dynasty. Interpretations of the word "Xia" vary, and the genesis of the name "Shang" is still under debate. In historical texts, the term "Shang" frequently appears alongside "Yin," and sometimes they are jointly referred to as "Yin Shang." The distinction between "Yin" and "Shang," as well as their interrelationship, represents foundational inquiries for any discussion regarding the Shang Dynasty's designation.

2.1 Shang and Yin: The Unclear Entanglement

During the Western Han Dynasty, the great historian Sima Qian wrote the comprehensive *Historical Records of China* which included separate Benji (biographic sketches of emperors) for the Xia, Shang, and Zhou dynasties. However, the names used are intriguing. The "Benji of Yin" follows the "Benji of Xia" but precedes the "Benji of Zhou." Qi (契), the founder of the Shang clan is referred to as the "Qi of Yin" at the beginning of the "Benji of Yin," which is similar to the "Qi (启) of Xia" in the "Benji of Xia" and the " Hou Ji (后稷) of Zhou" in the "Benji of Zhou." This

DOI: 10.4324/9781003510390-3

placement indicates that Sima Qian used the "Benji of Yin" to record both the early Shang history and the entire Shang Dynasty.

Before Sima Qian, the prominent Confucian scholars Confucius (Kong Qiu) and Mencius (Meng Ke) both exclusively used the term "Yin" in their works such as "the Analects," "Mencius," "the Great Learning," and "the Doctrine of the Mean."[2] However, after Sima Qian, possibly influenced by Confucius, Mencius, and Sima Qian, Han Yu, a renowned literary scholar from the Tang Dynasty who played a significant role in the study of Confucian classics, consistently referred to the Shang Dynasty as "Yin."

In contrast, during the Song Dynasty, there was a general preference for using the term "Shang." Even in previously written texts that used "Yin," the term was changed back to "Shang." Works such as Fan Zuyu's "*Tang Mirror*," Zheng Qiao's "*General Summary*," and Ye Shi's "*Notes on Learning*" all use "Shang." Neo-Confucian scholar Zhu Xi, in his annotations to the Four Books, intentionally avoided using the term "Yin" and replaced it with "Shang" throughout his annotations, except for two instances where "Yin" remained unchanged: "Learning the Rituals of Yin" and "I am capable of speaking about the rituals of Yin." In all other cases, "Yin" was uniformly replaced with "Shang."

The obvious reason for changing "Yin" to "Shang" during the Song Dynasty was to avoid the name taboo associated with Zhao Hongyin, the father of the founding emperor of the Song Dynasty, Zhao Kuangyin. Because of this name taboo, people in the Song Dynasty naturally couldn't use the character "Yin" when referring to the Shang Dynasty, like Confucius, Mencius, Sima Qian, and Han Yu did. Since they couldn't use the character "Yin," they had to use the character "Shang," or simply write "Yin" with a missing stroke. According to Chen Yuan's citation,[3] in the Yuan Dynasty, Hu Sanxing's *Commentary on the Zizhi Tongjian* stated: "In the *Book of Mencius*, it only says 'supervise Yin.' Now the *Zizhi Tongjian* says 'supervise Shang,' to avoid the temple name taboo of the Song imperial families."[4] Similarly, Zhai Hao's *Study of the Four Books* states in the chapter "Yin is Derived from the Xia Ritual": "Emperor Gaozong of the Song Dynasty changed the character 'Yin' to 'Shang' to avoid the name taboo of Xuanzu. The classics engraved on stone tablets of the Song Dynasty all use 'Shang,' but in the *Zhongyong*, the 'Yin' in the chapter of ' The rituals of Yin' is missing a stroke."

However, in historical records, the more common occurrence is the mixed use or combined use of "Yin" and "Shang." In ancient texts such as the *Book of Songs* and the *Book of Documents*, the term "Shang" is mentioned six times, while the term "Yin" is mentioned once. In the "Kanggao" and "Jiugao," the term "Shang" is mentioned once, while "Yin" is mentioned seven times. In the "Duoshi," the term "Shang" is mentioned twice, while "Yin" is mentioned twelve times. In the "Junshi," the term "Shang" is mentioned once, while "Yin" is mentioned eight times. In the "Biming," the term "Shang" is mentioned once, while "Yin" is mentioned four times. In the "Duofang," the term "Shang" is mentioned once, while "Yin" is mentioned three times. In the "Zuo Zhuan," both "Shang" and "Yin" are mentioned at different times. As for the combined use of "Yin" and "Shang," the "*Book of*

Songs–Da Ya" has multiple instances, such as "from there, Yin and Shang," "the journey of Yin and Shang," and "consulting you about Yin and Shang," with a total of seventeen
occurrences.[5]

Therefore, when looking at the surviving pre-Qin literature to modern works, the use of "Shang," "Yin," or the combination "Shang Yin," and even "Shang Yin" can be seen as quite arbitrary, without any consistent pattern.[6] However, names are not insignificant, especially when it comes to the name of a nation. When the country was founded, the national name had to be unique. The question is, does this uniqueness belong to "Shang" or "Yin?" Here, let's first consider the different viewpoints as expressed by various scholars.

1. The traditional view in history suggests that during the reign of Tang, the country was called Shang. It was renamed Yin after the capital was moved during the reign of Pan Geng. For chapter "Odes to Shang" of the *Book of Songs*, Zheng Xuan, a scholar from the Eastern Han Dynasty, explained, "Shang refers to the land granted to Qi." Similarly, Kong Yingda, a scholar from the Tang Dynasty, commented, "Shang was the grand title from the time of Cheng Tang, and it refers to the land granted to Qi." Zheng Xuan considers the land granted to Qi by Tang as the basis for the title. Furthermore, in the chapter of Pan Geng of *Shang Shu*, Kong Yingda noted, "Zheng Xuan said, 'the royal family of Shang moved here and called it Yin.' Zheng Xuan implies that the name Yin did not exist prior to this event." Sima Zhen of the Tang Dynasty, in his commentary on *Shiji* observed, "Initially, the Qi controlled Shang, but later, the descendants of Pan Geng moved to Yin. Yin, located south of Ye, became the recognized name throughout the country." The scholar Cui Shu of the Qing Dynasty, also indicated in his *Shang Kao Xin Lu*: "Many Confucian scholars believe that Pan Geng transitioned the name Shang to Yin." Consequently, some argue that "Shang" refers to the period from Cheng Tang's conquest of Jie until King Zhou's downfall, while "Yin" exclusively pertains to the era from Pan Geng's relocation to Yin until King Di Xin's downfall. Others believe that the period from Cheng Tang's overthrow of Jie to Pan Geng's relocation of the capital is called 'Shang,' the period from Pan Geng's relocation of the capital to the downfall of King Zhou is called 'Yin,' and the period from Cheng Tang's overthrow of Jie to the downfall of King Zhou is called 'Shang Yin.' Some also believe that the Shang Dynasty after the relocation of the capital or the Shang Dynasty in the former Yin territory is considered as the Yin-Shang period."

2. Cui Shu, in his book *Shang Kao Xin Lu*, posits that before Pan Geng's migration, the area was already known as Yin. After Pan Geng's move, the region continued to be called Shang. Yin and Shang are used interchangeably or in conjunction. Hence, there is no record of Pan Geng renaming the state. "Shang" was the original name of Tang's country, while "Yin" was the name of the capital city, which eventually became recognized as the imperial capital. Since Shang was situated within Yin, it was subsequently referred to by the name Yin.

3. In the chapter of "Zhouyu" in *Guoyu*, it is mentioned, "King Di Xin of Shang was greatly evil towards the people." Wu Zhao, a commentator from the Three Kingdoms period, explains, "Shang was the original name of Yin."

4. Since the 20th century, scholars have mostly based their arguments on the newly discovered oracle bone inscriptions from the Yin ruins. Luo Zhenyu believes that "according to the inscriptions, the Yin people referred to themselves as Shang and not as Yin. Even during the reigns of Wen Ding and Di Yi, albeit people lived north of the Yellow River, the country was called Shang ... There is no factual basis for the traditional division of Yin and Shang in old historical records."[7] Guo Moruo also later pointed out, "Based on the records in the oracle bone inscriptions, it is clear that the Yin people referred to themselves as Shang from beginning to end ... There is no such thing as Shang before the reign of Pan Geng and Yin after the reign of Pan Geng. The traditional classification of Yin and Shang in old historical works is entirely baseless."[8] Peng Bangjiong summarized, "In conclusion, based on literature and oracle bone materials, the Shang people called themselves Shang from a very early period. Even after Cheng Tang overthrew the Xia Dynasty, they continued to call themselves Shang. After Pan Geng, they were still referred to as Shang ... Considering the scientific nature of history, it is better to unify them under 'Shang.' This is in accordance with the historical reality of the Shang people and also aligns with the convention of categorizing dynasties by subsequent generations."[9]

5. In 1956, Chen Yuan argued in his essay "On the Shang Dynasty and Yin Dynasty" that "in our history textbooks, we should replace the term 'people of Shang' during the Shang Dynasty with 'people of Yin' ... because 'people of Shang' can easily be confused with merchants. If we use the term 'people of Shang' in the Yin Dynasty, it will imply that it was associated with merchants in the Yin Dynasty."

Based on the various arguments mentioned above, and considering the overall context, I would like to offer the following opinion, which tends toward agreement with the discussed perspectives:

Firstly, the explanation given by Wei Zhao that " Shang (商) is the original name of Yin (殷)" is correct. In other words, Yin (殷) is an alternate designation for Shang (商).

Secondly, Shang (商) is a self-designation used by the state's inhabitants, while Yin (殷) is a designation used by the people of Zhou and later generations to refer to the state governed by the Shang. Shang (商), Yin (殷), or Shang Yin (商殷) are terms additionally used in literature of the Zhou Dynasty and subsequent texts of later dynasties.

Lastly, Shang (商) was the initial self-designation, while Yin (殷) emerged as an alternative designation subsequently.

In conclusion, the entanglement between Shang (商) and Yin (殷) can be resolved as follows: "Shang" is the original and self-designated name, while "Yin" is an alternate and externally designated name. This situation is akin to the political entity of Liu Bei and Liu Shan during the Three Kingdoms period, which self-designated as "Han," but was referred to as "Shu" by others, and in retrospect, became known as Han, Shu, and Shu Han. However, this raises the questions: Why did Tang choose the state name "Shang," and why did later generations refer to it as "Yin"?

2.2 The Dark Bird: From Mortal to Divine

The origin and meaning of the name "Shang" can be explored from two perspectives: ancestry and etymology.

First, let's consider ancestry. In the poem "Xuan Niao" from the "Odes to Shang" in the *Book of Songs*, it is written: "Heaven sent down the Xuan Niao, which descended and gave birth to Shang." In this context, "Shang" clearly does not refer to a place. The question arises: How can a place "give birth"? The term appears to be a personal or clan name instead. The "Odes to Shang" was sung by the people of the Song state (descendants of the Shang clan)[10] during ancestral sacrifices in the Zhou Dynasty. It likely preserves elements of ancient hymns and can be regarded as credible historical evidence. Since no individual named "Shang" exists among the ancestors of the Shang, the name "Shang" must pertain to a clan, intricately connected with the "Xuan Niao," leading to the legend of the "Xuan Niao giving birth to Shang."

According to the *Shiji* (*The Records of the Grand Historian*), in the "Benji of Yin," "Yin Qi's mother was Jian Di, a daughter of the Emperor Shun's wife. When the couple were bathing together, they witnessed a Xuan Niao bird dropping an egg. Jian Di swallowed the egg, which resulted in her conception of Yin Qi."

The account specifies that Jian Di, the second wife of Emperor Ku, ingested an egg from a "Xuan Niao" and became pregnant, leading to the birth of Yin Qi, the progenitor of the Shang dynasty.

This entrancing legend of the "Xuan Niao giving birth to Shang" bears a semblance of historical authenticity. It mirrors the totemic beliefs of the early Shang people, who revered the Xuan Niao as their totem and held that their paternal forebears were Xuan Niaos. Such beliefs are not just chronicled in historical texts[11] but are also confirmed through artefacts like oracle bone inscriptions, bronzeware inscriptions, and bronze artefacts from the Shang Dynasty. For instance, a late Shang-era bronze vessel is inscribed with the composite characters "Xuan Niao Fu" (meaning "Lady Xuan Niao"). The "Xuan" character is fashioned as an "8," a figure frequently observed in bronzeware inscriptions, while the bird depicted on the right side is illustrated with its wings unfurled. According to researcher Yu Xingwu, the craftswoman of the pot venerated the Xuan Niao as her totem. She was a descendent of Jian Di and belonged to the Shang nobility.[12] Hu Houxuan also concurs that the Xuan Niao was undoubtedly a totemic symbol for the Shang people.[13]

So, what is the Xuan Niao? Scholars have various interpretations for "Xuan Niao," drawing upon its connotations of mystery, illusion, and darkness. Some believe it to be a swallow, while others argue it signifies a phoenix, with the prevailing belief aligning with the swallow. In the chapter of Odes to Shang in *Shi Jing*, the text reads, "Heaven-ordained Xuan Niao." Mao Heng of the Western Han Dynasty, interpreted this as: "Xuan Niao means a type of bird." Similarly, in the chapter of Bei Feng in the same book *Shi Jing*, the line " There flies Yan Yan," is followed by Mao Heng's explanation: "Yan Yan refers to a type of bird." In other words, Xuan Niao, and Yan Yan are terms associated with the same bird. Given that the upper body feathers of the Yan are blue-black (a shade denoted by Xuan), the bird was named for its appearance, and thus Yan is also known as Xuan Niao. Consequently, most scholars concur that the Shang clan revered the Yan (swallow) as their totem.

However, the argument for the phoenix also holds some weight. For instance, Qu Yuan, in his account of the Shang clan's origins and in "Tian Wen," poses the question, "Why is the lady delighted when Xuan Niao presents a tribute?" Yet, in "Li Sao," he describes something similar as "Yi Nv (beautiful woman) of You Li … Phoenix has received the decree." Hence, in Qu Yuan's writings, Xuan Niao is equated with the phoenix. Furthermore, during the Spring and Autumn period, Jie Yu, a maniac from the State of Chu, sang to Confucius, "Feng (Phoenix)! Feng (Phoenix)! How can one grasp your grace? For those who are gone cannot be seen, yet those who come can be pursued."[14] Confucius, a scion of the Song State and by extension the Shang clan, was likened to a phoenix by Jie Yu, a nod to the Shang clan's ancestral veneration of the phoenix. It could be that the earliest depiction of the phoenix was indeed black, hence it got the name Xuan Niao. Alternatively, the phoenix might have been envisioned as an amalgamation of various avian images that do not exist in reality but in the realm of myth, imbuing it with an illusory aspect, thereby earning the moniker "Xuan" and subsequently "Xuan Niao." Wen Yiduo, in his book *Myth and Poetry*, proposed that the phoenix was the totem of the ancient people of Yin.[15]

It is worth noting that there is an evolutionary relationship between the swallow and the phoenix. In the chapter of Er Ya in *Shijin,* it is stated: "Yan, the phoenix, its female is Huang." The term "Yan" here refers to the swallow, which is also called a phoenix.[16] The male is called Feng, the female is Huang, and together they are referred to as the phoenix. In *The Origins of the Gods* by He Xin, from the perspective of Chinese mythology, it is argued that the Xuan Niao may have evolved into either a swallow or a phoenix.[17] Additionally, in the *Dictionary of Chinese Mythology and Legend* compiled by Yuan Ke, under the entry for "Feng Huang," it is stated: "The swallow is black, hence called Xuan Niao ... From a black swallow, it was embellished and deified, giving rise to the divine bird, the phoenix, as described in the *Classic of Mountains and Rivers* and *Shuo Wen Jie Zi*."[18]

In conclusion, the Shang clan worshipped the Xuan Niao as their totem. Initially, the Xuan Niao was a swallow, a real bird. Later, through continuous embellishment, beautification, and deification, it became the phoenix, a fictional mythical bird. We can understand this evolutionary process as follows: The Xuan Niao (Swallow) giving birth to the Shang clan signifies that all members are born from the Xuan Niao, reflecting the primitive concept of equality during an era when societies may have still been matriarchal. The Xuan Niao (Phoenix) bestowing blessings implies a specific individual, referring to the offspring of Emperor Ku's queen, Jian Di, who conceived through the Xuan Niao. It also refers to the founder of the Shang clan, Qi, and the subsequent lineage of rulers and emperors who were born from the Xuan Niao. By this time, the Shang society had likely evolved to a patriarchal phase, and one expression of this transition is the development of a credible genealogy arranged according to patrilineal descent after Qi. In other words, the swallow totem carries a clear sense of primitiveness, representing the original totemic worship of the society. Conversely, the phoenix totem should be seen as a product of societal progress.

Establishing the phoenix totem laid the groundwork for "Shang" to become not only the clan name but also the national name. It is common for the names of primitive ethnic groups to relate to their totems, as discussed in the previous chapter on the Xia state's name. Likewise, the analysis of the Shang clan name can be traced back to the phoenix totem. Let's examine the oracle bone script for the characters "feng" (凤) and "shang" (商):[19]

In the oracle bone script, the lower part of the character "凤" closely resembles the body of a bird, while the upper part suggests the crest feathers on the head of a phoenix. Similarly, the character "商" in oracle bone script features the same crest feathers in its upper part, depicting the phoenix totem worshiped by the clan. Various explanations exist for the lower part of "商": Xu Zhongshu interprets it as a cave dwelling, Yang Yachang sees it as a house, and Zhang Guangzhi relays Ye Yusen and Yu Shengwu's belief that it signifies an altar.[20] Each explanation depicts a connection with the phoenix, dwelling in a cave, feathers above a house, or a phoenix image atop an altar. However, the interpretation that combines these elements, a phoenix image on an altar where worship rituals are conducted, may hold the most significance. It is likely that the character "商" originated from the worship of the phoenix totem by this group.

The provided text that you have been given is quite comprehensive, but there are a few points that can be improved for clarity, accuracy, and language flow. Here's a revised version of the text:

The term "商" (Shang) initially served as the name of a clan, which emerged following the establishment of the phoenix totem by the clan. Although the exact timing of its appearance cannot be precisely determined, it is improbable for it to have postdated the legendary ancestor of the Shang clan, Qi.[21] Moreover, the origin of the Shang clan's name is likely to be the eastern region, supported by the following key evidence:

Firstly, the dwelling place of Qi. " Wei River" in the *Shui Jing* and the *Di Wang Shi Ji* state: "Qi resided in Fan." Here, Qi refers to the legendary ancestor of the Shang clan, and Fan is identified as Fan County in the State of Lu in the chapter of Geography in *Han Shu*. Presently, it falls within the boundaries of Tengzhou City in south western Shandong Province, according to Wang Guowei.[22] Legends also suggest that the Shang clan migrated eight times from Qi to Tang. Scholars have mapped these migrations to predominantly south western Shandong and eastern Henan regions.

Secondly, the distribution of bird totems. The "Seventeenth Year of Zhao Gong" in *Zuo Zhuan* records that the Shaohao clan were connoisseurs of birds and named them accordingly. The presence of over a dozen different bird names is indicative of the eastern region's Shaohao clans adopting birds as totems, including numerous bird-named branches. Archaeological finds demonstrate that the Da Wenkou culture, centered around Mount Tai, corresponds to the prehistoric Shaohao clan's area, showcasing bird totems. Pottery artifacts from the Da Wenkou culture, such as tripod vessels with bird-like beaks and bodies, highlight the distinct attributes of the Da Wenkou culture pervasive in Shandong and northern Jiangsu regions over 5,000 years ago.

Drawing from these points, scholars have deduced a tribal connection between the Shang clan and the Shaohao clan group in the east. It is plausible that the original Shang clan was a branch of the Shaohao bird totem clan. The Shaohao clan primarily resided near modern-day Qufu in Shandong Province,[23] suggesting that the Shang clan's dwelling was likewise nearby or not far from this area. The assertion that "Qi resided in Fan" aligns with this geographic context. Consequently, it's reasonable to posit that the Shang clan's name originated in the south western region of today's Shandong.

The transformation from the clan name 'Shang' to the dynastic title "having the name under heaven" commenced with Tang. Known initially as Lv or Tianyi (and addressed as Taiyi and Gaozu Yi in oracle bone inscriptions), Tang ascended as Wu Tang or Cheng Tang after securing victory in eleven battles and toppling the Xia Dynasty. Upon establishing the Shang Dynasty, Tang exalted the clan's accomplishments and underscored the Shang's renowned ruling status. Furthermore, since the phoenix—a 'divine bird'—is associated with the Shang, opting for 'Shang' as the national title not only stemmed from the clan name but also implied sanctifying their power—a nuance likely contemplated by Tang when founding the dynasty.

It is noteworthy that, from the Shang Dynasty onward, the phoenix assumed an increasingly mystical and extraordinary persona. The *Classic of Mountains and Rivers* depicts it as a chicken-like bird, adorned in five colors, with "Virtue" emblazoned on its head, "Righteousness" on its wings, "Etiquette" on its back, "Benevolence" on its chest, and "Trustworthiness" on its belly. This bird's natural habits of eating, drinking, singing, and dancing, purportedly signify the advent of peace. "Shuo Wen Jie Zi" echoes this sentiment, calling the phoenix a 'divine bird.' Tian Lao describes it as a blend of several animals, encompassing all five vital colors and highlights its origin from the 'kingdom of Gentlemen in the East.' Its emergence was believed to herald serenity worldwide. This magnificent portrayal shares parallels with the cicada, which was noted previously as the source of the Xia Dynasty's insignia. Although the full magnitude of the phoenix's imagery and symbolism might not have been established during Tang's era, it is clear that the phoenix was no ordinary bird.

2.3 More About the Yin

The term "Yin" is closely associated with the Shang Dynasty and serves as an alternative name for it. After the Shang Dynasty, the Zhou people, and later historical texts referring to the Shang state, used this name. Why was this alternative name used, and what does the terminology signify? To keep the explanation concise, here is a summary of the author's perspective:

1. Yin derives from "Yi." Jiang Liangfu's article "Arguments on the Names of Yin and Shang," which considers ancient history, characters, pre-Qin classics, eastern cultural practices, among other sources, stated that "Yin" is argued to be the complex form of "Yi." This character denotes eastern tribes known for archery. "Yin" is seen as an evolution of the term, whereas "Yi" is the original form. Phonetically, the progression of "Yin" mirrors that of the pronunciation of "yi" (meaning clothing).[24] Xu Zhongshu pointed out in "*Some issues on the history of the Yin-Shang Dynasty*" that "The Zhou people referred to the Yin as Yi ... The pronunciations of 'Yi,' 'Yin,' and 'Yi' are similar, all representing different facets of ancient regional dialects." To put it simply, the Zhou people broadly labeled various eastern ethnic groups, including the Shang, as 'Yi,' while specifically designating the Shang as 'Yi,' which later became known as 'Yin.'[25]

2. Yin's name originates from place names. There are various theories about the origins of the name "Yin." Guo Moruo links "Yin" to the hunting grounds of Yin kings near modern-day Huai'an, referred to as Yin City. Wang Guowei, Fu Sinnian, Zhao Tiehan, and Miyazaki Ichisada, a Japanese scholar, associate it with the lower Yellow River or the broader Hebei region. Zou Heng's theory relates "Yin" to Wei, near today's Zhengzhou, Henan, while Yang Baocheng ties it to Anyang territory[26], which includes Yin ruins. These ideas resonate with earlier analyses suggesting the name "Shang" also stemmed from place names.

3. The Zhou Dynasty's usage of Yin doesn't imply negativity. Despite overthrowing the Shang, the Zhou Dynasty's references to the Shang Dynasty lacked negative connotations. Inscriptions like "Da Yi Shang" (Great Yi Shang) and phrases such as "Da Yin" (Great Yin) and "Da Bang Yin" (Great State of Yin) in Zhou texts exemplify this aspect. Furthermore, Zhou literature often humbly referred to the kingdom as a "small state" or "country," exemplified by the *Book of Documents*' phrases, "The heavens favor the tranquil king, who elevates our small state of Zhou," and "Utilize your many capabilities; though not meant for our small country, we cannot disregard the command of Yin." As noted by Yang Shengnan, this strategic humility helped the Zhou consolidate power by acknowledging the former Shang aristocracy in a symbolic sense, consequently garnering their support.[27]

4. Yin's neutrality in the Shang Dynasty context. Guo Moruo's assertion[28] that the Zhou's use of "Yin" or "Yi" to refer to the Shang people is malicious and lacks substantial evidence, as does Yang Shengnan's statement that such references are honorific.[29] The character "Yin," as explained in the Shuowen Jiezi, denotes the flourishing of music and thus has positive associations. Duan Yucai, a Qing Dynasty commentator, further interprets it to metaphorically signify abundance, greatness, numerousness, correctness, and centrality.[30] However, these are later interpretations, not the character's original significance, as likewise, was using

"Yin" as a positive country name developed over time, akin to the favorable connotations later linked to "Xia."

5. Despite later confusion and inconsistencies in the terms "Shang" and "Yin," two significant aspects should be noted: Firstly, Confucius, a Shang descendant, self-identified as a "Yin person" or "descendant of Yin," possibly finding the extended meaning of "Yin" more aesthetically and "culturally" appealing than "Shang." Secondly, throughout the Zhao and Song Dynasties, which emphasized "culture," there was a significant shift from "Yin" back to "Shang." Motivated partly by the desire to distance themselves firmly, and partly due to Zhao Kuangyin's Song association, and the auspicious implication of fire virtue for the nation,[31] the Song Dynasty preferred the original title of "Shang," seldom using "Yin" (see Figure 2.1).

6. Given that "Shang" is the dynasty's self-identified name and "Yin" the name assigned by others, we should adopt the principle of "the name chosen by the owner," leading to the correction of "*Historical Records–Annals of the Shang Dynasty*" to read simply *Annals of the Shang Dynasty*. Furthermore, the former Shang capital established by Pan Geng, referred to as "Yinxu" in "Beiji of Xiang Yu" of the *Historical Records* and known today as an archaeological site in Xiaotun Village, Anyang, Henan Province, should instead be called "Shangxu."[32] Therefore, "Shangxu" or "Shang City" should be recognized as the official name for the Shang Dynasty's capital for posterity.

Figure 2.1 On July 13, 2006, the Yin ruins in Anyang was inscribed on the World Heritage List

Notes

1 Xia-Shang-Zhou Chronology Project Expert Group, Summary of the Xia-Shang-Zhou Chronology Project 1996–2000 Phase Findings (Abridged Version), World Publishing Company Beijing Branch, 2000.

2 In the writings of Mencius, the character "Shang" is only used when quoting from the *Book of Songs* (Shi Jin). For example, in Mencius' "Li Lou," quotes from the Book of Songs: "The grandson of Shang, his beauty is incomparable."

3 Chen Yuan, "The Shang Dynasty and the Yin Dynasty," Editorial Work, Issue 18, August 1956, included in "Collected Academic Papers of Chen Yuan," Volume 2, Zhonghua Book Company, 1982.

4 " Temple name taboo of the Song Dynasty" refers to the fact that after Zhao Kuangyin founded the Song Dynasty, he posthumously honored his father Zhao Hongyin with the temple name "Xuanzu."

5 Zhu Yanmin, "A Study on Distinguishing the Names 'Yin' and 'Shang'," Journal of Nankai University, Volume 1, 1998.

6 Shi Suyuan, "A Brief Discussion on the National Name of the Shang Dynasty," History Teaching, Issue 7, 1981.

7 Luo Zhenyu, Annotated Study on Yin and Oracle Bone Inscriptions (Revised Edition), Preface by Luo Zhenyu, Oriental Society, 1927.

8 Guo Moruo, "The Slave System Era" – Chapter 2: "The Shang Dynasty as a Slave Society," included in "The Complete Works of Guo Moruo · Historical Compilation," Volume 3, People's Publishing House, 1984.

9 Peng Bangjiong, A Glimpse into the History of the Shang Dynasty, Chapter 1, Chongqing Press, 1988.

10 The State of Song was one of the feudal vassal states during the Zhou Dynasty. The founder of the state was Qi, the eldest son of Emperor Yi and the half-brother of Emperor Xin (Zhou). Qi was granted the fief of Wei (present-day Liangshan County, Shandong Province) during the Shang Dynasty and is commonly referred to as Duke Wei (Weizi).

11 "Book of Songs" (Shijin) ," Chu Ci" (Songs of Chu), including "Li Sao" and "Tian Wen," "Lüshi Chunqiu" (Annals of Lü Buwei), specifically the chapter "Initial Sounds," "Records of the Grand Historian" (Shiji), specifically the chapter on the Yin Dynasty, "Huainanzi" (Master Huainan), specifically the chapter on geographic features.

12 Yu Shengwu, "A Brief Discussion on the Origin of Totem and Religion and the Totem of the Xia and Shang Dynasties," Historical Research, Volume 11, 1959.

13 Hu Houxuan, "New Evidence of Bird Totems of the Shang Clan as Seen in Oracle Bone Inscriptions," Cultural Relics, Issue 2, 1977.

14 "Analects" (Lunyu), specifically the chapter "Wei Zi."

15 Wen Yiduo, Mythology and Poetry: Dragon and Phoenix, Zhonghua Book Company, 1956.

16 According to Wen Yiduo's "New Interpretation of Classical Poetry: An Exegesis of Li Sao" in "The Complete Works of Wen Yiduo," Volume 2, published by Sanlian Bookstore in 1982, there is a reference to the line "The phoenix, after receiving the official appointment." The commentary states: "The pronunciation of 'yàn hèn' (燕鷗) is similar; 'yàn' (燕) refers to the Yan kingdom, and 'hèn' (鷗) is a variant of 'yàn' (燕). In ancient times, 'yàn' (燕) was used as a generic term for birds, similar to how the term 'yan' (燕) is depicted as 'anhào yán' (匽若郾) in ancient bronze inscriptions. 'Hèn' (鷗) is synonymous with 'yàn' (燕), hence the phoenix is equivalent to the mythical bird Xuan Niao (玄鸟)." Hu Houxuan's "New Evidence of Bird Totems of the Shang Clan as Seen in Oracle Bone Inscriptions" includes the interpretation of the character "亥" in Wang

Hai's divination record, which looks like a bird with a crown-like shape. This interpretation also suggests that the Xuan Niao (玄鸟) can be referred to as the phoenix.

17 He Xin, "The Origins of Gods–Ancient Chinese Mythology and History," Chapter 4, Sanlian Bookstore, 1986.

18 Yuan Ke, Dictionary of Chinese Mythology and Legends, Shanghai Lexicographical Publishing House, 1985.

19 Institute of Archaeology, Chinese Academy of Sciences, Compilation of Oracle Bone Inscriptions, Volume 3 and Volume 4, Zhonghua Book Company, 1965.

20 Xu Zhongshu, "Issues on the History of the Yin and Shang Dynasties," Journal of Sichuan University, Volume 2, 1979.
    Yang Yachang, "On the Origin of the Shang Clan and Pre-Shang Culture," Northern Cultural Relics, Issue 2, 1988.
    Zhang Guangzhi, "The Origin of Shangcheng and the Shang Dynasty and Its Early Culture" in *Collection of Archaeological Papers in China*, Lianjing Publishing Company, Taipei, 1995.

21 Li Jianwu's "A Brief Discussion on the Seals 'Shang' and 'Juyu Fan'" in Zhongyuan Wenwu, Issue 3, 1986, argues that the term "Shang" in the seal inscription refers to the name of a clan, and it represents "the name of the clan from which the seals originated." Hu Axian's "Renaming China: Hu Axian's Discourse on National Names," in the third lecture "Fulfillment of the Dao," published by Zhonghua Book Company in 2013, discusses the significance of the name "Shang" and its association with the revered and appreciated mythical bird, the phoenix. Hu Axian suggests that there is a high degree of unity and coordination in both the content and form between the name of the Shang clan and the totem of the phoenix.

22 Wang Guowei, "On the Eight Relocations from Zi Qi to Cheng Tang," included in "*Collection of Observations in the Hall*" Volume 12, Zhonghua Book Company, 1959.

23 Zuo Zhuan, "*Fourth Year of Ding Gong*" states: "They assigned the people of Shang and Yan the title of Boqin and bestowed them land in the region of Shao Huang." The Western Jin Dynasty scholar Du Yu explained in his annotation that "Shao Huang Xu refers to Qufu, which is located within the city of Lu."

24 Jiang Liangfu, "Debating the Names of Yin and Shang," included in *Collection of Ancient Historical Papers*, Shanghai Ancient Books Publishing House, 1996.

25 According to Hu Axiang's "Naming China: Hu Axiang Explains National Names," in the third lecture, it can be understood as follows: "The character '夷' consists of two parts: '大' means 'people' and is like a person stretching their arms and spreading their legs; '弓' means 'bow and arrow.' Therefore, '夷' refers to the Eastern people who are skilled in archery. The Shang people originated in the lower reaches of the Yellow River in the Eastern region and tended to migrate, similar to nomadic pastoralists who are good at archery ... In other words, the later Zhou Dynasty based its naming on the characteristics and location of the earlier Shang people, using '殷' to specifically refer to the Shang Dynasty and '夷' as a general term for the Eastern ethnic groups, including the Shang people. In essence, Yin [殷] is not the name of a country, and the true name of the Shang Dynasty is still Shang [商]."

26 Guo Moruo, "The Slavery Age: Chapter 2 - The Yin Dynasty is a Slavery System;" Guo Moruo, "Introduction" of "Compilation of Divination Texts," included in "The Complete Works of Guo Moruo–Archaeology Volume 2," Scientific Publishing House, 1983.
    Wang Guowei, "On Yin," included in his work "Collection of Observations in the Hall" Volume 12.

Fu Siniian, "A Discussion on the East and West of the Yi-Xia," in "Collection of Studies by the Institute of Historical Linguistics," External Series 1 - "Celebrating the 65th Birthday of Mr. Cai Yuanpei," Volume 2, 1933.

Zhao Tiehan, "On the Five Relocations of Yin, Shang, and After Cheng Tang," in "Continental Journal," Volume 10, Issue 8, 1973.

Miyazaki Ichitei, "Ancient Chinese City-States and Their Tombs" and "Supplement," in "Studies in Oriental History" (Volume 4, 1970; Volume 2, 1971).

Zou Heng, "A Study on the Geographical and Legendary Interpretation of Xia Culture within its Distribution Area," included in the collection "Essays on Xia, Shang, and Zhou Archaeology."

Yang Baocheng, "Debating whether the Yin Ruins was the Capital of the Yin Dynasty," in "Yin Du Journal" (Volume 4, 1990).

27 Yang Shengnan, "The Origin of the Term 'Yin' in the Shang Dynasty," in "Historical Knowledge" (Volume 1, 1982).

28 Guo Moruo, "The Age of Slavery" - Chapter 2: "The Yin Dynasty was a Slave System"

29 Yang Shengnan, "The Origin of the Term 'Yin' in the Shang Dynasty."

30 Wang Chong, "Lunheng" (Discourses Weighed in the Balance).

31 See Chapter 15 of this book.

32 Xu Zhongshu, "The Yin and Shang Ethnicity and the Genealogy of the Yin Kings," included in the collection *Essays on Pre-Qin History*, Bashu Book Society, 1992. According to the book, "Xu" 墟 can also be written as "Xu" 虚 and is a term used to refer to the capital of the emperors and kings.

3 Zhou

Emphasizing Agriculture

In approximately 1046 BC, Ji Fa (known posthumously as King Wu of Zhou) led a campaign to overthrow King Zhou of Shang[1]. This marked the establishment of the Zhou Dynasty, the third dynasty in Chinese history. The Zhou Dynasty lasted for 32 generations and featured a total of 37 kings, spanning nearly 800 years. In 841 BC, it was recorded in Sima Qian's "Records of the Grand Historian" as the beginning of the "Republican" year, which denoted the start of precisely dated Chinese history. In 771 BC, during the reign of King You of Zhou, the Crown Prince's grandfather, Duke Shen, colluded with the Quanrong tribe and killed King You at the foot of Mount Li. The Crown Prince, Yi Jiu, was then chosen as the new king, known as King Ping. The following year, he relocated the Zhou capital to Luoyi (present-day Luoyang, Henan Province) in the Eastern Zhou region. The term "Western Zhou Dynasty" refers to the period before this relocation, from the rule of the 11th to the 12th kings. In contrast, the "Eastern Zhou Dynasty" denotes the period from the reign of the 21st to the 25th kings. During the Western Zhou period, the royal family held significant power, with the kings recognized as the leaders of the entire realm. However, during the Eastern Zhou period, the royal family's power gradually waned, and regional lords gained more political influence, diminishing the Zhou kings' authority to merely symbolic leaders. In 315 BC, King Shenjing of Zhou passed away, and his son Yan succeeded him as King Nan of Zhou. In 256 BC, the State of Qin destroyed the Zhou Dynasty[2]; with the death of King Nan, the last king of Zhou, and the dynasty came to an end. According to the "Geography Records" in the "*Book of Han*," "The Zhou Dynasty was the longest of the three dynasties, spanning over 800 years until the reign of King Nan, when it was conquered by the State of Qin."[3]

However, the history before the establishment of the Zhou Dynasty, which dates back to the ancient times, is equally long-standing. Based on different migration stages and traditional historical records, scholars have divided pre-Zhou history into four periods:

The first period is from the birth of Qi to Bu Zhu, Qi's son. Qi was the ancestor of the people of Zhou, who honored him as the cultivator of millet and bestowed upon him the title of Hou Ji with the surname Ji. It is said that Shun granted Qi land in Tai, where his descendants lived until the time of Bu Zhu. From the Han

DOI: 10.4324/9781003510390-4

Dynasty onwards, scholars believed that Tai was located in Wugong County, Shaanxi Province.

The second period is from Bu Zhu to Gong Liu, spanning three generations. Bu Zhu fled to the area of the Rong and Di tribes to escape the turmoil of the Xia Dynasty. The place to which he fled is said to be near present-day Qingyang City, Gansu Province, according to later geographical records.

The third period is from the migration of Gong Liu to Bin until Gu Gong Dan Fu, spanning ten generations. Bin was located near what is now Binxian and Xunyi counties in Shaanxi Province, with hardly any historical dispute regarding its location.

The fourth period is from the migration of Gu Gong Dan Fu to Qixia until King Wu of Zhou conquered King Zhou of Shang, spanning four generations. "Qi" refers to Mount Qi, the main peak of which is north east of Qishan County, Shaanxi Province. South of Mount Qi is Zhouyuan, where King Wu launched his conquest.

According to this account, the pre-Zhou period spanned roughly a thousand years. However, during the Xia and Shang eras, the Zhou ethnicity was still relatively obscure, and we find no written historical records attributed to them from that time. Consequently, Sima Qian's "*Records of the Grand Historian, Annals of Zhou*" provides detailed documentation of events following King Wu's overthrow of King Zhou, while the narratives preceding this are nebulous, particularly before the time of Bu Duo.

For instance, the "*Records of the Grand Historian, Annals of Zhou*" indicates that Bu Zhu was the son of Qi. Nevertheless, the Tang Dynasty's Sima Zhen, in his "*Critical Explanations in the Comprehensive Annotations of the 'Records of the Grand Historian,'*" raised a crucial point: "If Bu Zhu was indeed the son of Qi, then from King Wen to our time, there would be only fourteen generations spread across more than a millennium, which is inconsistent."

Furthermore, the "*Records of the Grand Historian, Annals of Zhou*" does not specify the origin of the name "Zhou." Zhang Shoujie of the Tang Dynasty, claimed in his "*Accurate Meanings in the 'Records of the Grand Historian,'*:" "Owing to the residence of the Taowang in Zhouyuan, the place was named Zhou." Additionally, in the southern Song Dynasty, Pei Yi of the southern Song Dynasty in his "*Comprehensive Annotations on the 'Records of the Grand Historian',*" relayed the words of Xu Guang: " There is a mountain to the north west of Meiyang in Fufeng, with Zhouyuan lying to its south." As for Huangfu Mi, he provided supporting testimony, saying, "Since they settled in Zhouyuan, the area started to be referred to as Zhou." Taking these various interpretations into account, one must question whether the name "Zhou" really originated from Gu Gong Dan Fu and was indeed derived from the region of Zhouyuan.

3.1 The Character 周 in Oracle Bone and Bronze Inscriptions and its Derivatives.[4]

The character "周" found in oracle bone inscriptions appears across various divinatory records and can manifest in two distinct forms. The first form includes shapes such as 囲 丗 囲 丗 丗, which modern script simplifies to the character 田. The second form incorporates shapes like 囲 囲 囲.[5] Many scholars do not differentiate these two forms of the character "周," interpreting both to represent the configuration of rice plants within a plot. However, in Luo Jiangsheng's *"Study on the Names of State Qin,"* a careful analysis reveals that the second form indeed depicts rice plants at the center of a field, whereas the first form portrays rice plants reaching the field's extremities. Thus, the intrinsic meaning of "周" is associated with "a field of rice plants" or "rice plants within a field," with the first form signifying "field" in a general sense and the second denoting specifically "within the field." Despite their divergent structures, both forms share an analogous semantic significance, serving as two variations of the same character.

The inscriptions of the character "周" in bronze scripts can similarly be divided into two styles. The first style includes forms such as 囲 囲 囲 that modern script simplifies to characters 田 and 丗. The second style encompasses forms 周 周 周 周 which modern script corresponds to characters 周 周 周 周 周 周.[6]

The first style is in alignment with the forms seen in oracle bone inscriptions, depicting a field of rice plants. The second style introduces the element of "口" (mouth), and some scholars consider it an expansion of the first style, suggestive of cultivated rice plants that provide food. Others regard the addition of "口" as symbolizing the foundation of state laws and ordinances. Under the former analysis, which adheres to the original significance, the character "周" retains its authentic interpretation. The latter perspective, which implies a subsequent semantic evolution of "周," departs from its primary connotation.

The original meaning of the character "周" relates to planting crops in the field, which offer sustenance and nourishment. This character also possesses derivations that incorporate the radical "口" (mouth),[7] a detail reflected in the oracle bone inscriptions of the Zhou Dynasty.[8] Within these inscriptions, "周" sometimes appears without the radical of "口," represented as 丗 丗 丗 丗, and at other times with it, as in 周 周, and so forth.[9] These variations correspond to simplified forms of the first type found in the oracle bone inscriptions of the Yin Ruins and the second type in the bronze inscriptions.

The composition of character "周," which follows the radical of "口," embodies the idea of cultivating crops to nourish people. History shows that people have always prioritized food, which is cultivated in fields (周)[10]. Hence, the fundamental concept of "周" as cultivating sustenance has evolved into broader, more intricate meanings. For instance, in the poem "Yun Han" (the Milky Way) from the *Book of Songs*, the line "靡人不周" was interpreted by Mao Heng of the Western Han Dynasty as this:" '周' means to save." Zheng Xuan of the Eastern Han Dynasty elaborated that "周" should be regarded as 賙, indicating that when the king was in need, everyone pitched in to help. In the "Monthly Ordinances" of the *Book of Rites*, Zheng Xuan explained "周" as insufficient supply. Thus, "周" conveys the concept of "赒给" (assisting those in need) and can also be expressed as "赒." Both "周" and "赒" retain usage throughout ancient and modern contexts. Originally, "周" signified the act of providing relief to the needy, but over time, its scope expanded to include meanings like "meticulous," "comprehensive," and "encompassing." This is evident in various interpretations of ancient texts, such as "meticulous" in *Shuowen Jiezi*, "comprehensive" in *Guangya*, and "surrounding" in *Xiao Erya*.

3.2 From the Name of a Clan and State to the Title of the Dynasty

There is no doubt that "Zhou" is the name of a clan and a state. But how was it chosen as a clan name and later designated as a title of the dynasty? What is the significance of "Zhou" being both a clan name and a title of the dynasty?

To answer these questions, it's crucial to understand the original meaning of the character "周" (Zhou). We need to rely on oracle bone and bronze inscriptions to comprehend its original connotation.

In these inscriptions, the character "周" (Zhou), outside of simplified Chinese, is related to fields and rice cultivation, as previously mentioned. Many modern sinologists and historians share this view:

Yu Yongliang observed, "In bronze inscriptions, '周' (Zhou) is depicted with the radical for 'rice' emerging from the center of a field."

Guo Moruo noted, "The character '周' (Zhou) is often crafted to resemble the shape of a field with crops."

Qi Sihe echoed, "In the oracle bone and bronze inscriptions from the Zhou Dynasty, the character '周' (Zhou) appears to mimic the form of a field."

Zhou Fagao explained, "It is the original character for '周原膴膴' in the poem 'Da Ya' from the Book of Songs, designed to symbolize something sown in a field."

Tan Jiefu stated, "In bronze inscriptions, '周' (Zhou) also resembles the shape of crops in a field."

Xu Zhongshu elaborated, "In bronze inscriptions, '周' (Zhou) features a 'field' radical, representing divided agricultural land, with a small dot in the center for the planted crops."[11]

The association of the character "周" (Zhou) with fields and planting is evident, affirming its agrarian roots. So when did "周" become a clan name? According to the "Emperor and Kings Chronicle" by Huangfu Mi of the Western Jin Dynasty, coupled with annotations by Liu Song's Pei Yuan and Tang Dynasty's Zhang Shoujie in the *"Records of the Grand Historian: Annals of Zhou,"* it is believed that "Zhou" originated from ancient times.

Before Gugong Danfu (King Tai of Zhou) moved to Zhouyuan, the clan was not yet named Zhou. This view, however, was challenged following the discovery of oracle bone inscriptions at the Yin ruins. The name "Zhou" had appeared before Gugong Danfu, during the reign of King Wu Ding of Shang, as evidenced by the Ji Mao divination: "Chong Zhen divined: Let the descendants follow the Qunhou Pu Zhou," and the *Bamboo Annals*, "In the twenty-first year of Yin Wu Yi's reign, Gugong Danfu of Zhou passed away." Wu Ding ruled approximately from 1250 BC to 1192 BC, succeeded by five rulers, ending with Wu Yi (circa 1147 BC to 1113 BC).[12] Consequently, the stance of Huangfu Mi and others lacks credibility.

Nonetheless, the Zhou Dynasty's connection with fields and agriculture, as suggested by the etymology of its name and symbolism of its power, indicates a profound link between the Zhou people and farming. This bond is further underscored by historical accounts which highlight agriculture as the paramount means of sustenance and driver of Zhou's expansion and eventual triumph over the Shang Dynasty.

3.2.1 Houji, the God of Agriculture.

The ancestors of a nation often have mysterious and miraculous legends about their births, and the same is true for the Zhou Dynasty's legendary figure of abandoned origin. According to the *"Records of the Grand Historian, Annals of Zhou,"* Zhou Houji, also known as Qi, was the child of Jiang Yuan, daughter of Tai. Jiang Yuan, a consort of Emperor Ku, ventured into the wild where she encountered the footprints of a giant. Compelled, she stepped on them and, consequently, felt as though she had conceived. Subsequently, she gave birth to a son. Perceiving him as an ominous sign, she abandoned him in a narrow alley where no animals would harm him. She moved him to a forest, where woodcutters found and cared for him. Later, she left him on ice in a ditch, only for birds to protect him with their wings. Realizing he was extraordinary, Jiang Yuan raised him as her own, naming him "Qi," which means "Abandoned" due to her initial intentions.

The stories of Jiang Yuan's unconventional pregnancy after stepping on a giant's footprints; Jiandi conceiving the Shang tribe's ancestor, Qi, after consuming a blackbird's egg; and Xiujie giving birth to the Xia tribe's ancestor, Yu, via caesarean section after eating Job's tears, share striking similarities. These tales reflect a matrilineal society where children recognized only their mothers. The transition to a patrilineal society, centering on men, began during the eras of Yu of the Xia tribe and Qi of the Shang tribe. During Qi's time, his tribe underwent a similar transformation. With the progression of agriculture and animal husbandry, along with the practice of exogamous marriage, the matrilineal system naturally evolved into a patrilineal one. Qi was pivotal in establishing the patriarchal system in his tribe. He took on the surname Ji, changing it from his maternal surname Jiang, setting a precedent for male lineage in his tribe. Consequently, Qi was venerated as the progenitor of the Zhou people.

The origin of the Zhou clan's name might also be traced back to Qi. As Tan Jiepu points out, "The name of the Zhou clan began with Houji."[13] Here, "Houji" refers to Qi. The act of Qi's abandonment also directly influenced the Zhou's clan name. According to Ji, it denotes millet (dehulled millet and unhulled as sorghum), primarily cultivated in the north west. The studies by Qi Si and Mao Shi into grain

Figure 3.1 Millet (grass grain)

names highlighted: "In ancient times, millet and sorghum were staple crops ... Millet, being tastier but yielding less per mu than sorghum, was thus more expensive and typically consumed by nobility, while commoners ate sorghum. In bountiful years, commoners could also partake in millet." Sorghum cultivation likely began with the Zhou, a north western ethnic group, potentially initiated by Houji (Abandonment) due to his significant contributions to its cultivation and high-yield selection, earning him the title "Houji" (Sorghum King). The Zhou people used Sheji (with She signifying land and Ji representing general crops or food) as a national emblem. Qi's name and crop, Ji, thus illustrate a profound connection between him, the Zhou, and their agricultural heritage. Qi Si's "The Valley Names in the Book of Songs" posits that "Ji is a valley name, yet the Zhou considered it their ancestor. Ji could be the totem of the Zhou." Qi's sophistication in Ji cultivation and technology bolstered the Zhou's pride in their ancestor, celebrated as the god of agriculture and the inventor of farming. Due to advanced agriculture, a defining trait, the Zhou rose to prominence, wealth, and power (see Figure 3.1).

Reviewing Zhou characters in oracle bone and bronze inscriptions suggests the term originally referred to Ji, the grain cultivated in fields during the initial stages of character development. If Ji was indeed the clan totem, it would become their emblem and namesake. It must be noted that with advancements in agricultural technology, the diversity of crops expanded beyond millet. The Zhou Dynasty's "*Shi Da Ya Sheng Min*" lauds Houji, stating, "Crawling on the ground, ascending hills, nourishment from the earth." The poem illustrates the artist's early fascination with learning and taste, cultivating a diverse array of plants like soybeans, ji, hemp, barley, and melons from a young age. Houji's farming techniques—from weeding to seeding to reaping—are depicted. His marriage to a Tai family woman and cultivated black glutinous millet are milestones, considered divine gifts celebrated through worship. These traditions persisted flawlessly through generations (see Figure 3.2).

Figure 3.2 Ji Wang Temple in Jishan, Shanxi Province

As "Shi Jing" (The Book of Songs) proclaims, the Zhou, since their ancestor Qi, were a pastoral society. They domesticated many crops and enhanced planting methods, inheriting and discovering various crop types. Hence, it's no surprise this agrarian culture adopted "Zhou" (fields and planting) as their clan name. By at least Duke Wu of Zhou's era, the fertile Tai region along the Wei River was known as Zhou, symbolizing their domesticated crops.

3.2.2 The Beginning of the Zhou Dynasty

The name of Zhou evolved from a clan name to a state name during the time of Gugong Danfu. The region where the state name of Zhou emerged was in the so-called "Zhouyuan." Based on the "*Records of the Grand Historian*" of the Zhou Dynasty and the accounts of "Shi–Daya–Gong Liu," "Shi–Daya–Mian," and "Shi–Lusong–Besong," we describe the historical facts about Gugong Danfu and the years surrounding his time.

In the 16th century B.C., the Zhou people, under the influence of the nomadic tribes, the Rong Di, temporarily abandoned agriculture. Gong Liu, the grandson of Bu Zhu, revived the agricultural practices initiated by Hou Ji, cultivated the land effectively, and produced abundant reserves. This agricultural tradition, heralded during the time of Hou Ji, was thus restored and advanced. Gugong Danfu, Gong

Liu's successor, was compelled to migrate due to Rong Di's invasion[14] and settled in Qixia. The area is depicted in the poetic ode "*Shi–Daya–Mian.*"

> Zhouyuan was vibrant and green, rich with blooming flowers and fragrant osmanthus.
> There, plans and pacts were made; a covenant with our turtle was forged.
> With steadfast labor, we built our domicile; we found solace and ceased to fret.
> We gazed left and right, demarcated boundaries, organized our land, and delineated our fields.
> From west to east, we tended to our governance, summoning the Ministers of Works and Education to establish our households.
> Our cords were taut, our rulers exact, and our temple was constructed meticulously.
> We erected the enceinte Gate, raised the court gate, and built the ancestral mounds.

On this original territory of Qixia—fertile and abundant—the crops, though some bitter, were as sweet as syrup. The ancient Duke, Gongsunfu, discerned the signs and chose to dwell here. The Zhou people developed irrigation systems, further enhancing their agriculture, and structured their community, carving out houses, cities, temples, and shrines. They appointed officials, delineated duties, and formalized governance, thus laying the groundwork for a state in its infancy. By this point, the Zhou clan had unequivocally established a state, with the ancient Duke Gongsunfu later posthumously honored as King Tai, regarded by the Zhou as the founder of their polity. However, around the 12th century BC, the Zhou state was quite unremarkable compared to the mighty Shang, positioned in the west and subjugated to other powers.

The development of the Zhou tribe into a state in the Qixia Plain was facilitated by the plain's natural advantages. Shi Nianhai describes the Qixia Plain (subsequently known as the Zhou Plain following the clan's resettlement) like this:

> Delineating its boundaries north of Qishan Mountain and south of the Wei River, the region, fed by numerous rivers on its western side and caressed by the meandering Qishui River, spanned most of Fengxiang, Qishan, Fufeng, and Wugong counties, stretching over 70 kilometers east to west and over 20 kilometers north to south, hugging the Wei River's contours.
>
> During that era, Zhouyuan offered ideal conditions for agricultural expansion, benefiting from a stable land surface, undulating valleys, plentiful water sources, a temperate climate, and fertile vegetation.
>
> The discovery of large-scale temple (or palace) building sites, remnants of bone workshops, and dense burial grounds in the area between Jingdang in Qishan County and the Huangdui and Famen communities in Fufeng County provides ample evidence that Zhouyuan had been the central habitation of the Zhou people since the early Zhou period.[15]

Positioned at the base of Mount Qi, Zhouyuan was well-situated to ward off invasions from northern barbarians. To the south east lay the lands of the Shang Dynasty, inclusive of Chongguo (now north east of Huxian County, Shaanxi Province) and Dangshe (now between Sanyuan and Xingping in Shaanxi Province). The vast territory, coupled with favorable natural and geographic conditions, enabled the Zhou tribe to develop agriculture and build up their strength. Mount Qi stood as a monumental symbol of the Zhou people's burgeoning development, and the fame of Zhouyuan commenced with the Zhou's habitation there. In Zhouyuan, the people of Zhou gradually fortified their state, setting the stage for their vision of "possessing the world." The "Book of Songs, Lu Song, Pei Gong" recounts: The grandson of Hou Ji, revered as the Great King, resided in the south of Mount Qi and began the clipping of the Shang dynasty.

Building on the substantial economic strength of the Zhouyuan, Gugong Danfu led the Zhou people in initiating the grand cause of "overthrowing the Shang Dynasty."

3.2.3 The Zhou Dynasty

Ji Fa overthrew the Shang Dynasty and established the Zhou Dynasty, which extended the national title from "Zhou" to "the ruler of the whole world." The role of agriculture in the genesis, development, expansion, and ultimately in becoming a dominant force in the world during the Zhou Dynasty has been significantly emphasized.

The monumental feat of toppling the Shang Dynasty was achieved through innumerable hardships, eventually accomplished by Ji Fa, the great-grandson of Gugong Danfu.[16]

Firstly, Ji Li, Gugong Danfu's third son, "upheld the legacy of Gu Gong, committed himself to righteousness, and therefore was followed by many nobles," repeatedly vanquishing the Rong people. In the 34th year of King Wu Yi's reign in the Shang Dynasty, Ji Li visited the Shang court, and the subsequent Shang ruler, King Wen Ding, appointed Ji Li as a governor[17], tasking him with coping with the Rong and Di in the west. However, as Ji Chang's influence grew, King Wen Ding, wary of this rising power, eventually assassinated him to remove a potential threat.

Following Ji Li's demise, his son Ji Chang took over and became the "West Duke" under the Shang Dynasty. "The West Duke emulated Houji and Gong Liu, adopting the laws of the ancient dukes, thus earning the allegiance of all vassals." Shang's Emperor Xin (Zhou) imprisoned West Duke Ji Chang but later released him thanks to the offerings of beautiful concubines and fine horses from Zhou ministers Tai Dian, Hong Yao, and San Yisheng. Furthermore, "he was bestowed with bows, arrows, axes, and spears, and granted authority to conquer and annex territories." Seizing this opportunity, Jichang subdued the Rong people, razed the states of Mixu, Li, Yu, and Chong, and established a flourishing city. He relocated the capital from Qixia to Feng. In comparison to Qixia, Feng was not only strategic-ally located for eastward expansion for the Zhou people but also surrounded by rivers and canals, with rich, fertile lands. Since ancient times, it has been renowned as a land of abundance. Even during the Han Dynasty, Dongfang Shuo described it as "rich in various cereals, fruits, mulberry, hemp, and bamboo arrows; fertile for crops like ginger and taro; and with abundant frogs and fish in its waters, ensuring that even the poor had their needs met and were free from the worries of hunger and cold."[18] By this time, the Zhou, though an ancient state, had a renewed destiny. The Zhou Dynasty had already amassed considerable strength and had made thorough preparations for the final campaign to "dethrone the Shang."

After a 50-year reign, Ji Chang passed away, and his son Ji Fa succeeded him. In the eleventh year (some sources say thirteenth year) of his rule, Ji Fa "commanded 300 chariots, 3,000 elite soldiers, and 45,000 armored troops to launch an offensive against the Shang," and "when the allied forces of the feudal lords assembled, they deployed 4,000 chariots and soldiers in the pasture." In the decisive Battle of Muye (currently south west of Qixian in Henan), the Shang's vanguard defected, and King Zhou "committed suicide by fire," precipitating the fall of the Shang Dynasty.[19] Ji Fa proclaimed that he had "fulfilled a grand mandate, overthrown the Yin (Shang), and received the Mandate of Heaven," thus founding the Zhou Dynasty. Henceforward, Zhou became known as "the sovereign of all under heaven" and endured for nearly 800 years.

In summary, since Qi cultivated and propagated a variety of crops, his progeny was characterized by the prominence of agriculture until Buzhu, hence "Zhou" became the clan name. From Gong Liu to Gugong Danfu, agriculture continued to evolve; particularly after Gugong Danfu moved to Qixia, the robust economic backbone provided by agriculture cemented the foundation of the kingdom, and the state name "Zhou" was established as a vassal to Shang. After three generations, the Zhou overthrew the Shang and established their own dynasty. Thus, the extensive history leading up to the Zhou Dynasty's establishment was marked by a continuous accumulation of crops in the fields, ongoing enhancements in agricultural techniques, and relentless cultivation of the land. Consequently, the Zhou clan's economy thrived, culture prospered, politics became structured, and military might intensified. The Zhou evolved from a minor state to a grand empire, eventually assuming dominion over the country. The title "Zhou" fittingly signified their adeptness in agriculture and their emphasis on its importance.

Interestingly, after the establishment of the Zhou Dynasty, some vassal and tributary states conferred by the Zhou also emulated their suzerain in naming their own countries. Qin, which would later overthrow the Zhou Dynasty, was one such vassal state.

Notes

1 There have been at least 44 different conclusions over the past two thousand years about the year of Ji Fa's overthrow of King Zhou and the end of the Shang Dynasty. The earlier ones suggest dates such as 1130 BC, while the later ones propose 1018 BC. Other commonly mentioned dates include 1122 BC, 1066 BC, 1057 BC, and 1027 BC. The most recent "Xia–Shang–Zhou Chronology Project" utilized various methods to narrow down the timeframe of King Wu's overthrow of the Shang Dynasty. These methods involved a comprehensive study of the radiocarbon dating of key archaeological sites, analysis

of eclipse records in oracle bone inscriptions, and examination of historical documents. Additionally, chronological sequencing based on bronze inscriptions and astronomical calculations related to King Wu's victory over the Shang Dynasty were considered. Finally, by integrating these findings, the best estimate for this significant event was determined to be 1046 BC. This conclusion is based on the report "Research on the Year of King Wu's Overthrow of the Shang Dynasty" by the Expert Group of the Xia–Shang–Zhou Chronology Project, published by the China World Publishing Corporation in 2000.

2 It should be noted that the "Western Zhou" mentioned in the last sentence refers to a small state during the Warring States period, which emerged after King Kao of Zhou (named Ji Wei) bestowed a fief to his younger brother, Jie.

3 If we start from 1046 BCE and count until 256 BCE, the total is 791 years.

4 Luo Jiangsheng's "Study on the Names of Qin State (published in *Literature and History*, Volume 38, 1994) provides a comprehensive explanation for this. This section primarily relies on that document while supplementing it with additional information.

5 Institute of Archaeology, Chinese Academy of Sciences, Compilation of Oracle Bone Inscriptions, Volume 2, Zhonghua Book Company, 1965.

6 Rong Geng, Compilation of Bronze Inscriptions, Volume 2, Science Press, 1959.

7 Hu Axiang's "Rectifying the Names of China: Hu Axiang Discusses National Names" (published by Zhonghua Book Company in 2013). Lecture 4 pointed out: "The law of the development of writing is from concrete to abstract, from complexity to simplicity, from randomness to standardization. Therefore, the character '周' should have gone through three stages: field of rice plants, in the field of rice plants, and cultivating rice plants in the field. The horizontal lines represent the distinct boundaries of the fields, and the four dots between the fields represent the crops. In simple terms, '周' means farming in the fields and making a living."

8 The term "Zhouyuan oracle bones" refers to a collection of oracle bone inscriptions from the Zhou people that were discovered in the Zhouyuan site, located at the junction of Qishan and Fufeng counties in present-day Shaanxi Province during the 1970s and 1980s. These inscriptions cover the period from King Wen to King Mu of the Zhou Dynasty and provide historical records from the early establishment of the Zhou Dynasty.

9 Wang Yuxin, An Exploration of Oracle Bones from the Western Zhou Dynasty (Chapter 6), Chinese Social Sciences Press, 1984.

10 In the fourth lecture of "Rectifying the Names of China: Hu Axiang Discusses the National Names", it is stated: "In the Book of Han, it is said that 'The ruler regards the people as heaven, and the people regard food as heaven.' This means that the foundation of a nation lies in its people, and the foundation of the people lies in their sustenance. These are irrefutable truths. The people depend on food, but where does food come from? Apart from the animal food obtained through hunting, herding, and fishing, the primary source is plant-based food obtained through agriculture. Therefore, clearing land, planting crops, harvesting grains, and nurturing the populace are the original and extended meanings of the character 'Zhou' (周).").

11 Yu Yongliang, Explanations of Diagrams for Divination in the Book of Changes: The Era and Authors, Journal of the Institute of Historical Linguistics, Volume 1, Section 1, 1928.

   Guo Moruo, Compilation of Divinatory Inscriptions, initially published by Tokyo Bun Kyudo in 1933, included in *The Complete Works of Guo Moruo–Archaeology Compilation*, Volume 2, Science Press, 1983.

   Qi Sihe, A Study of the Names of Places in the Book of Songs, Yan Jing Academic Journal, Issue 36, 1949.

Zhou Fagao, Interpretation of Bronze Inscriptions, Special Issue of the Institute of Historical Linguistics, No. 34, 1951.

Tan Jiefu, The Migration and Social Development of the Pre-Zhou Clan and the Zhou Clan, Literature and History, Volume 6, 1979.

Xu Zhongshu, The Rise of the Zhou Dynasty, included in *Essays on Pre-Qin History*, Bashu Publishing House, 1992.

12 For the dating of Wuding and Wuyi, please refer to the "Chronological Table of Xia, Shang, and Zhou" in the report "Xia-Shang-Zhou Chronology Project 1996–2000 Phase Results Report - Abridged Version" by the Expert Group of the Xia-Shang-Zhou Chronology Project.

13 Tan Jiefu, Migration and Social Development of the Pre-Zhou Clan and the Zhou Clan.

14 Qi Sihe, The Geography of the Western Zhou Dynasty (included in the book *Explorations in Chinese History* published by Zhonghua Book Company in 1981). It states that the Zhou people originated from the western borderlands and lived between the Rong and Di tribes. They were primarily engaged in agriculture and enjoyed abundant resources. The neighboring Rong and Di tribes, who were still in the nomadic stage, wandered in search of water and grasslands, lacking a fixed settlement. They were envious of the wealth and prosperity of the agricultural areas, and often sought to invade and plunder their resources. However, their lifestyle did not offer the same level of ease, abundance, wealth, and cultural development as the agricultural regions.

15 Shi Nianhai, "The Transformation of Zhou Yuan," and "Historical Geography and Archaeology of Zhou Yuan," included in *Collected Works on Rivers and Mountains*, Volume 3, People's Publishing House, 1988.

16 In accordance with *Records of the Grand Historian, Annals of Zhou* and related passages from *Bamboo Annals* and *Book of Songs*.

17 The position of the "mushi" was equivalent to the later "fangbo" in the Zhou Dynasty, serving as the chief of a regional vassal state.

18 This information can be found in the "Biography of Dongfang Shuo" in *Records of the Han Dynasty*.

19 According to the Xia-Shang-Zhou Chronology Project Expert Group's "Simplified Report on the Xia-Shang-Zhou Chronology Project 1996–2000: Phase III - Research on the Year of King Wu's Overthrow of the Shang Dynasty," the decisive battle, the Battle of Muye, was determined to have taken place on January 20th, 1046 BC, based on the combination of historical documents, archaeological information, and astronomical conditions. However, it is important to note that this interpretation is still not definitive and subject to ongoing research and discussion.

4 Qin

The Cattail (Forage Grass) for Raising Horses

After the eastern migration of King Ping of Zhou in 770 BC, the period commonly referred to as the "Eastern Zhou" began. During this time, the power of the Zhou royal family declined significantly, becoming far surpassed by some of the hegemonic states. Despite their weakened state, the Zhou royal family continued to claim the title of rulers of "all under heaven" in name, while the powerful states still rallied under the banner of "respecting the king and expelling the barbarians." For instance, as recorded in the *Annals of the Zhou* from the *Records of the Grand Historian*, in the forty-fifth year of the reign of King Nan of Zhou (270 BC), when Qin attacked Zhou, Prince Zhou Zui advised King Zhaoxiang of Qin as follows:

> The advisor suggested that attacking Zhou would be fruitless and only serve to incite fear in others. If the world fears Qin, they might join forces with Qi. Should Qin suffer defeat at the hands of Zhou, and if Qi were to unite the world under its banner, Qin would lose its dominance. Some advised the king to attack Zhou as a strategy to eliminate the Zhou Dynasty's lingering influence. However, this move could lead to the simultaneous downfall of Qin and the world, rendering any commands ineffective.

Zhang Shoujie of the Tang Dynasty explained this situation in his *Collected Interpretations of the Records of Historian*, saying: "Although the Zhou Dynasty retains its famed treasures, its land is narrow and offers no benefit to Kingdom Qin. If Qin attacks Zhou, it will tarnish the reputation of the Zhou emperor and instill fear of Qin throughout the world, prompting the vassals to unite under Kingdom Qi. If Qin's forces falter in Zhou, and Qi unifies the world, Qin's leadership will end." Despite the lack of emperor's authoritative voice, Zhou Zui's words highlighted that Zhou was still nominally the ruler over "all under heaven." At that time, the name "Zhou" was still synonymously used for the whole of China.

Fourteen years later, King Nan of Zhou passed away in the 59th year of his reign (256 BC). The written history in the *Records of the Grand Historian, Annals of Zhou* concluded the end of the Zhou Dynasty at this point. Zhang Shoujie's *Collected Interpretations of the Records of Historian* comments on the period that followed: "After King Nan's death, no clear ruler emerged for 35 years, and

DOI: 10.4324/9781003510390-5

the Seven Warring States vied for control. It was only with the rise of Qin Shi Huang [First Emperor of the Qin Dynasty] that the world was unified." Similarly, Sima Guang of the Northern Song Dynasty concluded in his *Zizhi Tongjian* with these lines such as "In this year, King Nan died," followed by the beginning of the "Chronicles of Qin," which starts in the 52nd year of King Zhaoxiang of Qin (255 BC). The *Commentary of Zizhi Tongjian* by Hu Sanxing of the Yuan Dynasty mentions: "Following the fall of the Western Zhou Dynasty, no suitable ruler emerged. Therefore, *Zizhi Tongjian* marks the death of King Nan as the symbolic unification of the world by Qin, beginning with King Zhaoxiang's reign."

In fact, during the period from the death of King Nan of Zhou in 256 BC to the unification of the Six States by King of Qin (Yin Zheng) in 221 BC, the Seven Warring States existed without a collective name throughout China. The time span from 221 BC to 206 BC marked the Qin Dynasty in the history of China.

In comparison with the Xia, Shang, and Zhou dynasties, the Qin Dynasty wielded the most tangible power. During the Xia, the royal capital was just surrounded by local tribes; in the Shang, local tribes existed alongside fiefs bestowed upon various lords. After the Shang's fall, the Zhou dynasty and Duke Zhou's successful Eastern Expedition prompted the widespread implementation of a feudal system. While the titles were commonly used terms during the Xia, Shang, and Zhou periods, the names didn't precisely match the political realities. However, starting with Qin Shi Huang, the first emperor of Qin, significant changes occurred. "He unified the four seas, made the Zhou Dynasty's authority weak and its territories lost to feudal lords. He forwent dividing the country by noble landholdings in favor of restructuring it into counties."[1] With policies such as the standardization of writing, chariot axles, and measures, the Qin Dynasty pushed for comprehensive national standardization. Henceforth, any territory under its domain was directly controlled by the emperor. The title "Qin" took on a new level of official status with the Qin Dynasty, reflecting both name and actual sovereignty.

The title "Qin," attributed to the Qin Dynasty, had a profound and ancient origin. As mentioned in the *Annals of Qin* in the *Records of the Grand Historian*, during the reign of King Xiao of Zhou, Feizi was granted land as a Fuyong (vassal) ,[2] and thus he founded the state of Qin, marking Qin's first political entity (state) around the early 9th century BC.[3] Many scholars later posited that the name "Qin" was derived from its geographic location. However, oracle bone and bronze inscriptions, as well as interpretations found in the *Shuowen Jiezi* (a dictionary of Chinese characters), suggest that the name "Qin" originated from the state itself. Such reasoning also challenges the assertion that the names of the Shang and Zhou dynasties stemmed from their respective states.

4.1 "Qin, the Name of the Forage Grass"[4]

The core issue in explaining the origin and meaning of the name "Qin" is to clarify the original meaning of the character "秦." According to the *Shuowen Jiezi* by Xu Shen of the Eastern Han Dynasty:

"It is the state that was bestowed upon the successor of Bo Yi. The land was suitable for growing grain; hence the character was formed from the radical '禾' and the simplified form of '春.' Alternatively, it is named after the grain it grows."

The annotation by Duan Yucai of the Qing Dynasty adds: "It is said that the character was formed from the radical '禾' and the simplified form of '春' because the land was suitable for growing grain. In the *Zhou Li*, it is stated that the valleys in Yongzhou are suitable for growing millet and grain. How could it be that only the valleys in Qin are suitable for growing '禾' (grain)? ... The original meaning of this character '秦' is not based on the association of pounding grain but is rather named after the land, as commonly passed down by the people. '秦, the Name of the Forage Grass' refers to another saying."

It is necessary to briefly explain *Shuowen Jiezi*, a dictionary by Xu Shen, which is frequently cited in this book. Xu Shen (approximately 58 AD–approximately 147 AD) wrote the *Shuowen Jiezi*, which was considered the most important academic work during the debate over the use of ancient and modern Chinese writing during the Han Dynasty. The "modern classics" referred to the Confucian classics transmitted by Han scholars, which were recorded in contemporary script (clerical script) and mostly did not have ancient texts from before the Qin Dynasty. They were passed down from teachers to students across several generations starting from the Warring States period and were not written down as a definitive version until the Han Dynasty. On the other hand, the "ancient classics" referred to Confucian classics written in the ancient script (a script that was used in the Warring States period by six states) before the Qin Dynasty and were interpreted by Han scholars.

As is well known, since Emperor Wu of the Western Han Dynasty implemented the cultural policy of "abolishing various schools and emphasizing Confucianism," Confucian classics were recognized, the position of professors of Confucian classics was established, and scholars competed to study these classics for the purpose of becoming officials. However, the modern and ancient classics not only differ in their writing styles but also vary greatly in content and interpretation, which caused a debate between the two schools. The problem was that this debate was not only academic but also critical as it affected the establishment of professors and the adoption of Confucianism as a governance principle. Xu Shen was a member of the ancient classics camp and believed that explaining ancient classics using the contemporary script was forced and lacked logical justification, whereas the ancient script had various meanings that necessitated identification and interpretation. Therefore, Xu Shen devoted his life to compiling the *Shuowen Jiezi* by using the ancient classics like *Book of Shizhou, Book of Cangjie,* and other ancient books to create a definitive analysis of the ancient Chinese script. The *Shuowen Jiezi* enriched and improved the "Six Categories" system of Chinese characters (namely, formation, semantic, compound ideographic, phonetic, loan, and transformed meanings) and established the method of clarifying the origin of Chinese characters by analyzing their structure and pronunciation. Thus, it achieved the objective of creating a basis for the objective interpretation of ancient literature to a considerable extent. On the other hand, the *Shuowen Jiezi* also preserved diverse ancient written materials and became an essential tool for later researchers of ancient Chinese history and culture. For example, in this book, the earlier discussion of the country names of the Xia, Shang, and Zhou dynasties; the explanation of the name of Qin in this chapter; and the argument about the name of the Han Dynasty in the following chapter all rely on the critical key provided by the *Shuowen Jiezi*.

How do we understand the citations related to the character 秦 in Xu Shen's *Shuowen Jiezi* and Duan Yucai's annotations? From the text, Xu Shen defines "Qin" primarily as "the state enfeoffed to the descendants of Boyi." However, he does not clarify whether this was a newly established name or a pre-existing one. Duan Yucai explains that "Qin" primarily refers to a geographical location and cites common understanding to support this, revealing a degree of uncertainty.

Considering Xu Shen's principles of analyzing character sound, form, and meaning, as discussed in the preface, he indeed seems to have drawn heavily from the views of ordinary people, while also using scholars' views for verification. It suggests that "the state enfeoffed to the descendants of Boyi" was the prevalent interpretation then, thus ascribed as the primary meaning. "Qin, the name of forage grass," likely came from public explanation and was deemed a secondary meaning.

A thorough examination of *Shuowen Jiezi* shows that, because "秦" falls under the radical of '禾'(grain), "the name of forage grass" should take precedence as the main meaning. Subsequent scholars, including Zhu Junsheng in his *Shuowen Tongxun Ding Sheng*, acknowledge this and adjust Xu Shen's definition of Qin as this: "Qin, a grain name, derived from 'grain' and 'threshing,' a pictogram. The meaning as a state name was applied later." Thus, "name of forage grass" was restored as the primary and initial meaning of "Qin." Similar support comes from Wang Shenxing's *Shuowen Bianzheng Juli*[5] and Japanese scholar Takada Chushu's *Ancient Zhouwen*.[6]

In the oracle bone script, the character 秦 was written as 𧗿, and 𧗿 in the bronze inscription of the Zhou Dynasty[7]. *Shuowen Jiezi* references oracle bone script from the Warring States period and the seal script from the Qin and Han dynasties. By comparison, the primary structure of 秦 remains consistent across oracle bone script and bronze inscriptions, indicating its original form. Despite changes in the seal scripts, some features of the original character have been preserved.

Analyzing the original form of 秦 in the oracle bone script and bronze inscriptions, the character denotes vigorously growing grain seedlings; the top part resembling grain ears reaching skyward; the two hands indicate manual harvesting. This highlights that "秦" was a distinct type of forage grass, cultivated unlike other grains.

Homophonic characters similar to "Qin," such as "榛," "蓁," "溱," "臻," "轃," and "捸," bear meanings that align with dense, clustered growth, the etymological essence of "秦."

Regarding the type of grain "秦" represents, "禾" holds dual meanings: the generic term refers to all flowering cereal crops ("秀" denotes flowering); and it refers to a specific cereal as well. "稷" being the known type of the most popular grain,

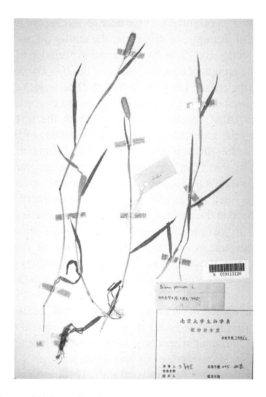

Figure 4.1 Specimen of high-quality forage grass Phleum pratense in the Poaceae family

it is evident that "禾" and "稷" never occur together in ancient texts. Qi Sihe notes that "禾" is a generic term for grain, the derivatives are all named after this radical. Including "秦," other grains also take their names from 禾. Over time, words such as "米," "粟," "糖," "苗," "稿," "秸," "秆," "科," "穰," "秀," and "穗" all originally denoted "禾" before expanding to general grain types.[8] Hence "秦" is actually a type of grain. The distinctive feature that sets it apart from other grains is its dense and clustered growth and the upward-facing ears (see Figure 4.1).

This kind of densely grown and upward-facing ears of grain has been examined by Luo Jiangsheng through field investigations and physical evidence. It has been found that the plant known as "Cao Gu"(grass grain) within Chinese folklore, also called "Mao Gu" or "Mao Wei Gu" (cattail), matches exactly the description of "秦."

Still cultivated in north west China, it is grown as fodder, sown densely without weeding, and fully harvested for livestock feed. Known as "grass grain" for its cultivation for forage or "cattail"[9] due to the similarity of its slender grain ears to a cat's tail, this mirrors the characteristics of grain's growth pattern of "Qin" (see Figure 4.2).

Figure 4.2 High-quality forage grass Phleum pratense in the Poaceae family

Considering the above, "Qin" is indeed the name of a grain. How then did "Qin," a grain used exclusively for animal feed, become the name of a state? In contrast to "Zhou," which was named after a human dietary staple, how did "Qin," the forage grass totally irrelevant to human dietary needs, acquire its status as a state name?

4.2 A Vassal State for the Breeding of Horses

Derived from the grain name, the character 秦 refers to both a type of grain and the name of a state. This association links the history of the people of Qin with their ancestral legends.

According to the "Annuals of Qin" in the *Records of the Grand Historian*, the establishment of the Qin state began with a man named Feizi, a vassal under the reign of the Zhou Dynasty.

Feizi resided on Quanqiu and excelled in the breeding of horses and livestock. The residents of Quanqiu informed King Xiao of Zhou of Feizi's talent, and the king enlisted Feizi to manage the royal horses between the Qian and Wei Rivers. Feizi's breeding program was successful, and the horses multiplied rapidly. Subsequently, King Xiao of Zhou declared, "Previously, Bo Yi managed Shun's livestock, which prospered immensely, leading to him being granted a territory and the surname Ying. Now, Feizi's descendants have also demonstrated mastery in livestock breeding, thus I will bestow upon them a territory as a vassal state." The land of Qin was granted, and Feizi's descendant was named Qin Ying.

Additionally, the *Records of the Grand Historian* briefly recounts the ancestral legend of the Qin people, mentioning that the first Qin ancestor was Nü Xiu, a granddaughter of Emperor Zhuanxu.

While weaving, Nü Xiu was struck by a black bird's egg, which she swallowed and later gave birth to a son named Da Ye. Da Ye wed the daughter of Shao Dian, Nü Hua, who bore a son named Da Fei. Da Fei supported Yu in managing the floodwaters and received Emperor Shun's recognition in the form of the territory Fuyou, being titled "Da Fei, Heir to Future Greatness." Acknowledged for his success in nurturing and domesticating birds and animals, Da Fei was granted the surname of Ying by Emperor Shun. He had two sons: Da Lian, the progenitor of the Bird clan, and Ruo Mu, the progenitor of the Fei clan. The Fei clan's great-great-grandson, Fei Chang functioned as King Tang's charioteer during King Jie of the Xia dynasty. The great-great-grandson of Dalian, known as Meng Xi and Zhong Yan, possessed bird-like bodies and human voices, serving Emperor Taiwu as charioteers.

The *Annals of Qin* in the *Records of the Grand Historian* further emphasizes the significance of the Zhongyu lineage within the Qin ancestry. The *Annals of Qin* outline the following details:

Zhongyu, offspring of Zhongyan, settled in the Western Rong and guarded the Western borders. His son, Fei Lian, and grandson, E Lai, both remarkably swift and formidable, served King Zhou of the Shang Dynasty. Upon King Wu of the Zhou Dynasty's defeat of King Zhou, both Fei Lian and E Lai were killed. Fei Lian's son, Ji Sheng, and grandson, Meng Zeng, were favored by King Cheng of the Zhou Dynasty. Their line endured through to Zao Fu, who, with his exceptional horsemanship, captivated King Mu of the Zhou Dynasty and was gifted four horses—Ji, Wenli, Hualiu, and Luer. King Mu also awarded him the town of Zhaocheng, thus beginning the Zhao clan's legacy. The offspring of Fei Lian, E Lai Ge, succumbed to an untimely death, but left behind a son named Nü Fang who fathered Pang Gao. Thereafter, Pang Gao sired Tai Ji, then Tai Ji fathered Da Luo, and Da Luo fathered Fei Zi. All enjoyed the patronage of Zao Fu, acquiring Zhaocheng and adopting the surname of Zhao.

According to the *Annals of Qin* in the *Records of the Grand Historian* and the legend of the ancestors of the Qin people before the establishment of the state by Feizi, we can draw the following conclusions through analysis:

1. Feizi was the earliest vassal of the Qin people, having been granted the title in the early 9th century BC. The real history of the Qin people and their family tree can only be traced after Feizi, while the period before Feizi is regarded as mostly legendary.

2. The debate concerning whether the Qin people originated from the east or the west has persisted for a long time. Advocates of the east migration theory include Wei Juxian, Huang Wenbi, Xu Xusheng, Zou Heng, Lin Jianming, Xu Zhongshu, Han Wei, and Mou Shishan, and so forth. Proponents of the west migration theory include Wang Guowei and Meng Wentong, and so forth.[10] Understanding the social and cultural characteristics of a people's origin and migration is crucial. However, as Li Ling has highlighted,

"The people of Qin had a defined range of residence and activity ... They did not belong to the various branches of the east ... They came from the Zhongyu branch, which settled in the western Rong area as early as the end of the Shang Dynasty. Therefore, at least from the end of the Shang Dynasty, the direct ancestors of the Qin people were influenced by western Rong culture and later by Zhou culture, thereby forming their own cultural identity. This can be confidently affirmed."[11]

Wang Guowei also stated, "At the end of the Shang Dynasty, there was a person named Zhongyu who had already settled in the western borders. It was not until the time of Da Luo and Feizi that there existed a recorded family tree, and the historical accounts became more credible."[12] In light of the economic and cultural characteristics of Qin and its level of social development, the establishment of Qin's national identity should also be understood on the premise that Qin was settled in the western border area.

3. "The Annals of Qin" in the *Records of the Grand Historian* clearly states that Feizi was able to become a vassal state because he raised horses for the Zhou Dynasty and achieved great success in breeding them. The term "vassal state" refers to the small states subordinated by the Zhou court. Therefore, the use of "Qin" as the national name and the Qin people being referred to as "Qin" originated at this juncture. What contributed to Feizi's success in horse breeding, besides his good techniques? "We should be pragmatic and acknowledge that solving feed problems was likely a major factor."[13]

"Qin" (dense-growing grain) is a common fodder crop today, but 3,000 years ago, during Feizi's era, the challenge was not so straightforward. At that time, "Qin" was an exceptional fodder crop. Utilizing the favorable natural conditions around the Quanqiu[14] and between the Qian and Wei Rivers, Feizi cultivated large quantities of millet to feed his horses, which led to the prosperity of the horse-breeding industry. Consequently, the Fei Zi tribe gained recognition from the Zhou Dynasty. It stands to reason that without effectively addressing the feed problem, even if Feizi and his people possessed extraordinary breeding skills, their success in horse breeding would have been unlikely.

In conclusion, we can assert that the ancestors of the Qin people, the Fei Zi tribe, were able to rear horses by planting "Qin," which led to their establishment as a vassal state under the Zhou Dynasty. To lay the fundamental groundwork for the state, they named the country "Qin."[15] Regarding the location of the vassal state, the land was also named Qin, as reference to the *Annals of Qin* in the *Records of the Grand Historian*.

4. From the story of Fei Zi establishing the Qin State by raising horses, we can decipher many doubts about the ancestral legends of the Qin people in later generations and understand some of the unique cultural traits of the Qin Dynasty. In the legends, the most noteworthy ancestor of the Qin people is Boyi, who is said in the *Records of the Grand Historian* to have "assisted Emperor Shun in taming birds and beasts, and many birds and beasts were tamed," and in the "Geographical Records" of the *Book of Han* to have "had no surname until Boyi, who was bestowed with the surname Ying."[16] Thus, the Qin people recognized

Boyi as their ancestral idol primarily due to his expertise and status as a specialist in raising and breeding crops, animals, and birds in ancient legends and having served as the official "Yu" of Emperor Shun, which was equivalent to the Minister of Agriculture and Forestry in later times. As a nomadic tribe in the western region, the Qin people, motivated by the desire to succeed, voluntarily worshipped Boyi as a spiritual idol of their tribe and gradually evolved him into their legendary ancestor.

In Qin culture, horses have a certain core status. The *Records of the Grand Historian* states, "Feilian is good at running, and Zhaofu is good at driving the chariot." Before Feilian and Zhaofu, Fei Chang, Meng Xi, and Zhong Yan were all imperial horse attendants, which shows that the ancestors of the Qin people were known for their skill in raising and driving horses. In addition, Wang Zijin's analysis of *The Classic of Mountains and Seas* highlights that "some inventions in the livestock industry with revolutionary significance all happened in Qin territory ... Veterinary medicine, horse training, and horse taming techniques, which have shamanistic characteristics, all originated in Qin territory, and should be seen as a sign that reflects a certain cultural commonality."[17] In the *Book of Songs*, there are also many poems that attest to the Qin people's love for their chariots and horses, such as "Chelin," "Sijin," "Xiaorong," and so on. Therefore, it is clear that Qin not only established its country by raising horses through Fei Zi but also had excellence in raising and driving horses as one of its defining cultural traits.

5. The geographic area where the state of Qin was established was called the "Qian-Wei convergence" region, rather than the "Qinting (Pavilion Qin) and Qingu (Valley Qin)" in Longxi as suggested by later scholars and the "Geographical Records" of the *Book of Han*.

The name "Qin" is derived from the vassal state of Fei Zi, but the exact location of Qin remained uncertain for some time. The lines in the *Annals of Qin* of the *Records of the Grand Historian* state, "the capital of Qin." *Collected Expositions of the Records of the Historian* by Pei Yin of the southern Song Dynasty quotes Xu Guang of the eastern Jin Dynasty, who says that Qin was located in today's Qinting (Pavilion Qin) in Tianshui of Gansu Province. Zhang Shoujie of the Tang Dynasty, in his *Collected Interpretations of the Records of the Historian*, citing the *Geographical Chorography* written in his time, claims that Qing Shui County in the Qin prefecture of the Tang dynasty was a settlement of Fei Zi's vassal Qin. *The Thirteen States Records* indicate that Qinting and Qingu were the same place. Yuan dynasty commentator Hu Sanxing, quoting Sui and Tang geographer Lu Deming, wrote that "Qin was a valley in Longxi, north east of Niaoshu Mountain in Yongzhou." "Geographical Records" of the *Book of Han* by Ban Gu of the Han Dynasty had already mentioned that Qin was a vassal state, with its capital in today's Qinting and Qingu in Longxi.

However, these claims do not correspond to the original text in the *Annals of Qin* in the *Records of the Grand Historian*. Firstly, as a vassal state, Qin should have been located close to the Zhou dynasty.[18] Secondly, although Sima Qian does not directly point out where Qin was located, he clearly states that in the fourth year of Duke Wen of Qin (762 BC), Duke Wen went to the "Qian-Wei convergence," where Fei Zi was granted his territory by Zhou and where he established his capital city. Li Ling's research concluded that this city was the same place as Fei Zi's Qin, which was located at the confluence of the River Qian and River Wei in the east of Baoji City, Shaanxi province.

Li's research has been widely accepted by many scholars, including Wang Hui, a disciple of Qian Mu, who stated, "Qin was at the Qian-Wei convergence, which is very clear."[19] Historian Shi Nianhai pointed out that the two valleys of the Qian and Wei rivers were "extremely important" for the later state of Qin.[20] In other words, King Xiao of Zhou assigned Fei Zi to breed horses in the "Qian-Wei convergence" region near Zhouyuan, and then granted the territory there, which later became a vassal state. Qin, a later unified dynasty, was established on this foundation and gradually became strong.

4.3 The Increasing Influence of the Title of Qin

From the early 9th century BC, when Fei Zi was made a vassal of the Zhou Dynasty, to the 26th year of King Zheng of Qin's reign (221 BC) when he unified the six states, the people of Qin embarked on a development journey spanning over 600 years. The twists and turns of this process are primarily documented in the *Annals of Qin* and the *Annals of the First Emperor of Qin* within the *Records of the Grand Historian*. Below, we mainly list key historical facts pertinent to the national status and geographical reach of Qin as recorded in these annals. From these records, the gradual rise in the influence of the Qin state becomes evident.

Fei Zi was ennobled with the Qin territory, starting a hereditary line continued by his descendant, Qin Zhong. King Xuan of the Zhou Dynasty appointed Qin Zhong as a senior official and tasked him with an assault on the West Rong, a campaign during which he met his end. "The Annals of the Twelve Feudal Lords" in the *Records of the Grand Historian* commence with the account of Qin Zhong.

After the demise of Qin Zhong, King Xuan of Zhou charged his son with leading an army of 7,000 soldiers against the West Rong, which culminated in success. Subsequently, Qin Zhong's eldest son was named the Grand Duke of Xi Chui and made his residence in West Quanqiu.

Upon the death of Qin Zhong's eldest son, who was posthumously titled Duke Zhuang, his second son ascended as Duke Xiang. The "Chronicles of Qin," supplementing the *Annals of the First Emperor of Qin*, begins with Duke Xiang. His tenure marked the recognition of Qin as a feudal state, a significant milestone in the history of Qin's progression. The Qingong Bo Bell, dating from the early Spring and Autumn period, was unearthed at the Taigong Temple in Baoji County, Shaanxi in 1978. The inscriptions of the Bell assert thus: "Qin Gong proclaimed: My forebears were graced with the Mandate of Heaven, which endowed me with land and conferred upon me a state." Here, "endowing with land" alludes to Fei Zi's territory grant, and "conferring a state" refers to Duke Xiang's elevation to a feudal lordship. These were pivotal moments in the collective memory of the Qin populace. The *Annals of Qin* also delve into greater detail regarding the events that followed:

> King You of Zhou replaced his heir with his consort Bao Si's son. Her infidelity incited rebellion among the lords of other states. Subsequently, the Western Rong and Qiang people invaded Zhou and killed King You at Lishan. Nevertheless, Duke Xiang of Qin dispatched forces to assist Zhou, displaying valor and subsequently earning honors for his contributions. As the Zhou resisted the Western Rong and retreated eastward to Luoyi, Duke Xiang provided an escort to King Ping of Zhou and was rewarded with the title of vassal, along with lands west of the Qin Mountains. Thereafter, Duke Xiang initiated his reign, affiliating with other state lords and presenting them with tributes of three white horses, three yellow oxen, and three fat sheep for sacrificial offerings at Xichou.[21] In the twelfth year of his rule, Duke Xiang engaged the Rong in battle near the Mountain Qi, where he met his demise. His son, Duke Wen, succeeded him as the ruler of Qin.

The *Annals of the Qin* record this event but do not provide a specific year. It is believed to have happened in the eighth year of Duke Xiang's reign, which corresponds to 770 BC, the first year of the Eastern Zhou in traditional Chinese history.

In the sixteenth year of Duke Wen's reign, he defeated the Rong army and "subsequently acquired the remaining Zhou territory up to the Mountain Qi."

After many generations, Duke Mu of Qin continued to expand the Qin territory. In the seventeenth year of his reign (643 BC), "Qin's territory extended eastward up to the Yellow River." In the thirty-seventh year of his reign (623 BC), "Qin used the plan of Youyu to attack the Rong and expanded its territory by 1,000 li, thereby dominating the Western Rong." The emperor sent Duke Zhao to congratulate Duke Mu of Qin on his successes with gifts of gold and drums, essentially acknowledging Qin's dominant position in the West. Later, Duke Xiao of Qin recounted, "In the past, Duke Mu cultivated virtue and martial prowess between Mountain Qi and Yong, conquered Jin to the east, set the Yellow River as the boundary, dominated the Rong and Di to the west, and extended his territory a thousand li. The emperor congratulated him, and the lords of the states commended him, laying the foundations for the future and shining brightly."[22]

After Duke Mu, there were sixteen rulers until Duke Xiao. At that time, Qi, Chu, Wei, Yan, Han, and Zhao were the six strong states east of the Yellow River, and there were more than ten small states between the Huai and Si rivers. Wei bordered Qin and had built a long wall, with Shang County to the north of Zheng and Binyang. Chu controlled Bashu and Qianzhong to the south of the Han River. With the Zhou dynasty in decline, the vassal states wielded their own political power and competed with each other. Qin, located in Yongzhou, did not participate in the competitions of the vassal states in the central plain, and was treated as a barbarous tribe. Duke Xiao then promoted benevolence, helped orphans and widows, recruited warriors, and clearly rewarded achievements. He issued a call for talent and Wei Yang, a citizen of Wei state (also known as Gongsun Yang), made great contributions to Qin and so was granted fifteen cities in Shangyu as a reward.

Henceforth, he was known as "Shang Yang." In the third year of Duke Xiao's reign (359 BC, or, according to some sources, 356 BC), Shang Yang initiated the first reform, which was followed by a second one twelve years later. After the reforms, "the people of Qin became rich and strong. The emperor rewarded Duke Xiao, and the vassal states congratulated him."[23] Qin gradually evolved into a powerful state and eventually became known as a "tiger and wolf state." Shang Yang's reforms laid a solid groundwork for Qin's later conquest of the six states.

After Duke Xiao, there were rulers such as Duke (King) Huiwen, King Wu, and finally King Zhaoxiang. During this period, with Qin's constant struggle for cities and land expansion, its status rose rapidly. In the second year of Duke Huiwen's reign (336 BC), the emperor congratulated Qin, and in the fourth year, he rewarded him for his achievements in governance and military. In the thirteenth year (325 BC), Duke Huiwen declared himself king. During King Wu's reign, he "wished to let his carriage pass through San Chuan (a tributary of the Yellow River) and concealed his ambition of usurpation." In the nineteenth year of King Zhaoxiang's reign (288 BC), Qin and Qi agreed to title themselves emperors, with Qin as the Western Emperor and Qi as the Eastern Emperor, but both later renounced their emperor titles. In the fifty-first year (256 BC), Qin destroyed the Western Zhou, and the royal family of Zhou was also eliminated. In the fifty-second year, the people of Zhou fled to the east, and the Nine Cauldrons (symbol of the ruling power) were taken by Qin. In the fifty-third year (254 BC), "guests from all over the world came to Qin." From then on, Qin took the place of Zhou and became the master of land under heaven.

After King Zhaoxiang's death, King Xiaowen succeeded to the throne but died after only one year. King Zhuangxiang succeeded him but also died after just three years. In 246 BC, following the death of King Zhuangxiang, his son Ying Zheng succeeded him and later became the first emperor of the Qin Dynasty.

When Ying Zheng (also known as Zhao Zheng) became the King of Qin at the age of 13, "Qin had already conquered Ba, Shu, and Hanzhong, and had established the Nanjun region by taking over Ying of the Yue. They had also conquered areas to the north including Hedong, Taiyuan, and Prefecture Shangdang, and to the east, they destroyed the Zhou dynasties and established the Prefecture Sanchuan." When Ying Zheng succeeded the reign, he continued to conquer the territories of the six kingdoms: Qin destroyed Han in 230 BC; conquered Zhao and captured the king in 228 BC; vanquished Yan in 226 BC and the king of Yan fled to Liaodong; conquered Wei in 225 BC, and Chu in 223 BC, capturing the king; and subdued the south, forcing the Yue state to surrender; Qin overcame Liaodong in 222 BC, capturing the king, and Dai in 221 BC. By this time, "King Zheng had been in power for 26 years and had established the 36 commanderies, proclaiming himself as Shi Huang (the First Emperor of Qin)." The Qin Dynasty had unified the whole country, and the name "Qin" became the common name for China at that time, establishing the foundation for the future territory of the country.

However, the Qin Dynasty, which was the first unified empire in Chinese history, created after more than 600 years of ups and downs, lasted only 15 years before it collapsed. "Five years later, the empire was reestablished under the Han Dynasty."

Notes

1 "Geographical Records" in the *Book of Han*
2 The term "fuyong" refers to the small states that were feudal vassals of the Zhou Dynasty. In the "Royal Regulations" of the *Book of Rites*, it states, "Those who do not align with the Son of Heaven but are attached to the feudal lords are called fuyong." The Eastern Han scholar Zheng Xuan commented, "Not aligning means not attending the court meetings. The term fuyong refers to small towns." The Tang Dynasty scholar Kong Yingda elaborated, "When it says not aligning means not attending the court meetings, it means that they are not allowed to participate in the gatherings between feudal lords and the Son of Heaven. When it says small towns referred to as fuyong, fuyong means city. It means that the small country is unable to communicate independently, so its state affairs are attached to a larger country, hence the term fuyong." Thus, originally, "fuyong" referred to small towns but later extended to refer to small states and their feudal lords who were subordinate to the vassals.
3 The reign of King Xiao of Zhou is estimated to have been from 891 BC to 886 BC. This is based on the *Chronology of Xia-Shang-Zhou* provided by the Xia-Shang-Zhou Chronology Project Expert Group's "Simplified Report on the Xia-Shang-Zhou Chronology Project 1996–2000: Phase III," World Book Publishing Company, Beijing, 2000.
4 This section is based on the revised version of "A Study on the Names of the State of Qin" by Luo Jiangsheng (published in the 38th issue of "Journal of Literature and History" in 1994), with some additional information included. The following section also incorporates many insights from Luo Wen's profound knowledge.
5 Wang Shenxing, Identification and explication of Shuowen Jiezi, appendix of the *Exploration of Chinese Characters and Cultural Traditions* by Huang Dekuan and Chang Sen, University of Science and Technology of China Press,1995.
6 Luo Jiangsheng, A Study on the Names of the State of Qin
7 Gao Ming, Compilation of the Ancient Characters, Zhonghua Book Company, 1980.
8 Qi Sihe, A Study on the Names of Valleys in the Book of Songs, Yanjing Academic Journal, Issue 36, 1949.
9 According to the information obtained from the research, it is known that the formal name of "Mao Wei Gu" is now called "Mao Wei Cao" (Cat's Tail Grass), also known as "Ti Mu Cao" (Ladder Pasture). This type of grass is adapted to cool and moist climates, grows to a height of about 1 meter, and generally has a lifespan of 6 to 7 years, although some can live up to 10 to 15 years. Its yield is measured in terms of green grass and ranges from 1600 kg to 2500 kg per acre. Donkeys and horses prefer to eat this type of grass, but sheep should not consume it excessively, as it can cause loss of appetite.
10 For further information, please refer to Chapter 2 of *History of Qin* by Lin Jianming, published by Shanghai People's Publishing House in 1981, and Chapter 2 of *Cultural Exploration of Records of the Grand Historian* by Wang Zijin, published by Hubei People's Publishing House in 1997.
11 Li Ling, The Early Urban Burial Sites of Qin as Seen in *Records of the Grand Historian*, Journal of Literature and History, Issue 20, 1983.
12 Wu Guo Wei, A Study on the Capital Cities of the State of Qin, Guan Tang Ji Lin, Volume 1-2, Zhonghua Book Company, 1959.
13 Luo Jiangsheng, A Study on the Names of the State of Qin.
14 The "Qianqiu" mentioned here refers to the Western Qianqiu, named so to distinguish it from the Qianqiu in the eastern Guanzhong region (the former capital of King Yi

of Zhou) which is located in the south east of Xingping City, Shaanxi Province. The Western Qianqiu is situated in the south west of Tianshui City, Gansu Province, and the north east of Lixian County.

15 In fact, such naming laws are not uncommon worldwide. For example, the country name Brazil originally referred to a type of redwood, Cameroon to a large crayfish, Mali to a hippopotamus, Spain to a wild rabbit, Brunei to a mango, and Liechtenstein to shining stones, among others. It can be seen that naming a country based on its natural resources is a common phenomenon. According to toponymic terminology, this is known as the characteristic naming method. Specifically, in the case of the vassal states mentioned in the text, the name "Qin" was chosen because the plant Qin played a crucial role in the establishment and foundation of their statehood.

16 In the "Book of Han: Treatise on Geography," Tang Yanshigu provided annotations stating that "Bo Yi" is an alternative name for "Bo Yi," as they have similar sounds. In addition, in the "Classic of Documents: Ode of Emperor Shun," Kong Yingda explained that the official is named "Yu," and the Emperor used the term to refer to the official's function, while "Zhen" is not an official designation.

17 Wang Zijin, Cultural Excavations of Shi Ji, Chapter 2.

18 *Annals of Qin* in *Records of the Grand Historian*: In the eleventh year of Duke Xian of Qin (around 374 BC), Dian, the historian of the Zhou Dynasty, met with Duke Xian and said, "The Zhou and Qin states were once united and then separated. After five hundred years of separation, they reunited, and seventeen years later, the Hegemon emerged." Similar references can be found in the *Annals of Zhou* and "*The Book of Enfeoffment*" in *Records of the Grand Historian*. The union of the Zhou and Qin refers to the Zhou royal family granting territory to Feizi near Qi Zhou. The time would be approximately during the reign of King Xiao of Zhou.

19 Wang Hui, "A Study on the Capitals of Zhou and Qin," Journal of Historiography, Issue 3, 1970.

20 Shi Nianhai, "Historical Geography and Archaeology of Zhouyuan," included in *He Shan Ji*, Volume 3, People's Publishing House, 1988.

21 "Chronicles of the Six States" in *Records of the Grand Historian*: "The Grand Historian read the 'Annals of Qin' and reached the part where the Quan Rong defeated King You of Zhou, and the Zhou Dynasty moved its capital eastward to Luoyi. It was at this time that Duke Xiang of Qin was first enfeoffed as a vassal lord, conducting state affairs in Xichou. The ambition of usurpation was evident."

22 According to "Chronicles of the Six States" in *Records of the Grand Historian*, Duke Mu of Qin was once hailed as one of the Five Hegemons of the Spring and Autumn period and was said to be on a par with Duke Huan of Qi and Duke Wen of Jin in terms of prestige and status. However, in the struggle for dominance in the Central Plains, Duke Mu of Qin did not emerge as a central figure. Until the end of the Spring and Autumn period and the early Warring States period, Qin had yet to play a leading role among the major powers in the Central Plains. This situation only began to change after the reform led by Wei Yang.

23 "Biography of Kings of Shang" in *Records of the Grand Historian*.

5 Han

"The Name 'Tianhan' (Milky Way) is Magnificent"

In 206 BC, King Ziying of Qin surrendered to the Chu general Liu Bang, marking the downfall of the Qin Dynasty, the first unified empire in Chinese history. In 202 BC, Liu Bang, the King of Han defeated Xiang Yu, the Hegemon-King of Western Chu, who then committed suicide at the Wujiang River. Liu Bang subsequently declared himself emperor at the North of Fanshui River and established the Han Dynasty, which succeeded the Qin Dynasty as the second unified empire in China.[1] The Han Dynasty continued until AD 9 when Wang Mang, a royal relative and regent, usurped the throne and renamed the country Xin. In AD 23, Xin was defeated by the rebellion led by Liu Xuan, who then restored the Han Dynasty with the reign name of Gengshi. In AD 25, Liu Penzi, a distant relative of the Han royal family, declared himself emperor with the support of the Red Eyebrow Army. Concurrently, Liu Xiu, another Han royal and a general under Liu Xuan, also declared himself emperor. Liu Xiu succeeded in unifying China, thereby establishing the Eastern Han Dynasty in AD 25. Liu Penzi was defeated by Liu Xiu in the same year, and Liu Xiu was later acknowledged as the legitimate emperor, restoring the Han Dynasty, which lasted until AD 220 when Cao Pi usurped the throne to establish the Wei Dynasty.

The 426 years between the fall of the Qin Dynasty (in 206 BC) and the usurpation of the Han throne by Cao Pi (in AD 220) saw various rulers who held the title of emperor, but their actual power varied. The state of Chu[2], for example, claimed to be the overlord of China but failed to substantiate this claim. The true sovereigns of China during their reigns were the Han[3] and Xin dynasties.

5.1 Xiang Yu Bestowed the King of Han on Liu Bang.

In February 202 BC, Liu Bang, the King of Han, became the emperor and established the Han Dynasty near Fanshui (north of the Fanshui River), in Dingtao, now located in the north western part of Dingtao County, Shandong Province. This year marked the fifth year of the Han Dynasty. Going back to 206 BC, Liu Bang, then the Duke of Pei, was crowned King of Han, marking the first year of the Han Dynasty. The crucial historical facts related to this event are found in "Biography of Xiao He," in the *Book of Han*:

DOI: 10.4324/9781003510390-6

Initially, the feudal lords made a pact to crown as king the one who would first enter the capital and defeat the Qin Dynasty. Liu Bang was the first to capture the Qin Dynasty, and Xiang Yu arrived later, with intentions to attack him. However, a peace was negotiated with Xiang Yu, who then proceeded to burn and destroy Xianyang, the capital of Qin. With Fan Zeng, he planned to relocate the Qin populace to the remote regions of Ba and Shu since they were strategically located and difficult of access. When Fan Zeng suggested that Ba and Shu were part of Guanzhong, Xiang Yu crowned Liu Bang as the King of Han and gave him a third of the Guanzhong territory. He then ordered the surrendering Qin generals to guard against Liu Bang. Therefore, Liu Bang harbored resentment and contemplated attacking Xiang Yu. Advised against it by Zhou Bo, Guan Ying, and Fan Kuai, it was Xiao He who countered, "The King of Han sees death as the worst outcome, but isn't it worse to be outnumbered and defeated in a hundred battles? The Book of Zhou warns of Heaven's punishment for those who don't embrace the gifts of Heaven; the term 'Tianhan [Heavenly Han]' is auspicious for you and carries a momentous weight. Only those like Tang and Wu, who swear allegiance to the many while serving the one, truly succeed. Thus, you should rule the Hanzhong, nurture its people, attract capable individuals, and annex Ba and Shu into your realm. Then, reclaiming the three Qin territories, one may conquer the whole country." Liu Bang, convinced, established his nation and appointed Xiao He as the prime minister.

As predicted by Xiao He, Liu Bang managed to retake the three Qin territories and eventually conquered the whole country. However, looking back to the beginning, why did Liu Bang become angry when he was bestowed the King of Han, and why would he listen to the advice of Xiao He and others to establish his own state? To understand this story, we need to go back to the Chen Sheng Uprising of 209 BC.

The downfall of the Qin Dynasty actually began with Chen Sheng and was completed by Liu Bang. In the *Chronologies of the Qin and Chu* of *Records of the Grand Historian*, it states, "The initial rebellion was led by Chen Sheng, the destruction of Qin was brought about by the Xiang family, the chaos was resolved, the tyrants were overthrown, and order was restored throughout the land. Eventually, the Han Dynasty emerged as the predominant power. In the span of five years, three rulers came to power."[4] The "three rulers" refer to Chen Sheng, Xiang Yu (controlling King Huai of Chu, later known as Emperor Yi of Chu), and Liu Bang. The sequence of events was filled with twists and turns, and drawing on the "Biography of Chen Sheng," *Annals of Xiang Yu*, *Annals of the First Emperor of Qin*, *Chronologies of Qin and Chu*, and *Annals of Emperor Gaozu* in the *Records of the Grand Historian*, and *Annals of Emperor Gao* of *Book of Han*, important historical facts have been arranged and analyzed as follows.

In 209 BC, during the first year of the Emperor II of Qin, Chen Sheng from Yangcheng (now located in Fangcheng County, Henan Province) and Wu Guang from Yangxia (now located in Taikang County, Henan Province) were conscripted, along with over 900 other people, to serve as soldiers stationed in Yuyang (now located south west of Miyun County, Beijing). While passing Daze Township in Qixian (now located in Liucun Town, south west of Suzhou City, Anhui Province), they encountered heavy rain that lasted several days, preventing them from arriving in Yuyang on time. According to the law of the Qin Dynasty, they would be executed for their tardiness. In response, Chen Sheng and Wu Guang decided to rebel, leading the 900 soldiers in an uprising. They quickly took control of Daze Township and Qixian, then moved east and north west separately. By the time the rebel army reached Chen County (now located in Huaiyang County, Henan Province), it had grown into a sizeable force with 600 to 700 chariots, over 1,000 cavalry soldiers, and tens of thousands of infantries. Chen Sheng proclaimed himself king, adopting the regnal name Zhangchu. At that time, the country was suffering under the tyrannical Qin rule, so the uprising received widespread support.

Among the rebels were county officials Liu Bang and Xiao He, warder Cao Can, butcher Fang Kuai, and musician Zhou Bo in Peixian (now located in Feng County, Jiangsu Province). They rebelled, killed the magistrate of Pei, and proclaimed Liu Bang the Peigong.[5] Xiang Liang (the son of Chu's famous general Xiang Yan) and Xiang Yu (Xiang Liang's nephew, with the given name Ji and the courtesy name Yu) from Xiaxiang (now located in Suqian, Jiangsu Province) killed the governor of Kuaiji (now a county in Suzhou, Jiangsu Province), with Xiang Liang appointing himself as the governor and Xiang Yu becoming his assistant.

The anti-Qin resistance centered around the Zhangchu regime established by Chen Sheng.[6] The term "Zhangchu" as seen in the *Records of the Grand Historian* and the *Book of Han* is interpreted by scholars as "restoring a great Chu state." As mentioned earlier, although the Chu state had been conquered, it still had the potential to rise again, so when Chen Sheng called for rebellion, the territory of Chu was vibrating, and the Guandong region was set ablaze with revolt. The rallying power of "Zhangchu" was unparalleled compared to that of the other five states in eastern China.[7]

In 208 BC, the second year of the Emperor II of Qin, "Chen Sheng, the king, ruled for six months" was assassinated by his charioteer Zhuang Jia, who then defected to Qin. Upon hearing the news, Xiang Liang convened other generals to discuss the situation at Xue, where Liu Bang also went and participated. Fan Zeng, a native of Juchao (now located in Tongcheng City, Anhui Province) and then 70 years old, went to persuade Xiang Liang.

> Chen Sheng's defeat was expected. When Qin conquered the six states, Chu received the lightest punishment. After King Huai of Chu surrendered to Qin without resistance, the people of Chu sympathized with him, and this sentiment persists to this day. Therefore, the Nangong of Chu declared, "Though Chu has only three clans left, if Qin falls, it will be Chu's turn to rise."[8] Unfortunately, Chen Sheng's first act was not to establish a Chu successor but to declare himself ruler, a decision that doomed his reign to brevity. Now, as you have risen in Jiangdong and the Chu generals eagerly vie for your favor, you, a Chu general for generations, are seen as the successor who is capable of restoring the state of Chu.

So, Xiang Yu accepted Fan Zeng's suggestion and found Xiong Xin, the grandson of King Huai of Chu, who was a shepherd among the common people, and "crowned him King Huai of Chu as it was what the people wanted."[9] The ceremony was held at Xutai (currently north east of Xuyi County, Jiangsu Province). Xiang Liang assumed the title of Lord Wuxin. During the Battle of Dingtao, Qin general Zhang Han defeated the Chu army, and Xiang Liang perished in battle. Zhang Han then moved north to cross the Yellow River and besiege Handan in Zhao.[10] King Huai of Chu moved the capital to Pengcheng (currently Xuzhou, Jiangsu Province) and appointed Xiang Yu as the Duke of Lu and Liu Bang as the Marquis of Wu'an. He ordered the generals, including Song Yi (former prime minister of Chu and a subordinate of Xiang Liang), Xiang Yu, and others to march north to rescue Zhao, while Liu Bang was ordered to go westward to search for any opportunity to enter Guanzhong. At that time, King Huai of Chu and the generals agreed that whoever entered Guanzhong first would become the king there.[11] However, the Qin army was strong and, riding on its victories, marched on relentlessly to the north. As a result, none of the generals could seize the opportunity to enter Guanzhong, much to Xiang Yu's chagrin, as King Huai of Chu had denied him the chance.

In 207 BC, the third year of the Emperor II of Qin, also the first year of King Ziying of Qin, Xiang Yu executed Song Yi for his delay in the military operations in Anyang and missing the opportunity of advancing. King Huai of Chu then appointed Xiang Yu as Commander-in-Chief. Xiang Yu burned his boats after crossing the Zhang River, and at Julu (currently south west of Pingxiang County, Hebei Province), he vanquished the main Qin forces. "Xiang Yu thus became the commander-in-chief and all the vassal lords submitted to him." Meanwhile, Liu Bang's western army seized Nanyang, took Wuguan, and marching to Lantian, defeated the Qin army.

The Qin Dynasty was teetering on the brink of collapse. Qin Prime Minister Zhao Gao coerced Emperor II of Qin into suicide and argued, "The former State of Qin had King Yingzheng as its ruler, and he declared himself the emperor of all under heaven. Now that the six states have reasserted themselves, and Qin territory has diminished, we should return to the title of king as before, rather than hold onto the vacuous title of emperor." He then instated the nephew of Emperor II of Qin, Prince Ziying, as the King of Qin.[12] However, King Ziying did not want to be Zhao Gao's puppet, so he accused him of collaborating with Chu to eliminate the Qin royal family and take control of Guanzhong. King Ziying had Zhao Gao executed, along with his family.

In 206 BC, after a 46-day reign, King Ziying capitulated to Liu Bang's forces at Bashang (currently east of the Bashui River, Xi'an, Shaanxi Province). King Ziying was compelled to adorn himself with a sword, a rope around his neck, and mounted on a white horse-drawn cart, he carried the imperial seal and proof of succession, signaling his surrender on the roadside. Liu Bang then occupied Capital Xianyang, secured the palace, the official treasury, and state apparatus, and retreated to Bashang. After over a month, when various vassal armies converged, Xiang Yu as the Commander-in-Chief, executed King Ziying together with all other Qin princes and nobility ... Thus, Qin was vanquished!

Following Qin's collapse, Xiang Yu dispatched messengers back to King Huai of Chu, who responded, "As promised," instructing Xiang Yu to honor the agreement that "whoever enters Guanzhong first will become the king." Nevertheless, Xiang Yu "coveted kingship for himself" and resented King Huai of Chu for barring his westward advance into Guanzhong and northward to rescue Zhao. He proclaimed, "It was Xiang Liang who crowned King Huai of Chu. Without our Xiang family's deeds, how could he have become the king with no military achievement? I shall apportion the land among the generals." Consequently, he "feigned reverence to King Huai of Chu, elevating him as Emperor Yi (pseudo-emperor), yet disobeyed his edicts," and proceeded to "parcel out the land and crowned himself king." He elevated the generals who had significantly contributed to the downfall of Qin and the aristocrats of the former six states to ranks of vassal kings, and he declared himself the Hegemon-King of Western Chu, with Pengcheng as his capital. He then exiled the pseudo-emperor to Chen County in Changsha and covertly ordered Ying Bu to assassinate him (in 205 BC).[13]

Grasping these historical events allows one to comprehend why Liu Bang was incensed upon being bestowed the King of Han.

Firstly, according to the agreement between King Huai of Chu and Xiang Yu, as well as other generals, Liu Bang should have been proclaimed the King of Guanzhong. However, Xiang Yu reneged on the agreement and instead bestowed Liu Bang as the King of Han, conferring on him rule over Ba, Shu, and Hanzhong, with Nanzheng as the capital. Xiang Yu's assertion that "Ba, Shu, and Hanzhong are also parts of Guanzhong territory," (recorded in the "Biography of Xiang Yu" in the *Records of the Grand Historian* as "Ba, Shu are also part of Guanzhong territory,") is a clear case of political manipulation. Although Guanzhong wasn't officially designated as a political region, and its boundaries were subject to various interpretations, during the Qin and Han dynasties, Guanzhong most commonly referred to the plains in present-day Shaanxi Province, bordered by the Qian River (which originates from Long County in today's Shaanxi Province) and the Yong River (in Fengxiang County) in the east, and the Yellow River and Huashan Mountains in the west—a definition that did not include Ba, Shu, or Hanzhong.

Secondly, in comparison to Guanzhong and the vast expanse of Guandong, the regions of Ba, Shu, and Hanzhong were considered remote. Han Xin commented on Liu Bang's status, "Xiang Yu appointed all the meritorious generals as kings, but only made you [Liu Bang] king of a remote place in Nanzheng, which was effectively a demotion." Given that all the officers and soldiers were from Shandong and longed to return home day and night, Xiang Yu's pronouncement was indeed harsh as if Liu Bang was "exiled since he had committed any offense,"[14] and Liu Bang's resentment was justified.

Thirdly, Xiang Yu proclaimed himself the Hegemon-King of Western Chu, reigning over nine counties in the Liang and Chu territories, with Pengcheng as his capital. The "nine counties" referred to were Donghai, Sishui, Kuaiji, Dongjun, Dangjun, Xuejun, Chenjun, Dongyang, and Zhangjun.[15] Pengcheng was a significant transportation hub in Guandong. With such a territory and capital city, if it were not for the later rebellion led by Tian Rong and some of Xiang Yu's miscalculations, it would have been possible to maintain control over the other feudal lords. Compared to the 18 kings, Xiang Yu, and his advisor Fan Zeng, particularly viewed Liu Bang as a threat because he was recognized for his benevolence and righteousness, had captured Guanzhong first and accepted the surrender of the King Ziying of Qin, had previously agreed to "the covenant of three chapters" on the condition that he would be made the king of Guanzhong, and had possessed considerable military strength and ambition for the entire nation. Thus, while Xiang Yu granted Liu Bang the title of King of Han, he simultaneously hindered him by strategically placing three states in the regions of Yong, Zhai, and Sai within Guanzhong to "guard against the King of Han at the borders" and further thwart Liu Bang's expansion northwards. He also installed Shen Yang as the King of Henan with Luoyang as his capital, and relocated King Bao of Wei to become the King of West Wei with Pingyang as his capital. Amidst this atmosphere of deep-seated distrust and obstruction, Xiang Yu and Fan Zeng believed that Liu Bang would be unable to turn the tide.

In light of the analysis above, it was certainly understandable for Liu Bang, a mere county chief under Emperor Yi of Chu, to feel indignant upon being named King of Han. However, when he was "enraged" and began plotting to attack Xiang Yu, the circumstances were not ripe for such action, the most apparent reason being that Liu Bang's forces were insufficient to challenge Xiang Yu's. At the time, Xiang Yu commanded an army of 400,000 which was regarded as formidable as a force of one million, whereas Liu Bang only had an army of 100,000 reputed to be 200,000 strong. Furthermore, the Chu soldiers were robust and instilled fear in the Han army. The family background and reputation of Xiang Yu, coupled with his close association with King Huai of Chu—who, despite wielding no actual power, was the nominal supreme leader of the coalition against Qin—were advantages that Liu Bang, with his modest origins, could not match. Aware of these realities, Liu Bang risked attending the Banquet at Hongmen and destroyed the plank roads through the Qinling Mountains to "demonstrate to Xiang Yu that he had no ambition to march eastward."

One detail that merits particular attention is that before Liu Bang departed for his kingdom in Nanzheng, Xiao He offered him insightful advice: "The term 'Tianhan' is remarkably auspicious." Wasn't there a saying about 'Tianhan' (Heavenly Han)? Such a beautiful and magnificent title indeed! Xiao He's counsel likely provided Liu Bang with a measure of solace amid his indignation and sense of powerlessness. It can be believed that Liu Bang's willingness to accept the title of King of Han, and his subsequent decision to name his empire "Han," were influenced by the suggestion from Xiao He.

5.2   Tianhan, Hanzhong and Hanshui

The "Biography of Xiao He" in the *Book of Han* says, "The term 'Tianhan' (Heavenly Han) is such an auspicious and magnificent title." Yan Shigu of the Tang Dynasty, annotated,

> "Meng Kang of the Three Kingdoms period said, it is an ancient saying, which
> means there is a river named 'Han' on earth, just like there is the Milky Way

in the sky, and the name is very auspicious and magnificent." Zan of the Jin Dynasty said, "The popular saying is 'Heavenly Han,' and the word 'Han' is always paired with 'Heaven.' This is also a beautiful name." Shigu agreed, "Zan's interpretation is correct. Heavenly Han refers to the Milky Way."

The so-called "ancient saying" originates from the poem Da Dong in the *Book of Poetry*, with the phrase "There is Han in the sky, shining and dazzling with brilliance." Mao Heng of the Western Han Dynasty explained that "Han refers to the Milky Way." The Milky Way is also known as Yun Han. In the poem "Yun Han," it is written, "The clouds gather in the Milky Way, shining and rotating in the sky." Zheng Xuan of the Eastern Han Dynasty stated that "Yun Han refers to the Milky Way." Kong Yingda of the Tang Dynasty interpreted it as "The Yun Han and the Han in Da Dong are the same; thus, it refers to the Milky Way." The so-called "popular saying" does not contradict the "ancient saying." During the Three Dynasties (namely, the Xia, Shang and Zhou dynasties), and through the Qin and Chu periods, everyone understood astronomy well. Phrases such as "The fireball is falling in July"(namely, the summer is passing and the weather turns cooler), "Three stars are in the household"(namely, the wedding joy), "The moon is rising in Hyades"(namely, there will soon be great rain), and "The dragon tail star hides behind the sun"(namely, the ritual of praying for blessings) were common.[16] It can be surmised that "Han" in astronomy refers to the Milky Way and was commonly used among the people during the Three Dynasties, Qin, and Chu.

Astronomically, "Han," also known as "Tianhan," refers to the Milky Way. Mentioning Han evokes the sky. Hence, "Han" is a magnificent name, and Liu Bang, upon Xiao He's advice, adopted the name since it was affirmatively auspicious. The "Commentary on the Mian River" in the *Commentary on the Waterways Classic* plainly states, " Emperor Gaozu of Han entered Qin, and Xiang Yu conferred the title of 'King of Han' on him. Xiao He said, 'Tianhan is a magnificent name.' Thus, they went to Nanzheng." Volume 22 in the *Yuanhe County and Prefectural Gazetteer* remarks, "After the fall of Qin, Xiang Yu bestowed the title of King of Han on Liu Bang. Gaozu intended to attack Yu, and Xiao He suggested, 'The name Tianhan is magnificent.' So they accepted it." In Xiao He's advice, the name "Tianhan" indeed holds significance (see Figure 5.1).

When Xiang Yu proclaimed Liu Bang as the King of Han, the primary reason was that he had conspired with Fan Zeng to establish the Kingdom of Han, based in Nanzheng, the capital of the Hanzhong Prefecture of the Qin Dynasty. The other kingdoms Xiang Yu established, except the Zhai Kingdom of Dong Yi, were named after their geographical locations, as seen in the following examples[17]:

- King Bao of Wei established the Kingdom of Wei in the west.
- King Cheng of Han established the Kingdom of Han.
- Zang Tu established the Kingdom of Yan.
- Tian Du established the Kingdom of Qi, based on the state destroyed by King Zheng of Qin.

Figure 5.1 A blue and white porcelain plum vase depicting Xiao He's pursuit of Han Xin under the moon, unearthed from the tomb of the Mu family in the Ming Dynasty in Nanjing

- King Xie of Zhao established the Kingdom of Dai, Zhang Er established the Kingdom of Changshan, Ying Bu established the Kingdom of Jiujiang, Wu Rui established the Kingdom of Hengshan, Han Guang established the Kingdom of Liaodong, and Tian Shi established the Kingdom of Jiaodong. These kingdom names derived from the commanderies of the Qin Dynasty.

Additionally:

- Shenyang established the Kingdom of Henan, which located in the south of the Yellow River; and Gong Ao established the Kingdom of Linjiang, whose capital was on the Yangtze River.
- Sima Ang established the Kingdom of Yin, whose capital, Chaoge, was the ancient capital of the Yin Dynasty during the Xia, Shang, and Zhou Dynasties.
- Zhang Han established the Yong Kingdom, named after Qin Yong County in its territory during the Spring and Autumn period.
- Sima Xin established the Kingdom of Sai, which either took its name from the important military area called Taolin Pass or named for "securing the safety of the Huai River and the Hua Mountains."

Xiang Chu established the Kingdom of Western Chu, based in Pengcheng. The "Biography of Emperor Gaozu" in the *Book of Han* notes, "Meng Kang said, 'Jiangling was formerly called Nan Chu (South Chu), Wu was Dong Chu (East Chu), and Pengcheng was Xi Chu (West Chu).' Commentator Yan Shigu confirmed, 'Meng's explanation is correct.'"

Thus, Liu Bang's Han was no exception, and the statement in "Biography of Emperor Gaozu" in the *Records of the Grand Historian* that "Pei Gong was bestowed as the King of Han," and Zhang Shoujie's *Collected Interpretations* are consistent with the name "Han" designated by Xiang Yu and Fan Zeng.

Hanzhong Prefecture was first established during the reign of Chu. In the seventeenth year of King Huai of Chu (312 BC), as *Records of the Grand Historian* records, a devastating battle occurred at Danyang where the Qin army overwhelmingly defeated Chu, killing 80,000 armored soldiers, capturing Grand General Qu Gai and Sub-General Fenghou Chou, among 70 others, and then seizing the Hanzhong Prefecture.[18] During the reign of the Qin Dynasty, the Hanzhong Prefecture, with its capital in Nanzheng, remained unchanged until Liu Bang was enfeoffed as the King of Han.[19]

As for the origin of the name "Hanzhong," the *Commentary on the Waterways Classic* states, "The Hanzhong Prefecture was named after the river Han." Zhang Shoujie's *Collected Interpretations of the Records of the Grand Historian* says, it was "named after the River Han." Undoubtedly the "Han" of Hanzhong Prefecture comes from the river Han. The character "Zhong" is interpreted by scholars as "middle and upper reaches." Shi Nianhai, discussing the situation at the end of the Warring States period, argued, "At that time, the middle and upper reaches of the River of Han were occupied by Chu, which had a Hanzhong Prefecture there. Qin only controlled Nanzheng and its nearby areas. When Qin conquered the Hanzhong Prefecture and established Nan Zheng as the capital, the name has been used ever since. Hanzhong city is situated upstream on the River of Han, and this reasoning underpins the city's name. The western boundary of the Hanzhong Prefecture during the reign of Chu is not precisely recorded."[20] Moreover, Ma Peitang suggests that the designation of Hanzhong Prefecture "might have been initially in Xicheng, occupying the middle section of the entire River of Han ... The county is situated between Bozhong and Dabie Mountains, with the commandery surrounding them, hence the name Hanzhong."[21]

The arguments mentioned above by Shi Nianhai and Ma Peitang are representative, while other similar assertions may be deemed unnecessary to discuss. In fact, such arguments appear rather contrived. Firstly, it is unclear when the Hanzhong Prefecture was established, from where it was governed, and the extent of its territory. Therefore, it seems presumptuous to directly pinpoint the "middle and upper reaches of the River of Han." Secondly, according to the *Book of Han*, Xicheng (currently north west of Ankang City, Shaanxi Province), listed as the first county under Hanzhong Prefecture, should, following convention, be the commandery's capital. However, the counties and commanderies listed in the *Book of Han* predominantly correspond to the timeframe between the years Yuan Yan (12 BC–9 BC) and Suihe (8–7 BC) under Emperor Cheng of Han. As Xicheng is thought to have been founded at the start of the Western Han Dynasty, the claim that Xicheng was administered from the Hanzhong Prefecture lacks substantiation. Even if it were so, this does not imply it spanned the middle of the entire River of Han; the location of Xicheng still falls within the upper reaches of the river.

According to Qing Dynasty scholar Wu Zhuoxin's *Supplement to the Geography Section of the Book of Han*, Volume 44, which references *Collected Annotations of the Records of the Grand Historian* that "the area was described as south of the Qin Nan Mountain, north west of Chu, and north of the River of Han, hence the name Hanzhong." Wu's rationale, positioning it south of the Qinling Mountains, colloquially referred to as Zhongnan Mountain, and north of the River of Han in Chu, also feels forced and ambiguous.

So, how should we interpret the name "Hanzhong?" The explanation becomes straightforward once we detach from the assumption that "Zhong" signifies 'midstream.' Deng Shaoqin noted that the Ba culture frequently used 'Zhong' as part of place names, such as Hanzhong, Bazhong, Langzhong, Zizhong, and Qianzhong.[22] Building upon this, Xue Fengfei explored the relationship between the Ba people and the River of Han basin, asserting that they inhabited the region during the Xia, Shang, and Zhou dynasties, expanding from downstream to upstream.[23] According to research by Sun Miao and others, the Ba people aided King Wu of Zhou in his conquest over the Shang Dynasty and were rewarded with their own kingdom. In the early Spring and Autumn period, the Ba centered around Western Hubei, bordering the State of Chu to the east, eventually retreating to Eastern Sichuan.[24] During the Warring States period, the Ba declared their kingship, but in 316 BC, King Huiwen of Qin conquered the Ba kingdom, establishing Ba County and governing it from Jiangzhou (present-day Chongqing's north bank of the Jialing River). Despite the sparse historical records making it challenging to pinpoint their domains, the Ba peoples' cultural footprint is discernible in Western Hubei, Southern Shaanxi, Eastern Sichuan, and Chongqing. Place names such as Ba County, Langzhong, Qianzhong, and Shizhong (the latter being a valley passing through the Qin Mountains) are vestiges of the Ba culture in pre-Qin toponyms. "Hanzhong" follows this pattern. In Ba language, 'Zhong' signifies a locale.[25] The ancient Ba term for 'place' is homophonic to "Zhong" in the Sinic languages,[26] hence its written form. Consequently, "Hanzhong," albeit transcribed using Sinic script, cannot be interpreted simply in a Sinic context. It is a bilingual toponym,[27] combining "Han" (a proper noun from the Sinic language) with "Zhong" (a common noun from the Ba language), denoting 'the place where the River of Han flows.'

As the phrase goes, "Breaking a pot to get to the bottom," since "Hanzhong" translates to 'the place where the River of Han runs,' what then is the story about the River of Han?

Firstly, the term "River of Han" was originally simply "Han," with "River" added later for clarity, akin to how ancient China's "Four Rivers"—the Yangtze, Huai, Yellow, and Ji—were later called the Yangtze River, Huai River, Yellow River, and Ji River, mirroring the general progression of geographical naming conventions.

Secondly, the character "Han" in "River of Han" holds an aesthetic significance. According to the ancient lexicon *Shuowen Jiezi*, 'Han' signifies flowing water, a notion Xu Shen adopted during the Eastern Han Dynasty. This description likely stems from the Warring States period work *Shang Shu*, which depicts "Mount Bozhong channeling the flowing water, henceforth running eastwards as the River of Han and also eastwards as the Canglang River." Here, "Canglang" refers to the water's hue, with "Canglang River" denoting the segment of the River of Han from Canglangzhou in Danjiangkou City, Hubei Province, to Xiangyang,[28] with "Bozhong" being a mountain in present-day Ningqiang County, Shaanxi Province. "Yang," in this instance, refers to the River of Han's source.

The spurious volume "Kong Anguo's Commentary on the Analects of Confucius" states, "From its mountain springs, the river initially bears the name Yang, taking the name Mian as it flows south-eastward, then adopting the name Han eastwards through Hanzhong." The River of Han emerges in contemporary Ningqiang County, Shaanxi Province, runs north east through Shaanxi's Mian County, joins the Mian River to the south west, and then flows eastward and south-eastward passing Nanzheng County and Hanzhong, before its confluence with the Yangtze River between Hankou and Wuchang in Wuhan City, Hubei Province. The River of Han, also referred to as Hanjiang, spans over 1500 km from its origin to the juncture with the Yangtze, making it the longest tributary of the latter.

Regarding Xu Shen's ancient text of 漢, it refers to the character used during the Warring States period. According to the annotations by Duan Yucai, "The character has the radical of 'huo' or 'da,' and thus resembles the present character 'guo' (国)." If we interpret the meaning of the characters in Xu Shen's ancient text based on their structure, the Han character signifies "a country that is nourishing and prosperous."

As for the small seal script version of the character "Han" used in Emperor Qin Shihuang's imperial edicts, which later became the standard form during the Han Dynasty, its original meaning remains uncertain. However, according to Duan Yucai's explanation, "Yang signifies thinness, and Han signifies abundance," which conveys a beautiful significance. When the Han River's water flow was weak and minimal, it was named "Yang" after the gentle ripples on the water's surface. But as the flow grew strong and abundant, it was named "Han" to reflect its magnificence and greatness (see Figure 5.2).

Of course, the character "Han" is most significantly beautified by its association with the "Heavenly Han" (Milky Way). During the Eastern Han period, Cai Yong composed "Han Jing Fu" to express his admiration for the Han River:

Oh, the vast and mighty river,
Pure and profound in its flow,
Named after the Heavenly Han River,
Supporting the weight of the earth.
Beginning in the mountains of Bozhong,
Flowing eastward to join with the Li River,
Gathering the waters of the Tang and Han Rivers,

Figure 5.2 Scenery of the Upper Han River

Blending the essence of the western lands.
Coursing through countless mountains and veering south,
Meandering down to Xiangyang,
Slicing through the Dabie Mountains in the east,
Unifying the lands of Jiang and Xiang with its spirit.
An untamed source birthing myriad of beings,
Dragons and snakes reveling within its depths.
Luminescent pearls hidden in the clams' shells,
Shimmering through the enigmatic continent's gloom.
A river brimming with treasures, obviating the need for turtles or fish.
Let us traverse this river from north to south,
Venturing through the expansive waves of its triple estuary.
Gauging the fortunes and shape of the dynasty,
Surveying the confluence of the Dongting Lake and the Yangtze River.

This excerpt praises the Han River's grandeur and profundity, with the phrase "named after the Heavenly Han River, supporting the weight of the earth" being particularly notable. This line implies that the earthly "Han" bears a stature equal to that of the heavenly "Han," underlying the parallels between them.[29] Flowing from north west to south east, the earthly "Han" courses between the Yellow and Yangtze Rivers, likely inspiring the name of the celestial "Han," which follows a similar trajectory. The "Heavenly Han" appears as a cloud-like band of light, resembling a

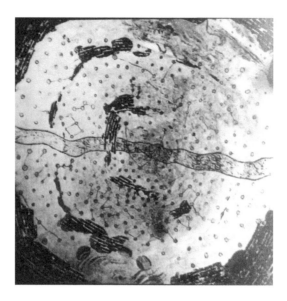

Figure 5.3 Ancient Chinese star map mural, with the Milky Way in the middle

river among the heavens, and is comprised of dense star clusters. It is also known as the "Tianhan" (Heavenly Han), "Yunhan" (Cloud Han), "Yinhan" (Silver Han), and "Xinghan" (Star Han)." Thus, the celestial "Han" and its associated appellations derive from the earthly river of the same name (see Figure 5.3).

5.3 A Few Conclusions and the Influence of the Title of Han

Regarding Liu Bang's coronation, the name of the country as Han, the origin and meaning of the name "Han," and some related issues, the following conclusions can be drawn:

Firstly, geographically speaking, the direct reason Xiang Yu and Fan Zeng named Liu Bang's kingdom as "Han" was that the capital of the kingdom was in Nanzheng, which had been the capital of Hanzhong Prefecture in the Qin Dynasty.

Secondly, linguistically speaking, with respect to the name of Hanzhong Prefecture, "Han" refers to the Han River, and "Zhong" means "place" in the ancient Ba language. Therefore, "Hanzhong" signifies "the place through which the Han River flows," not the commonly misconceived "the middle reaches of the Han River."

Thirdly, from a linguistic perspective, in the characters of the Warring States period and the Small Seal Script in the Qin Dynasty, regardless of their shape, pronunciation, or meaning, the character of "Han" is considered a beautiful word.

Fourthly, from an astronomical perspective, the word "Han" also holds a beautiful meaning, as the Milky Way in the sky bears a resemblance to the Han River on the ground. Therefore, the Milky Way is called "Han" or "Tianhan" in ancient and folk language. Conversely, since the terrestrial "Han" is correlated with the celestial, it is also deemed particularly elegant, known as "matching the sky with Han, this is a beautiful name."

Fifthly, from a psychological perspective, in accordance with the agreement that "whoever enters Guanzhong first will be king," Liu Bang, the King of Han, should have been crowned the superior king over Guanzhong. However, Xiang Yu violated the agreement and crowned Liu Bang as the King of Han. Liu Bang was angry yet powerless and, under the circumstances, he heeded the counsel of Xiao He and others to establish his kingdom in Nanzheng. During this process, Xiao He's advice—that the name "Tianhan" was exceedingly beautiful and magnificent— played a crucial role in comforting Liu Bang. This not only made Liu Bang accept the title of "King of Han" from Xiang Yu, but also influenced his decision to name his empire "Han" after unifying the whole country. "This subsequently became the imperial name of the Han Dynasty."[30]

Sixthly, from a perspective of influence, during the Chu-Han Contention, Liu Bang vanquished Xiang Yu and became the sovereign of the country. From that point on, "Han" served as the dynastic title for more than 400 years, though it was supplanted by "Xin" for a span of 15 years and subsequently only referred to one kingdom of the whole country (the "Shu Han" among the Three Kingdoms). The "Han" that Liu Bang founded, that Liu Xiu renewed, and that, in a sense, Liu Bei revived, not only became one of the most venerated country names in Chinese history but also exerted a profound and far-reaching historical influence:

1. "Han" has been adopted by numerous Chinese and non-Chinese founders of dynasties, such as Liu Yuan and Li Shou of the Sixteen Kingdoms, Liu Zhiyuan of the Later Han during the Five Dynasties period, and Liu Cunxu and Liu Chong of the Ten Kingdoms, as well as Chen Youliang during the latter part of the Yuan Dynasty. Its legacy surpasses that of the Xia, Shang, Zhou, and Qin Dynasties.
2. "Han" became a common designation for China beyond its borders. Although not as universally or continuously used as "Qin" (China, also known as "Cina" and "Sina"), it did exceed the prevalence of the name "Tang."
3. "Han" has evolved into the ethnic name for the core ethnic group in China from that time until today, including terms such as "Han people," "Han family," and "Han ethnicity."[31]

Notes

1 Regarding the name of "Liu Bang," a brief explanation is provided here to clarify any misunderstandings. It is generally believed that the given name of Emperor Gaozu of Han was originally "Bang" and the courtesy name was "Ji." However, this theory is worth questioning. Among his family members, friends, and in society at that time, he was commonly referred to as "Liu Ji," which means "Liu San" or "the third son of the Liu family." His two older brothers were called Liu Bo and Liu Zhong, which meant

"the eldest son of the Liu family" and "the second son of the Liu family," respectively. The name "Liu Bang" was probably adopted when Liu Ji ascended the imperial throne to emphasize his dignity, and it became his commonly used name thereafter. According to the *Shuowen Jiezi* with annotations by Duan Yucai, "邦" (Bang) refers to a country. "A large country is called 'Bang,' while a small country is called 'Guo'." (Note: Guo is another term for country.) Reference: Liu Xinguang, "A Brief Discussion on the Name 'Bang' for Emperor Gaozu of Han." Historical Studies Monthly, Issue 4, 1999. Of course, for the convenience of readers, this book still uses the name "Liu Bang." Similarly, in Chinese history, it was quite common for emperors to change their names upon ascending the throne. Although this book will touch upon some related instances, as they are not directly relevant to the main theme of the book, they will not be discussed in detail. However, it should be emphasized that this is a fascinating cultural phenomenon and an important historical fact.

2 After the fall of the Qin Dynasty in 206 BC, Xiang Yu pretended to honor the King Huai of Chu as the Emperor Yi of Chu while proclaiming himself the Hegemon-King of Western Chu. However, the following year, Xiang Yu killed the Emperor Yi of Chu. The Emperor Yi of Chu was merely a nominal ruler of the country, while Xiang Yu was only the leader of the feudal lords.

3 The commonly held belief about the chronological system of Chinese dynasties starting and ending is incorrect when it takes the year 206 BCE as the beginning of the Western Han Dynasty. In reality, in 206 BC, Liu Bang established the Kingdom of Han, which was just one of the eighteen kingdoms that Xiang Yu had appointed. It was only after Liu Bang defeated Xiang Yu and the feudal lords pledged allegiance to Han that Liu Bang ascended as Emperor and achieved the unification of China. This occurred in the fifth year of Liu Bang's reign as the King of Han, which corresponds to 202 BC.

4 In the "Preface" to the *Records of the Grand Historian* by Sima Qian, it is stated that within the span of "five years," the phrase was changed to "eight years." From the context, it refers to the period when Qin was overthrown and the Chu people rebelled. Xiang's family fell into chaos, and Liu Bang then supported righteousness and launched military campaigns. Within eight years, significant changes occurred, and the situation became complicated. Therefore, a detailed account of the *Chronology of the Qin-Chu Era* is provided in the fourth volume.

5 As for the title "Peigong," the *Annals of Emperor Gao* in the *Book of Han* explains that in ancient Chu, the term "Gong" was used as a title for county officials. When Chen She proclaimed himself the King of Chu, Liu Bang rose in response. Therefore, following the Chu system, Liu Bang was referred to as "Gong." This is based on the explanation given by Meng Kang in the Three Kingdoms period, as cited by Tang Yan in his annotations to the *Book of Han*.

6 The silk manuscript of the Twelve Earthly Branches unearthed from the Mawangdui Tomb No. 3, dating back to the 1970s, provides a chronological record of the transition of Qin and Han dynasties. It includes the reigns of various emperors but lacks the years of Qin Ershi (the second emperor of the Qin Dynasty). For more details, you can refer to Zhang Zhenglang's article titled "A Letter about the Issue of 'Zhang Chu'" published in the journal "Wenshizhe" in 1979.

7 Tian Yuqing, "Discussion on Zhang Chu," included in "*Explorations of the History of Qin-Han-Wei-Jin dynasties*, Zhonghua Book Company, 1993.

8 The *Annals of Xiang Yu* in *Records of the Grand Historian* states the following: "Yu Xi's *Zhilin* states, 'Nangong was a Daoist who understood the rise and fall of the times and knew about the downfall of Qin and the rise of Chu.' In the *Book of Han*, it is mentioned"

that the 'Nangong' contains thirteen chapters and that it was written by some Daoist from the Warring States period." Additionally, the term "sanhu" (three clans) is mentioned in the *Annals of Xiang Yu*. According to various explanations found in the annotations to the *Annals of Xiang Yu* in the *Records of the Grand Historian*, it can refer to the general discontent of the Chu people towards Qin, the three major families of Zhao, Qu, and Jing, or the Three Hu crossing point (located in modern-day Cixian, south western Hebei province) where Xiang Yu defeated the army of Zhang Han and Zhang Han surrendered, leading to the downfall of Qin. These different explanations can all be considered valid since they are essentially related to prophecies.

9 The *Annals of Xiang Yu* in *Records of the Grand Historian* quotes Ying Shao of the Eastern Han as saying: "Using a posthumous title based on ancestral appellation is in line with the people's expectations."

10 Zhang Er and Chen Yu, prominent individuals from the former state of Wei, installed Zhao Xie, a member of the royal family of the former state of Zhao, as the King of Zhao.

11 *Annals of Emperor Gaozu* in the *Records of the Grand Historian* and the *Annals of Emperor Gao* in the *Book of Han*. In the "Biography of Xiao He" in the *Book of Han*, it is mentioned that the one who first entered Guanzhong and overthrew Qin would be crowned as the ruler of that territory.

12 Historically, after Emperor Qin Shi Huang and the second Emperor of Qin, the designation "Qin" had already declined from being the title of the empire to that of a kingdom. This was a survival strategy devised by the Qin rulers at the time. However, even so, the Qin kingdom of the Ying family was unable to continue its existence. After the reestablishment of the Six States, the circumstances changed, and the anti-Qin forces would no longer allow members of the Ying family or former officials to retain their royal positions. The old regime of Qin was not recognized.

13 Regarding this matter, Tian Yuqing's analysis in his work "Discussion on Zhang Chu" states the following: Xiang Yu elevated King Huai of Chu to the position of Emperor Yi of Chu, replacing the legal status of the Qin emperor with that of the Chu emperor. He recognized the legitimacy of the imperial enterprise. Xiang Yu himself assumed the title of Hegemon King of Western Chu, continuing to act as the leader of the feudal lords ... He relocated Emperor Yi to Chen and then put him to death, temporarily leaving the title of Chu emperor in suspense, giving himself the opportunity to observe the situation and consider his actions ... His logical plan was to handle all the necessary post-war matters and then legitimately ascend to the throne as the Chu emperor. However, Xiang Yu did not take this step, and the situation quickly changed, causing him to shift from being proactive to being passive, and the opportunity to become the Chu emperor disappeared forever. The main reason why Xiang Yu couldn't become the "Chu emperor" was primarily due to his mishandling of Liu Bang during the enfeoffment of the Eighteen kingdoms.

14 In the *Collected Expositions of the Records of the Grand Historian*, Pei Yin of the Southern Dynasty quotes Wei Zhao from the Three Kingdoms period.

15 Yan Anqing, "The Uncertainties Regarding Xiang Yu's Western Chu Nine Commanderies and the Examination of Changes in the Territory of Western Chu," Historical Geography, Vol. 33, 2016.

16 Gu Yanwu, "Ri Zhi Lu," Volume 30, section of "Astronomy." The phrases of "fireball in July" can be found in the poem "Qi Yue" in the *Book of Songs*; "Three stars are in the household" can be found in the poem "Chou Miao" in the *Book of Songs*; "The moon is rising in Hyades" can be found in the poem "Jian Jian Zhi Shi" in the *Book of Songs*; and "The Dragontrail star hides behinds the sun" can be found in the *Zuo Zhuan*.

17 The following information sees reference in "Biography of Xiang Yu," " Biography of Emperor Gao," and so forth, and the collected annotations of the *Records of the Grand Historian.* "Biography of Emperor Gao" and "Records of Geography" in the *Book of Han*, as well as the annotations by Yan Shigu in the Tang Dynasty, the *Zizhi Tongjian* and the annotations by Hu Sanxing of the Yuan Dynasty. Zhou Zhenhe's "Geography of the Western Han Dynasty" (People's Publishing House, 1987 edition), and other references, combined with various historical facts of different countries. Additionally, Dushang Jun of Zhai is mentioned in *Zizhi Tongjian*, Hu Sanxing of the Yuan Dynasty annotated: "The above-mentioned commanderies are located in the north near the Rong and Zhai tribes, hence named after them."

18 In the *Shi Ji*, in the thirteenth year of King Hui Wen (312 BC), it is recorded that "Shuchang Zhang attacked Chu in Danyang, captured their general Qu Gai, beheaded eighty thousand soldiers, and also attacked Chu's territory in Hanzhong, acquiring lands of six hundred li and establishing Hanzhong Prefecture." Regarding the establishment of Hanzhong Prefecture, "Biography of Chu Families" should be considered the authoritative source. According to the *Strategies of the Warring States*: Strategy of Chu, it is mentioned, "Strategy of the invasion of Chu: Chu sent Zhao Shu with an army of one hundred thousand soldiers to Hanzhong. Zhao Sui defeated Qin at Zhongqiu, and Su Li said to Zhao Shu, 'If the king wants to make Zhao Sui conquer Qin, he must divide your army to strengthen his. Qin will know that your army is divided and will definitely attack Hanzhong.'" Taking these words into account, it is evident that Chu did have the Hanzhong Prefecture, where Zhao Shu stationed his troops.

19 *Commentary on the Waterways Classic* quotes from "Biography of Qi Jiu": "The name Nanzheng originated from Duke Huan of Zheng. Duke Huan died at the hands of the Quanrong, and his people fled to the south, hence the name Nanzheng." Furthermore, the establishment of Nanzheng as the commandery capital began after Qin's conquest, as explained in detail by Yang Shoujing and Xiong Huizhen in *Annotations of the Commentary on the Waterways Classic*, Volume 27.

20 Shi Nianhai, The Military Activities and Battlefield of the Qinling and Bashan Mountains in History, included in the *Collections of Rivers and Mountains*, Volume 4, Shaanxi Normal University Press, 1991.

21 Ma Peitang, A Study on the Return of Ba Shu to Qin, *Yu Gong*, Volume 2, Issue 2, 1934.

22 Deng Shaoqin, Exploration of the Historical Sites of Ba Shu, Sichuan People's Publishing House, 1983.

23 Xue Fengfei, Interpretation of 'Hanzhong', Chinese Place Names, Issue 3, 1992.

24 Sun Miao, Historical Records of the Xia and Shang Dynasties, Chapter 11, Section 3, Cultural Relics Press, 1987.

25 Xue Fengfei, "Interpretation of 'Han Zhong'.

26 The term "Zhuxia" is discussed in Chapter 23 of this book. Zhuxia, which developed into the later Han ethnic group, was the core and main body, and the characters of the Zhuxia language eventually became what are known as Chinese characters. For an overview of the linguistic regions of Zhuxia and neighboring ethnic languages during the "Book of Songs period" (roughly from the early Western Zhou Dynasty to the mid-Spring and Autumn Period, spanning over five centuries), please refer to the *Dialects and Chinese Culture* by Zhou Zhenhe and You Rujie, Chapter 4, Section 1, Shanghai People's Publishing House, 1986 edition. For specific information on the linguistic condition of the ancient Ba and Shu people, please refer to Tong Enzheng, Ancient Ba Shu, Sichuan People's Publishing House, 1979 edition, and Wen Shaofeng, "A Proposed Explanation for the Name 'Chengdu'," Social Sciences Research, Issue 1,1981.

27 Bilingual toponymy has been a prevalent phenomenon from ancient times to the present. For example, the Yarlung Tsangpo River, where "Tsangpo" is the transliteration of the Tibetan word for "river" in Chinese, combined with the general Chinese term "jiang"; in Qinghai Province, there is E'bao Dananshan, where "Dananshan" is in Chinese, and "E'bao" is the transcription of the Mongolian term, meaning "stone heap" with religious connotations.

28 Gu Jiegang, "Yu Gong (Complete Text with Annotations)," included in Hou Renzhi's compilation, Selected Readings of Ancient Chinese Geographic Works, Volume 1, Science Press, 1959

29 Yang Quan, *Theory of Physics* in the Jin Dynasty: "Stars are the brilliance of the primordial qi, and Han refers to the essence of water. When qi is released, the essence rises and flows, following the course of the river, known as the Milky Way or Cloud River." According to Yang Quan, the term "Han" refers to "Tianhan" or the Milky Way, which is the essence of water. Water is the foundation of the earth, generating vital energy, giving rise to the sun, moon, and stars, all of which rely on water for their existence. Yang Quan's theory about the relationship between heaven and earth might help in understanding the connection between the heavenly "Han" and earthly "Han." Additionally, Pi Ya, compiled by Lu Dian of the Northern Song Dynasty, contains the entry "Han" in Volume 20: "When water vapor is in the sky, it forms clouds; when the image of water is in the sky, it becomes the Han."

30 *Zizhi Tongjian* with annotations by Hu Sanxing of the Yuan Dynasty.

31 For the above three points, please refer to the following chapters for further details.

6 Xin

"Complying with the Heavenly Mandate"

In the orthodox view of Chinese history, the Xin Dynasty founded by Wang Mang has no historical position. According to Ban Gu's *Book of Han*, "from Emperor Gaozu's accession to the throne to the execution of Emperor Xiaoping by Wang Mang, twelve reigns and two hundred and thirty years had passed."[1] This means that the entire history from the first year of the Han Dynasty founded by Liu Bang (206 BC) to the fourth year of the Xin Dynasty founded by Wang Mang (AD 23) was included in the history of the Western Han Dynasty, while Wang Mang's regency and the 18 years of the Xin Dynasty could not have separate sections. "Unlike the vermilion, the color of purple and the leap month are just falsehood to be dressed up as truth."[2] Therefore, they were relegated to the end of the biographies section of the *Book of Han*, except for the "Narrative Biography." This treatment of the Xin Dynasty persisted after the Eastern Han Dynasty, as seen in the 60th volume of "*Zizhi Tongjian–Han Ji*," which covers the three years of regency of Wang Mang and fifteen years of a new dynasty of Xin.

However, this approach, represented by the *Book of Han* and the *Zizhi Tongjian*, is not appropriate for understanding and researching the history of Chinese dynasties. According to the "Biography of Wang Mang" in the *Book of Han* and the *Zizhi Tongjian*, in the fifth year of Yuanshi (AD 5), the 14-year-old Liu Yang reigned only for five years before being poisoned by Wang Mang. He was then designated posthumously as Emperor Xiaoping. The following year (AD 6), Wang Mang enthroned Liu Ying, a two-year-old descendant of Emperor Xuan of Han, as Crown Prince, Mang then acted as an "imperial substitute,"[3] and declared the "Jushe" era. In the eleventh lunar month of the third year of Jushe (AD 8), Wang Mang declared the "Chushi" era and claimed to have received the heavenly mandate. In the twelfth lunar month[4] of Jushe, Wang Mang ascended the throne with the title "Xin," making the first day of the first lunar month of the following year the beginning of the "Jian Guo" era. On the first day of the first lunar month in the Jian Guo era (AD 9), Wang Mang discarded the title of the Han Dynasty, deposed Prince Ruzi's position, and exiled him from the royal family of the Xin Dynasty. In the third lunar month of the fourth year of Dihuang (AD 23), Wang Chang and Zhu Wei uprose and declared Liu Xuan as emperor, ushering in a new era called "Gengshi." In the tenth lunar month, the uprising

DOI: 10.4324/9781003510390-7

troops captured the capital Chang'an and Wang Mang was killed by Du Wu, a merchant. In the third year of Gengshi (25 AD), "During summer, Fan Chong of the Red Eyebrows and others led a multitude of several hundred thousand people into the passes, establishing Liu Penzi and proclaiming him with an imperial title, attacking the Gengshi army, who then surrendered to them ... In June, Emperor Guangwu (Liu Xiu) ascended the throne, and it was only then that the ancestral temples and altars of the state were reestablished, and peace was finally restored throughout the land."

These facts unmistakably show that the Xin Dynasty was established after the Western Han Dynasty and should not be included within it. The period from the twelfth lunar month of the initial year (AD 8) to October of the fourth year of Dihuang (AD 23) corresponds to the Xin Dynasty's reign. During this period, the country was known as "Xin," which belonged to Wang Mang.[5]

Moreover, when studying the history of Chinese dynasties, the Xin Dynasty is often ignored and particularly special status must be recognized. I have previously pointed out in a television lecture aimed at the general public that "Wang Mang's replacement of the Han Dynasty and the establishment of the Xin Dynasty created the first example of a 'peaceful' change of dynasty in Chinese history. Prior to Wang Mang, changes of dynasty were the result of bloody wars—the Shang, Zhou, Qin, and Han dynasties all came to power through military conquest. After Wang Mang, for nearly a thousand years, changes of dynasty often resulted from non-violent political coups or involved minimal bloodshed, at least in form, such as in the Wei, Jin, Sui, Tang, and Song dynasties, where the emperor of the previous dynasty voluntarily abdicated. Either military or covert tactics could establish a dynasty. The history of China is characterized by these two types of changes of power. Wang Mang's Xin Dynasty was the first to be established through a covert coup, providing subsequent heroes and politicians with inspiration and enlightenment in terms of theoretical basis, specific methods, and policy design. The Xin Dynasty's influence was observed in subsequent generations, making this 'first example' worthy of consideration."[6] Thus, in traditional and modern Chinese historical chronicles, where the newly established Xin Dynasty has no "position," it is worth discussing the process of its establishment and the origin of its name in more detail.

6.1 "Originate from the Marquis of Xindu"

Wang Mang established a new dynasty named Xin, of which no annotation is provided in the *Book of Han*. The lack of annotation is, in itself, a kind of explanation. The meaning of the character "新 Xin" (new) is too obvious (it is the opposite of 'old,' signifying to replace the old with something new, to start afresh), so there is no need for annotation. This can be considered the semantic explanation for the new title of the country. In the Eastern Han Dynasty, the *Lun Heng* by Wang Chong states: "Wang Mang rose from the position of Marquis of Xindu, so the word 'Xin' represents the end of the old.'" In the *Zizhi Tongjian*, Hu Sanxing of the Yuan Dynasty annotated: "The new dynasty was named after the kingdom of

Xindu." Moreover, in Volume 29 of the *Notes on the History of the Twenty-Two Dynasties* by Zhao Yi of the Qing Dynasty, an interpretation is provided: "Wang Mang adopted the name 'Xin' because he was initially bestowed the Marquis of Xindu." This offers the geographical interpretation of the title "Xin."

Which interpretation is the truth, the semantic or the geographical? Or are both valid? Relatively speaking, the geographical interpretation is more readily accepted. In the " Biography of Wang Mang" of the *Book of Han*, it reads: "The emergence of the new Dynasty's prosperity began from two hundred and ten years of the Han Dynasty and at the ninth generation. It originated in Xindu, received signs from Huangzhi, commenced in Wugong, confirmed its fate in Zitong, completed its destiny in Badang, and extended its blessings to the twelve-words prophet. Heaven deeply and firmly protects and blesses the Xin Dynasty." The key phrase here is, undoubtedly, "originated in Xindu," which refers to the first year of Emperor Cheng of Han (16 BC), when "Mang was granted the title of Marquis of Xindu, with jurisdiction over 1,500 households in the capital of Xinye in Nanyang."[7] From that point on, Mang was regarded as a wise man.

Wang Mang (45 BC–23 AD) was the nephew of Empress Dowager Wang Zhengjun during the reign of Emperor Yuan of Han. After Emperor Cheng ascended to the throne, Wang Zhengjun was appointed as the Empress Dowager. Her father and brothers were all dukes and held positions of power. The Wang family boasted nine marquises and five grand generals. Meanwhile, Wang Mang and his brothers were five marquises and the sons of generals, leading lives of unbridled luxury and pleasure. Wang Mang had a unique position in the Wang family. His early experiences and his entry into the government are recorded in the biography of the *Book of Han*:

> Wang Mang's father passed away at a young age without any noble title. Wang Mang himself was of modest means and lived a simple life. He studied the classic text "Book of Rites" under the instruction of Chen Can, an expert in the text. He was dedicated to his studies and presented himself as a Confucian scholar through his attire. He was respectful to his mother and widowed sister-in-law and took good care of his nephew. He was adept at handling relationships with both superiors and subordinate officials. During that time, Wang Mang's uncle, the General-in-Chief Wang Feng, fell ill. Wang Mang attended to his uncle, tasting his medicines for him, not changing his clothes for months. As Wang Feng neared death, he entrusted Wang Mang to the care of his mother, the Empress Dowager, and the emperor Cheng. Wang Mang was then appointed as a Yellow Gate official (personal attendant of the emperor) and later promoted to the rank of Commanding Officer of Archers.

Wang Mang thus secured an official position. In 16 BC, upon the request of his uncle, the Marquis of Chengdu, and many renowned scholars, he had been bestowed the title of Marquis of Xindu, ascending to a noble rank. In 8 BC, Wang Mang succeeded Wang Gen as the Grand Marshal. After this appointment, Wang Mang had already distinguished himself among his peers and positioned himself as a key advisor following his uncles Wang Feng, Wang Shang, Wang Yin, and Wang Gen. He tirelessly persevered in his work and was "even more frugal and economical" to maintain a good reputation. In 7 BC, Emperor Ai ascended to the throne, with powerful courtiers Dong Xian and the influential Ding and Fu families dominating affairs. Consequently, Wang Mang lost his position as Grand Marshal and was made a Special Counselor and Attendant. In 5 BC, Wang Mang was dispatched back to his fief in Xindu (the present-day Jiu Nv city in southern Henan province). In 2 BC, he returned to Chang'an to serve the Empress Dowager Wang Zhengjun. In 1 BC, Emperor Ai had passed away, and Wang Mang was once again appointed Grand Marshal, taking charge of the Ministry of Personnel. Wang Zhengjun and Wang Mang then plotted to place the young Liu Kan, the nine-year-old son of King Zhongshan, on the throne as Emperor Ping, with Wang Mang assuming control over the court's political affairs.

After becoming a leading figure in politics, Wang Mang quickly began plotting to usurp the Han Dynasty. His first step was to order local officials in Yizhou to "request the barbarians outside the borders to offer white pheasants." The court ministers recognized Wang Mang's achievements by stating in the first year of Yuanshi:

> "Wang Mang has made great contributions and brought auspiciousness like the white pheasants in the reign of King Cheng of Zhou. According to the regulations of the sage kings, those who have made great achievements should be given honorary titles. Therefore, just as Zhou Gong, who served as a regent and devoted himself to the Zhou Dynasty, Wang Mang has made significant contributions to the stability of the country and should be awarded the honorary title 'Anhan Gong' (Duke of Stabilizing Han)."

The relationship between "requesting the barbarians outside the borders to offer white pheasants" and Wang Mang being named Duke of Anhan is elucidated by the *Taiping Yulan* (Imperial Encyclopedia of the Taiping Era) which quotes from the *Classic of Documents*: "To the south of Jiaozhi (present day Vietnam), there was a country named Yue Chang. During the six years when Zhou Gong served as regent, he created rituals and music, and there was peace throughout the whole country. Yue Chang presented a white pheasant to show their respect, which were translated three times into Chinese ... King Cheng accepted and gave it to Zhou Gong, who said, "How can I receive this gift?" The envoys replied, "I have received the request of the old people in my country, who said, 'we have favorable climatic weathers for a long time, which is a sign that there may be a saint in China. If there is one, we will go to pay him respects!'" It can be seen that Wang Mang's actions mirrored those of Zhou Gong. Zhou Gong advised the young King Cheng, governing the country and bringing peace. Similarly, Wang Mang's position at the time echoed Zhou Gong's, hence, just as Zhou Gong devoted to the Zhou Dynasty, Wang Mang contributed to the Han Dynasty. Likewise, Wang Mang's subsequent actions centered on using ancient examples to initiate reforms and ancient traditions to chart the course for the new.

After several rounds of declination, Wang Mang accepted the honorary title of Duke of Anhan and was promoted to Grand Tutor. Two years later (3 AD), Wang Mang's daughter became Empress to Emperor Ping of Han. The following year, he adopted the examples of Yi Yin of the Shang Dynasty and Zhou Gong of the Zhou Dynasty and was given the title "Zaiheng" (Chancellor). The next year, he received the Nine Bestowments[8], and another year later, he proclaimed himself as the "pseudo emperor."

Wang Mang's ascent to power from the Marquis of Xindu to Duke Anhan and finally to the pseudo emperor spanned more than 20 years. Xindu was not only the place of his rise but also the place of his resurgence. When he returned to Xindu, he remained prudent, strict with himself, and reclusive at home. His strictness extended to his family: Wang Mang even forced his second son, Wang Huo, who had killed a servant, to commit suicide. During the three years in Xindu, "more than a hundred officials submitted statements for the injustice of Wang Mang, saying he was fit to rule the country and it's totally unfair to be dismissed to his fief." Before receiving the Nine Bestowments, he wrote a letter stating:

"In the second year of Yuanshou, on one night in June, I was hastily summoned from the Marquis of Xindu to the Imperial Palace. On the day of Gengshen, I was appointed as the Grand Marshal, assuming the role of the Three Counselors of the state. In the first year of Yuanshi, on the day of Bingchen in January, I was appointed the Grand Tutor, awarded the title of Duke Anhan, and appointed among the Four Major Officials. This April, on the day of Jiazi, I was made Zaiheng, and took the position of Chancellor. I, Mang, prostrate myself, holding the title of Marquis of Xindu, Duke Anhan, Zaiheng, Grand Tutor and Grand Marshal, and have been graced with great glory."

In this way, Xindu was the place of Wang Mang's political rebirth as well as his initial rise to power. Wang Mang "did not forget his roots in Xindu,"[9] leading to the decision of "adopting a new title 'Xin,'" with the saying "originating from Xindu," just as Liu Bang rose to power in Hanzhong, which led to the dynasty being named Han.

However, the real complexity of the situation requires a further examination of the social and political context of the middle and late Western Han Dynasty. Considering Wang Mang's actions before and after he seized power to establish the Xin Dynasty, and the prevailing orthodox belief that "when an emperor receives the mandate to rule, he must choose a beautiful title to name the new dynasty," the naming of the new dynasty was not just derived from the fief Xindu or from the title Marquis of Xindu.

6.2 Replacing Old Virtues with New Ones[10]

As is well-known, after the reign of Emperor Wu of Han, the "Hundred Schools of Thought" were suppressed, and Confucianism—restructured with Dong Zhongshu's theoretical system at its core—became the dominant ideology of the

Western Han Dynasty. Within this system, the "Five Virtues" theory—outlining a correspondence between heaven and humanity—was a critical element. This theory posits:

Firstly, "heaven" possesses a will, and the emperor represents "heaven" in governing the populace. The emperor, though not absolute, must abide by "heaven," which communicates its will through auspicious or ominous signs. A virtuous ruler will receive favorable omens, signaling peace and harmony; a tyrant will be sent disasters as admonitions to amend his ways. A persistent refusal to change might result in heaven mandating another ruler. Both "reform" and "mandate-granting" are acts of compliance with heaven's will, differing only in scale and not in essence.

Secondly, heaven's rewards or punishments for the emperor depend significantly on his conduct toward the common people, society's bedrock. A diligent and kind ruler, who possesses virtue, enjoys heaven's mandate. Conversely, a ruler lacking virtue and governing poorly risks losing this mandate. History is replete with such fallen emperors, including those from the Xia, Shang, Zhou, Qin, and Han dynasties. "The righteous attacking the unrighteous" epitomizes a long-standing heavenly principle.[11]

Thirdly, "the righteous attacking the unrighteous" aligns with the traditional Five Virtues theory[12], meaning that "the righteous" may become "unrighteous" and be supplanted by a new "righteous" entity. likewise, "new virtues" may replace "old virtues," then be overwritten by subsequent "new virtues."[13]

Dong Zhongshu's theory carries intricate social and political implications. On one hand, the phrase, "The Son of Heaven receives the Mandate from Heaven, and the world receives the Mandate from the Son of Heaven,"[14] furnishes a theoretical underpinning for the legitimacy of Han Dynasty sovereignty. As long as the emperor is assiduous and takes care of his people, he can "secure the heavenly mandate indefinitely, perpetuating his rule."[15] On the other hand, the same theory paradoxically provided a pretext for subverting Han authority and justified Wang Mang's usurpation of power. These developments were closely tied to the societal and political conditions in the late Western Han.

The governance during the latter part of the Western Han waned. Commoners' status declined, and natural calamities were rife.[16] As governance faltered, concepts such as "transformation" and "reissuance of the mandate" gained traction among Yin-Yang scholars, Confucians, the ruling elite, and even the emperor himself. Imperial proclamations were rife with introspection, and efforts to enact change and "transform" were frantic. When these measures failed to ameliorate conditions, Emperor Ai of Han, influenced by the alchemist Gan Zhongke[17] and his disciple Xia Heliang, amended the era name to Taichu and proclaimed himself "Emperor Chen Sheng Liu Taiping "—a declaration of "reissuing the mandate."[18] Though his era name change was short-lived, the destabilization of Western Han rule was evident. Emperor Ai even once considered bestowing imperial power upon his favorite, Dong Xian, seemingly a move inspired by the "reissuing the mandate" ideology.

However, by the waning days of the Han Dynasty, loyalty to the dual concepts of "family and state" had greatly eroded, and the consensus was that old virtues would inevitably be supplanted by new ones. Detachment from Han familial virtues grew, with the whole society, including the imperial Liu clan, looking to embrace newer ideals.[19] It was in this context that Wang Mang emerged, positioning himself as the embodiment of this new virtue. Wang Mang's actions were exceptional: unlike local gentry who enslaved people, he held his son accountable for the death of a slave. Whereas aristocrats seized land voraciously, Wang Mang declined land from Xin Ye and repeatedly donated property to land-poor farmers through the Grand Minister of Agriculture. Moreover, Wang Mang "constructed tens of thousands of houses" and "recruited thousands of capable individuals throughout the whole country," gripping the attention of many in search of new virtues.

After Wang Mang came to power, new virtues replaced the old, and this became an obvious trend.[20] On the eve of the transition from the Han Dynasty to the Xin Dynasty, Ai Zhang from Zitong County presented a letter titled "The Red Emperor's Golden Letter Passes to the Yellow Emperor." According to the letter, the Red Emperor refers to Han, associated with the Fire Element[21], while the Yellow Emperor is linked with the Earth Element. Wang Mang referred to himself as "trusting in Huangdi, the ancestor of the Han dynasty." Therefore, Wang Mang's statement officially declared,

> "The spirit of the Red Emperor, the emperor Gao of the Han Dynasty, has received the mandate from heaven and passed the golden letter of the country to me. I am filled with awe and dare not disrespect it. In the year of Wuchen, I ascend to the throne as the true Son of Heaven and name my reign as 'Xin.' I change the calendar, the color of clothing, alter the sacrifices, introduce different symbols and implements used in ceremonies. I officially proclaim the 'New Ambassador of the Five Virtues' to receive the command of the Emperor of Heaven."

According to Wang Mang's "receiving the Mandate" from the Emperor Gao of the Han Dynasty, the transition of power was not the handover from Crown Prince Ying to Wang Mang, but a solemn event believed to be ordained by Han Gaozu – the handover from the Red Emperor to the Yellow Emperor. This was necessary either for the sanctity conferred by the Mandate from heaven or possibly because the heir was too young to perform the rites of abdication. In any case, the process of "receiving the Mandate anew," with new virtues supplanting the old, Earth virtues taking the place of Fire virtues, and "overthrowing Han to establish Xin, abolishing Liu and raising Wang," was finally complete. All of the mysteries surrounding Wang Mang's ascent to power centered around the title "Xin," which served as his symbol of power and cultural identity.

6.3 The New Policies, Naming Conventions, and Titles of the New Emperor

Wang Mang, who assumed power as emperor under the name Xin, was always in search of innovative ideas. This was apparent in the new name he chose for his dynasty, considered fitting for the fresh course he envisaged for the nation. Upon his ascension to the throne, he commenced a series of sweeping reforms, including changing the calendar, clothing, sacrificial system, flags, and even the implements used in ceremonies. His quest to inaugurate a new era captured the spirit of a "new king appointed by heaven."

Wang Mang was deeply committed to the new policies he introduced, tirelessly working day and night. Some of these policies, as described in Yang Xiong's *The Beauty of the Xin Dynasty* as follows: new flag designs, modifications to marriage and funeral customs, promotion of virtuous individuals among nine clans, reform of the system of deities, renovation of numerous temples, construction of new halls and platforms, implementation of new rituals, revision of the six Confucian classics, restoration and adjustments to the five nobility ranks, overhaul of the three fertile lands system, introduction of a new system of land ownership, liberation from slave labor, reform of the criminal justice system, and enhancements to the regulations concerning horses. Wang Mang's comprehensive reforms permeated every facet of society, including the systems of ancestral temples, national deities, vassal states, chariots, clothing, and legal penalties. As Gu Jiegang observed, "There was nothing that was not revised."[22] It was a bona fide "new age" that boasted the slogan "rule for billions of generations," and had perfected the system, addressing all necessary reforms. In this new epoch, Wang Mang had established unprecedented prestige. The morale of officials and bureaucrats was heightened; even the supernatural entities seemed to endorse his new reign. The populace welcomed the new order, and bandits and rebels found themselves impotent against the prevailing power of the regime. It was an exceptionally inspiring time![23]

In accordance with the atmosphere of reform and new policies, Wang Mang implemented significant changes to various titles, including those of central and local government officials, designations for different levels of nobility, names for prefectures, and tribal names for various ethnic groups. He underscored the importance of embracing novelty and change. For example, concerning names for prefectures, *Study on Official Positions in the Xin Dynasty* by Tan Qixiang noted that in renaming prefectures, "Wang Mang only considered historical significance, local geography, or topography in a very small number of cases. Instead, most of the new names were chosen based on their literal sounds, puns, or similar meanings, with some names reflecting opposite meanings. Some were chosen for sound similarities and others for their literal meaning." Additional changes involved appending terms such as 'city,' 'district,' 'hill,' or 'screen' to prefecture names and altering 'Han' to 'Xin' or 'Xin'(trust), and 'Yang' to 'Pavilion.'[24] The *Book of Han* states: "In the first year of Chushi (AD 8), Liu Jing, a Han imperial clan member and Marquis of Guangrao, submitted a memorial to the throne. In this memorial, he reported that in the seventh lunar month, Xin Dang, the magistrate of Changxing Ting (Pavilion/Village) in Linzi County, Qi Prefecture, had several dreams one night. He dreamed that a heavenly messenger came to him and said, 'I am a messenger of the heavens. The heavens have sent me to tell you that the regent should be real emperor.' Xin Dang did not believe the messenger, who then said, 'In your village, a new well will appear.' The next morning, Xin Dang discovered a new well more than a hundred feet deep. As a result, 360 prefectures changed their names, adding the word 'ting' to conform to the omen foreshadowing Mang's accession to the throne." The names "were changed so frequently that a single prefecture could be assigned up to five different names within one year, creating confusion among officials and citizens." Notably, amidst the extensive and repetitive renaming process, there was an underlying principle of imbuing names with positive meaning—names associated with 'governance,' 'peace,' 'happiness,' 'trust,' 'harmony,' 'goodness,' 'beauty,' 'kindness,' and 'prosperity' were chosen to reflect the hopes for a safe and secure nation. In contrast, names like 'fill,' 'cut,' 'flatten,' 'relieve' alongside words such as 'barbarian,' 'foreigner,' 'Di,' and 'Lu' were selected for borderland counties to underscore distinctions between 'Chinese' and 'non-Chinese' populations. The renaming was also done to adhere to the omen. Wang Mang's use of reign titles such as "Yuanshi" and "Chushi" and the establishment of his first new reign "Shijian Guo" were meant to symbolize 'renewal' and 'receiving a new mandate,' reinforcing his creation of a completely new state. Moreover, Wang Mang awarded many titles of 'Xin' to his officials in recognition of their accomplishments, including Wang Shun as Duke Anxin, Ping Yan as Duke Jiuxin, Liu Xin as Duke Jiaxin, and Ai Zhang as Duke Meixin—comprising the four Ministers. The three Chancellors then consisted of Zhen Han as Duke Chengxin, Wang Xun as Duke Zhangxin, and Wang Yi as Duke Longxin. The four Generals included Zhen Feng as Duke Guangxin, Wang Xing as Duke Fengxin, Sun Jian as Duke Chengxin, and Wang Sheng as Duke Chongxin, illustrating Wang Mang's focus on renewing norms.

However, through this extensive renomination and alteration of titles, Wang Mang's predilection for novelty and transformation is evident. Understanding Wang Mang's axiom that "a new title under heaven must be established" allows us to draw conclusions that align more closely with historical reality and Wang Mang's perspective. Wang Mang regarded himself as the "Emperor Xin," a title reflecting a departure from the past. For instance, when ascending to the throne, Wang Mang sent the beloved and trusted Marquis Anyang, Wang Shun, to request the imperial seal's transfer from the Empress Dowager. She rebuked him, saying:

> "Despite being part of the Han imperial family for generations and receiving great wealth and honor, they have shown no gratitude or loyalty. Now they seize control of the country, driven by opportunity and circumstance. Such individuals are unworthy of even dogs or pigs. How can they still consider themselves kin? If you claim to be the New Emperor, sanctioned by the Golden Chamber Covenant, having altered the calendar and attire, you should create a new seal to pass down through the generations. Why would you seek this ominous seal from a perished dynasty?"

The Empress Dowager's criticism implied that as the New Emperor, Wang Mang should have crafted a new seal to reflect the changes he had implemented. Additionally, references to the "New Emperor" were present in Wang Mang's "Imperial Decrees," as detailed in the *Book of Han*, even before his extensive renaming and title changes. The term likely originated from the concept of a

"New King" envisioned by Western Han scholars, including Dong Zhongshu in the *Chunqiu Fanlu* (Luxuriant Dew of the Spring and Autumn Annals). The New King was deemed a transformative figure, alluded to in quotes like "the Chronicles of Spring and Autumn state a new king will emerge" and "Confucius proposed a new king's way." Replacing the old king (Emperor Liu Kan and Emperor Liu Ying) with the New King (Wang Mang) symbolized the succession of old virtue by the new.

Furthermore, the word "Xin" encapsulates the enigma of Wang Mang's ascent to power. Orthodox thought from the Western Han era determined that "the king must choose a beautiful title under heaven for self-designation,"[25] as elaborated in the *Baihu Tongde Lun* (Evidential Analysis of Debates in the White Tiger Hall) from the Eastern Han Dynasty. The document posited, "Since all kings reign under heaven, distinguishing oneself is crucial. Altering the country's grand title showcases one's unique achievements. A king confirmed by heaven must select beautiful titles to clearly exhibit their divine mandate and intent for global recognition ... Therefore, a heaven-anointed king should adopt an auspicious name." For Wang Mang, "Xin" constituted the apt title, symbolizing his eagerness to "display his accomplishments" and "announce his reform and transformation to the whole country."

Lastly, Wang Mang's political career began as the Marquis of Xindu, from which the expression "the inauguration began at Xindu" derives. Yet, this was merely coincidental and not a decisive factor. Hu Shi contended that even without this title, Wang Mang was destined to become the Emperor of Xin. "Xin," as a dynastic title, signified not only a "glorious name" but also the sincerity and depth of the reforms, serving as a commendable appellation for Wang Mang's efforts.[26]

6.4 The "New Virtues" Give Way to Subsequent Newer Ones

History can sometimes be too cruel. Wang Mang, with his image of the New Virtue, became the best candidate for people of all social classes to look up to. He excitedly ascended the throne as the embodiment of the New Virtue. However, Wang Mang's New Virtue quickly became old and gave way to the subsequent New Virtue–the Eastern Han Dynasty, restored by Liu Xiu, which is "Genuine Fire Virtue, with a preference for red." Wang Mang's rise to power was accompanied by praise from "over eight thousand people extolling his achievements and virtues," and later, "nine hundred royal dukes and lords offering nine types of regalia," as well as "a total of four hundred and eighty-seven thousand, five hundred and seventy-two officials and citizens petitioning him."[27] But his fall was just as swift: a merchant named Du Wu killed him; a sergeant named Gong Bin beheaded him; and many soldiers fought over his body, with some even cutting and eating his tongue.

Why did Wang Mang rise and fall so rapidly, with such different outcomes? Historian Zhao Yi of the Qing Dynasty pointed out that:

> people often only understand Wang Mang's failure as being due to the people's
> loyalty to the Han Dynasty, but in fact, it was Wang Mang's own actions that

led to this. At first, he deceitfully named things to achieve his dark schemes, as a cunning and talented man would do. But when he became a usurper, he did not know how to govern and believed he could deceive and poison the people. He made enemies both within and outside the country, and as the state fell apart, he continued to stubbornly focus on his archaic practices, thinking that creating these rituals would bring peace to the country. He was preoccupied with these activities day and night, quoting and revising the teachings of the Six Classics, no longer paying attention to governance. But before he could finish creating these rituals, he was already beheaded.[28]

Ironically, the reason Wang Mang made enemies both inside and outside the country was precisely because he was so focused on tradition, and stubbornly pushed new policies and names.[29] His new policies created chaos, and his new names were confusing, leading to the large-scale failure of his reforms. "He caused foreigners as well as internal subjects to hold grievances against him ... The whole empire boiled over, and rebels and bandits rose up. Leading the way were Gengshi, Chimei (Red Eyebrows), and Guangwu (Liu Xiu), who were able to rally the whole country." Failed reforms are often worse than no reforms at all! Wang Mang's rise and fall were both due to a single word "Xin." What a tragedy!

After the fall of Wang Mang's Xin Dynasty, the Han became the new order. At that time, "people longed for Han" because emperors like Gaozu and Wudi had ruled with wisdom and benevolence, and even the slightly less virtuous emperors like Emperor Yuan, Cheng, and Ai had not been tyrannical towards their people. In contrast, under Wang Mang's rule, the people's longing for Han grew stronger due to his increasingly oppressive policies."[30] The rebellion of the Greenwoods and the Red Eyebrows, among other insurgent groups, rose up to restore the Liu family's rule and rebuild the Han dynasty. Wang Mang's usurpation of the Han dynasty was seen as an injustice by Liu family members, aristocrats, nobility, and gentry who supported the Han dynasty. Thus, restoring Liu Han rule was seen as a just and righteous cause. Against this backdrop, the Old Order of Xin faded away, and various people claiming to be Liu descendants like Liu Xuan, Liu Penzi, Liu Ying, Liu Ziyu (who pretended to be Wang Chang), Liu Wenbo (who pretended to be Lu Fang), Liu Yong, and others all claimed they were heirs to Han. Meanwhile, Liu Xiu, a brilliant descendant of Liu Bang and Liu Qi, emerged as a warrior leader following the prophecy of the Red Clump,[31] and by June of 25 AD, he became emperor upon ascending the throne in Hao, located in modern-day Baoding County, Hebei Province. Historian Zhao Yi of the Qing Dynasty observed that:

When examining those who had risen to power, it was either through claiming to be Liu family descendants or citing their support for the Han dynasty. Clearly, the people longed for Han, and this consensus made it easier for Guangwu to take the throne.[32]

In fact, when Liu Xiu declared himself emperor and named his new dynasty "Han," there were many others throughout the country who also claimed the title of emperor or king. However, over a decade later, in 36 AD, with extensive political experience, outstanding administrative abilities, and superior military strategy, Liu Xiu defeated all other contenders, and the title "Han" was unified under him alone. Emperor Guangwu of the Eastern (Later) Han thus became the founder of the dynasty just like Emperor Gaozu of the Western (Former) Han, and "Han" once again became the true national title, lasting a hundred and eighty-four years until 220 AD, when Cao Pi usurped the throne and established the Kingdom Wei.

Notes

1 "Narrative Biography," Book of Han
2 "Biography of Wang Mang," Book of Han
3 The term "pseudo emperor" refers to a puppet emperor, "imperial substitute" refers to an agent who handles specific affairs.
4 The date mentioned, the fifteenth day of the eleventh month, corresponds to December 31st, 8 AD, which means that twelfth lunar month (December) falls into 9 AD. Similar transitions between years are mentioned in this book in several other places (not further annotated to avoid repetition). For reference, you can refer to the appendix *Chronological Table of Chinese History* in various editions of *Cihai* (A Collection of Words) (compiled by the Editorial Committee of *Cihai* and published by Shanghai Lexicographical Publishing House). This table provides the corresponding dates in Chinese historical eras to the Gregorian calendar, starting from the year 1 AD.
5 Two points need clarification here: Firstly, the deposition of Ruzi Ying marks the end of the Western Han Dynasty. The *Zizhi Tongjian* uses "Jushe" and "Chushi" as the reign titles of Wang Mang. In fact, before Wang Mang ascended the throne and changed the dynastic title, he still adhered to the legitimate succession of the Han Dynasty. Therefore, "Jushe" and "Chushi" should be considered as the reign titles of Ruzi Ying. Secondly, the Eastern Han Dynasty officially began with the reign of Emperor Liu Xuan. However, Liu Xuan's reign was short-lived, and it was Liu Xiu who completed the unification within a span of around ten years. Hence, Fan Ye's *Book of the Later Han* does not acknowledge Liu Xuan's reign and does not include a separate biography for the Xin Dynasty. Instead, Liu Xuan and Liu Penzi's biographies are placed at the beginning of the biographical section, and the imperial biographies begin with Emperor Guangwu Liu Xiu's reign. In other words, Fan Ye considered Emperor Guangwu Liu Xiu's first year of the Jianwu era (25 AD) as the starting year of the Eastern Han Dynasty.
6 Hu Axiang, Rectifying the Name of China: Hu Axiang's Views on National Titles, Lecture 7, Zhonghua Book Company, 2013.
7 Biography of Wang Mang, Book of Han. This chapter contains numerous citations from this biography. Subsequent references will no longer be annotated individually to avoid repetition and complexity.
8 In "Biography of Wang Mang, Book of Han, Tang scholar Yan Shigu made the following annotation: "According to the *Lihan Wenjia*, it is recorded: 'The Nine Bestowments include chariots and horses, garments, suspended musical instruments, vermilion gates, raised steps at the front of the palace, warrior's armor, forged battle axes, bows and arrows, and fermented liquor made from black millet and aromatic herbs.' The 'vermilion gates' refer to large gates painted in vermilion red; 'raised steps at the front of the palace' are specifically carved steps under the eaves of the palace; and 'fermented liquor made from black millet and aromatic herbs' is a type of wine made from black millet and

tulip grass. In ancient times, emperors would bestow these nine items to feudal lords and ministers of great merit or influence, known as the 'Nine Bestowments.' Starting from Wang Mang, it became common for powerful ministers to receive the Nine Bestowments before usurping the throne."

9 Wang Chong, On Balance

10 This section is based on the research paper by Wang Baoding titled "The Influence and Conclusion of the Discussions on the Five Virtues of Dong Zhongshu" (published in the "Historical Studies Monthly" in the second issue of 1996), with some modifications and deletions.

11 Dong Zhongshu, Chunqiu Fanlu (Luxuriant Dew of the Spring and Autumn Annals)

12 The concept of the Five Virtues is rooted in the Five Elements, which refer to the five basic substances of earth, wood, metal, fire, and water. Ancient Chinese thinkers believed that these elements constituted the foundation of the world and used them to explain the origins of the world and various natural phenomena. During the mid-Warring States period, Zou Yan constructed a cyclical system based on the natural attributes of the Five Elements and extended it to the realm of social history to explain the succession of political power and dynastic changes. Emperor Qin Shi Huang consciously utilized this theory, designating the Zhou dynasty as the representative of the fire virtue, with water overcoming fire, thus making the Qin dynasty rise and locating it under the water virtue. This is known as the theory of the interdependence of the Five Virtues (in the order of wood, earth, water, fire, metal), which is suitable for describing dynastic changes through conquest. There is also the theory of interdependence of the Five Virtues (in the order of wood, fire, earth, metal, water), which is suitable for describing dynastic changes through abdication. The concept of the Five Virtues holds great significance in ancient Chinese political theory and practice. It was believed that a new dynasty would possess the corresponding virtue and would establish rituals and music based on that virtue.

13 Based on the writings of Liao Boyuan in "Shuo Xin: A Discussion on the Creation of Era Names and Its Reasons" (included in "The Collection of Yifen: Essays in Honor of Zhang Zhengliang on His 90th Birthday" compiled by the Editorial Committee of Zhang Zhengliang's 90th Birthday Memorial, published by Social Sciences Literature Publishing House in 2002), it is stated that "the sovereign receives the heavenly mandate to establish his reign, and every political action of the sovereign elicits a reaction from heaven. When the political governance deteriorates, disasters and anomalies occur. When political governance is enlightened, auspicious signs appear. Disasters and anomalies are signs from heaven to admonish or commend the sovereign. When the governance reaches a point of extreme decay and disasters and anomalies persist without introspection or repentance, then heaven changes its mandate and grants it to someone with virtue."

14 Dong Zhongshu, Chunqiu Fanlu

15 Biography of Dong Zhongshu, Book of Han

16 Tian Changwu and An Zuozhang, History of Qin and Han, Chapter 4, Section 1, People's Publishing House, 1993.

17 According to Biography of Li Xun, Book of Han, Gan Zhongke, an alchemist from Qi, during the reign of Emperor Cheng, produced the "Tianguan Calendar" and the "Baoyuan Taiping Classic" and claimed, "The Han dynasty has reached the final stage ordained by heaven and earth. It should receive a new mandate from heaven."

18 Annals of Emperor Ai, Book of Han

19 Qian Mu, in "A Biography of Liu Xiangxin and His Son" (Volume 5, Part 1 of *Ancient Historical Critiques*, Pu She Publishing House, 1935), pointed out that the belief in the transfer of yin and yang and the Five Virtues was prevalent at that time, which differed from later generations who advocated the eternal ruling of a certain emperor. During the usurpation of Wang Mang, many scholars who were well-versed in Confucianism praised his achievements and virtues and encouraged him to strive for progress. Although they may have sought favor and flattered him, it also reflected the trends of the time in academia. Liao Boyuan further stated in *Shuo Xin: A Discussion on the Creation of Dynastic Titles and Its Reasons* that the theory of the interaction between yin and yang and the Five Elements as a manifestation of the connection between heaven and humanity was prominent during the Western Han dynasty. Those who advocated this theory often held revolutionary views, asserting that the world does not belong to one royal family, but to all the people. They believed that the mandate of heaven was unpredictable and would be bestowed upon those with virtue.

20 During that time in the imperial court, Emperor Liu Kan was a child, and Empress Dowager Wang Zhengjun held the power. The influential Wang family, who had numerous descendants, held great power. Wang Mang, who was considered a paragon of morality, had total control, and his daughter was the empress of Emperor Liu Kan.

21 The issue of the virtuous cycle of the Five Virtues during the Han dynasty is highly complex. It was initially considered the Water Virtue, then changed to the Earth Virtue, and later changed to the Fire Virtue. For further details, please refer to Gu Jiegang, "The Politics and History in the Theory of the Five Virtues" in the Selected Essays on Ancient History, Volume 3, Zhonghua Book Company, 1996.

22 Gu Jiegang, "A Brief History of Academic Development in the Han Dynasty," Chapter 14. Dongfang Publishing House, 1996

23 Yang Xiong, "Juqin Meixin" (also known as "Rhapsody on Beautiful Qin"), included in Yan Kejun's compilation, Complete Works of Three Ancient Dynasties, Qin, Han, Three Kingdoms, and Six Dynasties, Volume 53. Zhonghua Book Company, 1958

24 Tan Qixiang, Study on Official Positions in the Xin Dynasty, Changshui Collection, volume 1, People's Publishing House, 1987.

25 Baihu Tongde Lun (Evidential Analysis of Debates in the White Tiger Hall)

26 Hu Songping, A Preliminary Draft of the Chronology of Mr. Hu Shizhi, consisting of four letters sent to Yang Liansheng between April and May 1956, Lianjing Publishing Company, Taipei, 1984

27 Zhao Yi, The Defeat of Wang Mang, Records of History: the Twenty-Two Dynasties, Volume 3.

28 Zhao Yi, The Defeat of Wang Mang, Records of History: the Twenty-Two Dynasties, Volume 3.

29 Wang Mang, who was hailed as the epitome of Confucian virtue, took the Western Zhou dynasty as a model. He insisted on referencing Duke Zhou in his speeches, following the rituals of the Zhou dynasty, and implementing the Zhou system. Wang Mang believed that by doing so, the Xin dynasty would recreate the prosperous era of the Western Zhou dynasty. However, this was the tragedy of Wang Mang, since history had already progressed to the Han dynasty, it was impossible to return to the Zhou dynasty. While Wang Mang seemed to advocate for novelty, in reality, his pursuit of innovation was divorced from practicality, exhausting people and wasting resources, ultimately exacerbating various contradictions in the name of restoration or reversion.

30 Zhao Yi, The Insurgents All Claimed to be Descendants of Han, Records of History: the Twenty-Two Dynasties, Volume 3.

31 The prophecy of the Red Clump was actually brought from Guanzhong by Qiang Hua, Liu Xiu's classmate in Chang'an. According to Li Xian's annotations of the *Book of Later Han*: Annals of Emperor Guangwu, from Emperor Gaozu to the early reign of Emperor Guangwu, it lasted a total of 228 years, precisely at the time of "four sevens." Fire virtue of Han refers to the fire as the main element of Han.

32 Zhao Yi, The Insurgents All Claimed to be Descendants of Han, Records of History: the Twenty-Two Dynasties, Volume 3.

7 Wei, Han and Wu

The Three Divisions of the Country

The unified Han Dynasty, restored by Liu Xiu, lasted until the seventh year of the Guanghe Era (184 AD), when the Yellow Turban Rebellion erupted, plunging the dynasty into a state of practical division. To suppress the rebellion, the central Han government was compelled to grant more power to prefecture governors and local officials. As a result, these prefecture governors and officials became fragmented forces that contributed to the disintegration of the Han Dynasty. In his commentary on the Records of Officials in the *Continuation of the Book of Han*,[1] Liu Zhao pointed out the following:

> The extensive regulations for respecting prefecture governors and local officials were ineffective in governing the state even for a single day. Consequently, the prefecture governors and local officials expanded their territories, undermining the emperor's authority in regions such as Min and E. Yuan Shao took control of Ji prefecture and extended his influence to Yan and Shuo. Liu Biao ruled Jingzhou and conducted ceremonial rites for Heaven and Earth. Cao Cao held Yanzhou, laying the groundwork for his imperial ambition. The downfall of the Han Dynasty can be traced back to these events.

Although the fall of the Han Dynasty cannot be solely attributed to these factors, the widespread conflicts among warlords across the country were integrally connected to the unchecked expansion of power by prefecture governors and local officials. Amidst these warlord conflicts, the Han Dynasty met its demise, and it was Cao Pi, the son of Cao Cao, who directly succeeded it.

In the year 220 AD, Cao Pi established the Wei Dynasty, succeeding the Han Dynasty. The success of Cao Pi relied on the strategic groundwork laid by his father, Cao Cao. In the second year of Xingping (195 AD), chaos erupted in Guanzhong, prompting Emperor Liu Xie (Emperor Xian of Han) to leave Chang'an and head east. Ju Shou advised Yuan Shao to lodge Emperor Xian, but the counsel was ignored. The following year, in the first year of Jian'an, Emperor Xian fled to Luoyang, where Cao Cao dispatched troops to escort the Emperor to Xu (present-day Xuchang in Henan Province). At that time, the landscape was divided with various warlords controlling different regions: Yuan Shao occupied

DOI: 10.4324/9781003510390-8

the prefectures of Ji, Bing, and Qing; Gongsun Zan held Prefecture Youzhou; Tao Qian, Liu Bei, and Lv Bu successively controlled Xuzhou; Yuan Shu commanded parts of Yangzhou; Liu Biao governed Jingzhou; Zhang Xiu ruled Nanyang; Sun Ce took over Jiangdong; Han Sui and Ma Teng controlled Liangzhou; Liu Zhang held Yizhou; and Gongsun Du controlled Liaodong. It wasn't until Cao Cao, commanding both Yanzhou and Yuzhou, seized power over Emperor Xian that the tide began to turn. With Emperor Xian in Xu, "the establishment of ancestral temples and the imperial system began." As Cao Cao held the emperor under his sway and commanded the allegiance of the nobility, he solidified his political dominance. Eventually, Cao Cao, Sun Quan, and Liu Bei vanquished the warlords and divided the realm into the three kingdoms of Wei, Wu, and Shu, respectively.[2]

The coexistence of the three kingdoms of Wei, Shu, and Wu, each representing an independent domain, marked the era known as the "Three Kingdoms." This was a divided age, with Wei, Shu, and Wu existing as distinct states, each with its unique lineage.

7.1 Wei: "Dangtu Gao, the Successor of Han" (He who Replaces Han Shall Be Covered in Wei)

The process of replacing Han was experienced through two generations of the Cao family, Cao Cao and his son Cao Pi. In 208 AD, Cao Cao was appointed as the Chancellor. In 213 AD, He was bestowed the title of Duke of Wei by Emperor Xian of Han. In 216 AD, Cao Cao was further elevated to the position of King of Wei.[3] In 220 AD, Cao Cao passed away, and his second son, Cao Pi, succeeded him as Chancellor and inherited the title of King of Wei. In the same year, Cao Pi declared himself emperor and established the Kingdom of Wei, with its capital in Luoyang, deposing Emperor Xian of Han (Liu Xie) to Duke of Shanyang, which marked the official end of the Han Dynasty.

Why did the Cao family choose to call their kingdom Wei after replacing Han? According to annotations of *Annals of Wei* in the *Zizhi Tongjian* by Hu Sanjing, it is stated that after Cao Cao defeated Yuan Shang and acquired Jizhou, he resided in Ye. Ye was the capital of the Prefecture Wei during the Han Dynasty, and Wei is a renowned name. Therefore, he was conferred the title of Duke of Wei, as predicted by the phrase "he who replaces Han shall be covered in Wei." The "Wei" in the phrase refers to the Kingdom of Wei. When Emperor Wen of Wei received the abdication of the emperor of Han, the country was officially named Wei.

From this, we can infer that Cao Pi's decision to name the state Wei was derived from Cao Cao's appointment as Duke of Wei and his association with the favorable meaning of "Wei" as a renowned name and the prophecy "he who replaces Han shall be covered in Wei."

According to the *Fengsu Tongyi* (Annotations of Literature and Customs) by Eastern Han historian Ying Shao, the ancestors of Wei were descendants of Duke Bi Gao, who used to have the same surname as the Zhou family. After King Wu of Zhou overthrew the Shang Dynasty, he granted Gao the fief Bi thus Gao got the surname Bi. His great-grandson was named Bi Wan, who served Duke Xian of Jin. Duke Xian conquered Wei and exterminated it, then bestowed the title upon Wan. The divination expert Bu Yan commented, "The descendants of Bi Wan will be great. 'Wan' signifies completeness or abundance, and 'Wei' represents a grand name. The emperor has the whole nation, while the vassals have a myriad of people. Now, by using a grand name that aligns with abundance, it is no wonder a large following is obtained." Additionally, in the *Huainanzi*, there is a line that says, "Therefore, dwelling above the rivers and seas while wandering beneath the grand halls of Wei Que." In the annotation by Gao You of Eastern Han, "Wei Que" is explained as "majestic and grand gates of the imperial court," indicating that "Wei" means towering and grand. This meaning of greatness for "Wei" has been in use since the Spring and Autumn Period, and with the title Wei, it symbolized the noble aspiration for a powerful state.[4]

Furthermore, the reason Cao Cao compelled Emperor Xian of Han to confer him with the title "Wei" is closely related to the prophecy of "Dangtu Gao, the successor of Han."[5] The earliest reliable appearance of this prophecy was found in letters exchanged between Liu Xiu and Gongsun Shu during the early years of the Eastern Han Dynasty. The line goes, "He who replaces Han shall be covered in Wei. Are you the one who possesses such loftiness?" Due to the ambiguity of this prophecy, it was interpreted differently and taken advantage of by various individuals. Some believed that this prophecy referred to someone named Dangtu Gao who would replace Han and hold the position of Chancellor.[6] Others thought that "Tu" meant the road, and since Yuan Shu's given name was Lu, he interpreted it as his name and given title, which coincidentally happened when he obtained the imperial jade seal from Sun Jian, prompting him to hastily declare himself emperor.[7] However, he was defeated by Liu Bei, whom he despised the most, and died in frustration.[8] As for the corresponding interpretation of Cao Cao being titled "Wei," it can be traced back to Zhou Shu's statement, "Dangtu Gao refers to Wei."[9] It means that "Wei" is the grand name, and "Tugao" signifies something towering. Therefore, the wise person took the association and spoke accordingly.[10] According to ancient customs, the magnificent towers and pavilions that stood high above the gates of emperors and vassals were called "Que" or "Guan." Due to their grand and towering presence, they were also known as "Wei Que." The phrase "Dangtu Gao" refers to tall buildings that face the main road, and "Wei Que" precisely fits this description.[11] Therefore, "Dangtu Gao" refers to Wei, and "he who replaces Han is Wei." At that time, Emperor Xian of Han was already under the control of Cao Cao, with the imperial robe becoming nothing more than Cao Cao's undergarment. It was evident to astute individuals that Cao Cao was the most likely candidate to replace the Han Dynasty. Cao Cao's appointment as Duke of Wei was in line with the prophecy, which provided a theoretical reason for the Cao family to replace Han. During the Eastern Han Dynasty, the position of Chancellor was not originally established, but Cao Cao became the first to hold the office, fitting the interpretation of the one who replaces Han as the Chancellor. Thus, following Cao Cao's lead, Cao Pi ultimately replaced Han and adopted the title Wei in accordance with the prophecy.

7.2 Han: The Only Legitimate Successor

In the year 221, in the fourth month of the year following Cao Pi's usurpation of the Han Dynasty and establishment of the Kingdom Wei, Liu Bei,[12] who had already assumed the title of King of Hanzhong after capturing Hanzhong in 219, declared himself emperor and established his capital at Chengdu, continuing the use of the title of Han.

It cannot be certain whether Liu Bei is truly a descendant of Liu Sheng, the King of Zhongshan and son of Emperor Jing of Han. On this matter, there is a meaningful passage in the annotations by Pei Songzhi of the Southern Song Dynasty in the *Records of the Three Kingdoms*: "I, Songzhi, consider that although Liu Bei claims descent from Emperor Xiao Jing, the lineage is ancient and the true nature of the ancestry is difficult to confirm. After inheriting the Han legacy, it is unknown which emperor he regards as the progenitor of his ancestral temple."[13] However, regardless of this uncertainty, Liu Bei leveraged his noble lineage as a member of the imperial family to rally support for the restoration of the Han Dynasty. Gradually, he formed a force that controlled one part of the divided realm, opposing Cao Cao and forming an alliance with Sun Quan. At that time, Cao Cao "claimed the title of Chancellor of Han and used the emperor as a pretext to conquer the four corners of the realm, exploiting the court for his purposes." Sun Quan "held control of the Jiangdong region, spanning thousands of miles." Although Liu Bei was situated in a strategically less advantageous location with limited territory and population, he claimed to be the legitimate heir to the Han Dynasty, providing him with considerable political leverage. Against this backdrop, Cao Pi's declaration as emperor, which included deposing Emperor Liu Xie and giving him the title Duke of Shanyang, made it inevitable for Liu Bei to inherit the Han throne, establish his own imperial position, and attempt to restore the Han Dynasty. Moreover, Liu Bei handled the situation quite effectively. It began with the rumors of Emperor Xian's death, upon which Liu Bei publicly mourned and donned mourning attire, bestowing upon Emperor Xian the title of Emperor Xiaomin posthumously.[14] Subsequently, there were numerous reports of auspicious signs, including the alignment of the sun and moon, with both civil and military officials strongly advocating for Liu Bei's ascension. It was after this sequence of events that Liu Bei transformed from King of Hanzhong into Emperor Liu Bei.

Based on the analysis above, Liu Bei's continued use of the title "Han" for his state was to demonstrate the legitimacy of his regime and its continuation of the Han Dynasty.[15] There is ample evidence directly related to Liu Bei's self-perception as the rightful ruler of Han, such as the account in "Book of Shu" in the *Records of the Three Kingdoms*, which details the petitions by Xu Jing, Zhuge Liang, and others urging Liu Bei to assume the imperial title.

Cao Pi usurped the throne, murdered the rightful ruler, extinguished the Han Dynasty, seized the divine seal, oppressed the loyal and virtuous, and ruled with extreme cruelty and injustice. Both living spirits and those passed were filled with anger and yearning for the return of the Liu clan. In this state of disarray, there was no emperor, plunging the nation into turmoil and leaving its people with no one to rely upon ... When Guan Yu besieged Fancheng and Xiangyang, the men of Xiangyang, Zhang Jia and Wang Xiu, presented Liu Bei with the jade seal. It had been hidden in the river Han, submerged in a spring, its brilliance lighting up the world, its divine radiance piercing through the heavens. The Han Dynasty, founded by Emperor Gaozu, now saw echoes of its beginnings with your rising from Hanzhong. Now, with the divine light of the imperial seal shining forth and emerging from Xiangyang, at the terminus of the River Han, it was to be bestowed upon the king, symbolizing divine favor for his ascension to emperor. This auspicious omen was not mere human contrivance ... It is hereby proclaimed that the king, the esteemed Lord, hails from the lineage of the King of Zhongshan, Emperor Xiaojing of Han. This noble lineage, blessed and favored by the heavens, has endured across generations. Your extraordinary talents, martial prowess, benevolence, accumulated virtues, and your love for the people and righteous officials have earned widespread admiration. Hence, it is only fitting for you to ascend the throne, continue the legacy of the two ancestors, inherit the virtues of Emperor Guangwu, and bestow great fortune upon the country.

Upon Liu Bei's ascension to the throne, he further expressed in the writing:

Han has ruled over this vast land for countless generations. In the past, Wang Mang usurped the throne, but Emperor Guangwu, fueled by righteous indignation, restored the imperial clan to its former glory. Now, with Cao Cao persisting in martial dominance, wantonly executing rulers and their descendants, a great chaos has ensued, flouting the will of heaven. Cao Pi, his son, extends his father's oppressive reign, unlawfully wielding the divine seal ... The state altar has fallen into neglect, and it is my sacred duty to restore it, to continue the legacy of the two mighty ancestors ... May the divine blessings be upon the Han Dynasty, bringing eternal peace to the four corners of the land.

Historical records state that the emergence of the jade seal from the river Han in Xiangyang resonated with the founders of the Han Dynasty, Emperor Liu Bang, and Emperor Liu Xiu. In doing so, Liu Bei became the "third founder" reviving the Han Dynasty, continuing the legacy of the "two founders," Liu Bang and Liu Xiu. Even the establishment of Liu Bei's reign as the Zhangwu era corresponded with Emperor Guangwu's earlier Jianwu era. Many later scholars recognized the importance of this symbolism, including Xie Bi of the Ming Dynasty, who wrote the *Chronicles of Ji Han* (Shu Han), and Wang Fuli of the Qing Dynasty, authoring *Five Records of Ji Han*. Both works affirm Liu Bei's Han (Ji Han) as the legitimate continuation of the Han Dynasty, linking directly to the Western Han (Former Han) under Liu Bang and the Eastern Han (Later Han) under Liu Xiu. Similarly, the *Continuation of the Later Han Dynasty* by Xiao Chang of the Southern Song Dynasty and Hao Jing of the Yuan Dynasty acted as extensions of Ban Gu's *Book of Han* (Former Han) and Fan Ye's *Book of the Later Han* (Later Han), acknowledging Liu Bei and Liu Shan as legitimate rulers, chronicling their reigns. If Liu Bei could perceive this recognition after his passing, he would surely rest content in the afterlife.

However, despite the centuries, Liu Bei, the big-eared lachrymose Emperor of Han, Zhuge Liang, the dedicated Chancellor, and Guan Yu, the loyal and righteous General, along with other devoted subjects of the Han Dynasty, would probably continue to lament in the realm of the dead! Because today, when expressing and studying the history of the Three Kingdoms, it has become customary to refer to the regime of Liu Bei and Liu Shan as "Shu Han" or simply "Shu." Take, for instance, the TV series "Romance of the Three Kingdoms," produced by China Central Television in recent years, where the flag of Kingdom of Shu (instead of Kingdom of Han) was consistently displayed throughout.

The designation of Liu Bei and Liu Shan's regime as "Shu" has historical origins and special considerations. At that time, amidst various factions contending for legitimacy, the regimes of Cao Wei and Sima Jin referred Liu Bei and Liu Shan's regime as "Shu." *Records of the Three Kingdoms* by Chen Shou of the Jin Dynasty, the most important official history for studying the Three Kingdoms period, is divided into three parts of "Book of Wei," "Book of Shu," and "Book of Wu," which record the histories of Cao Wei, Shu Han, and Sun Wu (Eastern Wu), respectively, with Cao Wei being regarded as the legitimate regime. Considering historical facts at that time, this is understandable.

Taking Chen Shou's approach, since the Sima clan rose to power through abdication rather than conquest, they needed to establish Cao Wei as the legitimate regime, or else they would undermine the legitimacy of the Jin Dynasty. As a loyal servant who transitioned from Liu Bei and Liu Shan to the Sima Jin regime, how could Chen Shou dare challenge this legitimacy? Consequently, instead of using the term "Han" for Liu Bei and Liu Shan's regime, the regional term "Shu"[16] was chosen to differentiate from "Book of Han," which recorded the history of the Han Dynasty of Liu Bang (known as the Western Han) and that of Liu Xiu (known as the Eastern Han). After all, establishing a dual "Book of Han" would easily have caused confusion.

Additionally, some scholars have noted that Chen Shou, born in Anhan County in Prefecture Baxi, belonged to an indigenous group in the Ba and Shu regions that had conflicts with the Liu Bei immigrants. Moreover, Chen Shou's father was executed by Zhuge Liang, yet Shou himself received leniency from Zhuge Liang. Therefore, Chen Shou's use of "Shu" instead of "Han" in the *Records of the Three Kingdoms* is also related to these factors (see Figure 7.1).

However, it must be emphasized that if we respect facts and the principle of using the owner's name, then the regime of Liu Bei and Liu Shan should be called "Han." Even in "Book of Shu," there are instances where the term "Han" is used without being replaced by "Shu." For example, the official documents in "Biography of Sun Quan" of "Book of Wu," which recorded the alliance between Liu Bei and Sun Quan, states as follows:

Figure 7.1 The author of this book is in front of the tomb of Emperor Zhao of Han (Liu
Bei) in Chengdu

The Nine Prefectures are in chaos; there is no unified authority; the people and
gods grieve, and there is no end in sight. When Cao Cao's descendant, Cao Pi,
acting as a despot, he committed evil deeds and usurped the throne. Pi continued
the wickedness as a mere figurehead, and obstructed our troops and seized our
lands without being punished ... Today, we have annihilated the wicked and
captured his associates. If it is not Han and Wu, then who will be responsible for
restoration? When eliminating evil and suppressing tyranny, one must expose
their crimes, divide and seize their lands first, so that the hearts of the soldiers
and the people know where to pledge their allegiance ... In the relationship
between Han and Wu, even though trust is fostered from within, the division
of territories and broken borders made it necessary to establish an alliance ...
From this day forward, after the alliance between Han and Wu, we should unite
our efforts, collaborate to eliminate the Wei traitors, save those in danger, aid
the suffering, share the hardships, and be united in likes and dislikes, without
wavering. If anyone harms Han, Wu will attack them; if anyone harms Wu,
Han will attack them. Each shall maintain their own territories and refrain from

invading each other. Pass this down to future generations, and the outcome will be as firm as the beginning.

It is apparent that in 229 AD when the alliance was established, the titles used by Liu Shan, Sun Quan, and Cao Rui were respectively Han, Wu, and Wei. Similarly, in the "Biography of Yang Xi" the "Book of Shu," when annotated *Biographies of Advisers of Ji Han* by Yang Xi in the 4th year of Yanxi (241 AD), Chen Shou did not change it to Biographies of Advisers of Shu, as "Ji Han" accurately represented the political regime of Liu Bei and Liu Shan at that time.

In summary, when discussing the regime of Liu Bei and Liu Shan today, we should not adhere to Chen Shou's historiographical approach under special political circumstances, where "Shu" was used instead of "Han." Instead, we should refer to historical facts and call it "Han" or use the previously established names "Ji Han" or "Shu Han." The long-standing practice of referring to Liu Bei and Liu Shan's regime as "Shu" carries a derogatory connotation and is highly inappropriate, as it impedes a correct understanding of the historical context at that time and disrespects Liu Bei, Zhuge Liang, Guan Yu, and other loyal subjects of the Han Dynasty, because the greatest political capital of those people lies in the legitimate symbol of the title "Han."

7.3 Wu: A "Stopgap Measure"

After Cao Pi declared himself emperor and established the state in 221, he conferred Sun Quan the King of Wu, who resided in Wuchang (present-day Ezhou, Hubei Province) at that time. In April of 229, Sun Quan ascended to the throne, and by September, he had moved the capital to Jianye (present-day Nanjing, Jiangsu Province), and the state was consequently named Wu. From then on, except for a brief two-year period from September 265 to December 266 (or January 267), when the capital was temporarily moved back to Wuchang, Jianye functioned as the capital of the Sun Wu regime.

Why did Sun Quan accept the title of King of Wu from Cao Pi? According to the "Biography of Sun Quan" in the *Records of the Three Kingdoms*, as annotated by Pei Songzhi and citing the *Annals of Jiangbiao*, the entire body of ministers of Sun Quan debated over the issue. They believed that he should claim the title of Grand General and Duke of Jiuzhou, rejecting the title offered by Wei. However, Sun Quan replied, "The title Duke of Jiuzhou has never been heard of in ancient times. In the past, Liu Bang also accepted the title of King of Han from Xiang Yu. It is just a stopgap measure. What harm is there?" Thus, he accepted the title.

From this, it becomes evident that Sun Quan's decision was grounded in an evaluation of the prevailing situation. Liu Bei claimed to be the legitimate successor to the Han dynasty and was supported by the populace, while Wei was the most powerful state with military supremacy. Sun Quan, caught between the two and unable to match them,[17] saw accepting the title as a strategic move under the given conditions. From Cao Pi's perspective, the rationale for bestowing the title of King of Wu on Sun Quan stemmed from the association of Sun Quan's territories in the Jiangdong region[18] with "Wu," a reference dating back to the Qin and Han dynasties and the Warring States period.[19]

The three kingdoms of Wei, Han, and Wu persisted until November 263, when Wei eventually overthrew the Han Dynasty. Thus, in some respects, the reconstructed "Ji Han" by Liu Bei, which symbolized a continuance of the Han regime, met its end. In December 265 (or January 266), Sima Yan declared himself emperor of Wei, renaming the State of Jin, with its capital remaining in Luoyang. Subsequently, in March 280, Jin conquered Wu, reuniting the fragmented parts. The unified empire of Jin spanned from central Korea in the east to the western rim of the Tarim Basin in the west, encroaching upon the southern borders of Vietnam in the south and reaching the shores of the Gobi Desert in the north. The title "Jin" was adopted as the new collective designation and common title for the whole country. The 60-year period (from October 220 to February 280) of ambiguous sovereignty and the absence of a unified title was relegated to history.

Notes

1 The name should be *Book of Later Han* instead of *Continuation of the Book of Han*. Fan Ye of the Southern Dynasty wrote the *Book of Later Han*, but he was imprisoned and died before completing the book. The current version of the *Book of Later Han* consists of eight sections and thirty volumes, which originally belonged to Sima Biao's *Continuation of the Book of Han* (with eighty articles including annals, records, and biographies; the annals and biographies are now lost), and later generations incorporated them into Fan Ye's *Book of Later Han*.

2 Many scholars believe that after the Battle of Chibi in 208 AD, the era of the Three Kingdoms began. However, this is not entirely accurate. It was after the Battle of Xiaoting in 222 AD that the situation of the Three Kingdoms truly solidified, and each kingdom established relatively stable borders. For more details, please refer to Hu Axiang's *Research on the Territories and Administrative Regions of the Six Dynasties*, Chapter One, published by Xi'an Map Publishing House in 2000.

3 In Chapter 3, Part 3 of the *Formation of the Sui and Tang Empires: A Historical Analysis* by Gu Chuan Daoxiong (translated by Li Jicang, Shanghai Ancient Books Publishing House, 2004), the author points out that during the Wei and Jin periods, there were many examples of the throne being bestowed upon close relatives of the emperor. The rare instances of the throne being given to those of a different surname indicated that a change in dynasty was imminent. At that time, it was highly possible for someone of a different surname to become emperor. The example of Cao Cao being titled King of Wei, as well as numerous powerful figures becoming emperors during the Jin, Northern and Southern dynasties, serve as evidence of this theory.

4 There is no direct relationship between the Wei in the Three Kingdoms period and the Wei kingdom in the pre-Qin era, so it is not discussed in detail.

5 The so-called "prophecies" refers to predictions about future events or facts, similar to the texts one would receive when consulting an oracle. Devout believers consider them as prophecies about the future or future generations.

6 For more details, please refer to the annotations by Li Xian of the Tang Dynasty, citing *Dongguan Ji* and *Huayang Guozhi*.

7 The meaning of "shu" and "lu" both imply a main road or route, while "dangtu" also carries the meaning of a main road, as seen in the idiom of "Daoting Tushuo" (hearsay).

8 Biography of Yuan Shu, Book of Later Han.

9 Biography of Zhou Qun, Book of Shu, Records of Three Kingdoms.

10 Biography of Du Qiong, Book of Shu, Records of Three Kingdoms.

11 To obtain a detailed explanation, please refer to the reference from the *Records of the Three Kingdoms*, annotated by Pei Songzhi of the Southern Dynasty.

12 Biography of Emperor Wen, Book of Shu, Records of the Three Kingdoms.

13 Biography of Emperor Wen in the *Records of the Three Kingdoms*, with annotations by Pei Songzhi of the Southern Dynasty. The annotations of Pei Songzhi also cite Yu Huan's "Brief Chronicle of Cao Wei," which mentions, "Bei (Liu Bei) was originally a descendant of the Marquis of Linyi." According to Ling Wenchao's research, in his essay "The Soul of the Great River: Xiangyang and Han River Culture Forum Papers" (published by People's Publishing House in 2015), it is identified that during the Han Dynasty, there were two Marquises of Linyi: Liu Rang, a descendant of King Xian in Changshan, and Liu Fu, a descendant of King Ding in Changsha. They were both descendants of Emperor Jing, but not of Liu Sheng, King Zhongshan. Considering Liu Bei's activities and his ancestors' proximity to Changshan, as well as the fact that Marquis Liu Rang of Linyi was executed by Emperor Guangwu for rebellion, it is more likely that Liu Bei was a branch of the Liu Rang lineage of Marquis of Linyi.

14 According to the *Annals of Emperor Xiaoxian* in the *Book of Later Han*, Liu Xie, the ruler of Wei, passed away in the second year of Qinglong (234 AD) and was posthumously honored as Emperor Xiaoxian.

15 Regarding the concept of "legitimacy" in ancient Chinese political theories, it is extensively documented and cannot be fully explained here. In general, the concept of legitimacy, in terms of bloodline succession, is contrasted with "branch lineages" and primarily signifies "direct lineage." In the context of fragmentation and the rise and fall of dynasties, it contrasts with "usurpers" and "illegitimate rule," representing the basic meaning of the "sole legitimate authority." A "legitimate" regime, at least nominally, obtains the qualification to govern the entire realm.

16 "Shu," the name of an ancient tribe and kingdom, located in the western part of present-day Sichuan Province, China. In the year 316 BC, it was annexed by Qin, and Prefecture Shu was established in that region.

17 According to Tao Yuanzhen's "A Study of Wu's Military in the Three Kingdoms" (Yan Jing Journal, Issue 13, 1933), it is mentioned that "Sun Jian died in battle before his achievements were accomplished. Sun Ce crossed the Yangtze River as a Captain. Sun Quan governed the prefecture as a filial and incorruptible prefecture governor. Their positions were still low, and their prestige was not yet established."

18 In "Geographical Records" of the *Book of Han*, it is stated, "The land of Wu has several districts. The present-day Kuaiji, Jiujiang, Danyang, Yuzhang, Lujiang, Guangling, Liu'an, and Prefecture Linhuai all belong to Wu."

19 As for the origin of the name "Wu" of the ancient kingdom before the Qin Dynasty, it is quite complex, and there are many scholarly discussions on the subject. References include Zhou Yan's "Interpretation of 'Wu'" and Yin Weiren's "On Tai Bo and Zhong Yong's Arrivals in Wu and the Issue of Ancient Customs," both in the Journal of Suzhou

University: Special Issue on Taihu Lake's Historical and Cultural Research, Volume 1, 1992. Zhou Guorong and Zhou Yan, "A Study on the Name 'Wu'," Journal of Suzhou University, Issue 3, 1992. Yin Weiren, "The Cultural Implications of the Title Wu," Academic Monthly, Issue 2, 1994. Although not elaborated here, it is understood that Sun Quan's Kingdom of Wu can be traced back to the pre-Qin kingdom of Wu.

8 Jin

The "Well-known Ambition" of Sima Zhao

The cold, merciless nature of history often manifests itself in its astonishing similarities, as in the case of power-seekers. After a certain period, their power is often wrested away by others. In 220 AD, when Cao Pi coerced Emperor Liu Xie of the Han Dynasty to abdicate in his favor, he likely did not anticipate that just over 40 years later, the Cao Wei Kingdom would face a similar fate. In early 266 AD, the ambitious Sima Yan, a powerful figure within the Cao Wei regime, coveted the imperial throne yet aimed to avoid the notoriety that came with usurpation. Following Cao Pi's example with the Han Dynasty, he coerced Emperor Cao Huan of Wei into "voluntarily" abdicating. Sima Yan feigned reluctance, transmuting usurpation into an ostensibly glorified act of abdication, and both parties were revered as benevolent rulers akin to Yao and Shun.

Cao Pi's usurpation of the Han and the establishment of the Wei provided a historical precedent known as the "Han-Wei transition." Sima Yan's usurpation of Wei and the establishment of the Jin mirrored this event, hence dubbed the "Wei-Jin transition." The only minor difference was that the "Han-Wei transition" spanned two generations with Cao Cao and his son Cao Pi, while the "Wei-Jin transition" was completed by three generations: Sima Yi, Sima Shi, Sima Zhao and Sima Yan.

With Jin's establishment through Wei's usurpation, the realm had not yet unified. However, in March 280 AD, Jin conquered Wu and became the new unified title of the realm. Jin retained this title until November 316 AD, when Emperor Sima Ye of Jin was captured by Liu Yao, a distinguished general of the Han regime founded by the Xiongnu. Tracing back, the establishment of the state name "Jin" dates to October 263 AD, when Sima Zhao was enfeoffed as the Duke of Jin by Wei. The proposal to enfeoff Sima Zhao with this title had been made even earlier, in May 258 AD. Regarding why Sima Zhao was granted the title of Duke of Jin, historian Hu Sanxing comments on the "Chronicle of Jin" of the *Zizhi Tongjian*:

> The Sima family hailed from Wen County in Henan. The emperor originally appointed Sima Yi (Emperor Xuan) to office; his successor, Sima Shi (Emperor Jing), was followed by Sima Zhao (Emperor Wen), who was enfeoffed as the Duke of Jin. Wen County of Jin, being the family's ancestral land, became the origin of the Jin Dynasty.

DOI: 10.4324/9781003510390-9

Here, "Emperor Xuan," "Emperor Jing," and "Emperor Wen" are posthumous titles later conferred by Sima Zhao and Sima Yan. After usurping Wei, Sima Yan posthumously honored the Sima family with these titles. According to Hu Sanxing, the enfeoffment of the Sima family drew from Wen County, the "original land of Jin." The connection between Wen County and Jin traces back to the pre-Qin period. Nevertheless, if the attribution of the dynastic title was solely because Wen County was the "original land of Jin," why did Sima Zhao's enfeoffment not encompass Prefecture Henei and Wen County? It seems that the relation of Wen County to Jin is a superficial phenomenon rather than the crux of the matter. The ennoblement of Sima Zhao as Duke of Jin and Sima Yan's choice to maintain the title Jin encapsulate a deeper significance.

8.1 Tracing the Origin: The State of Jin in the Pre-Qin Period

The State of Jin in the Pre-Qin Period was first established during the reign of King Cheng of Zhou in the 11th century BC. According to the "Biography of the Royal Family of the Jin Dynasty" in the *Records of the Grand Historian*:

> Ji Shuyu of Jin was the younger brother of King Cheng of Zhou. After the death of King Wu, King Cheng ascended the throne. The land of Tang was in chaos, and Duke of Zhou eradicated the rebels. Shuyu was then enfeoffed in the state of Tang, which was located to the east of the Yellow and Fen Rivers, covering an area of one hundred square miles, hence the name Tang Shuyu. The surname was Ji, and the style name was Zi Yu. Ji Shuyu's son, Ji Xie, became the Marquis of Jin.

Based on this, during the time of the initial enfeoffment of Ji Yu, the state was still named Tang.[1] However, after his son Ji Xie became the "Marquis of Jin," the state's name changed to Jin. The reason for changing Tang to Jin is explained in the *Collected Annotations of the Records of the Grand Historian*: "There was a river Jin in Tang, and when Ji Xie changed the name of his state, he was called Marquis of Jin." Additionally, *Collected Interpretations of the Records of the Grand Historian* quotes the *Treatise on Geography*: "Ji Shuyu's son Ji Xie moved and settled near the river Jin ... According to the *Maoshi Collection*, 'Ji Shuyu's son Ji Xie moved because there was a river Jin to the south of Yao's Ruins, and he changed himself to Marquis of Jin'." According to the "Geographical Records" of the *Book of Han*: the source of the river Jin is located south west of present-day Xuanweng Mountain in Taiyuan City, Shanxi Province. It flows north east through the ancient city of Yingxi and eventually merges with the River Fen. During the time of Ji Shuyu's initial enfeoffment, the territory was located around present-day Yicheng in southern Shanxi. At that time, the area near present-day Taiyuan was still inhabited by the Rongdi barbarians, so River Jin is likely a later name that originated from the State of Jin. Furthermore, River Jin is relatively short and, logically speaking, is not suitable as a basis for a state title.

Since the theory that the change of name from "Tang" to "Jin" due to the river Jin is uncertain, where did the name "Jin" come from? *Study on the Names of the State of Qin* by Luo Jiangsheng points out the following:

> Shuyu was granted fertile lands suitable for cultivating cereals and received a 'fine harvest,' which was highly praised by King Cheng and Duke Zhou. The original meaning of the character 'Jin' signifies the prosperous growth of grains, which corresponds to the concept of a 'fine harvest.' Thus, when his son Ji Xie succeeded to the throne, in order to signify that the 'fine harvest' was the foundation of the nation, the state was named 'Jin,' and his son Xie became known as the 'Marquis of Jin.'[2]

As stated in the *Records of the Grand Historian*: "A blessing from the heaven, Ji Shuyu received crops, exhibiting abundant growth. He presented them to King Cheng, who then commanded Ji Shuyu to deliver them to Zhou Gong in the eastern region. This event was recorded in *Gift of Crops*. After Zhou Gong received the crops, he declared it a favor from the Son of Heaven and recorded it as *Bountiful Crops*." This incident is also mentioned in the *Records of the Grand Historian, Annals of Zhou*. This strange and magnificent grain plant called 'crops' (specifically, millet) had multiple stalks growing from a single plant, with each stalk bearing one ear of grain. If this was widely cultivated, it would undoubtedly increase production greatly. People of that time believed this was a significant discovery related to the will of the gods and was crucial for national policy and people's livelihood. Therefore, the *Records of the Grand Historian* repeatedly recorded it in the *Annals of Zhou* and the *Descendants of Zhou Gong* to show its importance. The oracle bone script and bronze script forms of the character "Jin" (𣎔 𣎔, 𣎔 𣎔 𣎔)[3] further validate the credibility of Luo Jiangsheng's theory (see Figure 8.1)

However, the true origin of the name "Jin" is not well understood by later generations, leading to various interpretations of the meaning. Some explanations are based on the location of the river Jin,[4] while others are based on the extended meaning of the character "Jin" as "advance" or "progress."[5] It is worth noting that the Sima family, who established the Jin Dynasty in later generations, chose the name "Jin" for the country, which is closely related to the meaning of "advance" or "progress."

On the other hand, the reason Sima Zhao was titled Duke of Jin is that his fiefdom was within the old territory of the the State of Jin. The "old territory of Jin"[6] refers to the territorial range of the State of Jin during the pre-Qin period. When the the State of Jin was first established, it was just a small country with a territory of "a hundred miles to the east of the Yellow and Fen rivers," and its capital was located in Tang (now west of Yicheng County, Shanxi Province). In the early Spring and Autumn period, Duke Zhao of Jin divided and bestowed the fief of his uncle, Cheng Shi, in Quwo (now north east of Wenxi County, Shanxi Province), which led to a state of division. In 679 BC, Duke Wu of Quwo (a descendant of Cheng Shi) defeated Duke Xianhou (a descendant of Duke Zhao), unified the State of Jin, and the following year, the Zhou Dynasty bestowed the title of Duke of Jin upon him.

Figure 8.1 Statue of Shu Yu at the Jin Shrine in Taiyuan, Shanxi

In 677 BC, Duke Wu of Jin passed away, and his son Chong'er succeeded him, later known as Duke Xian. Duke Xian moved the capital to Jiang (now south east of Yicheng County, Shanxi Province) and gradually conquered surrounding small states, making the State of Jin prosperous. By the time of Duke Wen of Jin, internal reforms led to a strong and prosperous country, and it became a hegemonic power, occupying regions of the southern Taihang Mountains and the northern bank of the Yellow River, known as "Nanyang," amongst others. Duke Wen's successors, Duke Xiang and Duke Ling, moved the capital to Xintian (now north west of Quwo County, Shanxi Province), and the territory continued to expand, reaching its peak with the majority of present-day Shanxi Province, south western Hebei Province, northern Henan Province, and a corner of Shaanxi Province.

Subsequently, the six influential families of the Jin state (the Zhaos, the Weis, the Hans, the Zhis, the Fans, and the Zhonghangs) gradually grew stronger and competed with each other for power and territory. In 490 BC, the Fans and the Zhonghangs were defeated, and by 453 BC, the Zhi family was annihilated. As a result, the Han, Zhao, and Wei families divided the central, northern, and southern regions of what used to be the Jin state, leaving the Duke of Jin with only the cities of Jiang and Quwo. In the twenty-third year of King Weilie of Zhou (403 BC), the Zhou Dynasty officially recognized the Han, Zhao, and Wei families as feudal lords, which effectively marked the end of the Jin state. In 376 BC, the Han, Zhao, and Wei families jointly deposed Duke Jing of Jin and divided his territory. Jin would henceforth cease to be venerated,[7] and the territories divided from Jin came to be collectively known as "Sanjin" (the Three Jins).

In the historical narrative of the pre-Qin Jin state, two points are note-worthy. Firstly, the land known as "Nanyang." As recorded in the *Discourses on Governance of the States,* in 635 BC, King Xiang of Zhou granted Duke Wen of Jin fields in Nanyang that included the areas of Yangfan, Wen, Yuan, Zhou, Xing, Qi, Zu, and Zanmao. Wen soon became a county of the state of Jin (though briefly occupied by the Di barbarians), corresponding to present-day south west of Zhaoxian Town, Wen County, Henan Province. Secondly, the designation of "Sanjin" (the Three Jins). For instance, in the sixth year of King Xuan of Chu as mentioned in the *Records of the Grand Historian*: "Qin began to grow stronger, alongside the burgeoning Three Jins." Furthermore, the *Kaijuan Loude* by Lin Chunpu, mentions Volume 7, "Wei, Han, and Zhao split the land of Jin and were called Sanjin. However, Han and Zhao did not refer to themselves as the state of Jin; only Wei claimed the title ... both Jiang and Quwo belonged to Wei, and they claimed Jin as well due to tradition." Therefore, Wei, one of the "Three Jins" during the Warring States Period, could legitimately be called the state of Jin. Given the Sima family originated from the county of Wen and they established the Jin Dynasty, a historical link is suggested.

More significantly, in May of the third year of Ganlu (258 AD), Sima Zhao was granted the title of Duke of Jin, encompassing eight prefectures including Taiyuan, Shangdang, Xihe, Leping, Xinxing, Yanmen in Bingzhou, and Hedong and Pingyang in Sizhou. Sima Zhao initially refused the title nine times. In October of the third year of Jingyuan (263 AD), two additional prefectures, Hongnong and Fengyi in Sizhou, were included in his fiefdom, and Sima Zhao accepted the eleva-tion to Duke of Jin. The territories of Duke Sima Zhao's fief were nearly identical to those of the ancient state of Jin during the pre-Qin period. The lands, characterized as "stretching south to Huashan, north to Xing, east to Hukou, west across the Yellow River, covering an area of seven hundred li, all previously cultivated lands of Jin," were conferred to Shuyu, who was the ruler of all the unifying forces. Thus, to reward him for his stewardship, he was granted the title Duke of Jin, establishing it as a perpetual fiefdom for the Wei clan[8]. This decision by Cao Wei to use the former territories of the ancient state of Jin to confer to Sima Zhao suggests the origin of the title "Jin."

However, establishing a "perpetual fiefdom for the Wei clan" proved impos-sible for Sima Zhao. In March 264 AD, Sima Zhao was promoted to the King of Jin. Following Sima Zhao's death in August 265 AD, his son Sima Yan succeeded him as King of Jin. By December of that year, Sima Yan compelled the Wei rulers to abdicate, founding the Jin Dynasty, thereby fulfilling Sima Zhao's "legacy." The term "legacy" applies because Sima Zhao, during his lifetime, had coerced the Wei royal family to first appoint him as Marquis of Gaodu, then as Duke of Gaodu, and subsequently as Duke of Jin, discreetly revealing his ambition to usurp the Wei.

8.2 Gloss: From the Duke of Gaodu to the King of Jin

In August of 265 AD, just as Sima Zhao, the King of Jin, was preparing to declare himself emperor and replace the Cao Wei, he suddenly passed away. According to historical records in the *Book of Jin*, Sima Zhao was born into the prestigious Sima family of Wen County in prefecture Henei during the Han Wei period. The records state, "During the Chu-Han Contention, Sima Yi's ancestor Sima Ang served as a general for the state of Zhao and joined the rebellions in attacking the Qin Dynasty. After the fall of Qin, he was established as the King of Yin with the capital in Henei. During the Han Dynasty, this region became prefecture Henei, and his descendants thereafter resided there." Many of Sima Zhao's ancestors held high-ranking positions in the Han Dynasty. As for Sima Zhao's father, Sima Yi, he was described as "intelligent, strategic-minded, knowledgeable, and well-versed in Confucian teachings." Initially, Sima Yi looked down upon Cao Cao, whom he considered "an undesired eunuch remnant,"[9] and thus rejected Cao Cao's summons. However, after Cao Cao became Chancellor in the thirteenth year of Jian'an (208 AD), he resorted to coercive measures to appoint Sima Yi as a literary official. Throughout his career, Sima Yi served under three generations of the Cao family in the Han and Wei dynasties, holding various positions such as Chief Clerk of the Master of Records, Deputy Imperial Secretary, General Who Pacifies the Army, Director of the Secretariat, Palace Attendant, Commissioner, and Commander-in-Chief, even rising to Grand Tutor. Additionally, he received testamentary edict from Cao Pi and Cao Rui as a Senior Assistant Chancelor. In January of the tenth year of Zhengshi (249 AD), Sima Yi took advantage of Emperor Cao Fang and Commander-in-Chief Cao Shuang's absence from Luoyang during their visit to the royal Mausoleum of Emperor Ming (Cao Rui) in Gaoping. Sima Yi staged a military coup, killing Cao Shuang and his associates. From then on, Sima Yi completely seized control of the military and political power in Cao Wei, laying the groundwork for the future ascendance of the Sima family in replacing the Wei dynasty.

In 251 AD, Sima Yi passed away, and his eldest son, Sima Shi, continued to wield power. In 254 AD, Sima Shi deposed Emperor Cao Fang and installed Emperor Cao Mao, who was only 14 years old, on the throne. In 255 AD, Sima Shi died, and his talented younger brother, Sima Zhao, took full control of the government.

Sima Zhao was initially granted the title of Marquis of Xincheng in the year 238 AD. In 254 AD, when Cao Mao ascended the throne, Sima Zhao was elevated to Marquis of Gaodu, acknowledging his role in policy-making. In June of 256 AD, he was further promoted to Duke of Gaodu, with a territory spanning 700 li and was conferred with nine bestowments. However, Sima Zhao declined the offer. In May of 258 AD, he was again promoted to Duke of Jin, with the same territory and nine bestowments, as well as elevated to the position of Chancellor, which he declined again. The cycle of promotions and rejections continued for nine times, until April of 260 AD, Sima Zhao once again declined the rank and title.[10] In reality, during that time, "Sima Zhao's ambitions were well-known to the public."[11] His usurpation of the Wei regime was inevitable. His repeated refusals to accept the ranks and titles were simply formalities. On the other hand, Cao Mao was unwilling to accept being deposed and humiliated, so he resorted to desperate measures. On the night of June 7th, 260 AD, Cao Mao personally led the palace guards in an attack against Sima Zhao, who had anticipated the coup attempt. How could several hundred palace guards withstand Sima Zhao's forces? Consequently, Sima Zhao's supporter, General of the Guards Jia Chong, ordered Cao Mao's attendant, Cheng Ji, to assassinate Cao Mao in his carriage. With Cao Mao dead, Sima Zhao, on one hand, shifted the blame to Cheng Ji for the crime, executing him along with his entire family. On the other hand, Sima Zhao installed Cao Huan as the new puppet emperor, who was just 15 years old at the time.

In the spring of 263 AD, Sima Zhao launched an attack on the state of Shu through three separate routes. As news of his victories spread, Sima Zhao intensified his preparations for the establishment of a new dynasty to replace Wei. In October, he assumed the titles of Chancellor and Duke of Jin, and was offered nine bestowments. The following year, in March, he was further promoted to King of Jin, and in July, he began to establish the new rituals, legal systems, and bureaucratic structures. At this point, the new dynasty, known as "Jin," was on the verge of emergence. Tragically, in August of 265 AD, before Sima Zhao could formally ascend the throne as Emperor of Jin, he passed away at the age of 55. In December (or January of 266 AD), Emperor Cao Huan of Wei abdicated the throne in favor of Sima Zhao's eldest son, Sima Yan.[12]

Like peeling bamboo shoots layer by layer, we have finally uncovered the truth at the core: the origin of the Jin Dynasty under Sima's rule was fundamentally intended to fulfill the prophecy of "Dangtu Gao, the successor of Han," signifying a disdain for Cao Wei, a reverence for the Han Dynasty, and a distant continuation of the Zhou Dynasty. However, such a highly secretive, conspiratorial, and "cultured" intention akin to "Sima Zhao's heart" is probably not as widely known to the public as Cao Mao had suggested, is it?

Notes

1 The origin and history of the state of Tang are detailed in Chapter 11 of this book.
2 Luo Jiangsheng, "A Study on the Names of the Qin State," Journal of Literature and History, Volume 38, 1994.
3 Institute of Archaeology, Chinese Academy of Sciences, Compilation of Oracle Bone Inscriptions, Volume 7, Zhonghua Book Company, 1965.
    Rong Geng, Compilation of Inscriptions on Bronze, Volume 7, Science Press, 1959.
4 References include "Geographical Records," Book of Han; Maoshi Collection; Records of the Capitals of Ancestral States by Xu Zhicai from the Northern and Southern Dynasties; and Collected Annotations of the Records of the Grand Historian by Sima Zhen of the Tang Dynasty.
5 Liu Xi's *Shi Ming: Explanations of Place Names and Nations* from the Eastern Han Dynasty: "Jin means 'to advance.' Its territory is located to the north, so when it wants to attack the central plains, it advances south. It is also named after the river Jin, which flows swiftly onward."

6 *Annals of Emperor Wen,* Book of Jin.

7 "Biography of the Royal Family of Jin," Records of the Grand Historian.

8 *Annals of Emperor Wen* in the *Book of Jin.* According to the text, "Hua" refers to Mount Huashan in the jurisdiction of the Hongnong prefecture of Wei, located in present-day eastern Shaanxi; "Xing" refers to Mount Juzhu in the jurisdiction of the Yanmen prefecture of Wei, located in present-day northern Shanxi; "Hukou" likely refers to Mount Hukou in the jurisdiction of the Shangdang prefecture of Wei, located in present-day south east Shanxi; "He" refers to the Yellow River in the region between Shanxi and Shaanxi.

9 "Biography of Yuan Shao" in the Book of Wei in the *Records of the Three Kingdoms.* The text mentions the term " an undesired eunuch remnant," which refers to the fact that Cao Cao's father, Cao Song, originally had the surname Xiahou. However, he changed his surname to Cao because he was adopted by eunuch Cao Teng. However, recent studies in human genetics have shown that the genetic makeup of the Cao family is not consistent with that of the Xiahou family, casting doubt on the theory that Cao Song (Xiahou Song) was adopted by Cao Teng. References: Li Hui, "Tracing Cao Cao's Genes" and Han Sheng, "Historical Basis of DNA Investigation on Cao Cao's Family," both included in the book *Who Are We*, edited by Han Sheng and Li Hui, published by Fudan University Press in 2011. However, it is certain that, despite this, in the context of traditional historiography, Cao Cao's identity as a "an undesired eunuch remnant" remains undisputed.

10 *Annals of Emperor Wen,* Book of Jin.

11 "Record of the Illustrious Prince of Gaogui Township" in "Book of Wei" in the *Records of the Three Kingdoms.* Annotated by Pei Songzhi, a commentator of the Southern Song Dynasty, who cites the *Annals of Han and Jin Dynasties.*

12 The Wei-Jin abdication, spanning from Sima Yi, Sima Shi, Sima Zhao to Sima Yan, the three generations of the Sima family, is a significant event in the transfer of power from the Wei to the Jin Dynasty. It consisted of four stages: the rise of a powerful chancellor, the creation of public opinion, the establishment of procedures, and the benevolent treatment of the abdicated emperor. This can be seen as a transitional moment that built upon the establishment of new dynasties, following examples of Wang Mang's Xin Dynasty and Cao Pi's usurpation of the Han Dynasty, and paving the way for the proceeding dynastic transitions during the southern and northern Dynasties until Zhao Kuangyin's establishment of the Song Dynasty. See Hu Axian's "Reading History as a Drama: An In-depth Discussion of Chinese History" (published by People's Publishing House in 2014) for further reading on the Wei-Jin abdication.

9 The Sixteen Kingdoms and the Southern and Northern Dynasties
Turmoil, Rise and Fall

The Sima family's control over a unified empire was short-lived. Similarly, the Jin Dynasty had a brief existence. After the death of Emperor Wu of Jin in the year 290, the regional warlords fought for power, exterminating each other.[1] From 301 AD onwards, the situation escalated into a chaotic melee. The Upheaval of the Eight Princes lasted for a lengthy 16 years (291–306 AD), during which time barbarians took advantage of the situation and caused turmoil in the Central Plains.[2] Finally, in the year 304, the Xiongnu leader Liu Yuan and the Badi leader Li Xiong declared themselves emperors. Twelve years later, in 316, the Xiongnu general Liu Yao captured Chang'an, imprisoned Emperor Sima Ye (Emperor Min of Jin), and thus the Jin Dynasty was extinguished.

The year following the fall of the Jin Dynasty, in 317, Sima Rui, the Prince of Langya, former Chancellor, and Grand Commander (Commander-in-Chief of the Eastern Military Region), as well as the grandson of Sima Fang—the uncle of Emperor Wu (Sima Yan)—proclaimed himself the King of Jin in Jiankang (present-day Nanjing, Jiangsu Province). In the following year, 318, Sima Rui declared himself emperor, continuing the Jin title. However, this state of Jin was different from the previous Jin Dynasty, which had been a unified empire; this entity was a relatively stable regime but controlled only a portion of the territory it once had.

The revived Jin under Sima Rui is known as the Eastern Jin Dynasty. In 420, it ceded power to the Liu Song dynasty, marking the beginning of the so-called Southern Dynasties. The Southern Dynasties period ended in 589 when the Sui Dynasty unified the empire. Concurrently, during the Eastern Jin and the Southern Dynasties period, the territory to the north consisted of the Sixteen Kingdoms from 304 to 439 and the Northern Dynasties from 439 to 581. The term "Southern and Northern Dynasties" refers to this era from the establishment of the Liu Song dynasty in 420 to the unification under the Sui Dynasty in 589.

9.1 The Historical Overview

Now, let's address the historical overview of the Sixteen Kingdoms and the Southern and Northern Dynasties. This era was tumultuous with frequent changes

DOI: 10.4324/9781003510390-10

in leadership and boundaries. Here's a condensed summary focusing on the respective dynastic titles.

From the time Liu Yuan, the Xiongnu leader, declared himself the ruling King of Han in 304, until the unification of the Northern Liang by the Tuoba Wei in 439—a span of 135 years—various ethnic groups (including the Xiongnu, Xianbei, Jie, Di, Qiang, and Han) established their regimes amidst the chaos. This period is known as the era of the Sixteen Kingdoms. Here is a list of the related regimes, listed chronologically by their founding:

1. Han (Zhao): Liu Yuan declared himself the King of Han in 304, and Emperor of Han in 308. Under the reign of Liu Yao, he changed the title to Zhao (Former Zhao) in 319. The regime fell in 329 to the (later) Zhao.
2. Cheng (Han): In 304, Li Xiong declared himself the King of Chengdu, and in 306, he declared Emperor of Cheng. In 338, Li Shou changed the title to Han, which fell in 347 to the Jin Dynasty.
3. Liang: In 301, Zhang Gui declared himself the prefecture governor and was recognized by the Jin Dynasty. The regime, known as the Former Liang, continued independently after the fall of the Western Jin and was extinguished in 376 by the (Former) Qin.
4. Zhao (Later Zhao): In 319, Shi Le declared himself the King of Zhao, becoming the emperor in 330. The regime fell in 350 to the (Ran) Wei.
5. Yan (Former Yan): Murong Huang founded the Yan state in 337, with his son, Murong Jun, becoming the emperor in 352. The dynasty succumbed to the (Former) Qin in 370.
6. Wei (Ran Wei): Ran Min established the Wei dynasty in 350, which existed briefly until being overrun by the (Former) Yan in 352.
7. Qin (Former Qin): Fu Hong[3] founded the Qin state in 350, and with Fu Jian's coronation as emperor in 352, the dynasty lasted until 394, falling to the (Later) Qin.
8. Qin (Later Qin): Yao Chang declared himself the King of Eternal Qin in 384, then became emperor in 386. The dynasty endured until 417, capitulating to the Jin.
9. Yan (Later Yan): In 384, Murong Chui established the Yan state, which was overthrown by the (Northern) Yan in 407.
10. Yan (Western Yan): Founded in 385 by Murong Chong, this dynasty was short-lived, falling to the (Later) Yan in 394.
11. Qin: In 385, Qifu Guoren, a Xianbei leader, assumed the title of Grand Chanyu. In 388, Qifu Qiangui declared himself the King of Henan. In 394, he declared himself the King of Qin, establishing the Qin dynasty, which is known as the Western Qin. The dynasty fell in 431 to the Xia.
12. Liang: In 386, Lü Guang, a Di leader, assumed the title of Governor of Liangzhou. In 389, he declared himself the King of the Three Rivers. In 396, he declared himself the Heavenly King, establishing the Liang dynasty, which is known as Later Liang. The dynasty fell in 403 to the Later Qin.

13. Liang: In the year 397, Tufa Wugu, a Xianbei leader, proclaimed himself the King of Xiping, and the next year he changed his title to the King of Wuwei. In 401, Tufa Lilugu changed the title to the King of Hexi. In 408, Tufa Nutan again proclaimed himself the King of Liang, which is known as Southern Liang. In 414, it perished at the hands of the Western Qin.

14. Yan: In the year 398, Murong De, a Xianbei leader, proclaimed himself the King of Yan, and in 400, he declared himself emperor of Yan, which is known as Southern Yan. In 410, it perished at the hands of the Jin.

15. Liang: In the year 400, Li Hao proclaimed himself the Duke of Liang, with the state being named Western Liang. In 421, it perished at the hands of the Northern Liang.

16. Xia: In the year 407, the Xiongnu leader Liu Bobo proclaimed himself the Great Xia Heavenly King and Grand Chanyu, and in 418, he declared himself emperor, with the state being named Xia. In 431, it perished at the hands of Tuyuhun.[4]

17. Yan: In the year 407, Feng Ba installed Murong Yun (originally surnamed Gao, from the royal family of Goguryeo) as the Great Yan Heavenly King, and the state was named Yan. In 409, Murong Yun was killed by his subordinates, and Feng Ba ascended the throne as the Heavenly King, with the state retaining the name Yan. This period is known as Northern Yan. In 436, it perished at the hands of the Tuoba Wei.

18. Liang: In the year 401, the Xiongnu leader Juqu Mengxun proclaimed himself the Governor of Liangzhou, and in 412, he proclaimed himself the King of Hexi, and in 431, he proclaimed himself the King of Liang. The state was named Northern Liang. In 439, it perished at the hands of the Tuoba Wei.

These 18 regimes, summarized, are "Cheng" ("Han"), "Wei," "Xia," two "Zhaos" (Former and Later), three "Qins" (Former, Later, and Western), five "Yans" (Former, Later, Western, Southern, and Northern), and five "Liangs" (Former, Later, Southern, Northern, and Western). Among them, except for Ran Wei and Western Yan, the other 16 regimes are known as the "Sixteen Kingdoms."[5]

Following the historical period of the Eastern Jin and the Sixteen Kingdoms, it is known as the "Southern and Northern Dynasties." The Southern Dynasties include four consecutive regimes, namely Song (420–479), Qi (479–502), Liang (502–557), and Chen (557–589). Except for the period from November 552 to November 554, when Emperor Yuan of Liang, Xiao Yi, established Jiangling (present-day Jiangling County, Hubei Province) as the capital, the capital of the Southern Dynasties was generally in Jiankang (Nanjing, Jiangsu Province) for the remainder of the time. The successions of these regimes were achieved through "abdication." The Northern Dynasties began in 439 AD with the establishment of Wei (Northern Wei) by the Tuoba clans of Xianbei, which later split into Eastern "Wei" (534–550) and Western "Wei" (535–557) in 534 AD. Later, Northern "Qi" (550–577) replaced Eastern "Wei," and Northern "Zhou" (557–581) replaced Western "Wei." Northern "Zhou" then overthrew Northern "Qi," and in 581 AD, Northern "Zhou" was overthrown by the Sui Dynasty. In 589 AD, the Sui Dynasty unified the north and conquered the Southern Chen Dynasty, marking the end of the era of the "Southern and Northern Dynasties" and the emergence of a new unified regime in China.

However, as stated above, in terms of national titles, the 18 regimes of the "Sixteen Kingdoms" adopted a total of eight Chinese characters: Han, Zhao, Cheng, Liang, Yan, Wei, Qin, and Xia. The national titles of the "Southern and Northern Dynasties" include four characters in the Southern Dynasties (Song, Qi, Liang, and Chen), and three characters in the Northern Dynasties (Wei, Qi, and Zhou). None of these national titles were used throughout the entire country.

The establishment of the Yuwen clan's Northern "Zhou" came seven years after the foundation of the Gao clan's Northern "Qi." After coexisting for over 20 years, in 577 AD, Northern Zhou conquered Northern Qi, once again unifying the North. By 581 AD, Northern Zhou was overthrown by Yang Jian, founder of Sui, marking the beginning of the Sui Dynasty. In 589 AD, Sui conquered the Southern Chen dynasty, thus putting an end to the fragmented and separatist situation that had persisted for over 270 years following the disintegration of the Jin Dynasty. A unified central regime was re-established, and possessed a new collective title of Sui for "all under heaven."

Notes

1 "Biography of Zu Ti," Book of Jin. The reason of "princes contending for power" lies in the facts of granting large fiefs to the princes and allowing them to command troops and garrison. For more details, refer to Hu Axiang: "Research on the Territory and Administrative Division of the Six Dynasties," Chapter 2, Xi'an Map Publishing House, 2000.
2 "Biography of Zu Ti," Book of Jin.
3 According to "Biography of Fu Hong," Book of Jin, Hong's original surname was Pu. He changed his surname to Fu after possessing a prophecy predicting, "The throne will be handed to man with the surname Fu." His grandson Jian also had the characters "Grass Fu" on his back, which further reinforced the surname change to Fu.
4 Tuyuhun originally belonged to the Xianbei tribe and was the younger brother of Murong Hui, who was the ruler of the Xianbei. After Murong Hui succeeded to the throne, Tuyuhun led his tribe to migrate westward. During the Yongjia period of the Jin Dynasty, they crossed the Long Mountains and settled to the west of the River Tao. The leadership of Tuyuhun was passed down to his grandson Ye Yan, who then took his grandfather's name as their surname, clan name and the dynastic title.
5 At that time, there were also some small states, such as Chouchi (Di), Dai (Xianbei), Wei (Dingling and Zhai clans), Shu (Qiaozong), Tuyuhun (Xianbei), and others. No further details about them are provided.

10 Sui

Auspicious or Ominous?

In Chinese history, many dynasties and empires have repeatedly adopted certain imperial titles, even influencing regions beyond Chinese territory and becoming alternative names for the entire land. From this perspective, the national title of the Sui Dynasty stands out as unique: while it shows some continuity from the previous title, the characters used are different and carry distinct meanings, and with no successor. The Sui Dynasty spanned from January 589 to May 618. But the establishment of Sui slightly preceded this period, occurring in February 581. According to the *Annals of Emperor Jing, Book of Zhou*, in the first year of Dading (581), February, "Yang Jian, the King of Sui, claimed the imperial title of Emperor of Sui. The dethroned emperor retired to another palace and was conferred Duke of Jieguo by the Sui clan."[1] Have you noticed the change in Yang Jian's title from "King of Sui" to "Emperor of Sui?" Based on established rules derived from the numerous stories of "abdication" during the preceding Wei, Jin, Southern and Northern Dynasties, the title of nobility and the national title should remain consistent before and after the abdication. However, in this case, there is a change from "Sui" 随 to "Sui" 隋. What is the reason behind this change?[2]

10.1 Replacing Sui 随 with Sui 隋: Yang Jian's Discretion

Yang Jian adopted "Sui" as the title of his dynasty. According to historical accounts, this choice was likely influenced by Yang Jian's father, Yang Zhong, having held the title "Duke of Sui" under the Zhou dynasty. Yang Jian inherited this title and ultimately rose to become the "Emperor of Sui." As recorded in the "Biography of the Founding Emperor" in the *Book of Sui*: Yang Zhong's titles included "Great Minister of Public Works" and "Duke of Sui," and the like. Yang Jian initially served as the "Prefect of Suizhou," then inherited the title "Duke of Sui," was subsequently promoted to "King of Sui," and ultimately received the abdication from the Zhou dynasty. Similarly, the *Annals of Emperor Wen of Sui* in the *History of the Northern Dynasties* notes that in the first year of the Wu Cheng era, Yang Zhong was promoted to "Duke of Sui." Yang Jian first served as "Prefect of Suizhou," then as "Duke of Sui," and finally as "King of Sui." He expanded his influence

DOI: 10.4324/9781003510390-11

across "twenty prefectures, including Suizhou," and eventually the Zhou dynasty ceded power to him.

The passages from the *Book of Sui* and the *History of the Northern Dynasties* suggest that "Suizhou" (隋州) refers explicitly to the location known as Suizhou (随州). Founded in the year 554 by the Western Wei dynasty, Suizhou had its administrative center in Suixian County, Prefecture Sui, which was initially formed in 288 during the Jin Dynasty. Historical accounts tie Suixian County to the State of Chu (during the Pre-Qin period), the Qin Dynasty, and the Han Dynasty. The "*Geographical Records*" in the *Book of Han* indicates that Sui County belonged to Prefecture Nanyang and was known as "Sui, the ancient state." Presently, this area is governed as Suizhou City in modern Hubei Province. Thus, Suixian County, Prefecture Sui, and Suizhou are all historically linked to the ancient state of Sui (随). Given this context, the noble titles held by Yang Zhong and Yang Jian are correctly translated as "Duke of Sui" and "King of Sui," paralleling the terminology used in the *Book of Sui* and the *History of the Northern Dynasties*.

Cross-referencing with the *Book of Zhou* and *Zizhi Tongjian* highlights further inaccuracies in the *Book of Sui* and *History of the Northern Dynasties*. The "Biography of Yang Zhong" in the *Book of Zhou* mentions that in the first year of the Wu Cheng era, Yang Zhong was named "Duke of Sui." The *Annals of Chen* in the *Zizhi Tongjian* records that in the seventh month of the second year of the Guangda era, Yang Zhong, then the "Duke of Sui" under the Zhou dynasty, passed away, and his son Yang Jian succeeded him.[3] The *Zizhi Tongjian* further details that on the twelfth month of the twelfth year of the Taijian era, Yang Jian, as the Chancellor, expanded his realm to include "twenty prefectures including Anlu," leading to the establishment of the Sui Dynasty. In the thirteenth year of the Taijian era, Yang Jian began his tenure as Chancellor, oversaw all government affairs, received the nine bestowments, and established government offices.

These records from the *Book of Zhou* and *Zizhi Tongjian* affirm the discrepancies in the *Book of Sui* and *History of the Northern Dynasties*. Interestingly, in the *Annals of Emperor Jing* in the *Book of Zhou*, Yang Jian is referred to as "Emperor of Sui (随)" in February of the Dading era (581 AD). This title was recognized as "Emperor of Sui (隋)" five days later when the Zhou Emperor was dethroned as the Duke of Jieguo. Additionally, in the *Annals of Chen* in the *Zizhi Tongjian*, during the thirteenth year of the Taijian era, Yang Jian is abruptly designated as the "Emperor of Sui (隋)" and it is noted that the Zhou Emperor "abdicated to Sui (隋)."[4]

From this analysis, it is evident that Yang Zhong bore the noble title of Duke of Sui (随) and that Yang Jian progressed from Duke of Sui to King of Sui. The establishment of the Sui (隋) Dynasty was finalized when Yang Jian assumed control from the Zhou dynasty in February of 581 AD.

On the day Jiazi of February in 581 AD, the 41-year-old Yang Jian was busily engaged in state affairs within Chang'an. He transitioned from the Phoenix Mansion to the palace, donned the attire of a ruler, and received official documents and the imperial seal from Emperor Yuwen Chan of Zhou, who was merely nine years old. Afterward, dressed in a fine gauze hat and a yellow robe, Yang

Jian entered the Luminous Hall, adorned with ceremonial robes and a crown, to accept the congratulations and the shouts of "long live" from his officials. He then ascended the throne. On that significant day, Yang Jian also hosted rituals to honor his ancestors, declared a general amnesty, changed the era name, and chose "Sui" (隋) as the formal name for his new empire. Despite ascending as the King of Sui (随), Yang Jian renamed the country "Sui (隋)." Neither the *Book of Sui* nor the *History of the Northern Dynasties* or *Book of Zhou* elaborates on this decision. However, Li Fu, a late Tang Dynasty scholar, addressed the matter in *Li Fu Kan Wu* (The Rectification by Li Fu). Li noted that the name Sui 随 had negative associations in the Wei, Zhou, and Qi dynasties. Emperor Wen of Sui, disliking this, removed the radical "辶"[5] from the character to leave just 隋. Xu Zeng of the Southern Song Dynasty also discussed this in the *Neng Gai Zhai Man Lu*, stating that the character 隋 did not exist in ancient scripts.[6] Upon his ascension, Emperor Wen viewed the character 随 as a unsuitable label for the nation and deleted the radical "辶" to a new shape of "隋" due to the negative connotation signified by "辶" (to walk hastily).

Moreover, annotations by Hu Sanxing of the *Annals of Sui* in the *Zizhi Tongjian* suggest that Yang Zhong was granted the title of Duke of Sui for his merits under Emperor Taizu of Zhou. His son Yang Jian inherited this title and later the entire Zhou dynasty. The transition from 随 to 隋 is attributed to the dissatisfaction with previous names and the desire to remove the connotation of haste implied by the radical "辶."

These explanations, as provided by the three sources, have generally been accepted and passed down until today. Upon further analysis, the following understanding can be derived:

Initially, in Yang Jian's view, the Eastern Wei, Western Wei, Northern Qi, and Northern Zhou were all ephemeral dynasties, each lasting only 17, 23, 28, and 25 years, respectively. Naturally, he wished to avoid the same fate for his new dynasty—an existence marred by constant turmoil and brevity. The character 随 not only signifies the transient nature of the previous dynasties but also encapsulates a more critical aspect: its radical "辶" denotes instability and the gradual ebbing of fortune, an ominous omen indeed. This likely constitutes the core reason Yang Jian's decision of abandoning 随 when he ascended to the throne.

Secondly, Yang Jian also paid significant attention to another political "symbol" of the nascent dynasty—the reign title. Upon assuming the imperial mantle, he chose the reign title of "Kai Huang." In Buddhist scripture and also within Taoist tradition, "Kai Huang" are referred to as "opening ages." As stated in the *Book of Wei,* "Although the opening of ages is not confined to one, there are the names Yan Kang, Chi Ming, Long Han, and Kai Huang; these have been thus named." Additionally, the *Book of Sui* notes, "The initiation of dynasty is unhindered by the limitation to a single time span; hence the emergence of names like Yan Kang, Chi Ming, Long Han, and Kai Huang, together spanning forty-one billion eras." The reign title "Kai Huang" therefore originates from a Taoist backdrop,[7] bearing the auspicious connotation of innumerable years. During the Kai Huang period, the counties named Sui Kang, Sui Xing, Sui Hua, Sui Chang, Sui An, and Sui Jian[8] also emerged from a kindred mindset. With the reign titles and place names given such consideration, the national title of the new dynasty demanded equal deliberation from Yang Jian.

Nevertheless, the selection of a new Dynasty's name was not without constraints. By this point in time, the precedent—abdicating a worn-out dynasty and establishing a succeeding one—had been well established. Traditionally, titles from the preceding dynasty were adapted for the new dynasty, following the rationale, "Since the usage of titles from feudal states is customary, it caters to popular perception. It serves as a temporary measure to garner widespread consent with minimal disparagement."[9] Indeed, Yang Jian's predecessors, including Wei by Cao Pi, Jin by Sima Yan, Song by Liu Yu, Qi by Xiao Daocheng, Liang by Xiao Yan, and Chen by Chen Baxian from the Southern Dynasties, along with Qi by Gao Yang and Zhou by Yuwen Jue from the Northern Dynasties, all adhered to this custom. Yang Jian had no intention of deviating from this established practice, thereby avoiding superfluous confusion. Hence, his selection for the national title of the new dynasty was constrained—he could only follow existing feudal titles or apply minor alterations. Ultimately, he eschewed 随 in favor of 隋.

The advantages of substituting 随 with 隋 include the following: First, it eliminates the inimical radical "辶," as perceived by Yang Jian. Second, 隋 and 随 are minimally different in their character shapes and pronunciations. Additionally, 随 can readily be written as 隋. Third, the feudal titles Duke of Sui and King of Sui could be naturally integrated, thus adhering to the convention, "Initially, all were feudal lords, and when saintly virtues flourished, all nations followed suit, retaining their original titles unaltered."[10] Moreover, it serves to establish ancestral legitimacy for the dynasty. Thus, 隋 was a profoundly considered and meaningful choice for the new imperial moniker, indicative of a destiny diverging from the brevity of its predecessors.

10.2 Derision from Later Generations Regarding the Replacement of "随" with "隋"

Yang Jian could not have foreseen that the diligently contemplated national title 隋 would be subject to ridicule and scorn by later scholars and literati. Initially, Xu Kai from the Southern Tang Dynasty criticized in Volume 36 of the *Exegesis of Shuowen Jiezi*, "The extraction of the superfluous part of '随' to formulate '隋,' betokens mutilation. Its ominous implications are considerable." These critics were oblivious to the fact that the radical "辶" signifies movement, and its omission was merely due to ignorance. Did they aim to strip Heaven of its wisdom?

Subsequent scholars from the Song, Yuan, Ming, and Qing dynasties recognized and expanded upon Xu Kai's opinion. For instance, Wang Guangguo of the Song Dynasty, in Volume 10 of *Xue Lin*, wrote on the subject of the four sons of Sun Xiu: "According to the character lexicon, '隋' enunciated as 'suí' conveys disintegration, laxness, and laceration ... Emperor Wen of Sui neglected to scrutinize the character's form and coherence and acted in haste, provoking future eras to mock." Likewise, Luo Mi from the Southern Song Dynasty wrote in Volume 35 of *Lu*

Shi: "The word '隋' pertains to ritual items ... some also associate it with severing and shedding ... ultimately, the Sui empire disintegrated. Hence, its calamitous destiny seems prefigured by its appellation." Jiao Hong of the Ming Dynasty, in Volume 1 of *Bi Cheng*, mentioned the erroneous shift from "随" to "隋" – "Yang Jian's alteration of the national title from '随' to '隋' significantly differs in meaning and pronunciation." Wang Yinglin remarked: '随' denotes concordant movement, a sign of great fortune, whereas '隋' alludes to flesh being torn, significantly inauspicious. Such a haphazard alteration signified a deviation from tradition."[11] Similar views are echoed by many. Although "随" does not directly translate to peaceful walk nor can it be wholeheartedly deemed highly auspicious, the consensus categorizes Yang Jian's switch from "随" to "隋" as "haphazard" and "unlearned," a sentiment prevailing since the Five Dynasties and Ten Kingdoms era.

Indeed, the meticulous dissection of Chinese character nuances, weaving together phonetic, semantic, and graphic complexities, alongside the paramount importance accorded to nomenclature, is unparalleled. The inherent plasticity of Chinese characters in sound, shape, and meaning—comprehended through the Six Writing Categories—adds to the subtlety and sophistication of linguistics. Within such a paradigm, amplified by the enduring and intrinsic value of names, the exacting selection and finalization of nomenclature often fall under retrospective scrutiny and critique, emblematic of a distinguishing aspect of Chinese cultural heritage throughout its history.

For example, during the Three Kingdoms period, the erudite scholar Qiao Zhou, who was devoted to ancient learning, had an interesting discussion about the names of Liu Bei and Liu Shan. He said, "Liu Bei's name implies being 'prepared,' while Liu Shan's name implies being 'given.' So, it can be said that Liu is already prepared and should be given to others."[12] When the Shu Han dynasty eventually fell, people believed that Qiao Zhou's words were not unfounded.[13] Xu Kai also made a sarcastic remark about Yang Jian's lack of learning[14] because Yang Jian changed the national title to the inauspicious and ominous "Sui," which cannot ensure the longevity of the state's prosperity.

So, what is the meaning behind the characters 随 and 隋? According to various classical texts, both have multiple meanings. Besides being used as proper nouns (such as the name of a country, place, or surname), "随" can also mean "to follow," "along," "to comply with," "to allow," and so on.[15] "隋" also has various meanings. It can refer to the name for sacrifice, as mentioned in *Spring Officials* of the *Zhou Li*: "The great sacrifice ... praises 'Sui.'" According to the annotation by Zheng Xuan of the Eastern Han Dynasty, "Sui" refers to a type of ritual vessel shaped like an ax, and "Sui Qiong" refers to a specific ax, namely, one that is narrow and long, resembling an oval shape. "隋" can also mean a downward drop or descent, as mentioned in *Book of the Celestial Officials* in the *Shi Ji*: "To the west of the imperial court, there are five 'Sui' stars." According to Tang dynasty scholar Sima Zhen's *Collected Annotations of the Records of the Grand Historian*: "'Sui' means a downward drop; it also refers to a fall." However, the most common meaning of 隋, relatively speaking, is "broken flesh," which refers to the leftover sacrificial meat and food that should be buried after the ritual. As described in *Spring Officials* of the *Zhou Li*: "After the sacrifice, hide the 'Sui'." According to the *Shuowen Jiezi*: "'隋' means cracked meat." Therefore, Xu Kai's argument and the agreement of Wang Guanguo, Luo Bi, Wang Yinglin, Jiao Hong, and others are valid. This reasoning should be the background to the fact that the national title 隋 was indeed not recognized by later generations, and one of the pieces of evidence is that no dynasty was willing to use this national title. The key lies not in the short-lived image or the notorious reputation of the Sui Dynasty for exploiting the people's labor force, as the Qin Dynasty was even more short-lived and exploited the labor force more. Instead, it lies in the fact that Yang Jian's "bold modification" of the national title 隋 was deemed uncultured and a failed move by future emperors, generals, scholars, and intellectuals. The national title "隋" was even considered a dreadful prophecy of the division and downfall of the Sui dynasty![16]

However, the problem lies in the fact that when Yang Jian chose 隋 instead of 随, it was certainly not based on the meaning of "broken flesh" associated with 隋, it was more likely because 随 could be abbreviated as 隋 to save strokes in writing. Yang Jian directly used the abbreviated character 隋 as the official name of the country.

According to the *Huainanzi*: "The He clan's jade and the Marquis of Sui's pearl derive from the essence of mountains and abysses." And in the same text: "For example, the Marquis of Sui's pearl and the He clan's jade, if obtained, bring wealth, and if lost, bring poverty." This indicates that the precious pearl can also be referred to as "随珠" (sui zhu) or "隋珠" (sui zhu). Additionally, in ancient texts, the state or county of sui 随 are sometimes written as 隋. In the *Huainanzi*, it is mentioned that the Marquis of Sui refers to a lord from the eastern region of the Han Dynasty, belonging to the Ji clan. The Marquis of Sui encountered a large snake, treated it with medicine, and later, the snake repaid the favor by bringing a large pearl from the river, leading to the saying "the precious pearl of the Marquis of Sui." According to the *Shui Jing* (Waterways Classic) of the Han Dynasty, the River Yuan "flows south east past the Sui County in the west," as stated by Li Daoyuan in the *Commentary on the Waterways Classic*: "Now, the county is the ancient state of Sui." Hence, the pre-Qin state of Sui 随 can be written as 隋, and the County of Sui 随 in the Han Dynasty can also be written as 隋.[17]

Before the Sui Dynasty, "随" was often abbreviated as "隋" due to its stroke count. Regarding Yang Jian, it is possible that he abandoned "随" for "隋" because the radical "辶" in "随" carries ill connotations. This is the reason he chose "隋" as the name for his new dynasty.

Ironically, despite the prosperity of the Sui Dynasty (which became the dominant power in the year 589), it quickly declined and disintegrated, following the pattern of the Northern Zhou and Qi dynasties. The new unified empire of Tang was established shortly afterward. After the establishment of the Tang Dynasty, comments were made about the national title of the short-lived Sui dynasty. According to Gu Yanwu's *Jin Shi Wen Zi Ji* (Notes of Inscriptions on Ancient

Bronzes and Stone Tablets) from the late Ming and early Qing dynasties, with regard to the inscription of Huangfu Dan's tablet:

> The "Tablet of Huangfu Dan" inscription uses the character "随" instead of "隋." Similarly, the " Stele of Confucius Temple" by Yu Shinan, the "Inscription of the Sweet Spring in Palace Jiucheng" by Ouyang Xun, and the "Stele of Duke Li Wei" by Wang Zhijing and Emperor Gaozong, the "Stele of Mausoleum Shun" by Heavenly Empress, the "Stele of Wang from Huayang Temple" by Yu Jingzhi, and the " Stele of Shaolin Temple" by Pei Cui all exhibit this usage.[18]

In the early Tang Dynasty, strokes were frequently added to the title Sui 隋. Such changes contained political symbolism. Since the Sui Dynasty had a short duration, using the character 随 would seem appropriate, both in name and reality. Moreover, criticizing and surpassing its predecessor was a common phenomenon for a new dynasty in Chinese culture. As Cen Zhongmian pointed out, "Yang Jian inherited the title of Duke of Sui from his father Yang Zhong, hence he changed the dynastic title to Sui. Furthermore, he disliked the character 随 because it implied 'walking away hastily.' Therefore, he eliminated the radical '走' and adopted the rest of the character '隋.' In the Qing Dynasty, stone inscription experts often used the character '随,' which was used in the steles of the early Tang Dynasty, leading to doubts about the previous explanations. But with numerous stone inscriptions discovered in recent years, it has been found that the title '隋' was used in all inscriptions of the Sui Dynasty. Considering the tradition of criticizing their predecessors by new dynasties, it's not difficult to explain why the character '随' was frequently used in the early Tang Dynasty. However, after the early Tang, it became more common to use the title '隋,' while the other character '随' was rarely used. Without Yang Jian's modifications, we would not be able to explain these differences."[19]

To sum up, based on the original sources, Yang Jian, as the founder of the Sui Dynasty, adopted the character 隋 as the national title. This choice derived from the title of the Duke of Sui, initially granted to Yang Zhong and later inherited by Yang Jian, as well as Yang Jian's subsequent promotion to King of Sui. The historical origins of these titles can be traced back to the pre-Qin state of Sui (随).

Notes

1 According to the article "A Brief Study on the Name of the Sui Dynasty" by Ye Wei, published in the 11th issue of *Journal of Historiography of Peking University* in 2005, it is believed that in the early years of the Northern Song Dynasty, there were different spellings for "Duke of Sui" and "King of Sui" in the copied version of the *Book of Zhou*. Based on this, it is argued that "Yang Jian was originally appointed as the Duke of Sui and the King of Sui, and the name of the Sui Dynasty was derived from this." However, according to the references cited in the following text, both Li Fu from the late Tang Dynasty and Xu Kai from the Southern Tang Dynasty have already pointed out that Yang Jian changed his title from the character 随 to 隋, and their works predate the Northern Song Dynasty. Therefore, the doubts raised by Ye's article are unfounded. The interchangeable use of the two characters in many historical texts can be attributed to the

simplification of "随" to "隋," and the correct character for the official title of the Sui Dynasty founded by Yang Jian should be "隋."

2 Here is an explanation of the usage of the character "随" in this chapter. In simplified Chinese, it is written as "随," while in traditional Chinese, it is written as "隨." According to the *Shuowen Jiezi*, it is written as "𨕖." All characters related to "随" are derived from the radical "辵," which means "to walk hastily." Characters such as "迹" (trace), "巡" (patrol), "逝" (pass away), and "迅" (rapid) all belong to this category. In this chapter, both 𨕖 and "隨" are simplified as "随."

3 "Biography of Yang Zhong," *Book of Zhou*: Yang Zhong was posthumously named as Huan.

4 According to *Annals of Chen* in the *Zizhi Tongjian*, in the second month of the 13th year of the Taijian era, it is recorded that Yu Jicai, the commander-in-chief, advised the King of Sui to accept the heavenly mandate on the day Jiazi of the current month. The Grand Tutor Li Mu and the General Lu Ben also urged him to do so. As a result, Emperor Zhou issued an edict, resigning and moving to a separate palace. On the day Jiazi, Qi Chun, who served as both Grand Tutor and General, presented the credentials, and Zhao Jiong, the Senior Grand Tutor, presented the imperial seal and sash, and the abdication took place in favor of the Sui Dynasty." Note: The day Jiazi refers to the 13th day of the second month in the lunar calendar, which is also known as Jingzhe, meaning "awakening of insects."

5 The radical '走' should be '辵,' which means that the radical "辵" should be removed. In the *Shuowen Jiezi* by Xu Shen in the Eastern Han Dynasty, it is explained that "辵" means to walk or stop abruptly, while "走" means to hurry or rush. Therefore, there is a slight difference in meaning between "辵" and "走."

6 The statement "There was no ancient character for '隋'" is not accurate. The character "隋" did exist, as seen in Xu Shen's *Shuowen Jiezi* during the Eastern Han Dynasty.

7 In the "Biography of Wang Shao" of the *Book of Sui*, it is mentioned that Wang Shao wrote a memorial in the early years of the Kaihuang era, stating, "Furthermore, the reign title Kaihuang coincides with the year of Kaihuang in the 'Lingbao Jing' (Lingbao Scripture)." Yang Jian was "greatly pleased" and considered Wang Shao as extremely sincere.

8 "Geographical Records," Book of Sui.

9 This excerpt is from the *Annals of Emperor Shizu* in the *History of the Yuan Dynasty*, which discusses the naming of the Sui and Tang dynasties. The passage means that the national titles were derived from the names of the fiefdoms granted by the emperor, following the customs of the society. It was a temporary institutional arrangement that reflected a fair and just attitude, without any positive or negative implications.

10 "Biography of Cui Xuanbo," Book of Wei.

11 The statement "Wang Yinglin remarked" and so on, as mentioned in the "Kunxue Jiwen" by Wang Yinglin of the Southern Song Dynasty in Volume 13 of the *Examining Historical Records*, actually only quotes Xu Kai's words without adding anything new.

12 "Biography of Du Qiong," Book of Shu, *Records of the Three Kingdoms*.

13 In fact, Liu Bei had an adopted son named Liu Feng, and the combination of "Liu Feng" and "Liu Shan" forms the term "Fengshan," which refers to the ritual of offering sacrifices to Heaven and Earth and can only be presided over by an emperor.

14 In the "Biography of Emperor Gaozu" in the *Book of Sui*, historians in the early Tang Dynasty evaluated Yang Jian, stating that he had a suspicious nature, lacked scholarly knowledge, and did not appreciate poetry and literature. They also mentioned that he abolished schools.

15 When researching the etymology of words, you can refer to sources such as the *Shuowen Jiezi* with annotations by Duan Yucai from the Qing Dynasty, the *Guangya Dictionary*, the *Book of Changes* with commentary on the "Sui" hexagram, as well as various ancient and contemporary linguistic reference works.

16 As cited above, Xu Kai's statement and Luo Bi's remark belong to the same category of comments on the title Sui 隋.

17 In "A Brief Study on the Sui Dynasty's National Title," Ye Wei further pointed out that until the late period of the Northern and Southern Dynasties, and even on the eve of the establishment of the Sui Dynasty, there existed the usage of writing prefecture Sui (随) or Suizhou (随州) as Sui (隋) or "隋州," in stone inscriptions or documentary materials.

18 Gu Yanwu further explained: "In the past, both characters (随 and 隋) were commonly used in inscriptions. It was only after Sima Wen wrote the 'Comprehensive Mirror for Aid in Government' that the character '隋' began to be exclusively used." However, this analysis is not entirely accurate. Please refer to the following discussion by Cen Zhongmian.

19 Cen Zhongmian, History of the Sui and Tang Dynasties, section 1, "History of the Sui Dynasty" Volume 1, Zhonghua Book Company, 1982. Additionally, according to Takahashi Tsuguo's research article "A Study on the National Title '隋' " (published in the 44th issue of "Legal History Research" in 1995), which provides statistical data on Sui and Tang stone inscriptions, more than 90% of stone inscriptions in the Sui Dynasty use the character "隋," while less than 10% use the character "随." During the early Tang period until the reign of Emperor Xuanzong, the usage of the character "随" exceeded 80%. However, it gradually decreased after the middle Tang period, and in the late Tang period, the usage of the character "隋" again rose to nearly 90%.

11 Tang

Emperor Shen Yao's Aspirations and Self-Assessment

During the transition between the Sui and Tang dynasties, the situation in the entire country was turbulent. In 611, uprisings against the Sui Dynasty emerged across various regions. In Shandong, Hebei, and Henan, there were rebellions led by Wang Bo, Liu Badao, Sun Anzu, Zhang Jincheng, Gao Shida, Zhai Rang, and Xu Shijie, amongst others. Following these initial uprisings, numerous warlords rose to power and proclaimed themselves rulers. For example, in the ninth year of the Daye era (613), in December, Xiang Haiming declared himself emperor with the era name "Baiwu;" in May of the tenth year of the Daye era, Liu Jialun declared himself emperor with the era name "Dashi;" in December of the eleventh year of the Daye era, Zhu Can declared himself emperor of Chu with the era name "Changda;" Cao Shiqi claimed the title King Yuanxing with the era name "Shixing" in the same year; Lin Shihong declared himself emperor of Chu with the era name "Taiping;" in January of the thirteenth year of the Daye era, Dou Jiande proclaimed himself King Changle (later changed to King Xia) with the era name "Dingchou" (later changed to "Wu Feng"); in February, Li Mi proclaimed himself Duke of Wei with the era name "Yongping;" in March, Liu Wuzhou declared himself emperor with the era name "Tianxing;" in the same year, Liang Shidu declared himself emperor of Liang with the era name "Yonglong;" Guo Zihe claimed the title King Yongle with the era name "Zhengping" (or "Chouping"); in April, Xue Ju declared himself King of Western Qin with the era name "Qinxing;" in October, Xiao Yan proclaimed himself King of Liang with the era name "Mingfeng" (or "Fengming"); in May of the second year of Yining (618), Li Yuan declared himself emperor of Tang with the era name "Wude;" in September, Yuwen Huaji declared himself emperor of Xu with the era name "Tianshou;" in November, Li Gui proclaimed himself emperor of Liang with the era name "Anle;" in December, Gao Tangheng declared himself emperor of Dacheng with the era name "Falon;" Gao Kaidao claimed the title King of Yan with the era name "Shixing." In April of 619, Wang Shichong declared himself emperor of Zheng with the era name "Kaiming;" in September, Shen Faxing proclaimed himself king of Liang with the era name "Yankang;" Li Zitong claimed the title emperor of Wu with the era name "Mingzheng;" in January of 622, Liu Heita proclaimed himself King of Handong with the era name "Tianzao;" in

DOI: 10.4324/9781003510390-12

August of 623, Fu Gongshi declared himself emperor of Song with the era name "Tianming;" and so on.

As a result, the unity of the Sui Dynasty effectively lasted only until 611. The actual collapse of the Sui Dynasty can be traced back to March of the fourteenth year of the Daye era (618), when Yuwen Huaji assassinated Emperor Yang Guang of the Sui Dynasty in Jiangdu County (now Yangzhou City, Jiangsu Province), and May of the second year of the Yining era (618), when Li Yuan coerced Emperor Yang You of Sui into abdicating the throne in Chang'an. The establishment of a unified empire was completely lost, and the subsequent establishment of the Tang Dynasty marked the beginning of a new era of unity under single imperial rule.

From the perspective of the history of Chinese national titles, the name "Tang" has endured for a long time. Its beginning can be traced back to the fifth month of 618, when Emperor Yang You of the Sui Dynasty abdicated in favor of Li Yuan, who then assumed the title of emperor in Chang'an. After the war to pacify Jiangnan in 624, Li Shimin, known as Emperor Taizong of Tang, unified the realm. The end of the Tang Dynasty came on the first day of the fourth month of 907 when Zhu Wen deposed Emperor Ai (Li Zhu) and established the state of Later Liang. Between these bookends, in September 690, Empress Wu Zetian assumed the title of emperor during the reign of her husband Emperor Gaozong of Tang and changed the dynasty's name to Zhou. Then, in February 705, Emperor Zhongzong, the son of Emperor Gaozong, regained power and restored the dynasty's name to Tang. As such, the name "Tang" remained as the national title for approximately 289 years, distinguishing it from the short-lived national titles of Qin, Xin, Jin, and Sui. Similar to the influences of the national titles of Qin and Han, the name "Tang" has not only persisted to the present day but has also spread beyond the borders of China.

The origins of the enduring name and influence of the title Tang are explained in the annotations of the *Annals of the Tang Dynasty* of the *Zizhi Tongjian*, stating the following:

> The name "Tang" has ancient origins. According to Lu Deming, during the reign of King Cheng of Zhou, his maternal uncle Shuyu was granted the fiefdom of Tang. The land of Tang was where Emperor Yao and Emperor Shun, of mythological times, had their capitals. During the Han Dynasty, it was known as prefecture Taiyuan, located west of the Taihang and Heng Mountains in the ancient Jizhou, in the fields of Taiyuan and Hedong. The ancestors of the Li family, who later founded the Tang Dynasty, included Li Hu and Li Bi, among others, who had contributed to the Zhou Dynasty's campaigns against the state of Wei. They were all titled as "Pillar States."[1] When Emperor Min of Zhou received the abdication of the last Wei ruler, Li Hu had already passed away. However, his contributions were recognized, and he was posthumously granted the title of Duke of Tang. His son, Li Bing, inherited the title, and then his grandson Li Yuan, who rose up in rebellion, captured Chang'an and was subsequently appointed as king of Tang. Later, when Li Yuan accepted the abdication of the Sui Dynasty, the country was named Tang.

According to Hu Sanxing's explanation, the connection between Li and the title "Tang" as a country name is correct. It is also acceptable to consider Li Hu's post-humous title of the Duke of Tang as the direct source of the dynastic title "Tang." However, Hu's annotations did not address a crucial question: Why did the Emperor Min of Zhou confer the title Duke of Tang on Li Hu? Furthermore, Li Bing inheriting the title Duke of Tang, and Li Yuan himself being promoted from duke to king of Tang, are there any other reasons for Li Yuan using the title "Tang" as the country name?

11.1 Duke of Tang: The Posthumous Title of Li Hu

Li Hu, the grandfather of the founding emperor Li Yuan of the Tang Dynasty, is a significant historical figure. The *Imperial Genealogy* in the *Cefu Yuangui* (The Imperially Commissioned Encyclopedia of History, composed in the Northern Song Dynasty) briefly states the ancestry of Li Yuan and his establishment of the Tang Dynasty after the abdication of the Sui Dynasty:

> The Divine Emperor Shenyao (Yuan), Emperor Gaozu of the Tang Dynasty, surnamed Li, was from Didao, Longxi. His ancestors can be traced back to Li Hao, known as the King of Liangwu in the Liang Dynasty. After Li Hao's death, his son Li Xin inherited the position but was later overthrown by Juqu Mengxun. Li Xin's son, Zhong'er, fled to the south and served as the Governor of Prefecture Runan under the Song Dynasty. He later returned to Wei and was appointed prefect of Hongnong, later honored as the Prefectural governor of Yuzhou. Xi, his son, gained prominence as the commander of Jinmen and established himself in Wuchuan, serving as the military and civilian leader until his death, thus establishing the family's foundation. Xi's son, Tianci, served as an official under Wei and was honored posthumously as Duke Sikong during the Emperor Datong's time. Tianci's son, Li Hu, known as Emperor Taizu Jinghuan, was first conferred the title Duke of Zhaojun, then relocated and given the title Duke of Longxi. During Wei's abdication to Zhou, Li Hu recorded outstanding achievements and held the highest position, and thus he was posthumously conferred the title Duke of Tang. Hu's son, Li Bing, known as Emperor Shizu Yuanhuan, was initially titled Earl of Ruyang County and later inherited the title Duke of Longxi. During the abdication of Zhou, he succeeded his father as Duke of Tang. Gaozu, who was the crown prince during Emperor Yuan's reign, had Empress Yuanchen as his mother. At the age of seven, he inherited the title Duke of Tang. In the second year of Yining, he accepted the abdication of the Sui Dynasty and ascended the throne.

The traditional account of Li Yuan's ancestry mentioned above has many problems, but two points are particularly relevant and worth noting in relation to this chapter. Firstly, the ancestors of Li Tang were originally from Didao in Longxi (present-day Lintao County, Gansu Province), and later their family settled in Wuchuan (present-day Wuchuan County, Inner Mongolia). Secondly, Li Hu was initially conferred the title Duke of Zhaojun, then relocated and bestowed the title

Duke of Longxi, and later posthumously granted the title Duke of Tang. These two issues are interconnected, and the key lies in the problem of Li Tang's ancestors.

Regarding Li Tang's ancestors, Chen Yinke wrote several works, including "*Speculations on the Li Tang Clan* (1931), *Supplement to Speculations on the Li Tang Clan* (1933), *Discussions on the Issue of the Li Tang Clans* (1935), and *Miscellaneous Studies on the Historical Deeds of Li Tang and Wuzhou* (1936)[2]. The conclusions reached through examination and analysis are as follows:

Firstly, the claim that the ancestors of Li Tang originated from the Li family of Longxi after the Liang Dynasty's King Liangwu Li Hao, as stated in the *Cefu Yuangui*, the *Book of Tang*, the *New Book of Tang*, as well as the *History of the Northern Dynasties* and the *Book of Jin*, is all fabricated and false. Secondly, based on the records of the Guangye Temple Stele of the Tang Dynasty and volume 17 of the *Gazetteer of Yuanhe Prefectures and Counties*, it can be inferred that the ancestors of Li Tang hailed from the Li family of Zhaojun. If they were not a branch of the "fallen" Li family of Zhaojun, then they were a "counterfeit" branch. Thirdly, the transformation of Li's ancestral origin from Zhaojun to Longxi is related to the fundamental policy of "Guanzhong-centered governance" established by figures such as Yuwen Tai and Su Chuo during the Western Wei and Northern Zhou dynasties. Specifically, "When Li Hu entered Guanzhong and the division between the east and west was determined, they changed the surname and native village from Zhaojun to Longxi, motivated by similarities between the deeds of Li Kang and his ancestors. They further advanced the fabrication by claiming direct lineage to the West Liang and fabricated family connections to Wuchuan due to the Yuwen family" (see Figure 11.1) .

Figure 11.1 The tomb of the couple Chen Yinke and Tang Yun in Lushan Botanical Garden

Based on the aforementioned conclusions resulting from profound research, the following reasons can summarize the rationale behind conferring the posthumous title of Duke of Tang to Li Hu:

Firstly, according to *The Chronicles of Emperor Wu* in the *Book of Zhou*, in the ninth month of the fourth year of Baoding (564 AD), Li Bing was conferred the title Duke of Tang. Therefore, the conferral of the posthumous title Duke of Tang upon Li Hu would have occurred the same year,[3] eight years prior to Zhou accepting the abdication of the Wei Dynasty.

Secondly, the titles conferred upon Li Hu, including Duke of Zhaojun, Duke of Longxi, and the posthumous title Duke of Tang, relate to the ancestral origin and fabricated history. The connection between Duke of Zhaojun and Duke of Longxi is evident and requires no further discussion. The progression from Duke of Prefectures to Duke of Tang follows the same rationale. "In granting higher titles, the principle was to preserve the original title as much as possible. Therefore, when selecting names, they often looked for larger regions associated with the original title. If suitable names could not be found, they would search for larger regions adjacent to the original title. If no suitable names were available, they would abandon the original title's associated names and choose a new one."[4] Based on these principles, the ancient country names used for Li Hu's conferment, considering the ancestral connection, could have been Qin (related to Longxi prefecture), Jin, Zhongshan, Zhao, Wei, or Tang (all related to Zhaojun).[5] However, Wei was already the title of the Tuoba clan, and it could not be used. Zhongshan was deemed inappropriate for a higher title.[6] Additionally, with Yuwen Zhi as the Duke of Qinzhou, Yuwen Hu as the Duke of Jinguo, and Li Bi as the Duke of Zhaoguo, the names Qin, Jin, and Zhao were also unsuitable. Consequently, after eliminating these options, "if the official responsible for designing the title did not select a new name but still wanted to maintain a connection with the original name of the fief, Tang was the only choice. This is why Li Hu was posthumously conferred the title Duke of Tang."[7]

Thirdly, the ancient country name "Tang" relating to Zhaojun specifically refers to the Kingdom Tang founded by the legendary Emperor Yao's descendant, the Taotang clan.[8] According to the *Geographical Records* in the *Book of Han*, Tang County was under the jurisdiction of the Kingdom Zhongshan, and it is mentioned that "Mount Yao is to the south, River Tang is to the west." The annotations by Yan Shigu, as cited in the same book, state that it was the former Kingdom Tang, with Mount Yao located north east. Moreover, the annotations by Zhang Yan in the *Book of Han* for Wangdu County in Kingdom Zhongshan, saying, "Mount Qingdu is to the south of Mount Yao. From Mount Yao, one can see Mount Du, hence the name." Furthermore, according to the *Book of Wei*, "Terrace Yao" is in Guang'e County, South Zhaojun. According to Volume 17 of the *Gazetteer of Yuanhe Prefectures and Counties*, Guang'e County is the burial site of Li Tianci and Li Xi, Li Hu's father and grandfather.[9] This place is also mentioned in the inscription on the Guangye Temple stele, written by Yang Jin in the 13th year of the Tang Kaiyuan era, which refers to it as the "ancestral land of the royal family." Therefore, Li Hu was posthumously conferred the title of "Duke of Tang," drawing significance from the remnants of the Taotang clan of Emperor Yao that have been preserved in the Hebei region.

Li Hu's residence in the ancestral land of the Taotang clan, as well as his posthumous title of Duke of Tang granted by the Zhou Dynasty, has been elucidated above. As for the subsequent posthumous title of Duke of Tang bestowed upon Li Yuan, who later accepted the abdicated throne from the Sui Dynasty and adopted "Tang" as the name of his regime, it has more profound implications. In Volume 1 of the *Annotations on Daily Life during the Founding of the Tang Dynasty* by Wen Daya, it is stated that the founding of the Tang Dynasty began with Li Yuan.

> "Initially, the Emperor was promoted from the position of Minor Prefect of the Guards to the General of the Right Valiant Guards. He was then decreed to serve as the Imperial Peace Envoy of the Taiyuan region. He was given the authority to oversee the performance of the local civil and military officials, and had the power to demote or promote them as necessary, filling vacancies as he saw fit. From the region of Hedong and beyond, the Emperor was also tasked with the mobilization of troops and the suppression of bandits within his jurisdiction, which was during the time of Emperor Yang of the Sui Dynasty's visit to Loufan in the twelfth year of the Daye era. As the Emperor carried out his peace-making mission in Taiyuan, land of the common people and the aboriginals of the Tao Tang, he did not exceed his mandated territorial limits. He was privately delighted in this assignment, considering it a heavenly mandate. Throughout the places he journeyed, he showed leniency and kindness, and with the virtue and wisdom he possessed, he won people's hearts as naturally as a shadow follows its subject."

Wen Daya was a native of Qi County in Taiyuan. When Li Yuan raised his forces in Taiyuan, Wen Daya served as a staff officer in the General's Headquarters, responsible for handling administrative and literary matters. After Li Yuan proclaimed himself emperor, Wen Daya participated in the formulation of ceremonial rites and later became involved in confidential matters. In this light, the *Annotations on Daily Life during the Founding of the Tang Dynasty* not only provides abundant and detailed materials but also proves to be highly reliable. However, how did "the common people of Taiyuan" become "the ancient people of the Taotang clan?" How did the position of "Peace Envoy of Taiyuan Circuit" evolve beyond the original title of Duke of Tang? And what is the meaning behind the statement "privately delighted by this assignment, considering it a heavenly mandate?" All these questions are pertinent to the establishment of the title "Tang" as the ruler of all under heaven. To explore further, one must delve into the ancient historical legends concerning the Taotang clan, the descendants of Emperor Yao.

11.2 The Legend of Emperor Yao of the Taotang Clan and the Aesthetic Significance of the Term "Tang"

The figure of Emperor Yao is notably absent from Western Zhou literature, such as the *Book of Songs* and the *Book of Documents*. He emerges in works like *Tian*

Wen (Questions to Heaven), *Guo Yu* (Discourses on Governance of the States), and *Zuo Zhuan* (Zuo's Commentary on the Spring and Autumn Annals), as a character in stories about the abdication of rulers Yao and Shun. In these accounts, he is portrayed as a somewhat mediocre and unremarkable emperor. His name, "Emperor Yao," appears in the mythology of the *Shan Hai Jing*, but he is not included in the genealogy of ancient emperors in that text, indicating his relatively low position in early mythological legends. Yao becomes an exemplar of the ancient sage king and benevolent ruler particularly in Confucian and Mohist texts. Specifically, the Confucian school revered Yao and dedicated *The Canon of Yao* to extol his governance achievements, his virtues, and his abdication in favor of Shun, as well as the glorious legacy he left behind.

In the compiled genealogy *Imperial Lineage* from the late Warring States period, Yao is depicted as the third son of Emperor Ku, the great-grandson of the Yellow Emperor. In *Emperors' Lineage*, it is recorded that "Emperor Yao belonged to the lineage of the Tao Tang clan."[10] The *Records of the Grand Historian* follows this lineage and refers to him as "Emperor Tang." Henceforth in historical records, he came to be termed "Tang Yao," aligning his appellation with those of Yu Shun, Xia Yu, Shang Tang, and Zhou Wen Wang, becoming the "Emperor Tang" in the historical system of "Two Emperors and Three Kings" that was passed down from the late Warring States period, which included Tang, Yu, Xia, Shang, and Zhou. The *Virtues of the Five Emperors* in the *Book of Rites by Dai De* classifies Yao as the fourth emperor among the ancient "Five Emperors."

The legends of Yao are manifold and varied, and the information provided here is but a general overview. Regarding the term "Emperor Yao of the Taotang Clan," Liu Qiyu's *Four Entries on Ancient History* in the *Continued Analysis of Ancient History*"[11] illuminates several points:

Firstly, the oracle bone inscription for "Yao" 尧 depicts a person placed atop an unfired pottery mold, while "tao" 陶 and "yao" 窑 both refer to a pot made from fired pottery. Despite their different written forms, the three characters 尧, 陶, and 窑 likely shared the same ancient pronunciation of "tao." Thus, "Yao" 尧 could represent the founding deity of a clan named "Taotang," celebrated for significant achievements in pottery.

Secondly, the *Book of Documents* mentions a location called "Taoqiu," and the *Book of Han* depicts a place called "Dingtao" in Prefecture Jiyin. Archaeological discoveries indicate that the Longshan culture in Shandong province was renowned for its advanced pottery techniques, which included the production of thin, black pottery similar to eggshells. It is plausible that the "Taotang" clan, associated with the deity "Yao," originally thrived in the eastern regions.

Thirdly, the association of Yao with Tang originated from later legends that merged different historical accounts. Some said Yao was the son of Emperor Ku and was enfeoffed in Tang, while others claimed Yao resided in Tang before moving to Tao. This conflation led to the creation of the Taotang clan in texts like the *Guo Yu* and *Zuo Zhuan*. The *Shi Ben* (Emperors' Lineage) refers to Emperor Yao being from the Taotang clan.

Fourthly, the location of the "Tang" territory connected to Yao has been debated for centuries, with scholars during the Han and Tang Dynasties offering various theories.[12] The suggested locations include Jinyang and Pingyang in present-day Shanxi Province and Tang County in Hebei Province. Modern archaeological evidence, however, suggests that "Tang" was in the south western part of present-day Shanxi province.

Fifthly, the Tao tribe, skilled in pottery-making, was significant in ancient times. Their leader, Yao, took the name of an ancestral god, ruling a tribe or tribal alliance. Over time, Confucian texts, including the *Historical Investigations* (Shi Tong), idealized Yao, portraying him as a paragon of virtue and wisdom.

Remnants of Emperor Yao and the Tao Tang clan can be found in several Chinese provinces, including Shandong, Hebei, Henan, and Shanxi.[13] In Hebei, these remnants are linked to Li Hu's posthumous title as the Duke of Tang, given by the Northern Zhou Dynasty. In Shanxi, Li Yuan, the Duke of Tang (and later founder of the Tang Dynasty), claimed descent from the Tao Tang clan, asserting that his territory encompassed their ancient lands.

The legacies of Yao in Shanxi are concentrated primarily in Taiyuan and Pingyang areas. Various ancient texts suggest these locations were under Yao's dominion. The theory is that Yao and his descendants built their domain in the southern part of Shanxi, along the river valley of Fen. Yicheng, in particular, is identified with the Tang Kingdom of Yao's descendants during the Xia and Shang periods, later destroyed during King Cheng of Zhou's reign, who then created the Tang dukedom for his brother Ji Yu on the same lands.

Li Yuan, as the Ambassador of Pacification and Duke of Tang, felt divinely appointed due to the historical connection to the Tao Tang clan, considering Shanxi, with its traditions tracing back to Emperor Yao,[14] the inherent territory of his pacification and governance.

The naming of the country and Emperor Yao's association with the Tao Tang clan is addressed in the *Bai Hu Tong De Lun* (Debates in the White Tiger Hall), a text of the Eastern Han Dynasty, which explores the concept of emperors and how they are aligned with virtues and with heaven and earth. The term "Tang" is explained to represent expansiveness and grandeurs of morality, fitting descriptions of Yao's reign and influence.

In the *Lun Heng* (On Balance) by Wang Chong, it is suggested that names like Tang symbolize merits and virtues of an era, and it is affirmed that "Tang" implies something vast. According to the *Shuowen Jiezi*, "Tang" means significant and grand, representing greatness.[15] Furthermore, in the *Analects*, Confucius praises Yao's broad and unfathomable rule, thus associating grandeur with the term "Tang."

Great indeed was Yao as a sovereign! His shining virtue surpassed that of others, and it was only natural for Heaven to favor Yao. Broad and vast was his rule, such that the people could not fathom it. Great indeed was he in his success, radiantly brilliant in his accomplishments.[16]

Therefore, Yao's association with the term "Tang" encompasses both linguistic tradition and historical records. The use of "Dang Dang" to describe Yao's greatness reflects this association, and Gu Yewang's *Yu Pian* reiterates that "Tang" refers to Yao, embodying profound moral grandeur.

Based on this, "Yao" represents a sage king, whose great and boundless merits are expansive and vast. "Tang" serves as a poetic epithet that vividly expresses Yao's expansive and boundless greatness. When Li Yuan became the Ambassador of Pacification in Taiyuan in the 12th year of the Sui Dynasty's Daye era (616 AD), the land was already in turmoil. Hence, Li Yuan, the Duke of Tang, privately delighted in this appointment, considering it a divine gift (see Figure 11.2).

But what does "divine gift" mean? According to the *Annotations on the Beginnings of the Great Tang Dynasty*, in the 13th year of the Daye era, Emperor Yang of the Sui Dynasty ordered Li Yuan to remain in Taiyuan as the regional governor. Elated, Li Yuan, in a state of excitement, confided his thoughts to his second son, Li Shimin, saying, "Tang is indeed my country, and Taiyuan is its land. My coming here is a gift from heaven. If I am given such an opportunity and don't seize it, a calamity will befall us. However, if I can break through Lishan, overcome the Tujue, only then can I save the state in times of crisis." Notably, in the 11th year of the Daye era, Wei Dao'er led a rebellion and called himself Lishan Fei, amassing a force of over 100,000 followers. The following year, one of Lishan Fei's subordinates, Zhen Zhai'er, advanced towards Taiyuan. Additionally, the formidable external threat of the Turks had been prevalent

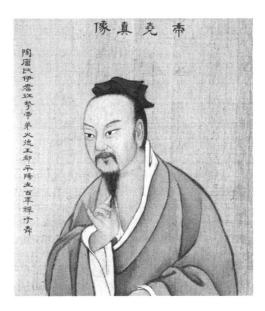

Figure 11.2 Image of Emperor Yao

since the Northern Zhou and Northern Qi dynasties. In terms of the phrase "jing-bang jishi" (safeguarding the state during troubled times), Li Yuan possessed the wisdom and capacity to govern the country and had long aspired to bring peace and stability. He envisaged his name being renowned in historical records. Furthermore, Taiyuan was considered a place of great destiny. Therefore, from the moment Li Yuan was appointed as the Ambassador of Pacification in Taiyuan, he harbored ambitions of disloyalty and separatism, and when he became the local governor of Taiyuan, he seized the opportunity to overthrow the Sui Dynasty, displaying valiant and decisive leadership, which ultimately established him as the dominant power.

Li Yuan, the Duke of Tang, had initially harbored disloyal intentions that were well-known among the "former people of the Tao Tang clan." It was only subtly hinted at in the early stages of his rebellion against the Sui Dynasty. However, it was not until 60 years later, in the fifth year of the Tang Xianheng era (674 AD), that his true intentions became widely known.

The "former people of the Tao Tang clan" were well aware of Li Yuan's intentions. During the early years of the Sui Dynasty, there was a folk song called "Peach and Plum Song," which went: "Peach and plum, do not speak rashly; the yellow heron flies around the mountains, gracefully turning in the flower garden." In Volume One of *The Annotated Records of the Founding and Living of the Great Tang Dynasty*, in the case of Wen Daya, it is stated: "Li, the same pronunciation of plum in Chinese, is the surname of the royal family; 'Tao,' the peach, should be translated as 'Tang' implying the Tang Dynasty. Thus, the Peach Blossom Garden is referred to as the prosperity of the Tang Dynasty. Graceful turns are related to the flags and banners. In the region of Fen and Jin, old and young, sing songs. Suddenly witnessing the realization, they cannot contain their joy."

Based on these accounts, the Duke of Tang, Li Yuan, was compared to Emperor Yao of the Tao Tang clan. He regretted not being able to fulfill the prophecy of "traveling a thousand miles in a single leap" to restore the former enterprise of the Tang Yao era. However, at least in the regions of Fen and Jin during that time, his intentions were as clear as "the heart of Sima Zhao, known to everyone."

The subtle hint of Li Yuan's aspirations during the early stages of his rebellion against the Sui Dynasty can be found in the *Annals of Tang* of the *Zizhi Tongjian*: "On the fifth day of the fifth month in the first year of the Wude era (618 AD), the King of Tang ascended to the imperial throne in the Taiji Hall ... Aligning with the Five Elements, he associates Tang with 'Tu' (Earth Virtue) and the color yellow."

On the surface, Tang adopted the Earth Virtue due to its inheritance from the Sui Dynasty, and hence, it's natural for it to associate with the color yellow. But in fact, there is deeper significance to the Earth Virtue of Tang and emphasis on the color yellow. It alludes to the fact that from the end of the Cao Wei Dynasty to the Sui Dynasty, the Southern and Northern dynasties were not unified and did not inherit the order of the Five Elements. Therefore, the Earth Virtue of Tang can be interpreted as a direct continuation of the Fire Virtue of the Han Dynasty.

For instance, Emperor Xuanzong of Tang issued a decree emphasizing the Tang Dynasty's lineage from the Han Dynasty, proclaiming that Wei, Jin, Zhou, and Sui were illegitimate rulers.[17] However, due to political considerations, this interpretation could not be openly stated during the initial stages of the transition of power when the realm had not yet been unified.

Additionally, the Biography of Sui Hong in the *Book of Han* records a letter from Sui Hong to Emperor Zhao of Han, which states, "My predecessor Dong Zhongshu once said, 'Even when there are succeeding emperors adhering to the principles of their predecessors, it does not influence the heavenly mandate of the sage ruler.' In the Han lineage, and as the descendants of Emperor Yao, there is a tradition of transmitting the state power. The Han Emperors should select talents throughout the empire and enthrone them.'"

Terms such as the "Han lineage" and "descendants of Emperor Yao" are complex and somewhat mystifying. However, its intention to conform to the situation at that time is unmistakable. In the fictitious historical framework contrived by Wang Mang, Liu Xin, and others, which later influenced subsequent generations, Emperor Yao of the Taotang clan was associated with the Fire Virtue.[18] Similarly, Li Yuan's association with the Earth Virtue and his affinity for the color yellow hearken back to his connection with "descendants of Yao." Liu Bang established the Han Dynasty and as a successor, Li Yuan founded the Tang Dynasty. The transition of imperial power is distinctive – from the Fire Virtue of the Western Han (Liu Han) to the Earth Virtue of the Xin Dynasty (echoing the shift from Yao's Fire Virtue to Shun's Earth Virtue). Now, it's the Fire Virtue of the Eastern Han passing to Li Tang's Earth Virtue, which also resonates with the legacy of "descendants of Yao."

From the preceding analysis, we can discern certain events during the timeline stretching from Li Yuan's uprising until he took the throne. In the third volume of the *Records of the Start of the Great Tang Empire*, memorials from civil and military officials urging Li Yuan to ascend are documented, featuring statements like "Your surname connects with that of Emperor Yao. None defy the celestial order," "Hymns of the Tang Dynasty and the Li family," "Merits breed succession," "Applauding and chanting for Tang, driving the Yang southward," and so forth. All these ideas are grounds of a plea based on the connection with the Taotang clan and Emperor Yao. Upon ascending to the imperial throne, Li Yuan proclaimed to the heavens the following edict, "I inherit the familial blessings and the worldly fortune that has been bestowed upon us. With ancestors both recent and ancient, their cumulative achievements and virtues are carried forth. Endowed with the privilege to walk upon the ruins, I establish my lordship upon the ancient lands of Tang," where "the ancient lands of Tang" refers to the former territories of the legendary Emperor Tang (Yao), and "the ruins" signifies the celestial region corresponding to the land of Tang in astrological terms.

Moreover, Li Yuan's motives became overt in the fifth year of Xianheng era (674 AD). On the day of Renchen in the eighth month of that year, Li Zhi and Wu Zhao proclaimed Li Yuan "Emperor Shen Yao," a title that unmasked his initial psychological intent to identify himself with the Emperor Yao as founder of the Tang Dynasty.

11.3 Li Yuan, the "Emperor Shen Yao"

As chronicled in *The Records of the Start of the Great Tang Empire*, the *Book of Tang,* and the *Zizhi Tongjian*, Li Yuan, styled Shude, was born in Chang'an in the first year of the Tianhe era (566 AD) in the Northern Zhou Dynasty. At seven, he inherited the title Duke of Tang. During the Sui Dynasty, he commanded the Qianqiu Army, ruling as provincial governor over Qiao, Long, and Qi, and holding prefecture over Xingyang and Loufan. He ascended to Deputy Supervisor of the Palace and later Assistant Minister of the Guard. In the eleventh year of the Daye era, he was named Grand Envoy to pacify and console Shanxi and Hedong, and the next year, to Taiyuan. Amid the faltering Sui Dynasty and nationwide turmoil, the prophecy stating "the Li family shall ascend to the throne" widely circulated.[19] In the thirteenth year of the Daye era, Li Yuan became prefect of Taiyuan, a significant military locus against Turkic threats, and on par with Chang'an and eastern Luoyang strategically.[20] In the sixth month of that year, Li Yuan declared his aim to lead a righteous army, establishing the General's Office and organizing three divisions. By the seventh month, his forces advanced from Taiyuan, claiming successive victories. In the eleventh month, they breached Chang'an.[21] On the day of Renxu in that month, Li Yuan established in Chang'an the 13-year-old Sui prince Yang You as emperor, initiating the Yining era, while still posthumously honoring Emperor Yang of Sui, who was in Jiangdu, as the Retired Emperor. On the day of Jiazi, Li Yuan was further ennobled from Duke of Tang to King of Tang. In the second year of Yining (618), in March, a mutiny broke out in Jiangdu where Emperor Yang was assassinated, and Yuwen Huaji proclaimed the Prince of Qin, Yang Hao, as a puppet emperor. On the day of Wuwu in May, Li Yuan forced Emperor Yang You to abdicate in his favor. On the following day of Jiazi, Li Yuan ascended to the throne as Emperor, establishing the Tang Dynasty, initiating the Wude era, and setting Chang'an as the capital. Subsequently, until the seventh year of Wude (624), the Tang Dynasty subdued rebels and local warlords, one after another—capturing Xue Rengui, executing Li Mi, arresting Li Gui, defeating Liu Wuzhou, capturing Dou Jiande, conquering Wang Shichong, apprehending Xiao Xi, beheading Liu Heita, and pacifying Fu Gongshi. The fractious warlords that had emerged in the wake of the Sui's decline were gradually vanquished. As a result, a united and imperial Tang Dynasty was formed, and the title "Tang" succeeded "Sui" as the common designation for the empire (see Figure 11.3).

Li Yuan, the founding emperor, ceded his throne to Li Shimin, his second son, in the eighth month of the ninth year of Wude era (626 AD). At seventy, the retired emperor expired in the fifth month of the ninth year of Zhenguan era (635 AD). The *Biography of Emperor Gaozu* of the *New Book of Tang* concludes his narrative.

Figure 11.3 Portrait of Li Yuan

He was posthumously honored as Emperor Taiwu and given the temple name Emperor Gaozu. In the first year of Shangyuan, his posthumous title was revised to Emperor Shen Yao. In the eighth year of the Tianbao period, his posthumous title was further expanded to Emperor Shen Yao, the Great Sage. Then, in the thirteenth year of Tianbao, it was extended to Emperor Shen Yao, the Great Sage, the Great Brilliant Filial Emperor.

The revision of Li Yuan's posthumous title to "Emperor Shen Yao" in the eighth month of the fifth year of Xianheng (the reign title changed to Shangyuan in this month) aligns with both his aspirations prior to declaring himself emperor and his self-assessment after ascending to the throne.[22] Before his ascension, Li Yuan harbored grand designs of restoring a golden age akin to that of Emperor Yao within the Tang Dynasty. Upon becoming emperor, he saw himself as a ruler of virtue and sagacity, emulating Emperor Yao. By adopting the title "Tang" for his country, he aspired to establish a dynasty grounded in ethical governance, striving for a greatness in virtue reminiscent of Emperor Yao's storied reign, with the aim of ushering in a period of tranquility and flourishing that would parallel the fabled era of Emperor Yao (see Figure 11.4).

However, a challenging development arose during the fifth year of the Xianheng era, while Li Yuan's grandson, Emperor Li Zhi (the ninth son of Li Shimin), was in power. Plagued by illness, Emperor Li Zhi entrusted a considerable portion of imperial affairs to Empress Wu, also known as the Martial Empress. During this

Figure 11.4 The stone tiger at the Mausoleum Xian of Li Yuan, Emperor Gaozu of the Tang Dynasty

period, Empress Wu posthumously honored Li Yuan as Emperor Shen Yao and Empress Dou as Empress Tai Mu Shen. Duke Xuanjian (Li Xi) was posthumously honored as Emperor Xuan, Empress Zhang as Empress Xuan Zhuang, King Yi (Li Tianci) as Emperor Guang, and Empress Jia as Empress Guang Yi. Emperor Li Shimin was honored as Emperor Taizong, the Holy Emperor of Literature and Martial Arts, while Empress Changsun was honored as Empress Wen De, the Holy Empress of Virtue. More importantly, Empress Wu also adopted the titles "Tian Huang" (Heavenly Emperor) and "Tian Hou" (Heavenly Empress) for Emperor Li Zhi and herself, audaciously positioning themselves as supreme rulers. Though "Tian Huang" and "Tian Hou" were ostensibly used as unique titles to differentiate from those of previous emperors, Hu Sanxing incisively interpreted these titles as manifestations of Empress Wu's aspirations for prestige and authority.[23] This pursuit of esteem would propel Empress Wu's rise from "Heavenly Empress" to "Holy Mother, Divine Empress" and at one point, she even entertained the notion of transitioning the ruling dynasty from Tang to Zhou.

Notes

1 The so-called "Eight Pillar States" are described in Volume 16 of the *Book of Zhou*, which discusses the position of the Grand General of the Pillar States. It states that before the sixteenth year of the Datong era, there were a total of eight individuals who held

this position. Emperor Taizu was in charge of all government affairs and commanded the armies both in the capital and on the frontlines. Prince Xin of Guangling, Wei clan's esteemed relative, only had the responsibility of maintaining order within the palace. The other six individuals each supervised two Grand Generals and were in charge of commanding the imperial armies, providing a defense against external threats. At that time, they enjoyed great prestige and were unmatched in their status. Hence, when referring to influential families, they were collectively referred to as the "Eight Pillar States." According to this, among the Eight Pillar States, Yuwen Tai, a powerful figure in Western Wei, held the highest position, while Yuan Xin was more of a nominal figure, with the actual authority held by the other six Pillar States. Based on this, we can see the extent of Li Hu's influence and prestige. Additionally, according to Volume 16 of the *Book of Zhou*, Li Hu held the titles of "Commissioner-in-Chief, Grand Commandant, Grand General of the Pillar States, Grand Commander-in-Chief, Left Deputy Director of the Imperial Secretariat, Imperial Commissioner of the Longyou Region, Imperial Preceptor, and Founding Duke of Prefecture Longxi." Li Hu passed away in the seventeenth year of the Datong era of Western Wei (551 AD).

2 Chen Yinke, Collected Works of Jin Ming Guan, Shanghai Ancient Books Publishing House, 1980.

   Chen Yinke, Essays on the Political History of the Tang Dynasty, Volume 1, Shanghai Ancient Books Publishing House, 1982.

3 The citation from *Zizhi Tongjian* with Hu Sansheng's commentary states it was during the time of Emperor Min of Zhou, which is actually an error.

4 Chen Yinke, Discussions on the Issue of the Li Tang Clans, included in the Collected Works of Jin Ming Guan.

5 According to ancient Chinese history, the state of Qin in pre-Qin times held control over the region of prefecture Longxi. According to legends, the country established by Emperor Yao was also referred to as Longxi. In addition, in pre-Qin times, the states of Jin, Zhongshan, Wei, and Zhao also had periods of ruling over the territory of Zhaojun.

6 Chen Yinke points out the complexities in his essay, stating, "The name Zhongshan was used as a title for the Duke of Zhongshan during the Northern Wei Dynasty, as well as the title for the governor of the prefecture during the Northern Zhou Dynasty. However, when referring to these titles, the term 'jun' (郡) is omitted, such as using 'Zhongshan Wang' (King of Zhongshan) or 'Zhongshan Gong' (Duke of Zhongshan). Before Emperor Wu changed his title from Tian Wang (Heavenly Prince) to Emperor in August of the first year of the Wucheng era in the Northern Zhou Dynasty, the highest noble rank was the duke of a state. So, when Yuwen Hu was promoted from the Duke of Zhongshan Jun to the Duke of State, he was not given the title 'Duke of Zhongshan Guo.' This was not only because the name of Zhongshan was considered smaller compared to Jin, but it was also influenced by the customs of the Wei Dynasty, as they wanted to make a distinction. Hence, the title 'Duke of Zhongshan Guo' was not used in this context."

7 Chen Yinke, Discussions on the Issue of the Li Tang Clans.

8 In the pre-Qin era, there were three different states referred to as Tang. The first was the legendary state of Tang of Emperor Yao. The second was the state of Tang founded by Duke Ji Yu, the younger brother of King Cheng of Zhou (Note: in Chapter 8, there is a discussion on changing the name to Jin by Ji Xie). The third was the state of Tang of the Ji clan, which was one of the states established during the Zhou Dynasty. This state of Tang was located in the vicinity of Tang County, north west of Suizhou City in present-day Hubei Province. It was conquered by the state of Chu in 505 BC. The reason for affirming that the title of Duke of Tang held by Li Hu originated from the state of Tang of

Emperor Yao is that, firstly, the Tang under Shu Yu was short-lived, and secondly, there was a great geographical distance between it and the state of Tang that was destroyed by Chu.

 9 In the *Gazetteer of Yuanhe Prefectures and Counties*, in volume 17, it is mentioned that the county was originally named Guang'a during the Han Dynasty, then abolished during the Later Han Dynasty, and later reestablished as Guang'a County during the Northern Wei Dynasty. It also mentions the imperial mausoleums: Emperor Xuan, the 13th generation ancestor, built Liu Ling with a height of four zhang and a circumference of 80 zhang. Emperor Guang, the 12th generation ancestor, built Qiyun Ling with a height of four zhang and a circumference of 60 steps. Both mausoleums are located south west of the county, 20 li away, and share a perimeter of 156 steps.

10 According to the historical account in the "Ancient Music" in the *Lüshi Chunqiu*, the lineage of the Taotang clan preceded the Yellow Emperor, while Yao (Emperor Yao) came after the Yellow Emperor. There was originally a distinction between the two. However, the book *Shiben* mistakenly refers to Yao with the title of "Taotang clan."

11 Liu Qiyu, Continued Analysis of Ancient History, China Social Sciences Press, 1991.

12 In the context of the Han Dynasty's Taiyuan Commandery and Jinyang County, the Eastern Han scholar Zheng Xuan, in his commentary on the *Book of Songs*, stated that Tang was the ancient capital of Emperor Yao and that it corresponds to the present-day location of Taiyuan and Jinyang. He mentioned that Yao originally resided there before moving to Pingyang in Hedong. This view is supported by Ban Gu's *Book of Han* from the Eastern Han Dynasty, Du Yu's annotations on the *Spring and Autumn Annals* from the Western Jin Dynasty, and Li Daoyuan's *Shui Jing Zhu* from the Northern Wei Dynasty. On the other hand, the *Shi Ji* presents an alternate theory of east of the River Fen, and Zan of the Jin Dynasty and Yan Shigu of the Tang Dynasty, in their annotations on the *Book of Han*, propose the Yong'an theory. The *Shiben* and the *Collected Annotations of Shi Ji* support the theory of E, and the *Collected Interpretations of Shi Ji* support the theory of Pingyang. *Treaties on Geography* by Li Tai of the Tang Dynasty advocates the theory of Yicheng, while other theories include the theory of Yutai in present-day Shandong and the theory of Tangxian in present-day Hebei.

13 Liu Qiyu, Discussing the Origin of Xia Culture from the Original Settlement of the Xia People in Southern Shanxi, Continued Analysis of Ancient History.

   Wang Wenqing, The Possibility of the Taosi site as a Cultural Remnant of the Taotang Clan, Huaxia Civilization, Volume 1, edited by Tian Changwu, Peking University Press, 1987.

14 Geographical Records, Book of Han.

15 According to the analysis of oracle bone and bronze inscriptions, the character "唐" is composed of "庚" above and "口" below. The upper part "庚" represents a wind cabinet used to separate chaff from grain, while the lower part "口" signifies a vessel for storing grain. The original meaning of "唐" is "to receive and store grain under the wind cabinet." It is likely that the meaning of "magnificent" or "grand" emerged from the concept of separating chaff through the blowing wind. For further details, see Chen Zheng, Discussion on the Etymology of Characters, Guangxi People's Publishing House,1986.

16 Translated into vernacular Chinese, it can be rendered as follows: "Confucius said: How great is Emperor Yao! How lofty is he, with only heaven above him. Only Yao can emulate Heaven. The benevolence of Yao is so extensive that the people do not know how to praise him enough. How magnificent are the achievements of Yao! How splendid is the system of rituals and etiquette established by Yao!"

17 Tang Fengyan, The Feng Family's Notes on Events, Volume 4.
　　Biography of Wang Bo, Book of Tang.
18 Further details can be found in Chapter 5 and Chapter 6. Additionally, Gu Jiegang
　has compiled a "Genealogy Chart of the Yao Descendants in the Early Han Dynasty,"
　which includes Yao, Jianming, Liu clan, Liu Lei, Shi Wei clan, Du clan (Du Bo), Xi
　Shu, Shi Hui, Liu clan, Feng Gong, Zhi Jia (Huan), and Emperor Gaozu of Han. It is
　also mentioned "Shi Wei clan ... Tang clan." For more information, refer to Gu Jiegang,
　"Political and Historical Aspects of the Five Virtue Cycles," Gu Jiegang's Collection of
　Essays on Ancient History, Volume 3, Zhonghua Book Company, 1996.
19 Emperor Yang Guang of the Sui Dynasty suspected that Li Hun, the Duke of Cheng,
　was conspiring with his second son Min and would fulfill the prophecy. As a result, he
　exterminated their entire clan.
20 Hu Axiang, et al., A Brief Overview of Military Geography in Chinese History: The
　Land That Must Be Contended for by the Military, Hehai University Press, 1996.
21 The following incidents mentioned in Volume 2 of the *Annotations on Daily Life during
　the Founding of the Tang Dynasty* are worth noting in relation to the establishment of
　the Tang Dynasty: On the day of Jiazi in the seventh lunar month, an old man dressed
　in white robes met Li Yuan and addressed him as "Emperor of Great Tang." In August,
　on the day of Xinchou, a turtle-shaped green stone was discovered in Taiyuan with
　natural cinnabar inscriptions that read "Li Zhi will last for a myriad of generations."
　Li Yuan proclaimed, "This is a heavenly decree, bestowing ten thousand blessings."
　On the same day, a man named Kong Shanle from Xingping presented a bountiful
　harvest and offered it as a tribute. Li Yuan exclaimed, "A bountiful harvest is an auspi-
　cious sign. I have heard of such prophecies. It happened in the time of Emperor Yu and
　was achieved in the later generations by Shu Yu. Now, the Tang family is fortunate to
　witness this divine blessing. This gift from Xingping, presented by Shanle, is a remark-
　able occurrence." The phrase "Jia He Wei Rui" (auspicious grain as an omen of good
　fortune) and its relationship with the Tang Dynasty are discussed in detail in Chapter 8
　of this book
22 As it is well known, posthumous titles are honorary names given based on the achievements
　and virtues of the deceased, serving as a final judgment and evaluation. The system of
　posthumous titles originated during the Western Zhou Dynasty. Emperor Qin Shi Huang,
　however, abolished the practice of posthumous titles because he believed it had the draw-
　back of "sons judging their fathers and ministers judging their lords" (*Annals of Qin Shi
　Huang, Records of the Grand Historian*). He proclaimed himself as the "First Emperor,"
　with the intention of establishing a dynasty that would last for countless generations.
　The Han Dynasty later reinstated the system of posthumous titles. Regarding the posthu-
　mous titles of emperors, terms like "Wen" (cultured), "Wu" (martial), "Jing" (revered),
　"Ming" (illuminating), "Lie" (heroic), "Rui" (wise), "Kang" (prosperous), "Zhuang"
　(exemplary), and others are considered positive and commendatory. Terms like "Hui"
　(benevolent), "Ling" (enlightened), "Li" (cruel), "Yang" (extravagant), and others are
　considered negative and derogatory. Terms like "Ai" (mourning), "Huai" (sorrowful),
　"Min" (compassionate), "Dao" (lamenting), and others carry a sympathetic connotation.
　On the other hand, terms like "Xian" (offering), "Gong" (respectful), "Shun" (obedient),
　and the like, belong to the category of mockery from the victor to the defeated. Initially,
　posthumous titles consisted of a single word, but due to the difficulty of summarizing
　the achievements of an emperor in a single word, the practice of using multiple words
　for posthumous titles was developed. In the case of Li Yuan, the initial title "Emperor

Taiwu" clearly commended his achievements in founding and establishing the dynasty. The revised title "Emperor Shenyao" reflected the later emperors of the Tang Dynasty viewing Li Yuan as the reincarnation of Emperor Yao, considering him the contemporary equivalent of the ancient sage Emperor Yao. This reflects the alignment between Li Yuan's aspirations prior to proclaiming himself as emperor and his self-perception after assuming the imperial position.

23 Annals of the Tang Dynasty, *Zizhi Tongjian*, with commentary by Hu Sanxing of the Yuan Dynasty.

12 Zhou

The "Ancient Ancestor Ji Zhou" of the "Empress of the Holy Mother"

In August of 674, Emperor Li Yuan, founder of the Tang Dynasty, was posthumously named "Emperor Shen Yao." Empress Wu Zhao, who played a pivotal role, was concurrently bestowed with the title "Heavenly Empress." In September 690, Empress Wu Zhao renamed the dynasty from Tang to Zhou, and she became known as the "Divine Emperor of the Holy Mother." Subsequently, in February 705, Li Xian, her son with Li Zhi, reinstated the title to Tang.

The rationale behind Wu Zhao's decision to change the dynastic title from Tang to Zhou is not clearly recorded in historical documents. We are left to speculate based on various hints and clues.

Initially, in the first year of the Zaichu era (690), Wu Zhao invented a new character for her name, "Zhao," symbolizing the radiant sun and moon over the Divine Land.[1] The familiar epithet "Wu Zetian" arose after Emperor Li Xian honored Wu Zhao with the title "Grand Holy Emperor of Ze Tian" in the second month of the first year of the Shenlong era (705). In November, Wu Zhao was given the title "Grand Holy Empress of Ze Tian" according to her legacy. Emperor Xuanzong, Li Longji of the Tang Dynasty, later modified it to "Empress Ze Tian," which was subsequently expanded to "Holy Empress Ze Tian."[2] For the purpose of consistency I n this text, she will be primarily referred to as "Wu Zhao," her original name.

12.1 From Tang to Zhou: Diverse Explanations

Wu Zhao's father, Wu Shiyue, was from Wenshui in Bingzhou (present-day eastern Wenshui County, Shanxi Province). Initially a timber merchant, he served as a sergeant in the Yingyang camp during the late Sui Dynasty. Li Yuan, progenitor of the Tang Dynasty, "traveled through Fen and Jin, often lodging at his house. When the Banner of Righteousness was raised, Wu Shiyue joined the cause to pacify the capital."[3] At the dawn of the Tang Dynasty, he was made Minister of Public Works and later held governorships in Yuzhou, Lizhou, and Jingzhou. Wu Zhao's mother, Lady Yang, hailed from Huayin in Hongnong and was a daughter of Yang Da, a member of the Yang clan who served as General of the Right Military Guard and Minister of left Guanglu during the Sui Dynasty, and was posthumously granted the title of Minister of Personnel and the Marquis of Shi'an. After marrying his

DOI: 10.4324/9781003510390-13

first wife, Xiangli, Wu Shiyue wed Lady Yang. Through this union, they had three daughters, with Wu Zhao as the second daughter.

The rise of Wu Zhao to the palace and her ascension to empress are chronicled in the *Old Book of Tang*, within the Biography of Empress Ze Tian, as follows:

> Initially, at fourteen, Emperor Taizong (Li Shimin) summoned Wu Zhao to the palace because of her famed beauty, bestowing upon her the title "talented maiden." Upon Emperor Taizong's demise, she took vows as a nun at Ganye Temple. Emperor Gaozong (Li Zhi) encountered her there and recalled her to the palace, first elevating her to Luminous Consort, then to Concubine Chen. In the sixth year of Yonghui, upon the deposition of Empress Wang, Wu ascended as empress. Emperor Gaozong declared himself Heavenly Emperor, with Empress Wu assuming the title of Heavenly Empress. Known for her wisdom and literary acumen, Empress Wu actively engaged in politics. Suffering from frequent dizziness and headaches since the fifth year of Emperor Gaozong's reign (Xianqing era), he left all matters of state in the hands of the Empress for detailed adjudication. Henceforth, for several decades, she exerted imperial authority, jointly honored with the emperor as the "Dual Saints."

It is generally accepted that Wu Zhao's title of "Heavenly Empress" was a precursor to her covert revolutionary designs. Still, even prior to this initiation, her remarkable capabilities had been manifested. In the fourth year of Xianqing (659 AD), four years after her coronation as empress, Emperor Li Zhi, debilitated by headaches and impaired vision, gradually began to concede political control to Wu Zhao.[4] Accordingly, a decree issued mandated the transition of the *Records of Clans* to *Records of Surnames*. The *Zizhi Tongjian* details in the sixteenth volume of the Tang Annals for the fourth year of Xianqing:

> Initially, Emperor Taizong commissioned Gao Shilian and others to compile the *Records of Clans*, which was deemed fitting at the time. The book, however, neglected the origins and ambitions of the Wu clan; hence, Xu Jingzong and others petitioned for its revision. Consequently, Kong Zhiyue and others from the Ministry of Rites were appointed to refine the document, instituting a clan-based hierarchy of nine tiers, with the Wu clan ranked first, and other clans allocating into eight tiers according to their bureaucratic standing in the Tang Dynasty.

The 200-volume *Records of Surnames* has been lost, yet according to Volume 36 of the *Tang Hui Yao* (Laws and Institutions of the Tang Dynasty), the Wu clan and other distinguished lineages, such as Duke Xi, who abdicated the throne to Tang and ennobled as the Duke of Xi, were prioritized in the first tier. Consequently, both the paternal and maternal families of Wu Zhao were distinguished at the highest tier among the nine.

Belonging to the prestigious first tier implied either a notable familial heritage or an enduring lineage. Although Wu Zhao's maternal family was not directly descended from the Sui royal family, they wielded considerable clout, which is not elaborately discussed here.[5] Additionally, the *Genealogy of Chancellors* in the *New Book of Tang* reveals:

The Wu clan descended from the Ji clan. The youngest son of King Ping of Zhou bore with the character Wu in his hand, which thereafter became his surname. In the Han Dynasty, a military official named Wu served as the Prince of Zhao's consort … (spanning 19 generations) to the general of Northern Pacification, minister of the Five Weapons, and Duke of Jinyang, Qia, ennobled separately as the Marquis of Daling, granted 50 hectares of land and making his home there ... (spanning six more generations) to Wu Shiyou, Minister of Works, Duke of Yingguo.

Daling County, located north east of modern-day Wenshui County in Shanxi, was known as Shouyang County during the Northern Wei Dynasty. It was renamed Wenshui County during the Sui Dynasty. In the first year of the Chang'an period in the Zhou Dynasty (701), a monument named "Inscription for Emperor Gao of the Great Zhou, the Supreme, Filial, and Wise"[6] was established for Wu Shiyou. It reads:

Qi Feng (Duke Wen of Qi) received his mandate, and King Wu of Zhou sheathed the spears of the battlefield at Shang; Qiao Bo laid the foundation, and King Wen moved the ancestral cauldrons to the Han palace … Emperor Gao of the Great Zhou, the Supreme, Filial, and Wise, was a native of Wenshui, Taiyuan. His ancestors originated from the youngest son of King Ping of Zhou, who had the character "Wu" in his hand; hence, they adopted it as their surname and resided in Zhu Village of Pei County. The sixth-generation ancestor, Qia, served in Wei and was enfeoffed in Jinyang. His descendants settled in Wenshui and continued the family lineage.

The *Yuanhe Xingzuan* (Compilation of Surnames in the Yuanhe Era) by Linbao of the Tang Dynasty includes similar accounts. Accordingly, the Wu family, which was initially a timber merchant, ascended to become a new privileged and powerful family. With Wu Zhao as the empress, they even entered the high-ranking noble class and were recognized for their "good background," claiming descent from the youngest son of King Ping of Zhou (see Figure 12.1).

Note that Wu Zhao's maternal clan, the Yang family, also claimed descent from the Zhou Dynasty and the Ji clan, according to the "Monument of Emperess Gao of the Great Zhou, the Supreme, Filial, and Wise"[7] and the *Genealogy of Chancellors* in the *New Book of Tang*. The Ji clan was the royal family of the Zhou Dynasty. Both of Wu Zhao's paternal and maternal clans traced their origins to the Ji clan of the Zhou Dynasty, making them descendants of emperors of the Zhou Dynasty. Wu Zhao ascended to the throne and claimed emperor, changing the Tang Dynasty to Zhou; this should be considered the primary reason, namely, to highlight the origin of her clan.

This reason, though sometimes considered coincidental or even absurd by later generations, was underscored at the very beginning of Wu Zhao's Zhou Dynasty. For example, just four days after the renaming of the country to Zhou, "Emperor

Figure 12.1 The Temple of the Holy Mother of Empress Wu in Wenshui, Shanxi

Li Dan was appointed Crown Prince and bestowed the surname Wu"; on the fifth day, "seven temples for the Wu clan were established in the divine capital."[8] The seven temples include the progenitor Jichang, Emperor Wen of Zhou; the insightful ancestor, Ji Wu, the youngest son of King Ping of Zhou; Wu Shiyue, the venerable Emperor Gao, and the divine lords of the other four generations of the Wu clan.[9] Moreover, Wu Zhao once decreed changes from state to prefecture, but because the word for state (州) is homophonous with Zhou (周), some people said, "Your Majesty has initiated the revolution by abolishing the state, which is not auspicious," Wu Zhao promptly halted this. Wu Zhao also enacted that all of the Wu clan throughout the empire be exempt from taxes and corvée, changed Wenshui County to Wuxing County, allowing the common people and their descendants to inherit and restore their property. Such measures all belong to the clear actions of elevating "Zhou" and honoring "Wu."

The second reason for Wu Zhao's shift from the Tang Dynasty to the Zhou Dynasty was related to the feudal title of her father, Wu Shiyue. According to the "Monument of Emperor Gao of the Great Zhou, the Supreme, Filial, and Wise" and the *Zizhi Tongjian*, after Li Yuan initiated the uprising in Taiyuan during the 13th year of the Daye era of Sui, Wu Shiyue was first titled Duke of Kaiguo in Shouyang County. In the third year of the Wu De era of the Tang Dynasty, he was promoted to Duke Yingguo. After his death in the ninth year of the Zhenguan era, he was posthumously named Minister of Rites, with the title Duke of Loyalty and Filiality. In the sixth year of the Yonghui era, Wu Zhao was proclaimed empress. The following

February, Wu Shiyue was posthumously named Minister of State, and was bestowed the title Duke of Zhouguo. Later, Wu Shiyue was posthumously promoted to Grand Commandant and King of Taiyuan. In the first year of the Guangzhai era (684 AD), the Ancestral Hall of Wu Clan was built in Wenshui,[10] transferring the title of Grand Commandant and King of Taiyuan to Wu Hua, Wu Shiyue's father, while Wu Shiyue was posthumously honored as Grand Tutor and King of Wei. In the Yongchang era (689 AD), Wu Shiyue was posthumously honored as the Loyal and Filial Grand Emperor of Zhou. Subsequently, in September, Wu Zhao changed the Tang Dynasty to the Zhou Dynasty. This change followed the traditional practice of using feudal titles to signify a transition from the enfeoffment to the royal status during the Wei, Jin, Southern and Northern Dynasties, as well as the Sui and Tang Dynasties.

The third reason Wu Zhao used "Zhou" as the new title was to emphasize the legitimacy of succession from the Ji clan and the Zhou Dynasty. In the eleventh month of the first year of Yongchang era, Wu Zhao issued the "Decree of Amnesty at the Beginning of the New Era," which stated:

The people of the Xia Dynasty had their sovereign's mandate, yet it did not match the land rectification of the Shang Dynasty; the land rectification of Shang had its own distinction from the celestial mandate of the Zhou ... It is for this reason that I earnestly follow the rites and classics to fulfill the will of my predecessors. Now, considering the sequence of the three mandates, our state has obtained the celestial mandate. It is proper to establish the eleventh month as the first. Upon examination of the various arts, the rationale is clear. It is appropriate to designate the eleventh month of the first year of Yongchang as the first month of the first year of the new era and the twelfth month as the new intercalary month. Next year, the first month will be changed to January.

Following the tradition of the Ji Zhou Dynasty, the eleventh month was set as the standard start of the new year.[11] This was a deviation from the Tang Dynasty custom of the first month as the standard start of the new year. By reestablishing the Zhou Dynasty's system, Wu Zhao clearly demonstrated her respect and affiliation with the Zhou Dynasty, before even declaring herself emperor or founding her own state. This move was a clear attempt to align herself with the cultural and political legacy of the Zhou Dynasty.

As Wu Zhao adopted the system and calendar of the Zhou Dynasty, it became inevitable that changes would follow in how the Tang Dynasty regarded the descendants of the (Northern) Zhou and Sui dynasties. In the Tang Dynasty, these descendants were recognized as "nobles" and "honorable guests." Under Wu Zhao's reign, in addition to adopting the Zhou calendar, she altered the treatment of the Zhou and Han Dynasties' descendants. Now, the descendants of Shun, Yu, and Cheng Tang received the same reverence as the five ancestral generations from the Yu, Xia, Shang (also known as Yin), Zhou, and Han dynasties. This shift sought to adhere to the venerable practice of honoring a nation's founding ancestors.

Moreover, it underscored the continuity of the Wu Zhou imperial rule and its ties to the heritage of the three eras of the Ji Zhou Dynasty.

There were two significant developments concerning Emperor Wu Zhao's embrace of the system of the Zhou Dynasty. Firstly, in the third year of Xianqing era, she reformed several traditional ceremonies and instituted new rites, which deviated from long-held customs.[12] In the second year of Yifeng, she introduced the "Five Rites" modeled after the *Rites of Zhou*. Secondly, in the inaugural year of Guangzhai, upon declaring herself the sovereign, she restructured the six government departments (Personnel, Revenue, Rites, Military, Justice, and Public Works) into the six ministries (namely Heaven, Earth, Spring, Summer, Autumn, and Winter). Provincial offices, temples, and various official positions were renamed to better reflect the principles of the Zhou Dynasty. These overhauls revealed Wu Zhao's ambition to emulate the splendor of antiquity and perpetuate the legacy of the triumvirate of the Ji Zhou epochs.[13]

In conclusion, prior to her "revolutionary" measures, Wu Zhao had laid out extensive groundwork. This involved affirming the noble bloodlines of her Wu family and her mother's Yang family as descending from the Ji clan, granting her father Wu Shiyue, posthumously, the noble title of Duke of Zhou, and later labeling him the "Loyal and Filially Pious Great Emperor." She retraced the lineage of the Xia, Shang (Yin), and Zhou dynasties according to the chronicles of the Three Dynasties, with Zhou appropriately placed as the ruling lineage. She adhered to the rituals of Zhou and employed its calendar. Thus, should Wu Zhao choose to supplant the Tang Dynasty, she was well-prepared to found her dynasty under the name of Zhou.[14] Her profound affinity with the Zhou Dynasty had primed the concept of adopting "Zhou" as her country's appellation for imminent realization.

12.2 The Title of "Holy Mother Divine Emperor"[15] with Considerable Strategic Flexibility

On the solid groundwork of her meticulous preparations, Wu Zhao's revolutionary move to dethrone the Tang Dynasty and proclaim the Zhou Dynasty bore resemblance to Wang Mang's establishment of the Xin Dynasty during the erstwhile Han Dynasty. The *Zizhi Tongjian* specifically in the *Annals of Tang*, documents a momentous incident in the ninth month of the first year of the Chu Yuan era (690 AD):

> On the day of Bingzi, Fu Youyi, an imperial aide hailing from Ji County, led a contingent of over nine hundred individuals from the Guanzhong region to the imperial capital, presenting a petition for renaming the country as Zhou and for adopting the imperial surname of Wu. The Empress Dowager rejected the proposal and elevated Fu Youyi to a palace attendant's rank. Nonetheless, following his persistent appeal, sixty thousand officials, royal kin, societal elites, commoners, tribal leaders, monks, and Taoist priests all submitted memorials echoing Fu Youyi's plea to change the state's name and the imperial surname to Wu.

Four days post-petition, Wu Zhao granted their request. Two days henceforth, on the celebratory ninth day of the ninth month—aligning with the Double Ninth Festival—Wu Zhao publicly announced the transformation from the Tang Dynasty into the Zhou Dynasty and inaugurated the Tianshou era, heralding the birth of the Great Zhou Empire. At this pivotal juncture, Wu Zhao was 67 years old, having dedicated over half a century to this historic milestone.

Wu Zhao's engagement with the Li family of the Tang imperial court commenced in the eleventh year of Zhenguan era (636 AD), when she entered the palace as a 14-year-old concubine. Following Emperor Taizong, Li Shimin's demise in the twenty-third year of Zhenguan (649 AD), Wu Zhao was compelled to leave the palace and adopt the monastic life in the Buddhist nunnery. In the second year of Yonghui era (651 AD), Empress Wang, confronted by Consort Xiao's growing influence, orchestrated Wu Zhao's return to the imperial residence. Within the palace walls, Wu Zhao executed her strategies with precision, using her foes against one another, tirelessly climbing the sovereign echelon, ultimately overtaking Consort Xiao and Empress Wang, until she claimed the throne as the empress in the sixth year of Yonghui era.

Wu Zhao, upon becoming the new empress, was not content with merely holding the title. Preceding her, both Empress Dugu, consort to Emperor Wen of the Sui Dynasty, and Empress Changsun, consort to Emperor Taizong of Tang, had engaged actively in politics. With similar ambitions, Wu Zhao sought to also exercise political power. Additionally, the chronic illness[16] of Emperor Li Zhi provided her with the opportunity to partake in decision-making processes. Leveraging these circumstances, Empress Wu progressively expanded her political influence and ambition. In the eighth month of the fifth year of the Xianheng era (674 AD), under the guise of honoring the ancestors of the Li Tang imperial family and acknowledging Emperor Li Zhi, she conferred upon herself the exalted title of "Heavenly Empress," marking the first step in her covert coup.

In the twelfth month of the first year of the Hongdao era (683 AD), Emperor Li Zhi passed away. He was posthumously granted the title "Great Emperor of the Heavenly Sovereign" and the temple name Gaozong. Li Xian, Gaozong's seventh son, ascended the throne. Wu Zhao, as Li Xian's mother, attained the status of "Empress Dowager." According to Gaozong's will–which stated that the Empress's counsel should be sought in matters of national significance–Wu Zhao had a legitimate basis to govern. In February of the following year, Wu Zhao deposed Li Xian, granting him the title Prince of Luling, and instead installed Li Zhi's eighth son, Li Dan, as emperor. Wu Zhao, as his mother, presided over the state affairs from behind a screen at court gatherings. She ruled as Empress Dowager for five years, during which she suppressed the insurrection led by Xu Jingye, aimed at reinstating Li Xian. Wu Zhao appointed draconian officials, encouraged denunciations, and subdued dissenters who defied her.

In the fourth month of the Chuigong era (688 AD), Wu Chengsi inscribed proclamations on white stone–"The Holy Mother Reigns, Eternal Prosperity for the Empire"–and circulated a fabricated tale of its discovery from the River Luo. In the fifth month, Wu Zhao further elevated herself with the prestigious title of "Holy Mother Divine Emperor."

This title, "Holy Mother Divine Emperor," was symbolic and laden with profound meaning. "Holy" and "divine" signified Wu Zhao as the incarnation of sanctity and divine right, ordained to rule over the earthly domain. "Mother" and "emperor" reflected her dual role, being both the mother of the sitting emperor and the sovereign herself. At this point, she effectively acted as the ruler and was positioning herself to formally assume the title. Yet, she hesitated to oust the figurehead emperor, Li Dan, preferring to gauge the realm's response. The title "Holy Mother Divine Emperor" afforded her strategic flexibility–she could eventually drop "mother" to solely claim the mantle of "emperor," or retain the dual title as needed.

Nonetheless, Wu Zhao's ambitious motives met with staunch resistance from the Li Tang royal lineage. In the eighth month of the year, Li Chong, governor of Bozhou, and Li Zhen, governor of Yuzhou, retaliated by mobilizing forces. Meanwhile, Li Yuanjia, the governor of Zhangzhou, and Li Yuangui, the governor of Qingzhou, covertly plotted their support. Wu Zhao dispatched her military, decisively quelling the revolts. This action removed the last impediments to her Dynasty's impending change. In September of 690 AD, Wu Zhao formally ascended the throne, abdicating the Tang Dynasty and inaugurating the Zhou Dynasty, now revered under the title "Divine Holy Emperor."

This title, "Divine Holy Emperor," evolved from her previous title, omitting "mother" while keeping "holy" and "divine" to perpetuate Wu Zhao's divine persona. This aura was instrumental in captivating the populace and legitimizing her claim to the throne.

The legitimization of Wu Zhao's rule, alongside the transition from Tang to Zhou, was characterized by her adept manipulation of public perception, and she particularly leveraged her affiliation with Buddhism. Lady Yang, mother of Wu Zhaoling, was a devoted Buddhist, and Wu Zhao herself was "greatly reverent towards Buddhist teachings and desired to embrace them."[17] Incidentally, Buddhism provided Wu Zhao with a significant influence on power and became a theoretical tool enabling her imperial ambition. Chen Yinke's *Wu Zhao and Buddhism* elaborates on this connection:

> The Confucian doctrine restricts women's involvement in governance ... Wu Zhao, in her pursuit to transition from Tang to Zhou, harnessed Buddhist symbols and predictions. Although original Buddhist scriptures demeaned the status of women, such views shifted over time. In subsequent Mahayana Buddhism texts, discussions included women attaining enlightenment and becoming Chakravartin, or 'wheel-turning,' holy kings. In promoting herself, Wu Zhao circulated the "Dayun Jing" (Great Cloud Sutra), recognized as a Mahayana text of the time.

The "Dayun Jing," from the Later Liang Dynasty, mentions in its fourth volume, "The Buddha tells Queen Pure Light ... despite being a woman, you will rule a large kingdom beneath the Chakravartin King." The sixth volume predicts, "Seven hundred years after my Parinirvana, a small country in southern India will witness

... the birth of a princess. Following the king's unexpected death, officials will request her regency. Upon accession, she will conquer the world, and Jambudvipa will unite under her rule, unopposed." This provided a foundation for sycophantic monks like Huaiyi and Faming to reinterpret these scriptures with fresh commentaries, positing Wu Zhao as the reincarnation of Maitreya Buddha and rightful leader of the human world. Court scholars such as Ji Yingfu and Song Zhiwen zealously championed these ideas. Hence, Wu Zhao not only relied on favorable omens and celestial commands but also on Buddhist "symbols and predictions" that rationalized the need for a "revolution." Following the coup's success, an edict mandated the erection of a "Dayun Temple" in each capital and province soon after, enshrining the "Dayun Jing" and authorizing monks to publicly interpret it. Moreover, during the second year of the Tianshou era (691 AD), the "Regulations on the Superiority of Buddhism over Daoism" were enacted.

The grand cloud unfolds the secret of the glorious kingdom; it is a symbol of prosperity and the manifestation of extraordinary achievements. It heralds the beginning of a revolutionary era and initiates the course of renewal.

As is well-known, the emperors at the beginning of the Tang Dynasty all claimed Laozi (Li Er) as their distinguished ancestor. Emperor Gaozong (Li Zhi) even posthumously honored Li Er with the title of Emperor Xuan Yuan, thus establishing Daoism's supremacy over Buddhism. Accordingly, since Buddhist "talismans and prophecies" became so closely intertwined with the Wu Zhou revolution, it was inevitable that Buddhism would be revered while Daoism was suppressed.

Moreover, after the revolution, the titles bestowed upon Emperor Wu Zhao of the Zhou Dynasty, such as the Holy Emperor of the Divine Golden Wheel, the Holy Emperor of the Divine Golden Wheel Transcending Antiquity, the Holy Empress Ci of the Divine Golden Wheel Transcending Antiquity, and the Holy Emperor of the Heavenly Commissioned Divine Golden Wheel, all bore connections with Buddhism (with the "Divine Golden Wheel" being an emblem of the Buddha's radiance) and Maitreya Buddha (the name "Ci" refers to Maitreya, following its Sanskrit interpretation). The mention of "Heavenly Commissioned" reflects a similar emphasis on the Confucian concept of divinely sanctioned imperial authority, much like Wu Zhao's agenda in renaming the era "Tianshou," marking her initiative to overhaul the Tang order and underscore that the ruler's mandate was heaven-bestowed (see Figure 12.2).

To encapsulate, Wu Zhao's remarkable ascent commenced in 636 AD when she was selected to join the imperial harem, culminating in her revolutionary seizure of the Tang Dynasty in the year 690 AD. Her extraordinary path unfolded over a span that included 11 years as a talented maiden, 4 years in religious seclusion as a Buddhist nun, 3 years graced with the rank of Zhaoyi (one of the nine concubines of the second rank), 28 years as the empress consort, and 7 years as the empress dowager. Ultimately, transcending the limitations of her gender in an epoch dominated by imperial male sovereignty and a patriarchal social order, Wu Zhao emerged as the sole and unchallenged female emperor throughout the extensive annals of China's dynastic history.

Figure 12.2 The Luohan Buddha in the Fengxian Temple of the Longmen Grottoes in Luoyang, believed to be the incarnate form of Emperor Wu Zhao

In the first month of the year of Shenlong (705 AD), amidst the backdrop of the "Coup of the Five Princes" and her own severe illness, Emperor Wu Zhao ceded the imperial throne to the Crown Prince Li Xian.[18] Once Li Xian became emperor, he did not hastily erase Wu Zhao's imperial title but continued to honor his abdicated mother with the title of "Grand Holy Emperor of Ze Tian."

In February of 705, Li Xian "restored the title of Tang, maintaining everything as it was before including the altars of earth and grain, the ancestral temples, imperial tombs, suburban sacrifices, military flags, official uniforms, names of the heaven and earth, sun and moon, terraces, and official titles, all in accordance with the customs prior to the Yongchun period. The divine capital remained as the Eastern Capital, the Northern Capital was the Supreme Commander's Mansion in Bingzhou, and Laozi was still venerated as the Emperor Xuan Yuan."[19] Thus, the Li Tang Dynasty was restored, and the Wu Zhou Dynasty became a thing of the past.[20]

Again in November of 705, the then nominal and 82-year-old "Holy Emperor Zhao of Heaven" Wu Zetian passed away in solitude, leaving very contemplative final wishes: her burial with the imperial title removed, referred to as "Grand Holy Empress of Ze Tian." The groundbreaking Empress who established herself, Wu Zetian, was most concerned at her last moments with being posthumously worshiped at the ancestral temples of the Li family and being interred with her husband, Emperor Gaozong, at Qianling Mausoleum, abandoning the imperial title and reverting to the position of an empress named after her husband. This surely reflects the power of traditional patrilineal inheritance, ancestor worship, and Confucian teachings. Of course, Wu Zhao's infinite wishes entrusted in the temple offerings from Zhou to Tang ultimately could not be realized. The restored Li Tang Dynasty, while enduring in name until March 907, was eventually supplanted by Zhu Wen's Later Liang Dynasty.

Notes

1 At the same time or around that time, Wu Zhao also modified the writing of approximately 20 very important characters (天, 地, 日, 月, 年, 君, 臣, 圣, 人, 国, and the like.), such as 地 being written as 埊, 国 as 圀, and so forth. These characters later became known as the "Wu Zhou new characters."

2 In other words, "Zetian" is neither Wu Zhao's given name nor the characters representing her name. Therefore, referring to Wu Zhao as "Wu Zetian" is a combination of surname and honorific title, a rather unconventional designation.

3 Biography of Empress Wu Zetian, Old Book of Tang. For the sake of brevity, the following citations in this chapter are mainly taken from "Biography of Empress Wu Zetian" in the *Old and New Book of Tang*, as well as from the *Zizhi Tongjian* (Comprehensive Mirror for Aid in Government) and the annotations by Hu Sanxing.

4 In *Annals of Tang* in the *Zizhi Tongjian*, in October of the Fifth Year of Xianqing, it is recorded: "The emperor initially suffered from severe dizziness and heavy head, unable to see clearly. When court matters were reported, sometimes he would have the empress make decisions. The empress, being intelligent and knowledgeable in literature and history, handled her affairs with great wisdom. As a result, she began to be entrusted with political matters, sharing power with the ruler." Hu Sanxing's annotation stated: "The historical account reveals the shift of Tang Dynasty's power to the empress, and it was during this time that her influence solidified."

5 Please refer to "Biography of Prince Xiong of Guande" in the *Book of Sui* and "Biography of Yang Shao" in the *History of Northern Dynasties* for more details.

6 In the second year of the Shengli era of Zhou (699 AD), the name of the mausoleum of Wu Shiyue was changed to Panlong Terrace, thus this stele is also known as the "Panlong Terrace Stele." The text was composed by Li Qiao and approved by Wu Zhao. It can be found in Volume 249 of the *Complete Works of Tang*.

7 In Volume 239 of the *Complete Works of Tang*, there is the "Inscription and Preface for the Great Zhou's Supreme Filial and Wise Empress Dowager Stele," written by Wu Sansi.

8 In 684 AD, the Eastern Capital Luoyang was renamed as the Divine Capital, but in 705 AD, it was restored to its former name.

9 According to Zhang Zhaoyuan in the "Records of Rituals" of the *Old History of the Five Dynasties*, he believed that during the reigns of Emperor Gaozong and Empress Wu Zhao, the Tang Dynasty adopted the title of Zhou, established seven ancestral temples, and retroactively honored Duke Wen of Zhou as their progenitor. Zhang regarded this as the misguided behavior of flatterers who lacked understanding of historical truth. The establishment of the ancestral temple for the Wu family by Empress Wu Zhao was seen as a departure from established norms and was ridiculed by many.

In addition, in Hu Sanxing's annotation of the *Annals of Tang* in the *Zizhi Tongjian*, he pointed out that Empress Wu "distantly claimed ancestral connections to the Zhou royal family, which was a serious distortion. Would Duke Wen of Zhou truly approve of these sacrificial rites to the ancestors?"

10 According to the "Royal Regulations" of the *Book of Rites*, the emperor would have seven ancestral temples, while the feudal lords would have five. Empress Wu Zhao originally intended to follow the request of Wu Chengsi and establish seven ancestral temples for the Wu family. However, her ministerial officials advised against it.

11 "正" represents the beginning of a year, while "朔" represents the beginning of a month. "正朔" refers to the New Year's Day.

12 Changsun Wuji, an elder statesman and trusted minister during the reign of Emperor Taizong, and also the uncle of Emperor Gaozong, strongly opposed the establishment of Empress Wu Zhao. In the fourth year of the Xianqing era, he was falsely accused of plotting rebellion and was forced to commit suicide.

13 According to the perception of the people in Tang Dynasty, only the Zhou and Han dynasties were considered golden ages. Among them, the Zhou Dynasty was regarded as superior to the Han Dynasty. It was said that "the Zhou Dynasty used the way of kings, with a single teaching and people following it, while the Han Dynasty was a mix of hegemonic rule, with strict laws and regulations, but also filled with hypocrisy and worldliness. Therefore, being praised by close relatives is better than being feared, and the Wen and Jing eras are inferior to the Cheng and Kang eras" (Zhang Shuo's "Response to the Critiques of Verse Scholars," in the *Complete Works of Tang*, Volume 224).

14 In the year before establishing the state title as Zhou, Wu Zhao issued the "Decree of Amnesty at the Beginning of the New Era" (Volume 96 of the *Complete Works of Tang*), which stated: "Confucius said, 'If there is someone who can continue the Zhou dynasty, it can be known even after a hundred generations.'" … From the Wei Dynasty to the Sui Dynasty, almost four hundred years have passed, with numerous emperors and empresses, dozens of families rising to power. They all claimed to uphold the principles of kingship but established their own private authority, initially relying on deception and force before emphasizing benevolence and righteousness. Their achievements did not surpass those of small vassal states, and their virtues did not shame the hegemonic ambitions. Even though they managed to unify the feudal lords for a period, uniting the regions, the establishment of the Jin Dynasty by Emperor Wu of Jin, and the greatness and accomplishments of Emperor Wen of Sui cannot compare to the achievements of the Qin Dynasty. So how can someone as insignificant as me take the place of the three great dynasties?"

   Examining the meaning of the text, it can be inferred that Wu Zhao's revolution was in response to the statement in the "Analects of Confucius" about "continuing the Zhou dynasty." The "Inscription for the Great Zhou's Supreme Filial and Wise Emperor" mentions the "sacred Zhou dynasty" and the unique connection with the divine, receiving the mandate for a thousand sacrifices and shining for hundreds of generations. This aligns with Wu Zhao's intentions. Furthermore, in Wu Zhao's view, none of the states from the Wei Dynasty to the Sui Dynasty can be considered as the third great dynasty. Naturally, their state names were not suitable for adoption. Additionally, in terms of the meaning and significance of the state title, "Zhou" is a noble and inspiring choice that is not inferior to "Tang" and may even surpass it.

15 This section refers to the scholarly works of Sun Yongru, titled "Wu Zetian's Titles and Politics," presented at the Fifth National Academic Conference on Wu Zetian in October 1994, and Chen Yinke's "Wu Zhao and Buddhism," included in the "Collected

Manuscripts from the Gold-Bright Hall, Volume 2," published by Shanghai Ancient Classics Publishing House in 1980.

16 "The chronic illness (feng ji)" could possibly be severe hypertension and dysfunction of the vestibular system."

17 Wu Zhao, "Preface to the Holy Teachings of the Tripitaka," the Complete Works of Tang, Volume 97.

18 Zhang Jianzhi, Cui Xuanwei, Jing Hui, Huan Yanfan, and Yuan Shuji led the imperial guards into the forbidden palace, executed Wu Zhao's inner favorites Zhang Changzong and Zhang Yizhi, and welcomed Crown Prince Li Xian to the throne. The five of them were subsequently all ennobled as kings. This event is historically referred to as the "Coup of the Five Princes."

19 Annals of Emperor Zhongzong, Old Book of Tang. The Yongchun era, from February 682 to December 683, was the last reign title of Emperor Gaozong (Li Zhi).

20 Interestingly, although Li Xian restored the state title to Tang, he still retained the era name of Shenlong and did not claim to be the restorer of the dynasty. In June 710, Li Xian passed away, and his son Li Chongmao ascended the throne, only then did the era name change to Tanglong.

13 Five Dynasties and Ten Kingdoms
Inheritance and Division

On the first day of the fourth month in the year 907, the Great Tang Dynasty founded by Li Yuan came to an end when Emperor Li Zhu abdicated to Zhu Wen, who then took the imperial throne and established the Liang Dynasty. The Liang Dynasty marked the beginning of the "Five Dynasties," which were successively followed by the Tang, Jin, Han, and Zhou dynasties. This period lasted for a total of 54 years, culminating in the usurpation of the Zhou Dynasty by Zhao Kuangyin, who established the Song Dynasty in January 960. To distinguish these five regimes from previous dynasties, they were respectively referred to as the Later Liang, Later Tang, Later Jin, Later Han, and Later Zhou. All were located in the Central Plains and claimed legitimacy. Historians later regarded them as legitimate, integrating their histories into the epoch known as the "Five Dynasties and Ten Kingdoms Period."

Almost concurrently with the "Five Dynasties," various separatist regimes arose across the southern regions, along with the Northern Han in Hedong, collectively known as the "Ten Kingdoms." The Ten Kingdoms period concluded in May 979 when Emperor Zhao Kuangyi of the Song Dynasty vanquished the Northern Han, reuniting the empire.

The "Five Dynasties and Ten Kingdoms Period" between the unified Tang and Song dynasties represented another era of fragmentation akin to previous periods such as the Three Kingdoms, the Sixteen Kingdoms of the Eastern Jin Dynasty, and the Southern and Northern Dynasties. Whereas the Central Plains experienced incessant conflict and fleeting reigns during the Five Dynasties, the nine southern kingdoms and the Northern Han generally had longer periods of stability due to their respective policies emphasizing border security and the welfare of their people. Each of these disparate states originated from varying circumstances and bore certain similarities. The briefly summarized historical accounts given here draw upon sources such as the Old and New *History of the Five Dynasties*, the *Zizhi Tongjian*, and further annotations from Hu Sanxing of the Yuan Dynasty, as well as the *Spring and Autumn Annals of the Ten Kingdoms* by Wu Renchen of the Qing Dynasty.

DOI: 10.4324/9781003510390-14

13.1 Succession of the Five Dynasties:

1. Liang: In April 907, Zhu Wen,[1] formerly known as a Jiedushi (governor of one or more provinces in charge of both civil and military affairs during the Tang Dynasty) in Xuanwu, crowned himself emperor and made Bian (present-day Kaifeng, Henan) the capital. This new state was named Liang, harking back to a time when it was known as Liang during the Warring States period. Initially part of the rebel forces under Huang Chao, Zhu Wen defected to the Tang when he realized Huang Chao's regime was failing. With Li Keyong, he quickly subdued Huang Chao's forces in merely two years, but later plotted to assassinate Li Keyong—his very benefactor—only to be discovered and become enemies with the Li family. From that point on, Zhu Wen controlled Henan while Li Keyong controlled Shanxi. Later, Zhu Wen managed to seize control of the Tang imperial court, eradicated the regional warlords in Hebei, and executed the eunuchs who surrounded the Tang emperor. With the removal of these two scourges — the regional warlords and the eunuchs — the Tang Dynasty effectively came to an end.

   Zhu Wen's hometown was in Wugou of Dangshan, Songzhou (present-day Dangshan County, Anhui), which during the Warring States period was part of the state of Liang. The Tang Dynasty appointed Zhu Wen as the governor of Xuanwu, with the administrative center in Bianzhou (modern-day Kaifeng, Henan), which was also ancient Daliang.[2] As Zhu Wen's power grew, he was ennobled as King of Liang, and when he eventually founded his own dynasty after deposing the Tang, he established the state title as Liang.

2. Tang: Li Cunxu, son of Li Keyong, established the Later Tang Dynasty. The Li family hailed from the migrating Shatuo[3] nobility and initially had the surname Zhu Xie. Following the Turks' defeat by the Tang, the Luo and Pugu Turkic tribes were relocated under Xue Yantuo's governance. Emperor Taizong (Li Shimin) conquered Xue Yantuo and established a Governor's office there. When Tubo captured this office, chieftain Zhu Xie Jinzhong led his people eastward and eventually perished while being pursued by Tubo forces. Zhu Xie's eldest son Zhiyi returned to Tang and led the "Shatuo Army," renowned for its cavalry archery prowess. Zhiyi's successor, Chixin, later took part in quelling Pang Xun's rebellion during Emperor Yizong's reign, and was awarded for his loyal service with titles "Commander-in-chief of the Shanyu Protectorate and Military Governor of the Zhenwu Army." He was also granted the royal name Li Guochang, and henceforth enrolled as a subject.

   Li Keyong, son of Li Guochang, supported the Tang against Huang Chao before being appointed as the Military Governor of Hedong, based in Taiyuan, and later titled King of Jin. Post-Tang usurpation by the Later Liang, Li Keyong and his son Li Cunxu contended with the Later Liang for the Central Plains. In April 923, Li Cunxu proclaimed himself Emperor, establishing the state known as Tang (historically referred to as Later Tang). His choice of the Tang name was clearly an exploitation of favorable conditions given that the imperial Li family of the Tang Dynasty had conferred the Li surname and recognized their subject status. Both Li Keyong and Li Cunxu considered themselves descendants of the Tang dynasty, using the call to "restore the Tang" as their rallying cry, believing themselves to be the rightful successors of the Tang with a divine mandate to rule China.[4] In October 923, Li Cunxu finally conquered Later Liang and made Luoyang his capital.

3. Jin: The Jin Dynasty's founder, Shi Jingtang, was a member of the Shatuo tribe. His father, Nie Lengji, had served Li Guochang and Li Keyong and had risen to military school officer. Under later Tang Emperor Mingzong, Shi Jingtang[5] advanced through the ranks to become Prefect of Taiyuan, Garrison Commander of Beijing, and Jiedushi of Hedong, wielding significant military power from his Taiyuan base.

In November 936, with the support of Khitan Emperor Yelü Deguang, Shi Jingtang was proclaimed Emperor of Jin (later known as Later Jin) outside Liu Lin, the north gate of Taiyuan. As a condition of their alliance, Shi Jingtang promised to cede the sixteen cities of Youzhou and Jizhou to the Khitan (the official handover took place in 938) and offer an annual tribute of 300,000 bolts of silk. He recognized the Khitan ruler as the "Father Emperor" and referred to himself as the "Son Emperor." In the intercalary eleventh month, Jin conquered Later Tang. In 937, the Jin Dynasty established its capital in Bianzhou. According to Hu Sanxing's Annotations in the first volume of *Annals of Later Jin* in the *Zizhi Tongjian*: "The Shi family originated from the north and followed the King of Jin to Taiyuan, rising to power in the Central Plains from Taiyuan. As Taiyuan was the seat of government for Jin, the Khitan followed suit, and thus the state was named Jin."

4. Han: In early 947, the Khitan entered Bianzhou and appointed Shi Zhonggui (the nephew of Emperor Shi of Later Jin) as the Marquis Fuyi, leading to the downfall of Later Jin. In February, the Khitan changed the state name to Liao. Liu Zhiyuan, the Garrison Commander of Beijing and Jiedushi of Hedong of Later Jin, ascended the throne in Taiyuan, denouncing the incompetence and political corruption of Shi Zhonggui and aiming to continue the Jin legacy and gain the support of former Jin officials. Liu Zhiyuan abandoned the era name Kaiyun used by Shi Zhonggui and retained the era name Tianfu used by Shi Jingtang, without changing the state name. In March, faced with widespread resistance from the people of the Central Plains, the Khitan Emperor left Bianzhou and returned north, while Jin's civil and military officials relocated to Taiyuan. In June, Liu Zhiyuan entered Bianzhou and renamed the state as Han (Known as Later Han), and the following year, he established the era name as Qianyou. Liu Zhiyuan's decision to change the name from Jin to Han was based on geographical, ethnic, and personal considerations. From a geographical perspective, having already possessed the Central Plains and established the capital at Bianzhou, the name "Jin," with its strong regional connotations, seemed rather narrow. From an ethnic standpoint, the Jin had compromised on a significant principle by submitting to the Khitan (Liao) under the nominal designation of "son." Furthermore, examining the situation from their own position,

Liu Zhiyuan "originally belonged to the Shatuo tribe and resided in Taiyuan. Upon gaining control of China, he adopted the surname Liu, thus claiming to be a descendant of King Huaiyang, Liu Bing, the eighth son of Emperor Xianzong (Liu Zhuang) of the Eastern Han Dynasty, and he named his state 'Han.' He traced his lineage back to Emperor Gaozu (Liu Bang) as the high ancestor, and Emperor Guangwu (Liu Xiu) as the founding ancestor." In this way, facing the context of a powerful foreign adversary in the Khitan to the north, multiple states vying for power to the south, and a surge in ethnic sentiment in the Central Plains region, Liu Zhiyuan's assertion of lineage from Liu Bang, Liu Xiu, and Liu Zhuang and adopting "Han" as the state name served multiple purposes: it asserted the legitimacy of his reign, underscored the national righteousness, and demonstrated a claim to a heritage with distinct origins.

5. Zhou: Less than five years after the establishment of Later Han, a power struggle ensued within the court. Emperor Liu Chengyou of Han plotted against Guo Wei, the military commander stationed in Yedu (present-day north eastern Daming County, Hebei). Eventually, Guo Wei led his troops south, entered Bianzhou, and Liu Chengyou was killed by unruly soldiers. This marked the end of the Later Han and the rise of Guo Wei's Zhou Dynasty. Guo Wei, originally from Yaoshan, Xingzhou (present-day Longyao County, Hebei), had served as the military commander and chief of staff in the Capital Yedu of Later Han, as well as the Jiedushi of Tianxiong and the leading chancellor. In January 951, Guo Wei ascended the throne, set his capital in Bianzhou, and named his state Zhou (known as Later Zhou). According to the *Annals of Emperor Taizu of Later Zhou* in the *Old History of the Five Dynasties,* upon his ascension to the imperial throne, Guo Wei declared: "I am a distant descendant of the Ji clan, a progeny of Guo Shu. With accumulating blessings and meritorious deeds that resonate with the light of heaven, my profound virtue has extended through a hundred generations, and now the great mandate has once again been bestowed upon my modest self. Thus, it is fitting for my newly established state to be named 'Great Zhou.'" Additionally, in the *Annals of the Later Zhou* of the *Zizhi Tongjian*, Hu Sanxing's commentary states: "The Zhou Dynasty claimed descent from Guo Shu of the ancient Zhou. During the Spring and Autumn and Warring States periods, historical records referred to the descendants of Guo Shu who had their own states as 'Duke Guo,' but later they were called 'Duke of Guo.' The sounds 'Guo' and 'Zhou' are phonetically similar. Gong Ziqi, a high-ranking official of the Yu state, stated: 'Guo Zhong and Guo Shu were venerable uncles of King Ji.' As the Guo clan originally took its surname from the Zhou dynasty, it was thus appropriate to name the new state 'Zhou.'" Ten years later, in January 960, the Later Zhou was supplanted by the Song Dynasty.

13.2 Division of the "Ten Kingdoms"

1. Wu. In August 892, Yang Xingmi, a native of Hefei in Luzhou (present-day Hefei, Anhui), secured the position of Jiedushi of Huainan and took control of Yangzhou (present-day Yangzhou, Jiangsu). In March 902, having held the

traditional Wu region of Huainan and Jiangdong, he was granted the title of King of Wu by the Tang Dynasty. In April 919, Yang Xingmi's second son, Yang Wo, ascended the throne as the King of Wu, and established a royal court with officials, ancestral temples, imperial shrines, and palaces. The state observed civil and military practices conforming to those of the emperor. In November 927, Yang Xingmi's third son, Yang Pu, became the emperor, maintaining the title of Wu, with its capital at Jiangdu (present-day Yangzhou, Jiangsu). In October of the year 937, Xu Zhigao accepted the "abdication" from the emperor of Wu, leading to the demise of Kingdom Wu.

2. Tang: In October 937, Xu Zhigao was enthroned at Jinling (present-day Nanjing, Jiangsu), initially adopting the state name of Qi. Born with the surname Li and a native of Xuzhou, he was orphaned at an early age and adopted by Yang Xingmi. Subsequently, he became the adopted son of Xu Wen, the Chancellor of Wu, thus changing his surname to Xu. Following Xu Wen's death, Xu Zhigao gradually assumed control over Wu's political landscape. Initially titled Duke of Xunyang, his title was changed to Duke of Yuzhang, and he was later promoted to King of Donghai. In 935, he was named King of Qi, with Sheng and Run as his fiefs.[6] In 937, as the King of Qi, Xu Zhigao accepted the "abdication" from Emperor Yang Pu of Wu and renamed the state Qi. However, in February 939, Xu Zhigao renamed the state to Tang (known as Southern Tang), adopted the surname Li, with the given name Yi and the style name Ming. He fabricated a genealogy to claim descent from the Tang Dynasty. The *Annotation of Zizhi Tongjian* by Hu Sanxing recorded that, in the second year of Tianfu, "Xu Zhigao professed to be a descendant of the royal family of Li, and took the grand title of the Tang Dynasty, thus changing the country's name to Tang."[7] Southern Tang existed until November 975, when it was replaced by the Song Dynasty.

3. Wuyue: Qian Liu, founder of the Kingdom Wuyue, was a Lin'an native in Hangzhou (north of today's Lin'an City, Zhejiang Province). Toward the end of the Tang Dynasty, he earned distinction in quelling the Huang Chao Rebellion. In September 893, he was appointed Jiedushi of Zhenhai and Governor of Runzhou (located in present-day Zhenjiang City, Jiangsu Province, which was not then under control of the Qian family). Qian Liu eventually took command over the thirteen prefectures of the two Zhejiang provinces. In October 896, he received further elevation to the position of Jiedushi of Zhenhai and Zhendong. In May 901, the title of King of Pengcheng was conferred upon him. The following year, the Tang Dynasty commended, "Qian Liu, the King of Pengcheng, possesses wisdom and martial prowess capable of pacifying the people and settling turmoil; his virtue is such that he can assist in national governance. His domain includes the former territory of King Goujian of Yue." Consequently, Qian Liu was appointed King of Yue. In April 904, he requested to be titled King of Wuyue, but the imperial court declined, instead asserting, "When King Fuchai of Wu faced instability, he dared not supplant the Zhou Dynasty. When Sun Quan of Eastern Wu sought power, he still recognized the Han Dynasty. Likewise, with your repute and virtue within this great nation, you

will surely assist in overcoming adversities and rectifying the realm, achieving unification." Hence, Qian Liu was named King of Wu. In May 907, recognizing the traditional regional designation "Wuyue,"[8] the Later Liang Dynasty conferred upon Qian Liu the title of King of Wuyue. While some may have advised refusal, he accepted, remarking, "How could I not emulate Sun Quan's accomplishments?" Consequently, the Qian family established Hangzhou as its capital, wielding the dual titles of Wu and Yue for the kingdom that lasted until May 978. Qian Liu's grandson, Qian Chu, then surrendered to the Song Dynasty, bringing the Kingdom Wuyue to its close.[9]

4. Chu: The founder of the Kingdom Chu was Ma Yin, a native of Yanling in Xuzhou (present-day Yanling County, Henan Province). In September 896, the Tang court appointed Ma Yin as the Governor of Tanzhou (located in present-day Changsha City, Hunan Province). By 898, he was promoted to the position of Jiedushi of Wu 'an. By 899, Ma Yin had consolidated his control over the regions north of the Five Ridges and had extended his authority over all of Hunan. In April 907, Zhu Wen usurped the Tang Dynasty and founded the Later Liang Dynasty. Ma Yin was granted the title of Duke of Chu for sending envoys, offering tributes, and his efforts in persuading others to recognize the new dynasty, as his domain was within the historical boundaries of the state Chu during the Qin Dynasty. In June 927, the Later Tang Dynasty further recognized Ma Yin as the King of Chu. In August, he established the Kingdom Chu with Changsha as its capital, built palaces, and formed a government mirroring the imperial court. The Kingdom Chu fell to the Southern Tang Dynasty in November 951.

5. Min: In August 886, Wang Chao, hailing from Gushi in Guangzhou (present-day Gushi County, Henan Province), seized control of Quanzhou and submitted to the Tang Dynasty, receiving appointment as the Governor of Quanzhou. In May 893, he asserted control over Fuzhou and proclaimed himself "Liuhou" (regent).[10] Recognizing his dominion over the five provinces of Fujian, the Tang court named him Guanchashi (Commissioner) of Fujian. In September 896, he was honored as the Jiedushi of Weiwu. After Wang Chao's death due to illness in 898, his brother Wang Shenzhi succeeded him. In April 904, Wang Shenzhi was ennobled as the King of Langya. In 909, the Later Liang Dynasty titled him King of Min. In 926, Wang Yanzhan, Wang Shenzhi's son, capitalized on the Later Tang Dynasty's instability, declaring Min a perennial kingdom and establishing the Kingdom Min in October. He announced himself as King of Min and organized his court in the manner of an emperor. Wang Yanjun, Wang Yanzhan's brother, succeeded the throne in January 933, sustaining the Min dynasty and selecting Changle (current Fuzhou, Fujian Province) as the capital. The historical legacy, tied to Minyue and the Seven Min tribes, influenced the choice of "Min" as the name of the kingdom. The Southern Tang Dynasty conquered the Min Kingdom in August 945.[11]

6. In 904 AD, Liu Yin, from Pengcheng (present-day Xuzhou City, Jiangsu Province), was appointed as the Jiedushi of Qinghai during the Tang Dynasty. In May 907, after pledging loyalty to the Later Liang Dynasty, he was named

King of Dapeng. As noted in Hu Sanxing's comments on the *Zizhi Tongjian*, since Emperor Wu of the Song Dynasty, Liu's family had flourished south of the Yangtze River, adopting "Liu from Pengcheng" as their surname. In October 908, Liu Yin became the Jiedushi of both Qinghai and Jinghai. Renamed as the King of Nanping in April 909, he rose to King of Nanhai in 910, securing rule over Lingnan. After Liu Yin's demise in 911, his sibling Liu Zhi succeeded and severed ties with the Later Liang Dynasty in 915. Liu Zhi ascended the throne in Panyu (now Guangzhou, Guangdong Province) as the ruler of Yue, a name resonating with the Hundred Yue territory, in August 917. Liu Zhi had a particularly strong fixation on titles and names, "and he was fond of grandiosity." After he ascended the throne, he first changed his name to Yan, then to Gong, and then again to a newly created character Yan 龑, which was coined from the meaning of "the flying dragon in the sky" found in the *Book of Changes*. This obsession with titles and names was also reflected in the name of the state. In November of 918, Liu Yan changed the name of the state to Han (historically known as Southern Han). The reasons behind changing the state's name from Yue to Han included: firstly, Yue had an overly distinct regional characteristic, and the region of Baiyue had been traditionally considered a land of barbarians; using Yue as the state's name lacked grandeur. Secondly, since Liu Yan himself hailed from Pengcheng, and his brother Liu Yin had been conferred the title of King of Dapeng, it was meaningful to note that the Liu family of Pengcheng included the Emperor Liu Yu of the Southern Dynasty, who claimed descent from the 21st generation of Liu Jiao, Prince Chuyuan, a brother of Emperor Gaozu, Liu Bang. Thus, by adopting Han as the name for his regime, Liu Yan had historical foundations and familial reasons to do so. Thirdly, Liu Yan "felt ashamed to be the chief of barbarians and also denouncing emperors of the Central Plains as governors of Luozhou."[12] Liu Yan's ambition was not merely to rule over Lingnan but to replace "the emperors of the Central Plains," an aspiration that could not be encompassed by the name Yue. Lastly, since the end of the Tang Dynasty, "the world was in chaos, the scholars from the central court thought of the remote regions beyond the mountains as places of refuge, and many traveled there. Notable officials from the central plains who were exiled to the south often had descendants who lived on, or contemporary officials who were caught in tumults and could not return; they all stayed in the region beyond the mountains." As Liu Yin was courteous to and appreciative of learned men, Liu Yan also relied heavily on these scholars and dignitaries from the central plains. Abandoning Yue in favor of Han—a name politically more prestigious and ethnically more authentic—was likely in line with the desires of this group of officials, helping to consolidate his rule. In February of the year 971, Han was conquered by the Song Dynasty.

7. In October 891, Wang Jian, who hailed from Wuyang (presently Xiyang County in Henan Province), became the Jiedushi of the south western province of Sichuan. By October 897, Wang Jian had extended his control to encompass the south eastern part of Sichuan, known as Jiannan Dongchuan, effectively ruling the entire province as we know it today.[13] In August 903, he was bestowed the

title of King of Shu by the Tang Dynasty. In 907, amidst the turmoil of the Later Liang Dynasty, Wang Jian proclaimed himself an independent sovereign and established his capital in Chengdu, using the regnal name of Shu (historically known as Former Shu). In 916, the ruler of Shu, Wang Jian, revised the era name to Tianhan and temporarily adopted the regnal name of Han. However, in the first year of the Tianhan era, and specifically in December, he announced a general amnesty and reverted to the next year's era name Guangtian, along with the regnal name of Shu.

Wang Jian initially adopted the title of Shu due to his dominion over the Shu territory, aligning himself with its historical significance as the King of Shu. The ancient state of Shu during the pre-Qin era spanned the western part of today's Sichuan Province, north of the Yangtze River, and the south western area of Shanxi Province. Following the Han Dynasty, the term 'Shu' broadly referred to the region Shu in the pre-Qin era. Thus, when Wang Jian declared himself emperor, he chose to maintain this time-honored title. The transient switch to 'Han' was an attempt to align with Liu Bei's legacy and resonate with the local sentiment towards the Han Dynasty overseeing the Shu people. Nevertheless, according to the "Biography of Wang Jian" in the *Old History of the Five Dynasties*, the name 'Han' was less fitting due to Wang Jian's surname, making the title temporary until reverting back to Shu. Ultimately, in November 925, the Later Tang Dynasty overran the Former Shu.

8. Shu: Following the Later Tang Dynasty's conquest of the Former Shu in November 925, Meng Zhixiang, originating from Longgang of Xingzhou (now Xingtai City, Hebei Province), was appointed the prefect of Chengdu and served as the Jiedushi of Jiannan Xichuan. By February 933, Meng Zhixiang had also taken on the role of Jiedushi for Jiannan Dongchuan and Xichuan, and was honored with the title of King of Shu. In the intercalary month of January 934, Meng Zhixiang declared himself emperor in Chengdu and preserved the regnal name of Shu (historically referenced as Later Shu). The Song Dynasty brought about the conquest of the Later Shu in January 965.

9. Nanping (Jingnan): In May 907, Gao Jichang, a native of Yanshi in Shaanxi Province (currently Dongnan Township of Shan County in Henan Province), was named the Jiedushi of Jingnan by the Later Liang Dynasty and garrisoned in Jiangling (now Jiangling County, Hubei Province). The Later Liang Dynasty conferred upon Gao him the title of King of Bohai in August 913. The Later Tang Dynasty then bestowed upon Gao Jixing[14] the title of King of Nanping in March 924, and historically, he is associated with both Nanping and Jingnan. The Song Dynasty absorbed the Nanping territory in February 963 since Gao Jixing's dominion previously formed part of the state Chu during the pre-Qin era, and the region was known as State of Jing[15] during the pre-Qin, Qin, and Han dynasties. In the *Spring and Autumn Annals of the Ten Kingdoms* by Wu Renchen of the Qing Dynasty, it is noted that "At the beginning of the Song Dynasty, Lu Zhen compiled the *Chronicles of the Nine Kingdoms*, and he did not include Nanping, reasoning that since it was confined to just a corner around Jiangling, it did not warrant recognition as an independent state. Later, Zhen's

grandson Lun continued the work and produced the *Chronicle of Jingnan*, which finally completed the *Chronicles of the Ten Kingdoms.*" During the reign of Emperor Shenzong, Liu Shu authored the *Annals of the Ten Kingdoms*, evidently following the example of the *History of the Five Dynasties*. Therefore, despite Gao Jichang never claiming the imperial title, later histories often consider his state one of the "Ten Kingdoms."

10. Han: In January of the year 951, Guo Wei founded the Later Zhou Dynasty as a successor to the Later Han Dynasty. Liu Chong, the younger brother of Emperor Gaozu of the Later Han, and the military governor of Beijing and commander of Hedong Circuit declared himself emperor in Taiyuan. He continued using the regnal title of the Han Dynasty, thus establishing the Northern Han Dynasty, as denoted in historical records. This action was emblematic of the legitimate continuation of Liu Zhiyuan's legacy and was also a denunciation of the Later Zhou's illegitimacy. As the Emperor professed, "We carry on with the pursuits of our forebears, who have now fallen. We are compelled to assume this title," implying that the current dynasty recognized the decline of its predecessor and sought to perpetuate the imperial lineage. In May 979, the Song Dynasty ended the Northern Han Dynasty's rule.

Notes

1 Before assuming the title of emperor, this person's original name was Wen, which was later changed to Quan Zhong. After becoming emperor, the name was changed again to Huang.

2 During the Warring States period, King Hui of Wei moved the capital from Anyi (now north west Xia County, Shanxi Province) to this place. Later, the name of the capital became the name of the country, which is why Wei is also called Liang. For more details, please refer to the *Records of the Grand Historian* and the *Studies of the Seven States*, Volume 5, by Dong Yue of the Ming Dynasty.

3 The Shatuo tribe was a separate branch of the Western Turkic Khaganate and originally resided in the Western Regions. During the middle to late Tang Dynasty, some of them migrated to the central plains.

4 According to *Annals of Tang Dynasty* in the *New History of the Five Dynasties*, after Li Cunxu proclaimed himself emperor, he established seven ancestral temples in Taiyuan. Among them, four ancestral temples were dedicated to the emperors of the Li Tang Dynasty (Emperor Gaozu Li Yuan, Emperor Taizong Li Shimin, Emperor Yizong Li Ci, and Emperor Zhaozong Li Ye). Later, when Li Siyuan (a member of the Shatuo tribe and originally named Miao Jile, adopted son of Li Keyong) assumed the imperial title as the regent of Later Tang, there was a discussion about whether to establish a new national name as it was believed that "the fortune of the Tang Dynasty has faded, and it is appropriate to establish a new national name." Li Siyuan asked his attendants, "What should be the national name?" They replied, "The late emperor bestowed the surname Tang upon us, and we seek revenge for Tang. After succeeding Emperor Zhaozong, we are still called Tang. The people of the Liang Dynasty do not want your Majesty to be called Tang." Li Siyuan said, "I served my ancestor (Li Guochang) at the age of thirteen, who treated me as his own children. I also served Emperor Wu (Li Keyong) for nearly thirty years, and the former emperor (Li Cunxu) for over twenty years... The

foundation of Emperor Wu is my foundation, and the empire of the former emperor is my empire as well. How can we be of the same family but different nations!" At that time, the Minister of Personnel, Li Qi, also expressed his opinion, saying, "If we change the national name, then the former emperor will become a passerby. Where will the imperial ancestral temple find its support!" Therefore, the national name of Tang was retained unchanged (referring to *Annals of Later Tang* in the Zizhi Tongjian, and *Annals of Emperor Mingzong* in the *Old History of the Five Dynasties*.

5 In Hu Sanxing's annotation of *Annals of Later Jin* in the *Zizhi Tongjian*, he stated: "He was surnamed Shi, but the origin of how he acquired this surname is not known."

6 In the year 915, Xu Wen, a powerful minister of the Kingdom Wu and a native of Qushan in Haizhou, was granted the title of Duke of Qi. Qushan in Haizhou is located in the south west of present-day Lianyungang City, Jiangsu Province, and is part of the traditional "Qi" region. Xu Wen was granted the title of Duke of Qi based on this. In 919, Xu Wen was further promoted to the title of King of Donghai. In 927, after Xu Wen's passing, he was posthumously honored as the King of Qi.

7 According to *Annals of Later Jin* of the *Zizhi Tongjian*, there is a mention of Xu Zhigao taking the throne of Wu and adopting the national name of Tang in the second year of Tianfu. However, it is doubtful if this information is accurate. This is in accordance with the *Annals of Emperor Liezhu of Southern Tang* in the *Annals of the Ten Kingdoms*.

8 The ancient states of Wu and Yue were centered around the present-day areas of Jiangsu and Zhejiang, with interconnected territories and similar customs. Since ancient times, Wu and Yue have been collectively referred to as the "land of Wu Yue."

9 It is worth noting that the Qian family of Wu Yue never claimed the imperial title; therefore, in a nominal sense, they were not independent kingdoms. Similar to this, there is Chu and Nanping, among others, which are referred to as the "Ten Kingdoms." For more details, please refer to the subsequent information.

10 During the middle to late period of the Tang Dynasty, when the sons or trusted officials of military governors (jiedushi) acted as deputies, they held the titles of "Jiedu Liuhou" or "Guancha Liuhou," which roughly translate to "Governor's Deputy" or "Observer Deputy." Afterward, the imperial court would often appoint them as official military governors (jiedushi) or observers (guanchashi) to assume the full responsibilities of the position.

11 In February 943, Wang Yanzheng, the Prince of Fusha in the Kingdom Min, declared himself emperor in Jianzhou (modern-day Jian'ou City, Fujian Province) and adopted the national name Yin. He engaged in conflict with his brother, Emperor Wang Yanxi. In March 944, a minister named Zhu Wenjin killed Wang Yanxi and proclaimed himself as the King of Min. In early 945, the old loyalists of Min killed Zhu Wenjin and invited Wang Yanzheng to become the Emperor of Min. Wang Yanzheng retained Jianzhou as the capital but changed the national name from Yin to Min.

12 Biography of Liu Zhi, the Old History of the Five Dynasties. Here, "emperors of the central plains" refers to the Tang Dynasty established by the Shatuo tribe in Luoyang.

13 During the Tang Dynasty, there was a military governorship of the Jiedushi of Jiannan. Later, it was divided into two military governorships: Jiannan Dongchuan (Eastern Sichuan) and Jiannan Xichuan (Western Sichuan), commonly known as Dongchuan and Xichuan (Liang Chuan). After the Song Dynasty defeated the Later Shu, the region was divided into two circuits: Xia (Gorges) and Xichuan. It was later further divided into four circuits: Yizhou, Zizhou, Lizhou, and Kuizhou, collectively known as the Chuanxia Four Circuits. It was later simplified to be called Sichuan Circuit. During the Yuan Dynasty,

the Sichuan Administrative Province was established. This is the origin of the present-day name Sichuan Province.

14 The name Gao Jixing is actually Gao Jichang, who changed his name to avoid the taboo of the Later Tang Dynasty founder Li Guochang.

15 In ancient times, the State Chu was initially established in the Mountain Jing (present-day western Nan Zhang County, Hubei Province) during the Western Zhou Dynasty. The origin of its national name is described in the *Shuo Wen Jie Zi*: "Chu, a clump of trees, also known as Jing. It consists of the radical 'lin' (forest) and has the phonetic 'pi'." Chu is like a foot (pi) among the clump of trees (lin). Duan Yucai, in his commentary on the *Shuo Wen Jie Zi*, suggests that "Chu" and "Jing" are different names for the same concept. State Chu was alternatively referred to as "Jing" or "Jing Chu," indicating the association with plants similar to the Jing (common name for certain plants). Gu Jiegang, in his article "Discussion on Ancient History in Response to Mr. Liu Hu," argues that the people of Chu established their country in the forest, which was filled with Jing (thorns), thus giving rise to the name "Chu," which is also linked to the plant called "Jing." Xu Zhongshu, in his work "Further Discussion on Bashu Culture," points out that the people of Chu planted a type of thorny bush called "Wood of Chu" around their villages as a defensive measure, hence the name. In the book *The Bamboo Slips of the Warring States Period in the Collection of Tsinghua University*, compiled by Li Xueqin, in the section of "Chu Residences," it is recorded that Bi Li, the wife of Xue Xiong, the first monarch of Chu, faced difficulties during childbirth and died after a Cesarean section, while the child, Li Ji, survived. After Bi Li's death, the witch-doctors buried her wrapping with Jing branches. To commemorate Bi Li, later generations named their country "Chu." This further confirms that the national name "Chu" is derived from the plant "Jing."

14 Song

Moments of Serendipity

As mentioned above, from May 979 to February 1127, the Song Dynasty can be considered the dominant power in China during that time. This period of dominance began in January 960 with the founding of the Song Dynasty and lasted until its end in February 1279. In January 960, only nine years after Guo Wei's rebellion and the establishment of the Later Zhou Dynasty, Zhao Kuangyin staged a military coup in Chenqiao, draped with the imperial yellow robe, established the Song Dynasty, and adopted the reign title of Jianlong. This marked the end of the "Five Dynasties" period and the beginning of the Song Dynasty. By that time, the era marked by a swift turnover of rulers beginning with Wang Mang's seizure of the Han Dynasty, followed by successive waves of turmoil, including multiple abdications during the Five Dynasties period, had finally settled. In February 963, the Song Dynasty conquered the Kingdom Jingnan. In January 965, they conquered the Later Shu. In February 971, they absorbed the Southern Han. In November 975, they annexed the Southern Tang. In May 978, the Kingdom Wuyue surrendered to the Song Dynasty. Finally, in May 979, the Song Dynasty conquered the Northern Han. The downfall of the Northern Han marked the end of the "Ten Kingdoms" period and the reunification of the Central Plains under the Song Dynasty.

After the reunification of the Central Plains, the imperial rule was known as the Northern Song Dynasty, which lasted until the Jingkang Incident in 1127 when it fell to the Jin Dynasty. In May of the same year, Prince Kang of Song, Zhao Gou, ascended the throne in Nanjing (present-day Shangqiu City, Henan Province) and adopted the reign title of Jianyan. The restored Song court after the Jingkang Incident is commonly referred to as the Southern Song Dynasty, as it ruled from its southern capital, paralleling the Eastern Jin Dynasty, which was established after the War of the Eight Princes during the Western Jin Dynasty.

During the Southern Song Dynasty, while confronting the Jin Dynasty in the north, it maintained control over approximately half of the historic Chinese territory. In January 1234, after the fall of the Jin Dynasty, the Mongols declared war on the Southern Song. In January 1276, Emperor Gong of Song surrendered the imperial seal and submitted a surrender letter to the Mongol-led Yuan Dynasty,[1] resulting in the invasion of Lin'an (present-day Hangzhou, Zhejiang Province) by the Yuan forces. In March 1279, at the Battle of Yamen, the Song forces suffered

DOI: 10.4324/9781003510390-15

a definitive defeat, and the Chancellor, Lu Xiufu, accompanying Emperor Bing, drowned himself and the young emperor in the sea, thus bringing an end to the Southern Song Dynasty.

The unified imperial dynasty established by Zhao Kuangyin, known as the Song Dynasty, had its capital at Kaifeng (present-day Kaifeng City, Henan Province). The relatively secure imperial court rebuilt by Zhao Gou had its capital at Lin'an.[2] The distinction between Northern Song and Southern Song arises from the geographical locations of their respective capitals–Kaifeng in the north and Lin'an in the south. However, both dynasties were known by the same dynastic title, "Song," without differentiation.

In the history of Chinese national titles, "Song" has significant importance in two aspects:

Firstly, starting from the Song Dynasty, the origins of dynastic titles in the Central Plains—such as Song, Yuan, Ming, and Qing—were no longer related to nobility titles. This contrasted with the situation in previous dynasties, where many dynastic titles were derived from the titles of prior regimes. The main reason for this change lies in the nature of dynastic transitions, with internal abdication or "Shan rang" within the ruling elite being common previously, while the Song and later dynasties mainly rose to power through external conquest or rebellion.[3] In the book: *China: Tradition and Transformation*, American scholars John K. Fairbank and Edwin O. Reischauer noted that "the Song Dynasty perfected the civil service system, leading to greater stability within the Chinese government. Zhao Kuangyin's coup in 960 was the last instance of a Chinese emperor being overthrown by generals, empresses, or powerful ministers. After 960, such internal usurpations ceased, and dynasties instead were overthrown by foreign conquests or popular uprisings."[4]

Secondly, it can be argued that, comparatively, the national title "Song" and its associations with fire, virtue, and the color red have had a significant impact on the latter part of Chinese history, influencing movements such as the "Song Loyalist" movements against the Yuan Dynasty and the Red Turban Rebellion, as well as the "Restore Ming" movement and the activities of the Heaven and Earth Society during the early Qing period. These historical phenomena demonstrate the continuing legacy and influence of the Song Dynasty's emblematic attributes.

14.1 The Title "Song" Originated from the Name of the Governing Prefecture

In the *Annals of Emperor Taizu* in the *History of the Song Dynasty*, it is recorded that "in the spring of the first year of Jianlong, in the first month on the Yisi day, there was a general amnesty, and the era name was changed. The official name of the country was established as Song."

Additionally, in Volume One of the *Collected Imperial Edicts and Commands of the Song Dynasty*, there is a decree titled "Decree of General Amnesty upon Emperor Taizu's Ascension to the Throne." It states:

In ancient times, King Wu of the Zhou Dynasty established grand titles to conform with the will of the people. Emperor Liu Bang of the Han Dynasty and Emperor Li Yuan of the Tang Dynasty took their titles from their noble positions and the establishments of their respective kingdoms. Therefore, the country's name should be 'Da Song' (Great Song).

These records indicate that, in accordance with historical tradition, rulers of China often chose national titles that conveyed legitimacy, conformity, and adherence to the will of the people. However, the specific reason for the choice of the national title "Song" is not explicitly stated in these documents.

Historical records such as the *Annals of Emperor Shizong* and *Annals of Emperor Gong* in the *Old History of the Five Dynasties*, and *Annals of Emperor Taizu* in the *History of the Song Dynasty* reveal that Zhao Kuangyin, born in 927 in Zhuozhou (present-day Zhuozhou City, Hebei Province), was from Jiamaying of Luoyang. He and his father, Zhao Hongyin, commanded the Forbidden Army during the Later Zhou Dynasty.

In the sixth year of the Xiande era (959), in June, Emperor Shizong of Zhou, Chai Rong, appointed Zhao Kuangyin as Commander of the Imperial Army and conferred upon him the titles of Imperial Preceptor and Jiedushi of Zhongwu. After Chai Rong's death, his seven-year-old son, Chai Zongxun (Emperor Gong of Zhou), ascended the throne. In July, Zhao Kuangyin was appointed as the Jiedushi of Songzhou and retained the previous titles. He was further ennobled as the Marquis of Kaiguo. The following year, in January, with the support of his army, Zhao Kuangyin forced Chai Zongxun to abdicate, and the Song Dynasty was established, succeeding the Later Zhou Dynasty.

According to Volume One of the *Compilation of the Continuing Chronicle of Zizhi Tongjian*, Zhao Kuangyin's usurpation of power from the Later Zhou was relatively swift and smooth. On New Year's Day of the seventh year of the Xiande era (960), the border regions falsely reported that the Khitan and the Northern Han allied forces were invading from the north, and the Chancellor of the Later Zhou Dynasty, Fan Zhi, dispatched Zhao Kuangyin to lead the army against the enemy. On the second day, the vanguard departed, and on the third day, the main army left the city and stayed overnight at Chenqiao Courier Station (present-day Chenqiao Town, Fengqiu County, Henan Province). From early morning on the fourth day until evening, a mutiny among the soldiers took place. With the support and instigation of Zhao Kuangyi (Zhao Kuangyin's younger brother) and Zhao Pu (the secretary of the Guiding Army), Zhao Kuangyin was dressed in the yellow robe of sovereignty. He then returned to the capital with his troops, where the court officials prostrated themselves, and he assumed the position of emperor (see Figure 14.1).

The key to Zhao Kuangyin's usurpation lay in his significant position as the chief Commander of the Imperial Army stationed in front of the palace. Emperor Shizong of Zhou, Chai Rong, created the Dian Qian Bureau, with the chief officer being the Dianjian, who commanded the central imperial guards—a formidable

Figure 14.1 The place where Zhao Kuangyin donned the yellow robe at Chenqiao Relay
Station

force that not only safeguarded the palace but also served as the main military force
for territorial conquest.

During the late Tang Dynasty, the prolonged rule of regional warlords led to a
situation where military officers seized power and proclaimed themselves as feudal
governors. This trend continued during the Five Dynasties and Ten Kingdoms
period, culminating in the self-proclamation of emperors. Zhao Kuangyin leveraged
this situation, swiftly proclaiming himself the sovereign and choosing "Song" as
the national title, primarily because he personally governed a prefecture called
"Songzhou." As confirmed in Volume One of the *Compilation of the Continuing
Chronicle of Zizhi Tongjian*, Bi Yuan of the Qing Dynasty clearly states, "A decree
was issued to establish the national title as 'Song,' derived from the name of the
prefecture he governed."

Prefecture Songzhou was initially established in the 16th year of the Kaihuang
era of the Sui Dynasty (596 AD) with its capital in Suiyang (renamed Songcheng
in the 18th year of the Kaihuang era, present-day Nanshi, Shangqiu City, Henan
Province). It was renamed Prefecture Liang in the third year of the Daye era of
the Tang Dynasty but reverted to Songzhou in the fourth year of the Wude era. In
the first year of the Tianbao era, it was renamed Prefecture Suiyang but returned

to Songzhou in the first year of the Qianyuan era. From the mid-Tang Dynasty on, Songzhou was a seat of Jiedushi, successively hosting the Xuanwu Army and the Guiding Army.[5]

In July 959, Zhao Kuangyin, previously the Jiedushi of the Guangwu Army (governing Xuzhou, present-day Xuchang City, Henan Province), was appointed as the Jiedushi of the Guiding Army to defend the capital. Given that the Guiding Army was based in Songzhou, he was also referred to as the Jiedushi of Songzhou.[6] Consequently, as the supreme commander of a regional military force, Zhao Kuangyin had direct control over Songzhou and stationed his troops there.

Although Zhao Kuangyin served as the commander of the central imperial guards stationed in the capital, with little direct involvement in Songzhou over 100 kilometers away, holding the title of Jiedushi of Songzhou was prestigious and signified the highest regional office he had attained before seizing power from the Later Zhou Dynasty. Consequently, the phrase "the nation's fortune soars to Song"[7] gained currency, underscoring why "Song" was chosen as the dynastic title.

Upon declaring Song as the dynastic title, Songzhou's status soared. *The Treatise on the Nine Regions during the Yuanfeng Era* records that in the third year of Jingde era (1006 AD), Songzhou was promoted to Yingtian Fu, and Songcheng County to Cichi. By the seventh year of the Dazhong Xiangfu era (1014 AD), Yingtian Fu became Nanjing, with Songcheng County named Zhengchi. Despite being at the same administrative level as the prefecture state, the status of Fu was superior. "Yingtian" encapsulated the sentiment of the country's fortune favoring Song, as affirmed in the "Decree to Elevate Songzhou to Yingtian Fu," which highlighted Songzhou as the emperor's foundational land. The decree emphasized respect for sacred ancestors and a plan initiated with auspicious intentions. Significant in the imperial examinations, where the imperial guards and talented individuals were marshaled per imperial mandates, the title "Yingtian" aptly celebrated Divine Martial accomplishments and the dynasty's ascendancy.[8] "Nanjing" functioned as the capital outside of the Eastern Capital, Prefecture Kaifeng. The decree invoked the nation's ancestral artistry and a historical lineage that tracked back through Binyang and Chongling, paralleling the Tang Dynasty's origins in establishing a new capital.[9] With Zhengchi and Cichi ranking highest among counties, the extraordinary elevation of Songzhou and Songcheng County reaffirmed the fact that the national title "Song" originated there.

14.2 Coincidences and Tenuous Analogies Often Yield Post Hoc Interpretations

Zhao Kuangyin's role as the Guiding Army's commander in Songzhou may have been a chance event in the country's eventual naming. Yet, this simple fact fell short of the Song literati's cultural and psychological expectations. For them, the grand title had to embody deeper cultural significance. The historical, geographical, astronomical, and etymological coincidences provided various possibilities for the people of Song to create associations and provide explanations that were more culturally meaningful.

14.2.1 Coincidence One: Songzhou was the ancient state of Song's capital during the pre-Qin era

Established as Songzhou in the 16th year of Kaihuang era during the Sui Dynasty, the county seat changed to Songcheng two years later. Its nomenclature harkens back to the pre-Qin state of Song. The *Records of the Grand Historian* recount how Prince Wei was installed in Song by Duke Zhou to maintain the Yin Dynasty's ancestral sacrifices. The founder of the Song Dynasty, known as Qi (or "Kai" to avoid taboo with Emperor Jing of Han, Liu Qi), was a half-brother to King Zhou of Shang. Initially titled Prince Wei, he fled turmoil in the Shang Dynasty and eventually surrendered to Zhou. Crowned Duke of Song and recognized as Shang's successor, he established the Song capital in Shangqiu,[10] strategically placed to assimilate Shang's descendants and maintain Zhou's influence. With the capital's shift to Pengcheng in the Warring States period, Song persisted for 800 years until State Qi conquered it in 286 BC. Thus, the literati connected the imperial Song Dynasty to the ancient capital of Song, although they considered this linking initially undesirable, as it related to surrender. Yet, such lineage tracing continued, reaching back to Gaoxin's eldest son, Yan Bo,[11] an ancestor of the Three Dynasties.

14.2.2 Coincidence Two: Yan Bo resided in Shangqiu and worshiped the Great Fire

In the complex and elusive lore of ancient history, it is commonly believed that Qi, the progenitor of the Shang Dynasty, was the offspring of Emperor Ku and Queen Jiandi. This detail appears in the *Annals of Yin* in the *Records of the Grand Historian*:

> Qi of Yin, born to Jiandi, a daughter of secondary consort Lady Youji to Emperor Ku.

The assertion of Qi being Emperor Ku's son is corroborated by other historical texts, such as the *Lineage of Emperors*, the *Book of Rites* by Dai De, and the *Chronicles of Emperors*. According to the *Annals of the Five Emperors* in the *Records of the Grand Historian*, Emperor Ku was among the revered Five Emperors and a direct descendent of the Yellow Emperor. Emperor Ku was also recognized as Gaoxin. As the *Shuowen Jiezi* confirms, "Xie, son of Gaoxin, who was Minister of Education under Yao, stands as the progenitor of Yin." Moreover, Mao's commentary on the *Book of Songs* from the Western Han Dynasty records, "Tang's ancestor, daughter of Jiandi, was coupled with the Yellow Emperor's descendant, Emperor Gaoxin ... from whom Qi was born."

In this genealogy, Yan Bo was Gaoxin's eldest son and a distant forebear of the Shang clan. *The First year of Duke Zhao* in the *Zuo Zhuan* states,

> In bygone times, Gaoxin sired two sons. The elder was Yan Bo; the younger, Shi Shen. Residing in Kuanglin, the siblings clashed, leading to war. Subsequently, losing imperial favor of the Hou Di, Yan Bo resettled to Shangqiu to oversee

celestial observations of Chen. Hence, the Shang people deemed this meaningful, associating celestial observation of Chen with the Shang constellation.

Thus, the correlation between Gaoxin, a Shang ancestor, and his firstborn, Yan Bo—relocated to Shangqiu as a stargazer—further amplifies the narrative constructed by Song literati about the Song nation's title and its cultural import.

In the *Ninth Year of Duke Xiang* in the *Zuo Zhuan*, it is stated:

The Duke of Yan Bo safeguards the flame in Shangqiu. They honor the Great Fire through rituals, tracking its cycles diligently. Xiang Tu is the successor of Yan Bo. The people of Shang discern omens of calamity and defeat through fire.

Based on the two pieces of evidence from the *Zuo Zhuan*, we can cross-verify and provide some explanations as follows:

Firstly, Hou Di, which refers to 'Tao Tang Shi,' is identified as Emperor Yao. The *Annals of the Five Emperors* in the *Records of the Grand Historian* states that Emperor Ku took a daughter of the Chen Feng clan as his wife, and she gave birth to Fang Xun, who was Emperor Yao.

Secondly, 'Zhu Chen,' meaning 'the worship of the great fire,' is explained in the *First Year of Duke Zhao* in the *Zuo Zhuan* with a commentary by Du Yu of the Western Jin Dynasty: "Chen refers to the great fire." The great fire is the second star (Antares) in the heart of the Scorpius constellation, a red first-magnitude star, thus named "the great fire." "Zhu Chen" implies using the great fire star as the reference point, tracking its trajectory to determine time intervals, also known as "measuring time by the fire." Yan Bo, the brother of Emperor Yao with a different mother, was the Minister of Fire, responsible for the worship of the fire star.

Thirdly, the *Annals of Yin* in the *Records of the Grand Historian* records that in the three generations preceding Shang's founder, there were Qi, Zhao Ming, and Xiang Tu. Yan Bo lived in Shang Qiu and oversaw the star of Chen, and Xiang Tu relocated to Shang Qiu as the successor. Therefore, "Shang worships the great fire" and "Chen as the star of Shang" suggest that the Shang Dynasty used the great fire as the primary star for their rituals; the great fire was the tribal star of the people of Shang.

Remarkably, Yan Bo, custodian of the star of fire and its worship, settled in Shangqiu[12]—future capital of the successor state of Song, sprouted from the Weizi. "The Seventeenth Year of Duke Zhao" in the *Zuo Zhuan* mentions, "Song is the realm of the Great Chen." Here, "Great Chen" mirrors the star of Chen and the Great Fire. The *Book of Han* reveals, "Zhou granted Weizi dominion over Song, now Suiyang—home of the Tao Tang clan, under Yan Bo's stewardship" (see Figure 14.2).

The intricate historical ties above lend depth to the interpretation of Zhao Kuangyin's country-founding act, championing the principle of fire virtue. Initially declared upon founding the state, "Officials proclaimed reception of Zhou's relinquished power, signifying wood virtue preceding fire. Thus, our sovereign shall embody fiery virtue, brandishing red, performing sacrifices in the month of

Figure 14.2 Yanbo Terrace in Shangqiu

Xu."[13] Such "wood virtue of Zhou" insinuates inheriting water virtue from the late Han Dynasty; as *Book of Zhou* in the *Old History of the Five Dynasties* asserts, "Upon founding, the state shifted from water to wood virtue." This statement rigidly observes the Five Virtues' politico-philosophical cycles. Nevertheless, given the tie of Yan Bo with the star of Chen, and the association with the Song Dynasty, the Zhao and Song fire virtue is grounded in an extensive historical narrative. Like Zhao Kuangyin, the Lord of Suiyang, naturally embraced the fire virtue, leading to monumental country-founding achievements. These feats trace back to the Shang Dynasty's splendid heritage across three generations.

14.2.3 Coincidence Three: "Song" and "Shang" can be Interchangeably Referred to Each Other

Yan Bo, the progenitor of the Shang Dynasty, made his home in Shangqiu where he performed the rite of the Great Fire. Successor Shang ancestors followed this precedent, underscoring the eminent status of Shangqiu during their reign. After the fall of the Shang to the Zhou Dynasty, the major territorial divisions under King Cheng of Zhou were overseen by Duke Dan of Zhou. He bestowed upon Weizi Qi the duties of "continuing the Yin (Shang) legacy" and "upholding the sacrifices of the Yin."[14] This clearly identifies Shangqiu as an appropriate location. The enigma that arises, though, is why Weizi Qi christened his state "Song." No elucidation is provided by the *Book of Documents*, the *Book of Songs*, nor the *Records of the*

Grand Historian. In the Eastern Han Dynasty, the *Explanations of Names* by Liu Xi posits:

> Song, meaning "to send," situates near the Huai and Si rivers, with a proclivity towards the south east. It is envisioned as a repository for the descendants of Yin, as if it were a site transmitting impurities, tasked with directing envoys eastward to the ocean.

According to this interpretation, the notion of Song as a "site of impurities" requiring "envoys to be dispatched seaward"[15] does not quite resonate with the original motive of placating the Shang populace, conferring the state of Song, and honoring the Shang rites. Delving into the *Shuowen Jiezi*, we find it states, "Song entails an offering, derived from 'roof' and 'wood,' and sounds akin to 'send.'" Though Song shares phonetic similarities with "send," its significance aligns more closely with the gloss provided by scholars like Xu Xuan of the Northern Song Dynasty in his commentaries on the *Shuowen Jiezi*: "Wood symbolizes the material from which a shelter for humans is fashioned."[16] This correlates with the term "Ju," signifying dwelling or residing, coming from the parts 'corpse' and 'table.' "Ju" represents the contentment of settling in after finding an appropriate abode. In essence, based on the etymology of the character, Song epitomizes a place of habitation, a domicile. Given the Zhou Dynasty's reverence for tradition, the bestowment of Song, the perpetuation of Shang rites, plus the desire for Harmony among the Shang—including those once in defiance like Wugeng—the state under Weizi was christened Song. This naming can thus be interpreted as having significant import.[17]

In more recent times, Wang Guowei's "Interpretation of the Shang Dynasty" introduces an alternative viewpoint concerning the investiture of Weizi as the Lord of Song:

> When Weizi was enfeoffed, there was no renaming of the state; he inhabited Shangqiu, the land of his forefathers. Thus, the state was known as Song, but it was simultaneously referred to as Shang.[18] Throughout the Zhou Dynasty, it was commonplace to interchange Song with Shang. I conjecture that Song and Shang shared phonetic similarities, and initially, the state may have borne the name Shang. Subsequently, to distinguish it from the overarching Shang Dynasty, folks began calling it Song.

Wang Guowei implies that the original appellation of the state of Weizi was Shang, being also recognized as Song. Yet, my estimation is contrary. Just as Duke of Zhou, having enfeoffed descendants of Shun, opted not for the title Yu but Chen, and descendants of Yu, upon his enfeoffment, was not dubbed Xia but Qi. In this vein, with Zhou's replacement of the Shang, it would be improper to name the new state Shang, a name once signifying imperial dominion. Dubbing Weizi's domain of Shang might breed conflict with the established sovereignty of Zhou. Thus, selecting the dissimilar yet phonetically related character of Song was a judicious alternative. What's more, it became routine to use Song and Shang synonymously.

Regardless of the semantics behind "Song" for the State of Song, it's an irrefutable historical fact that during the early Zhao-Song era, phrases like "Song, the successor of Shang," "Shangqiu, the heartland of Song," and "Song, Shang, Shangqiu—three appellations for one locality, which is also the Suiyang County of the State of Liang"[19] were well-known among scholars. The historical archives on music before the fourth year of Emperor Yangxi in the Song Dynasty (987 AD) as recorded in the *Tai Ping Imperial Geographic Gazetteer* affirm: "Songzhou was the dwelling of Yan Bo, Gaoxin's scion, it is the provincial metropolis today ... King Wu conferred the Weizi lineage in Song." There is also mention of Songcheng County, "once the Weizi lineage's settlement, and the helm from which Xiang Tu, the grandson of Qi governed. In the Spring and Autumn Period, it served as the capital city of the State of Song," and the location of the mausoleum of Weizi. Driven by such evidence, early Song Dynasty intellectuals further postulated that Zhao Kuangyin, begotten of "Hong Yin," who "rooted his establishment in Suiyang" and "ascended in Song," was predestined to adopt Song, a name steaming from the Shang legacy, as the sovereign title of his dynasty.

14.2.4 Coincidence Four: Zhao Kuangyin's Father's Name, Hong Yin

According to the *Biography of Taizu* in the *History of Song*, Emperor Taizu, Zhao Kuangyin, was the second son of Zhao Hongyin. It is recorded that Zhao Hongyin was brave, and skilled in both horseback riding and archery. During the Later Tang Dynasty, Emperor Zhuangzong appointed him commander of the imperial guards. In the Later Han Dynasty, he was promoted for his achievements to become the chief commander of the Holy Guard. After the fall of the Later Han Dynasty, he entered the Zhou Dynasty and became the commander of the First Iron Cavalry, then the commander of the Right Brigade, and later the defense commissioner of Yuezhou. His various official positions included acting Minister of War, and he was granted the title of prefect of Tianshui County. He shared command of the imperial guards with his son, Zhao Kuangyin. He passed away in the third year of Xiande and was posthumously honored as the Military Commissioner of Wuqing and as Grand Commandant.

As described in Chapter 2 of this book, the Shang Dynasty among the three ancient dynasties was also referred to as "Yin." Sima Qian's *Records of the Grand Historian* recounts the early history of the Shang Dynasty in the *Biography of Yin*. The fortunate convergence of the name Zhao Hongyin with the propitious meaning of "Hong Yin" as "Great Yin," corresponding to "Great Song," along with the restoration and magnificence of "Yin" symbolizing "Song," became significant for culturally learned scholars when interpreting the Song Dynasty's nomenclature. This seemed to suggest it was predestined that Zhao Kuangyin would become the emperor who would revive the Shang Dynasty.

In conclusion, the state of Song, named after Zhao Kuangyin, who became the military governor of Songzhou under the Later Zhou Dynasty, has seen its name interpreted in increasingly comprehensive and complete ways due to various coincidences, acquiring a greater depth of complexity and mystique.[20] This interpretation supports the "Sacrificial Rites of Song" excerpt found in the *Records of Anomalies in Luoyang* by Qin Zaisi from the early Song Dynasty:

Emperor Ku had four consorts; one bore Emperor Zhi, another Emperor Yao, one the progenitor of the Yin [Shang Dynasty], and another the progenitor of the Zhou. The descendants of Yin were enfeoffed in Song, which is present-day Shangqiu; the current Majesty, having formerly served as a military governor in Suiyang under the previous dynasty, established a new sovereign state, hence adopting the name 'Great Song.' Prior to this, the father of our emperor was named Hongyin, which is now proved to have been prophetic; 'Hong' signifying the greatness that was to come, and 'Yin,' the foundation of the Song. 'Huang' [imperial] is a fortunate sign heralding the imperial destiny. Today, the capital is founded amidst great fire, with the Song identified with the fire element, inheriting the mantle from the Zhou dynasty with the virtue of fire as its guiding principle. According to astrology, the star of Heart represents emperors, truly aligning with the land of the Song. Today, the ancestral temples of the Gaoxin clan are located thirty li from the Song city. Such a confluence of cosmic and earthly Yin and Yang and human affairs is indeed exceedingly rare throughout the ages.[21]

The information about Emperor Ku's consorts is recorded in the book *Chronicles of Emperors*. Furthermore, during the early years of the Southern Song Dynasty, the *Continuation of the Compendium of Miscellaneous Knowledge* by Li Shi corroborates Qin Zaisi's theory. It states that "the current Majesty, who was previously assigned to fortify Suiyang during the preceding dynasty, instituted the founding of the Great Song Dynasty. Furthermore, he established the capital amidst the great fire, hence the Song is associated with the fire element. According to astronomy, the Heart star is symbolic of emperors; it is truly within the Song's realm of influence. Such a profound alignment of heaven, earth, and humanity is exceedingly rare throughout history." From this perspective, the explanation of the title Song and the concept of fire virtue were evidently prevalent throughout the Song Dynasty.

However, it is important to recognize that this explanation, encompassing history, geography, contemporaneous events, family lineage, the five elements, and astronomy, appears to have arisen subsequently and may be considered a retrospective interpretation.

The interpretation of the national title and the concept of Virtue Destiny can significantly influence contemporary politics and culture, as can be affirmed by the examples mentioned above. Another point worth noting is that after the Southern Song Dynasty fell to the Yuan Dynasty, the title of Song and the concept of Fire Virtue continued to serve as dual banners advocating for the nationalism of the people of Han. For instance, at the end of the Yuan Dynasty, rebels like Xu Shouhui and Han Lin'er both used "Song" as their title and adhered to the principle of Fire Virtue. Later on, the dynastic title "Ming" chosen by Zhu Yuanzhang, and its complex relationship with "Da Song" and Fire Virtue, presents another intriguing topic. This issue is discussed in detail in Chapter 17 of this book.

Notes

1 In the year 1271, Kublai Khan, the Mongol Emperor, established the national title as "Da Yuan."

2 In the year 1129, Hangzhou was elevated to the status of Lin'an Prefecture and became the de facto capital of the Southern Song Dynasty after 1138.

3 In 2002, the entrance examination for doctoral students majoring in Chinese ancient history at Nanjing University included a question on "A General History of China."

4 Fairbank J.K. & Reischauer E, China: Tradition and Transformation, translated by Chen Zhongdan and others, Chapter 6, Jiangsu People's Publishing House, 1992.

5 In the second year of Jianzhong era during the Tang Dynasty, Jiedushi of the Xuanwu Army was established in Songzhou, and in the beginning of Xingyuan era, the governance of Jiedushi was shifted to Bianzhou. During the Five Dynasties, it was once again named the Xuanwu Army. During the Tang Dynasty and at the beginning of the Northern Song Dynasty, it was called the Guide Army.

6 The Jiedushi would govern a few prefectures, sometimes two or three, or more than ten. Among them, the Jiedushi would directly govern one prefecture, while the remaining were called "supporting prefectures."

7 In "Rituals and Calendars" of the *History of the Song Dynasty*, Xie Jiang, the Chief of the Guanglu Monastery, submitted a memorial in the fourth year of Tianxi era.

8 Collected Imperial Edicts and Commands of the Song Dynasty, Volume 159.

9 Wang Yinglin, Yu Hai (Jad Sea), Volume 16, Four Capitals of the Song Dynasty: Nanjing.
    The term "Art Ancestor" refers to Zhao Kuangyin, "Bintu" and "Chongling" refer to the land where the Zhou Dynasty and the founder emperor Liu Xiu of the Eastern Han Dynasty rose to power, and "Jinyang" refers to the place where the Tang Dynasty began its enterprise.

10 Wang Guowei's article "On the Shang Dynasty" (included in the book *Collected Writings by Guantang*, Volume 12, published by Zhonghua Book Company in 1959) states: "The ancient State of Song was actually called Shangqiu. 'Qiu' means emptiness, and the name Shangqiu in Song refers to the same as the southern Huai River being called Yinxu."

11 Pang Pu, Examination of the History of the Song Dynasty, Chinese Culture, issue 1, the Chinese Academy of Arts, 1989.

12 In the south west of Shangqiu City today, there is Yan Bo Terrace, commonly known as Huoshen Terrace or Huoxing Terrace. The existing buildings were constructed during the Song and Yuan dynasties, with repairs carried out in the Ming and Qing dynasties.

13 Compilation of the Continuing Chronicle of Zizhi Tongjian, Volume 1.

14 *Annals of the Yin Dynasty* in the *Records of the Grand Historian* states, "Conferred Weizi in Song to continue the Yin dynasty," while the *Book of Music* states, "they enfeoffed the descendants of Yin in the land of Song," and the "Biography of Duke Zhou of Lu" states, "Enfeoffed Weizi in Song to carry out the worship of Yin." Similarly, in the "Biography of Chen Qi," it states, "After the fall of Yin, the Zhou Dynasty enfeoffed its descendants in Song," and so on. According to the *Records of the Grand Historian*, Yin is referred to as Shang, which is explained in the second chapter of this book.

15 This carries a certain sense of appeasing the plague god.

16 Xu Shen, Shuowen Jiezi, with annotations by Xu Xuan, China Bookstore, 1989.

17 Wang Xiantang further elaborated on this in his work "The Fire and Candle Seen in Ancient Characters" (completed in 1945, published by Qilu Press in 1979). In the chapter "Divinities and the Ancestor Temple," he suggests that the character "Song" is a variant of the character "Zong." "Zong" represents the divinities arranged in the radical ⼧, while

"Song" represents the divinities arranged in the radical 木 within ⼧. Since Shangqiu was the old capital of the Shang Dynasty, where the ancestor temple was located, the name of this place could be called "Song." Additionally, the enfeoffment of Weizi was primarily for the purpose of worship, hence the name of the fiefdom was also called "Song." "Song" thus signifies divinities and ancestor temples. This can also be seen as another perspective.

18 There are numerous examples supporting the association of "Song" with "Shang." This can be attributed to either self-designation or designation by others. For more details, refer to Wang Guowei's article "On the Shang Dynasty."

19 "The First year of Duke Zhao," "The ninth year of Guke Xiang" in the *Zuo Zhuan*, annotated by Du Yu of the Western Jin Dynasty; and cited by Tang Kong Yingda in his commentary on Du Yu's *Exemplifications of the Spring and Autumn Annals*.

20 According to the *Compilation of the Continuing Chronicle of Zizhi Tongjian*, Volume 22, in the eleventh month of the sixth year of Taiping Xingguo era (981 AD), there is a record stating, "Prior to this, there was a person named Qin Zaisi who submitted a memorial requesting not to grant pardons again." Qin Zaisi was a person from the early Song Dynasty.

21 Qin Zaisi, "Luozhong Ji Yilu" (Records of Anomalies in Luoyang), compiled by Tao Zongyi, included in the "Shuofu" edition, and referenced in the Complete Collection of Ancient and Modern Books.

15 The Great Yuan

How Grand is the Primal Beginning of Creativity

In February 1279, with the fall of the remaining Song Dynasty territories, the first Chinese national regime ruled by a non-Han ethnic group was established,[1] adopting "Da Yuan"(Great Yuan) as its official title.[2] The term "Da Yuan" had been in use since November 1271, during a period when the Mongols were consistently victorious in their campaigns against the Southern Song Dynasty. 'Da Yuan' became the formal appellation for the Central Plains dynasty from February 1279 and remained in use until August 1368.

On July 27, 1368 (according to the lunar calendar), Emperor Toghon Temür, ruler of the Yuan Dynasty, fled north to the expansive grasslands of Mongolia. On August 2, the Ming army[3] captured the capital city, Dadu[4] (today known as Beijing), signifying the conclusion of Yuan rule in the Central Plains. Thus, after more than 160 years of the Mongol Empire's and the Yuan Dynasty's dominance, the Mongolian nomads ultimately retreated to their ancestral grasslands in the north.

15.1 The Great Yuan is Distinct from the Mongol Khanate

The founders of the Yuan Dynasty were the Mongols, a grassland ethnic group with a lengthy history. As far back as the 5th and 6th centuries, the Shiwei tribe, with linguistic and ancestral connections to the Donghu people, inhabited the grasslands stretching from what is now Hulunbuir in the east to the Nen River Basin in the south and reaching the lower Ergun River in the north. By the 7th and 8th centuries, the Shiwei tribe had evolved considerably. According to the *Chronicles of the Northern Barbarians* in the *Old Book of Tang*, there was a Shiwei clan known as the "Mengwu Shiwei," where "Mengwu" was the initial Han translation of "Mongol." Subsequent Chinese texts featured approximations like "Menggu" and "Monggu." The first instance of "Mongol" in writing appeared in the *Records of the King Yang on the River* by Xu Mengxin during the Southern Song period. By the Yuan era, "Mongol" had become the standard representation. Research by scholars suggests that, in the ancient Mongolian language, "Mongol" might have implications of "stupid and weak," yet it could also signify proudness, strength, celestial beings, and even baldness.[5] Initially designating a clan or tribe, by the 13th century, a new ethnic group known as "Mongol" emerged on the broad grasslands

DOI: 10.4324/9781003510390-16

from the headwaters of the Kerulen, Orkhon, and Tula rivers to the Hulunbuir region in the east, heralded by the establishment of the Great Mongol Empire.

The founder of the Great Mongol Empire was Temujin (1162-1227), the chieftain of the Mongol Kiyad tribe. In the late 12th and early 13th centuries, the valiant and militarily adept Temujin unified the significant nomadic tribes of the Mongolian steppes, becoming the most powerful leader of the grasslands. In 1206, at the source of the Onon River (present-day Kerulen River),[6] Temujin summoned his kin, offspring, cavalry, attendants, and tribal chiefs to a kurultai (a Mongolian 'assembly'). During this gathering, he raised nine white banners, accepted the title "Genghis Khan,"[7] thereby marking the formal establishment of the Great Mongol Empire.

At its peak, the Great Mongol Empire's domain spanned from the Xing'an Mountains in the east to the Altai Mountains in the west, extended northward past Lake Baikal, and reached as far south as the Yin Mountains (see Figure 15.1).

After founding the Great Mongol Empire, Genghis Khan expanded his ambitions to the wider world and gradually introduced a system of feudalism. The Great Khans, successors of Genghis Khan, sustained an agenda of military conquests. Alongside their rule over their own domains, they granted territories to their loyalists, creating Khanates (termed "Uluses" in Mongolian), which functioned as sovereign feudal states or principalities. These Khanates, led by military and political chiefs invested with lands by the central Mongol Empire, were directly answerable to the Great Khan, reporting their populations and financial

Figure 15.1 The statue of Mongolian cavalry at the Mausoleum of Genghis Khan in Inner Mongolia

resources. Thereby, a suzerainty relationship existed between the Great Khan and the Khanates.

During the reign of Genghis Khan (1206-1227) and his successor Ögedei Khan (Genghis Khan's third son, 1229-1241), the suzerain-vassal relationship between the Great Khan and the Khanates could be maintained. However, as the struggle for power and authority among the Khans intensified, this political relationship began to disintegrate. During the reign of Möngke Khan (the eldest son of Ögedei Khan, 1251-1259), the Mongol Empire had de facto split into the Empire of the Great Khan (which officially became known as the "Great Yuan" in 1271) and the Three Great Khanates (the Chagatai Khanate, the Golden Horde, and the Ilkhanate), each pursuing its own path of independent development.

The three Great Khanates of the Mongol Empire, along with the later Ilkhanate, had territories that extended from Central Asia and West Asia to Europe. At its peak, the Chagatai Khanate (misidentified as the Golden Horde – the Golden Horde and Chagatai Khanate were separate entities) reached from the lower reaches of Ebinur Lake and the Irtysh River in the east to present-day Russia, Ukraine, Belarus, and other regions in the west. It bordered Lake Balkhash, the Caspian Sea, and the Black Sea to the south, and approached the Arctic Circle to the north.[8] During the heyday of the Chagatai Khanate, their territory expanded eastward from present-day Turpan and the Lop Nur region in Xinjiang to the lower reaches of the Amu Darya in the west, reached the Irtysh River in the north, and extended south beyond the Hindu Kush mountains.[9] During the zenith of the Ögedei Khanate, their domain stretched from present-day Kashgar and the Talas River Valley in Xinjiang in the west to Turpan in the east, bordered the upper Irtysh River in the north, and encompassed various cities along the southern routes of the Tianshan Mountains.[10] The Ilkhanate, founded by Hulagu Khan, the grandson of Genghis Khan, encompassed territories from the Amu Darya and Indus Rivers in the east to the Khorasan region of present-day Iran. From there, it extended westward, crossing the Tigris and Euphrates Rivers, reaching as far south west as Basra in present-day Iraq. It bordered the Indian Ocean to the south and the Caucasus Mountains to the north.[11]

The Mongol Khanate that spanned the Eurasian continent is not the same concept as the "Great Yuan." The "Yuan" dating system in Chinese history began in 1271 when Kublai Khan declared himself emperor of the "Great Yuan." However, Kublai Khan's ascension was contested by his younger brother Ariq Böke. In March 1260, Kublai Khan held a kurultai (a gathering to elect a leader) in Kaiping (now on the north bank of the Dongshandian River in Zhenglan Banner, Inner Mongolia), which deviated from Mongolian tradition that required all princes of various lineages to gather at the source of the Onon, Kherlen, and Tuul rivers. Thus, although Kublai Khan and the subsequent Yuan emperors were nominally the supreme rulers of the Mongols, the established independent khanates viewed the Great Yuan emperor as a symbolic figure. The succession of these khanates also nominally required recognition from the Great Yuan emperor, but this was largely symbolic as the Great Yuan's territory did not include the vast regions of the independent khanates.

Under the Great Yuan, based on the Mongol heartland and the Central Plains, the empire's territory far surpassed that of the Han and Tang dynasties at their peaks. For instance, in 1280, the year after the Song Dynasty's fall, the extent of the Great Yuan included the following territories: in the north, from the Ertz River in the west to the Sea of Okhotsk in the east, encompassing present-day Siberia, the Ili River basin, the lower reaches of the Heilongjiang River, and areas east of the Ussuri River, including Sakhalin Island; in the north east, it controlled part of the Korean Peninsula; in the south west, Tibet, Yunnan, as well as regions such as present-day Kashmir and Bhutan along the southern foothills of the Himalayas, north eastern Myanmar, northern Thailand, and northern Laos; and to the east, it extended to the sea, governing the Penghu Islands and Jeju Island in present-day Korea.[12]

The vastness of the Great Yuan is recorded in the *Geographical Records* of the *History of the Yuan Dynasty*:

> Compared to the systems of feudalism, prefectures, and counties of the Han, Sui, Tang, and Song dynasties, all of which enjoyed prosperous rule over the entire nation, none could surpass the expanse of the Yuan Dynasty. The Han Dynasty was thwarted by northern barbarians, the Sui Dynasty could not subdue the eastern tribes, the Tang Dynasty faced off against western barbarians, and the Song Dynasty was perennially challenged by threats from the north west. On the other hand, the Yuan Dynasty emerged and expanded its frontiers to the northern deserts, included the Western Regions, subdued Western Xia, annihilated the Jurchens, subjugated Goryeo (Korea), established suzerainty over the Southern Champa kingdom, and ultimately extended its dominion southward to Jiangnan (the Yangtze River region), unifying the entire country.

Regarding the events mentioned:

- In 1206, Temujin (Genghis Khan) founded the Great Mongol Empire.
- In 1218, the Western Liao (Kara-Khitan Khanate) was absorbed into the empire.
- In 1227, the Western Xia regime was conquered.
- In 1234, the combined Mongol and Southern Song forces defeated the Jin Dynasty.
- Goryeo (present-day Korea) became a vassal state of the Mongols during the reign of Genghis Khan, and the Mongols exerted control over Goryeo for a prolonged period.
- In 1254, the Kingdom Dali was subdued (along with the submission of various Tibetan groups).
- In 1276, the Song Dynasty capitulated, and by 1279, the last vestiges of the Song Dynasty were eradicated. Thus, the unification of the entire nation took place.

The Central Plains Dynasty born from the division and transformation of the Great Mongol Empire was the Yuan Dynasty, and "Great Yuan" was the title adopted for the unified nation after the Song Dynasty had fallen.

15.2 The Evolution of Titles of the Mongol Khanate

As previously noted, in 1206, Genghis Khan (Temujin) established a nation on the grasslands named Yeke Mongghol Ulus, which translates to "Great Mongol State" or "Great Mongol Empire." In November 1271, Kublai Khan, who was the de facto Great Khan of the Mongols, declared the official dynastic title "Great Yuan" in Han territory.

The terms Yeke Mongghol Ulus, "Great Mongol State," and "Great Court" all referred to the state ruled by the Mongol Khans. "Great Court" was commonly adopted as a shorter and informal title. However, these terms had varying contexts and were applied in different geographic regions. Here is a brief summary:[13]

15.2.1 *Yeke Mongghol Ulus*

The Mongols adopted a national title during Genghis Khan's era. The title of Yeke Mongghol Ulus, which can be rendered as "Great Mongol Nation" or "Great Mongol Empire,"[14] adheres to a pattern in Chinese history where non-Han powers often adopted ethnic or tribal names as their state titles. As the official state name of the Mongol Khans, Yeke Mongghol Ulus was widely used in formal documents, especially in diplomatic communications.

The oldest extant historical record containing the full Mongolian name Yeke Mongghol Ulus appears in a seal document used by Güyük Khan (the eldest son of Ögedei Khan, who reigned from 1246 to 1248) in a letter to Pope Innocent IV in 1246. The first half of the seal document states, "By the will of the eternal sky and the mandate of heaven, the decree of the Great Mongol Nation to the entire world" (Möngketngri-yin küchüdür Yeke Mongghol Ulus undalai-in Qanuγrlγ).

It's notable that even after the adoption of the state name "Da Yuan" in 1271, the term Yeke Mongghol Ulus remained in use in Mongolian texts and persisted without change until the fall of the Yuan Dynasty. For instance, the Han-Mongol Unity Stele of 1335 features the inscription "Dai On Yeke Mongghol Ulus" (meaning "Great Yuan, Great Mongol Nation"). The Han-Mongol Unity Stele of 1346 also uses the term "Yeke Mongghol Ulus." Moreover, the Han-Mongol Unity Steles of 1338 and 1362 include the phrase "Dai On Kemeke Yeke Mongghol Ulus" (meaning "the Great Mongol Nation known as the Great Yuan"). Even during the Ming Dynasty, Mongol political entities on the grasslands continued to refer to themselves as Yeke Mongghol.

15.2.2 *Great Mongol State*

"Great Mongol State" served as the official Chinese name for the early Mongol Khans' dominion. As noted in Yelu Liuge's biography within the *History of the Yuan Dynasty*, this Chinese designation was embraced as early as 1212, concurrent with the Mongols' initial onslaught against the Jin Dynasty. Furthermore, in the *Miscellaneous Records of the Imperial Court since the Jianyan Era*, authored by Li Xin in 1216 during the Southern Song Dynasty, the phrase "Great Mongol Nation" is referenced, solidifying its adoption before that time. Nevertheless, the transition to "Great Yuan" in 1271 relegated the term "Great Mongol State" to obsolescence.

Marked by strong ethnic implications, "Great Mongol State" signaled foreign domination, which influenced its application scope. Examination of available historical documents indicates a predilection for its use in diplomatic discourse rather than common parlance among the Han Chinese. Before 1271, official communications with entities like the Jin, Southern Song, Goryeo (Korea), and Japan frequently incorporated "Great Mongol State."

15.2.3 Great Court

In juxtaposition to the official "Great Mongol Nation," the denomination "Great Court" or "Da Ting" in Chinese, although somewhat informal, permeated widespread use among the Han demographic in China. It likely represents a streamlined translation of "Yeke Mongghol Ulus," eschewing the ethnic identifier "Mongol" and interpreting "ulus" as "court," reflecting the Chinese perception of governance. As a result, "Great Court" assumes the guise of a more Sinicized Mongolian state name.

Evidence of "Great Court" usage dates back to approximately 1221, as detailed in the section of "National titles and Era Names," in the *Record of Mongols and Tartars* by Zhao Gong (published in 1222). Zhao described the Mongol regime as "Great Court," reflecting Mongolian script he had encountered. There's speculation that its emergence postdates 1217, subsequent to Mongol General Mukhali's incursion into the Jin Dynasty and the establishment of a capital at Yanjing[15] (modern-day Beijing). During this phase, the Mongols, while predominantly nomadic and steppes-centric, initiated overt conquests of Han China, aiming to reinforce colonial governance. Simultaneously, they began assimilating Chinese customs, among them, the "Great Court" nomenclature, emblematic of their supremacy over the Han people of the Central Plains.

Notwithstanding, "Great Court" lacked the formal gravitas of conventional Chinese state names and, within the Chinese language realm, also connoted reverence for the extant dynasty. With the inception of "Great Yuan" as the formal state name in 1271, terms like "Great Court" and "Great Mongol Nation" waned into disuse.

15.3 Interpretation of the Title "Great Yuan"

The meaning behind the national title "Great Yuan" is elucidated in the "Decree on the Establishment of the National Title," which states, when translated into vernacular language: "I have decided to use 'Great Yuan' as the title, adopting the meaning of 'great indeed is the primal unity' from the Qian hexagram in the *Book of Changes*. This 'primal unity' is the element that shapes and encompasses the ever-changing forms of the natural world, the origin bestowing upon it its inherent achievements." The Qian hexagram in the *Book of Changes* describes "Qian, the creative," achieving supreme success, fostering perseverance. The

Commentary expounds: "Great indeed is the primal unity of the Creative, which furthers one to be steadfast and upright in conduct, to align with the laws of heaven and earth."

From this interpretation, "Yuan" emerges as the most esteemed virtue among the four within the Qian hexagram, signifying the inception of all things. As the primordial essence of the universe and master of celestial virtue, "Yuan" harmonizes with the Mongolian tradition of revering the heavens. The first hexagram (☰), Qian, symbolizes the heavens and is also identified as one of the sixty-four hexagrams denoting the positive or robust elements. The Mongolian reverence for the heavens, propagated through the Shamanism embraced by Genghis Khan, venerates the eternal heavenly god, "Changshengtian," or the Eternal Heaven. The convergence of "Yuan" with Qian encapsulates the essence of "Eternal Heaven," aligning with the celestial worship of the Mongolian people.

Moreover, "Yuan" echoes Kublai Khan's vision laid out in the "Decree on the Establishment of the National Title:" "I unify the myriad nations and underscore the virtue of benevolence. I preserve the original systems and pursue harmony between heaven and humanity." This spotlight on unity and harmony resonates with the Han Chinese, who hold peace, righteousness, morality, and the unity of heaven and humanity in high regard. Thus, the state title "Great Yuan" embodies a cultural emblem of Kublai Khan's Sinicization efforts, touching upon the psychological needs of the Han Chinese populace.

It is notable that the character 元 (Yuan) encompasses additional positive connotations. Embodied in the original sense, "Yuan" signifies the head or leader,[16] extending also to "beginning." The *Shuowen Jiezi* dictionary elucidates: "Yuan, meaning beginning." As associated with the Qian hexagram in the *Book of Changes*, it states, "Yuan is excellence in leadership." Hence, "Yuan" articulates the notion of "excellence" or "goodness." In the phrase "大哉乾元" (great indeed is the primal unity), "元" embodies "greatness." The commentary by Kong Yingda of the Tang Dynasty reveals that the phrase mirrors the expansive nature of the energy of yang, the breadth of the substance of hexagram Qian, and the origin of all existences. The use of "大哉乾元" conveys the enormity and significance of the primal unity, ensuring the preservation of its essence, hence it is proclaimed as "great."

Consequently, "元" is frequently used to symbolize "great" or "big." In the context of "大哉乾元," "元" inherently signifies "great." Undoubtedly, Liu Bingzhong, a scholar proficient in the *Book of Changes*, contemplated this meaning when proposing the national title.

The distinction of "元" as "great" is manifest in Kublai Khan's "Decree on the Establishment of the National Title:" "Emperor Taizu Shengwu of the Great Ancestral Yuan Dynasty bears the divine emblems of Qian, ascends to lead the northern lands with martial spirit, and executes the imperial mandate with divine might. His voice resounds to the heavens, augmenting our lands magnificently. The expanse of the imperial domain is unparalleled in history." Indeed, as of 1271, the Mongol Empire had already extended over the Mongol heartland, Western Xia, the Jin Dynasty, the Dali Kingdom, the Tubo Empire, as well as territories from the

Western Liao and Southern Song Dynasties. In possessing such a vast and majestic empire, selecting the name "Great Yuan" aptly reflects its magnificence.

The ingenuity here lies in the connection between "大" (big/great) in "元" (Yuan) and the earlier mentions of "Great Mongol Empire" and "Great Court," fostering seamless continuity. As noted in the *Introduction to the Compendium for Governance*,

Throughout history, no nation has paralleled the splendor of our dynasty. Emperor Shizu initially altered the title from 'Great Mongol' to 'Great Yuan,' acknowledging that other dynasties' origins or feudal territories paled in comparison. Thus, 'Yuan' denotes 'big or great.' Since the character 'great' alone fails to capture the entirety; 'Yuan' signifies supreme greatness. Such refined craftsmanship in this decision opens up resources amassing myriad years. Who, then, could cast doubt upon its credibility?[17]

This passage meticulously illustrates the intentional selection of "Yuan" to symbolize the empire's eminence and importance. It underscores the transformation from "Great Mongol Empire" to "Great Yuan" as a substantive shift that reflects the empire's unrivaled scope. The continuity and association between these majestic titles underscore the empire's immense authority and historical significance.

Furthermore, the three official Chinese titles of the Mongol Great Khans are ingeniously interconnected, as each encompasses the notion of "greatness" denoted by "大" (dà). The character "元" (yuán), while also conveying "greatness," provides a richer and more nuanced meaning bolstered by its literary and historical context, in contrast to the more straightforward "大" (dà).

The adoption of "大元" (Great Yuan) for the national title, along with the reign titles of subsequent Mongol emperors, including Kublai Khan's "至元" (Zhì Yuán), Temür Khan's "元贞" (Yuán Zhēn) and "大德" (Dà Dé), and Öljei Temür Khan's "至大" (Zhì Dà), all resonate with the theme of "greatness" and align with the ideology embedded in the "乾" (Qián) hexagram of the *Book of Changes*.

These titles attest to the fact that the Mongol Empire, upon conquering the Central Plains, not only adopted naming conventions like reign, temple, and state names from the Han nationality but also drew inspiration from the venerable classic of Han, the *Book of Changes*. The *Book of Changes*, or Yi Jing, also called Zhou Yi, is acknowledged as the primary text among the "Six Classics" by Ban Gu in the *Treatise on Literature* in the *Book of Han* during the Eastern Han Dynasty. It bears noting that Neo-Confucian scholars of the Song Dynasty esteemed the *Book of Changes* as the preeminent work among the "Thirteen Classics." Additionally, the *Book of Changes* opens with the phrase "乾元亨利贞" (The Creative Principle of Qian is the origin of all things, bringing success, prosperity, and continued progress through perseverance).

Since Kublai Khan's reign, the Mongols' evolution from nomadic conquerors of the steppes to a legitimate ruling dynasty within the Central Plains is apparent in their adoption of the title "Great Yuan" as a token of sovereignty. Nonetheless, the title of "Great Yuan" persisted even after the rise of the Ming Dynasty in 1368. Mongol Khanates, led by Tuqa-Timur[18], his offspring Ayurbarwada Buyantu Khan,

Toghto, and their heirs, continued to use the title "Great Yuan" (known as the Northern Yuan). In 1388, the Northern Yuan's claim to legitimacy faltered after Toghto's assassination by his Chancellor Yesüder, leading to the relinquishment of the title "Great Yuan."[19]

Notes

1 In January 1276, Emperor Zhao of the Song Dynasty surrendered the imperial seal and a submission letter, leading to the downfall of the Southern Song Dynasty when the Yuan army entered Lin'an. For further details, please refer to Tan Qixiang's article "Annotated Chronology of Chinese History: From the Beginning to the End of Each Dynasty" in Historical Research, Issue 6,1991.

2 It is important to note that the formal state name of the Yuan Dynasty is "大元" (Dà Yuán), where "大" (dà) means "great" and "元" (yuán) is a shortened form. The use of "大" (dà) before the state name started with the Yuan Dynasty, while in earlier dynasties, the use of "大" (dà) was an honorific title. As stated by Zhu Guozhen in his work "Miscellaneous Sketches of the Rising and Falling of Dynasties" in Chapter 2 on state names: "The addition of '大' (dà) before the state name started with the non-Han Yuan Dynasty, which was followed by our dynasty (the Ming Dynasty) ... The terms '大汉' (Dà Hàn), '大唐' (Dà Táng), and '大宋' (Dà Sòng) were used by subjects and foreigners as honorary terms. Recently, in the book *Research on the Succession of Dynasties* published in Xin'an, the addition of '大' (dà) was found in reference to the Han, Tang, Song, and Sima Jin dynasties, thus deviating from its original usage (Tang steles also used the term '巨唐' (jù táng), where '巨' means 'large'). The Song Dynasty was referred to as '皇宋' (Huáng Sòng), where '皇' (huáng) also means 'great.' Liu Yueshi's memorial also mentioned '天祚大晋' (Tiān zuò dà Jìn), indicating 'great' as well." Similarly, in the book *The Mongol Empire and the 'Dà Yuán* by Jin Haodong (included in the compilation "Yuan History of Tsinghua University," edited by Yao Dali and Liu Yingsheng, Commercial Press, 2013), it is emphasized that "'大元' (Dà Yuán) was originally a two-character state name. However, as seen in examples like '皇元' (Huáng Yuán) and '我元' (Wǒ Yuán), the two-character state name '大元' (Dà Yuán) became mixed with the examples of '大汉' (Dà Hàn) and '大唐' (Dà Táng), resulting in the understanding of '大' (dà) as an adjective with a sense of superiority, making '元' (yuán) seem like a one-character state name." Similarly, "明" (Míng) and "清" (Qīng) are also shortened forms, while "大明" (Dà Míng) and "大清" (Dà Qīng) are the official full titles.

3 In January 1368, Zhu Yuanzhang ascended to the throne in Yingtian Fu (present-day Nanjing in Jiangsu Province) with the state name "大明" (Dà Míng), meaning the Great Ming Dynasty.

4 In the Mongolian language, the capital city was called "Khanbaliq," meaning the city of the Khan.

5 For further details, please refer to Han Rulin's "Names of the Mongols" in his compilation " Collection of QiongLü," published by Shanghai People's Publishing House in 1982. Additionally, Yang Xianyi's "The Original Meaning and Source of Mongolian Names" in his compilation "Translations and Miscellaneous Writings" is also a valuable resource for understanding the meanings of Mongolian names. This compilation was published by Sanlian Bookstore in 1983.

6 In this translation, some important place names are presented with their contemporary names and annotations for clarity. Generally, the modern names are used to facilitate the understanding of readers.

7 The meaning of "成吉思" (Chéngjísī), also known as "Chinggis," varies. It can be interpreted as "strong," "great sea," "heaven," and so on. As for the term "汗" (hàn), it originally referred to the leader of a tribe or tribal confederation and later evolved to mean "monarch." Previously, the northern ethnic groups such as the Rouran, Göktürks, and Uighurs used the term "汗" (hàn) to refer to their highest ruler.

8 In the 15th century, the Qara Del Khanate gradually split into several khanates, including Siberia, Kazan, Crimea, and Astrakhan. The rule of the Qara Del Khanate came to an end in 1480.

9 In the mid-14th century, the Chagatai Khanate divided into two parts, the East and the West. The Western Chagatai, under the rule of the noble Timur, evolved into the Timurid Empire, while the Eastern Chagatai fragmented into several smaller states, which were subsequently conquered and ceased to exist.

10 In 1309, the Golden Horde, also known as the Ulus of Jochi, was conquered by the Chagatai Khanate, but later regained independence.

11 In 1335, the Ilkhanate gradually started to fall into a state of fragmentation. By the end of the 14th century, it was incorporated into the Timurid Empire.

12 The territory of the Yuan Dynasty later contracted. If we take the year 1330 as a reference, its north western extent was limited to the Hami region in present-day Xinjiang. The north eastern part, including a portion of Korea, contracted within the eastern boundary along the lower reaches of the Yalu River. Its western border was the Tieling area in the present-day Anbyon region of Gangwon Province in Korea.

13 The following information is synthesized from Xiao Qiqing's "On the 'Da Chao': The Han-Written National Title of Mongolia Before the Founding of the Yuan Dynasty" (Hanxue Yanjiu, Vol. 3, No. 1, Taipei, 1985). Original sources are not cited here.

14 Jin Haodong's "The Mongol Empire and the 'Da Yuan'" indicates that "we cannot find a definite record of the formal proclamation of this national title." Additionally, Chen Xiaowei's "Reexamining the Issue of the Creation Year of the National Title 'Da Mongol' " (Zhonghua Wenshi Luncang, 2016, No. 1) argues that the year Xīn wèi (1211) saw the establishment of the national title "Da Mongol," which was closely related to the historical context of the Mongolian campaign against the Jin Dynasty. This event held significant strategic importance and had far-reaching historical implications for the Mongol Empire.

15 After 1153, Yanjing (present-day Beijing) became the capital of the Jurchen Jin Dynasty, known as Daxing Fu. In 1214, the Jin Dynasty relocated its capital to Nanjing (present-day Kaifeng, Henan Province). However, in 1215, the Mongols captured Yanjing (formerly known as Daxing Fu) and retained the name Yanjing.

16 Yang Shuda: Collection of Exegetics of Yang Shuda, Volume Two, Chinese Academy of Sciences, 1954.

17 Introduction to the Compendium for Governance, included in Anthology of Yuan Texts by Category, volume 40.

18 *The History of the Ming Dynasty* identifies Tuogusi Temur as the son of Aiyu Shi Lidala, which may be a mistake. For reference, please consult "Mongolian Genealogy, Volume 12" by Gao Wende and Cai Zhichun, published by the Chinese Academy of Social Sciences Press in 1979.

19 Yasoqadir's abandonment of the title "Great Yuan" is closely related to the history of the founding of the Yuan Dynasty. Yasoqadir was originally a descendant of Ariq Böke.

After Kublai Khan defeated Ariq Böke, he established the Yuan Dynasty. However, over 120 years later, Yasoqadir, a descendant of Ariq Böke, assassinated Kublai Khan's descendant, Tug Temür, and seized the position of Khan (known as Zöregtu Khan). From then on, Yasoqadir no longer used the title of "Great Yuan." For more details, please refer to Cai Meibiao's article "Mongolia and the Title of the Great Yuan in the Ming Dynasty," included in the collection of papers from the Second International Academic Discussion on the History of the Ming and Qing dynasties, compiled by the Editorial Committee, published by Tianjin People's Publishing House in 1993.

16 The Great Ming

"In the Radiant Light of the Buddhas"

On the fourth day of the first lunar month in the year 1368, under the warm sun and gentle breeze of Zhongshan, Zhu Yuanzhang, the King of Wu, worshipped heaven and earth and ascended the imperial throne. He proclaimed the title of the empire as "Da Ming,"[1] meaning "Great Brightness." He established the era name as Hongwu and chose Yingtian (modern-day Nanjing, Jiangsu) as the capital.

Later that year, on the twenty-seventh day of the seventh lunar month, the formidable army of the Great Ming launched a northern expedition and captured Tongzhou (now Tongzhou District in Beijing). On that night, Emperor Shun of Yuan, along with his empress, concubines, the crown prince, and some ministers, fled from Dadu (present-day Beijing) through the Jiande Gate. Dadu was then occupied by the Ming army on the second day of the eighth lunar month.

The emperor's flight and the Ming army's occupation of Dadu marked the end of the Yuan Dynasty and the ascent of the Great Ming as the new ruling power.[2]

The Great Ming's reign ended in 1644.[3] On the nineteenth day of the third lunar month of that year, Li Zicheng, the King of Dashun, captured the capital city (Beijing).[4] The Ming Emperor Zhu Youjian hanged himself in the Shouhuang Pavilion on Jingshan. Then, on the thirtieth day of the fourth lunar month, Li Zicheng abandoned Beijing and retreated westward. The Qing Dynasty's[5] Prince Regent, Dorgon, entered the capital on the second day of the fifth lunar month, marking the beginning of the ruling of Qing over the central plains.

16.1 The Revolt Against the Yuan and the Restoration of the Song

In the previous chapter, we noted that the Yuan Dynasty was the first nationwide regime ruled by a non-Han ethnic group in the history of China. Near its end, the Yuan faced crises and rampant corruption. This situation was vividly portrayed by the popular folk song "Zui Taiping Xiaoling," (A Short Lyric of the 'Peaceful' Society)[6] which captured the social climate of the time:

> The mighty Yuan Dynasty was plagued by unchecked power among treacherous officials.

DOI: 10.4324/9781003510390-17

Mismanagement of the Grand Canal led to economic turmoil, stirring the Red Turban Rebellion.

Corruption and harsh punishments within the official system caused popular grievances.

Exploitation and the buying of power led to widespread suffering.

Thieves turned officials, and officials turned thieves—no distinction between wisdom and folly. How pitiable and lamentable!

This verse of short lyric, known from the capital to the south of the Yangtze River, indicates that political corruption, societal malaise, and pronounced class and ethnic conflicts marked the decline of the Yuan Dynasty. The mismanagement of the policy of "Kaihe" and "Bianchao" triggered "the source of chaos" and played a direct role in the demise of the Yuan Dynasty in the Central Plains.

The term "Bianchao" refers to the policy of massive printing of new currency of the Yuan court in 1350 to remedy financial issues, resulting in inflation and surging prices. "Kaihe" refers to the policy of repairing and managing the Yellow River. The river had seen multiple breaches, significantly impacting the national economy and the people's well-being. In April 1351, 150,000 laborers were conscripted from locations such as Bianliang (present-day Kaifeng) and Daming, along with 20,000 soldiers from Prefecture Luzhou and other forces, for forced labor for river management. While the river management was crucial, the officials' harsh treatment and embezzlement of provisions enkindled intense resentment among the conscripted workers.

Against this backdrop, Han Shantong,[7] leader of the White Lotus sect in Bailuzhuang of Yongnian, Hebei (situated in south east present-day Yongnian County, Hebei), seized the opportunity. He had long "prophesied a period of great chaos and the coming of Maitreya Buddha. The prophecies found a willing audience among the Henan and Jianghuai populace."[8] Han Shantong spread children's rhymes claiming, "A stone man with one eye will provoke the Yellow River, and the world will revolt." He also clandestinely buried a stone figure with one eye at the river worksite. When the stone figure was unearthed by unsuspecting workers, the inscription on its back read, "Do not underestimate the single-eyed stone figure; when it emerges, the world will revolt." The discovery caused great commotion at the Yellow River worksite. The following events are documented in the *Annals of Emperor Shun* in the *History of the Yuan Dynasty* for May of the eleventh year of the Zhizheng era (1351).

A mystic named Liu Futong from Yingzhou sparked a revolt and overtook the city. Initially, Liu Futong, together with Du Zunda, Luo Wensu, Sheng Wenyu, Wang Xianzhong, and Han Yao'er, disseminated deceitful claims that Han Shantong was the eighth-generation descendant of Emperor Huizong of Song, and thus the rightful ruler of China. They made a grand oath over the slaughtered bodies of a white horse and a black ox, signifying their resolve to raise an army and create upheaval. When officials uncovered their conspiracy and attempted to arrest them, Liu Futong initiated a rebellion. Han Shantong was captured, and his wife Yang and his son Han Lin'er fled to Wu'an.

The uprising erupted hastily and spontaneously. When the workers at the Yellow River construction site heard the news, they joined Liu Futong's ranks. Because the rebel army used red cloth as their distinguishing mark, they were known as the "Red Turban Army" or "Red Army" by the common people. They were also called the "Incense Army" due to their association with the White Lotus sect's practice of burning incense in religious ceremonies.

Liu Futong's uprising prompted responses in various regions. In Xuzhou, individuals such as Zhima Li, Peng Da, and Zhao Junyong, amongst others, rose up. In Haozhou (located north east of present-day Fengyang County, Anhui), Guo Zixing, Sun Deyan, Zhu Yuanzhang, and others led insurrections. In Xiangyang (now Xiangfan City, Hubei), figures including Wang Quan, Meng Haima, and others emerged. In Qishui (present-day Xishui County, Hubei), Xu Shouhui, Peng Yingyu, Ni Wenjun, and others initiated their own uprisings. Additionally, in areas not directly linked to the Red Turban Army, individuals like Fang Guozhen from Zhejiang and Zhang Shicheng from Gaoyou took advantage of the turmoil to start their own rebellions.

The fall of the Yuan Dynasty's foundation at the hands of the Red Turban Army uprising is indisputable. It is important to note that the use of red cloth as a symbol by Liu Futong and the claim that Han Shantong was the eighth-generation descendant of Emperor Huizong of the Song Dynasty, and thus the rightful ruler of China, were fraught with significant symbolism.[9]

Liu Futong, the leader of the White Lotus sect in Yingzhou (now Fuyang City, Anhui), utilized the organizational structure and teachings of the sect to underpin the uprising. Amidst the complex ethnic conflicts of the late Yuan Dynasty, both Han Shantong and Liu Futong initiated the rebellion, drawing on the teachings of the White Lotus sect. They also politically pressed for the restoration of rule of the Han nationality, placing particular emphasis on the re-establishment of the prosperous Song Dynasty. Their actions were symbolic: the color red, which symbolizes the fire virtue (huode) in White Lotus sect teachings, was prominently adopted by the Red Turban Army, with its soldiers donning red headbands and waving red flags, signifying the resurgence of the Zhao-Song virtue. Moreover, Han Shantong falsely proclaimed himself to be the eighth (or even ninth)[10] generation descendant of Emperor Huizong, while Liu Futong declared himself Liu Guangshi, a renowned Song Dynasty general, announcing their intention to support the restoration.[11] These declarations were tactical; showcasing their allegiance to the legacy of the fallen Song Dynasty to further their current cause.

The uprising's widespread influence and success can be attributed to the political resonance of the Red Turban Army's appeals.

In essence, the Anti-Yuan Movement at the time found inspiration in the Song Dynasty, a sentiment that was not exclusive to personalities like Han Shantong and Liu Futong. According to the *Annals of Emperor Shun* in the *History of the Yuan Dynasty*, in May of the twelfth year of the Zhiheng era (1352), it states,

> Numerous bandits in Henan frequently invoke the name of the defunct Song Dynasty as a pretext
>
>   …

The sentiments of the Han nationality, who were subordinate under the reign of the Yuan, are so clear. There has been a longstanding axiom, "Since ancient times, the Chinese civilization in Central Plains has been highly esteemed, while the barbarian tribes were regarded as inferior."[12] The Han were considered the legitimate successors of the Central Plains. Yet, throughout the Yuan Dynasty, their status was exceedingly undermined.

The Yuan government classified the people under its rule into four distinct categories: Mongolians, Semu people, Han people, and Southern people. This system enforced rigid racial policies, which impacted the selection of officials, the imperial examinations, and even the meting out of punishments. The Mongolians enjoyed the highest privileges, with the Semu people next in line (including the Halaj, Qiangchuan, Tangut, Alasha, Tufan, Qangli, Uyghur, Huihui, Naiman, Oirat, Sakaf, Volga, Ongud, Jürmed, Qashqai, and so forth.). Subsequently, the Han people comprised those originally under Jin Dynasty rule, along with Jurchen, Khitan, Goryeo, and other ethnicities. The Southern people, primarily the remaining Han people from the Southern Song Dynasty, were ranked last. The inequalities fostered by this system led to sporadic uprisings and attempts to restore Song rule following the collapse of the Southern Song in 1279.[13] In the waning years of the Yuan Dynasty, the political choice to oppose Yuan authority and reinstate orthodox Han rule became prevalent among the warlords. For example:

- In October 1351, Xu Shouhui declared himself emperor, founded the State of Qishui (today's Xishui County, Hubei), claimed the title "Great Song," and adopted the era name of Zhiping.
- Zhang Shicheng titled himself King of Cheng in Gaoyou in 1354 (present-day Gaoyou City, Jiangsu), established the Dazhou State, and utilized the era name of Tianyou.
- Chen Youliang murdered Xu Shouhui in May 1360, proclaimed himself emperor and embraced the title "Great Han" with the era name of Dayi, founding his capital in Jiangzhou (now Jiujiang City, Jiangxi).
- Xu Shouhui's general, Ming Yuzhen, declared himself emperor in Chongqing in March 1362, adopted the title of "Great Xia," and used the era name of Tiantong.
- In February 1355, Liu Futong enthroned Han Lin'er, alleging his status as the ninth-generation descendant of Emperor Huizong of the Song Dynasty, and used the moniker "King of Light Junior." The capital was set in Bozhou (currently Bozhou City, Anhui), adopting the Song designation and the era name of Longfeng.

The states named Song, Zhou, Han, and Xia were all prominent designations historically employed by Chinese dynasties or empires, serving as potent anti-Yuan emblems. During the period, these names were strategic choices made by the warlords intending to consolidate support and reestablish Han rule. "Song" held a particularly poignant resonance due to its not-too-distant fall. The army of Xu Shouhui and that of Han Lin'er represented the key forces of the Red Turban Army in the southern and northern regions, respectively.[14]

The overarching aim of the warlords' anti-Yuan campaign, coined as "expelling the barbarians and restoring China,"[15] signified the triumph of their crusades. The non-Han Yuan Dynasty retreated to the steppes, relinquishing claims to centrality in the Central Plains' geographical and cultural legacy. In its wake, the establishment of a Han-led government persisted in the Song's line of legitimate succession. Yet, the aspiration to wholly "reinstate the Song" went unrealized. Zhu Yuanzhang, who originated from humble beginnings in Huaiyuan, initially served under "King of Light Junior" (Han Lin'er), contesting the Yuan rule under the Song banner. He eventually founded the dynasty known as Great Ming, assuming control from the Yuan and unifying the post-restoration. However, the derivation of the title "Great Ming" adopted by Zhu Yuanzhang requires further clarification.

16.2 "The Emergence of the King of Light": King of Light Junior and the Emperor of the Great Ming

Previously, it was acknowledged that the revolts against the Yuan stemmed from the political impetus to reinstate Han governance or reestablish the Song Dynasty. It is necessary to consider the intimate association between the Red Turban Army and the White Lotus Sect. That Han Lin'er was lauded as the "King of Light Junior" and Zhu Yuanzhang acclaimed himself as the "Emperor of the Great Ming " can be traced to the White Lotus Sect.

Originating from the Pure Land Buddhist tradition, the White Lotus Sect promulgated the veneration of Amitabha Buddha. Its founder, Mao Ziyuan, hailed from Kunshan in the Prefecture Pingjiang (current Kunshan City, Jiangsu). During the early Southern Song Dynasty, Mao Ziyuan, following more than two decades as a monk, established the White Lotus Repentance Hall on Lake Dianshan. There, he "urged both men and women to cultivate pure karma in unison, naming himself the Patriarch of the White Lotus and gaining the congregation's veneration."[16] This event marked the genesis of the White Lotus Sect. In the era of Qiandao of the Southern Song, the sect's influence mushroomed rapidly after an imperial audience between the retired Emperor Zhao Gou and Mao Ziyuan, resulting in bestowed honors and widespread expansion of the sect.

White Lotus doctrine directly succeeded the Pure Land Buddhist tradition. According to Chinese Buddhism, Pure Land thought comprises two major schools: Maitreya's Pure Land and Amitabha's Pure Land. The former venerates Maitreya Buddha, whereas the latter is devoted to Amitabha Buddha. Both schools subscribe to the notion of a Pure Land, striving for rebirth within this realm through devout practice.

Since the Eastern Jin Dynasty, Maitreya Pure Land belief has gradually declined, while Amitabha Pure Land belief has become the mainstream.[17] Specifically, within the White Lotus Sect, devotees revere Amitabha Buddha and aim to be reborn in the Pure Land, which is the Western Paradise where Amitabha Buddha resides. They propagate the idea that "the mindful recitation of Amitabha Buddha's name brings about his appearance, and limitless bliss is omnipresent."[18]

Mao Zeduan, the founder of the White Lotus Sect, developed the practice of communal recitation of the Buddha's name within the Pure Land tradition. He also emphasized the relationships between teachers and disciples within the sect. This organizational innovation profoundly influenced the subsequent development of the White Lotus Sect.

During the Yuan Dynasty, the White Lotus Sect flourished, its temples spreading through various regions. Some temples accommodated thousands, or even hundreds of thousands, of devotees. This widespread presence led to the saying, "the branches and leaves of the White Lotus are spread all over the world."[19] In the first year of the Zhida era under Emperor Wuzong (1308 AD), the government issued an order to ban the White Lotus Sect due to its anti-Yuan activities. However, in the fourth year of the Zhida era, during the intercalary seventh month, Emperor Renzong issued a decree to reinstate the sect's legal status. By the mid to late Yuan period, the belief in Maitreya Pure Land,[20] closely connected with the White Lotus Sect, infiltrated the group. This greatly influenced the sect, with followers not only believing in "the appearance of Amitabha" but also widely accepting the proclamation of "the descent of Maitreya."

The tightly organized, long-standing, immensely influential, and complex White Lotus Sect became a tool in some anti-Yuan uprisings during the peculiar social and political context of the late Yuan Dynasty. The sect's teachings, preaching "the descent of Maitreya" and "the appearance of Amitabha" in the Pure Land, awakened the people's aspirations for a better future under oppressive rule. This religious background played a significant role in the rebellions organized by Han Shantong and Liu Futong.

According to the *Strategies of Great Planning* by Gao Dai of the Ming Dynasty, it states:

> Han Shantong was born into a distinguished White Lotus family. It was said that his grandfather's influence through the White Lotus gatherings and incense burning inspired Han Shantong to proclaim that the world would face great chaos, Maitreya Buddha would be reborn, and the King of Light would emerge. The people in Henan and the Jianghuai region readily believed his teachings.

Furthermore, the *Treasure Trove of Famous Mountains* by He Qiaoyuan of the Ming Dynasty states:

> Han Ling'er, the son of Han Shantong, a thief from Xu region, gained followers through his family's influence in the White Lotus gatherings. At the end of the Yuan Dynasty, he began to proclaim that chaos would engulf the world, Maitreya Buddha would be reborn, and the King of Light would appear. These proclamations stirred the people in the Jianghuai region.

The *Annals of Emperor Shun* in the *History of the Yuan Dynasty* presents a slightly similar account. However, it differs in that the official version was cautiously edited by Ming Dynasty officials who wished to eschew mentioning the personal name and the dynastic title of the founder of Ming. Therefore, it omits the concept of "the appearance of the King of Light."[21] Yet, in reality, this concept is intricately tied to the origin of the dynastic title "Da Ming" (Great Ming). Zhu Yuanzhang, the emperor of the Great Ming, ascended with the support of "Xiao Mingwang" (King of Light Junior).

Considering the literary works from the end of the Yuan Dynasty to the beginning of the Ming Dynasty, Han Lin'er was referred to as the "Xiao Mingwang" (King of Light Junior). Han Lin'er was the son of Han Shantong, so if the son was called the "Xiao Mingwang," it is likely that Han Shantong was known as the "Mingwang" (King of Light) or "Da Mingwang" (King of Light Senior) during his lifetime. Whether it was Mingwang, Da Mingwang, or Xiao Mingwang, all titles originated from Han Shantong's proclamation of the "appearance of the King of Light." Given that Han Shantong was a follower of the White Lotus Sect, which preached the "descent of Maitreya" and the "appearance of Amitabha" at the end of the Yuan Dynasty, it can be inferred that the "Mingwang" mentioned by Han Shantong likely referred to Amitabha Buddha. In fact, this was the case.

Amitabha refers to Amitabha Buddha. The primary scripture that followers of the White Lotus recite is the "Infinite Life Sutra," which states:

> The Buddha said: "Amitabha Buddha's radiance is bright, surpassing the sun and moon by countless times. He is the king of all Buddha's radiance, thus known as the Buddha of Infinite Life and the Buddha of Infinite Light ... His radiance illuminates all realms, including the darkest and most hidden places in the world."

Since Amitabha Buddha is referred to as the "king of all Buddha's radiance," synonymous with the "King of Light," it naturally implies that the "appearance of the king of Light" is the manifestation of Amitabha Buddha. The king would manifest because the world is in great chaos, and the red-colored king of Light will come to this world to save all beings. After the arrival of the king of Light, there will be no suffering or injustice, and a realm of ultimate bliss replete with dignity, purity, abundance, and beauty will be established. Furthermore, Han Shantong, hailing from a prestigious White Lotus family, associated both the "descent of Amitabha Buddha" and the "appearance of the king of Light." Therefore, the notion of the "appearance of the king of Light" can only originate from their teachings—the White Lotus sect's doctrine (see Figure 16.1).[22]

Han Shantong was captured and executed shortly after his rebellion. In February 1355, Liu Futong welcomed Han Shantong's son, Han Lin'er, to Bozhou and honored him as the "Xiao Mingwang"(King of Light Junior). Clearly, by assuming the title of King of Light Junior and using the dynastic title "Song," Han Lin'er was carrying on his father's cause. On one hand, he established the political legitimacy for the anti-Yuan efforts and the revival of the Song Dynasty, and on the other hand, he embraced the White Lotus sect's ideology of the "appearance of King of Light." The "army with red turbans"[23] symbolized both the fiery virtue associated with

Figure 16.1 Thangka of Amitayus Buddha

the Song Dynasty and their religious beliefs since Amitabha Buddha, the "King of Light," is connected with the color red.

The regime led by the King of Light Junior, Han Lin'er, known as the Regime Longfeng of Song, lasted for 12 years. In the 15th year of the Zhizheng era (1355 AD), they established the capital in Bozhou in February and later moved it to Anfeng (present-day Shouxian County, Anhui) in December. In the fourth year of the Longfeng era (1358 AD), Liu Futong captured Bianliang (the former capital of the Northern Song Dynasty, present-day Kaifeng, Henan), prompting Han Lin'er to move from Anfeng to Bianliang to establish a new capital there. However, by the following autumn, Bianliang had fallen, leading to their retreat to Anfeng. In the ninth year of the Longfeng era, Zhu Yuanzhang, who had been conferred the title of Duke of Wu by Han Lin'er, commemorated the King of Light Junior and Liu Futong to Chuzhou (present-day Chuzhou, Anhui). By December of the twelfth year of the Longfeng era (1366 AD), Zhu Yuanzhang, under the pretext of escorting Han Lin'er and Liu Futong to Yingtian, secretly ordered his general, Liao Yongzhong to drown them in the Guazhou River, thus marking the end of the Song regime.

With the collapse of the Song Dynasty came the rise of the Ming Dynasty. In January 1368, Zhu Yuanzhang declared himself emperor with the dynastic title "Da Ming" (Great Ming). The title "Da Ming" bears a clear connection to the honorific "Xiao Mingwang" (King of Light Junior) bestowed upon Han Lin'er, the Emperor of Song. Sun Yi of the Ming Dynasty wrote in his article "An Outline of the Early Ming Dynasty" in the *Anthology of Dongting*: "The dynastic title 'Da Ming' inherits the mantle of 'Xiao Ming' from Han Lin'er." This connection is intrinsically linked with Zhu Yuanzhang's own ascent to power.

Zhu Yuanzhang (1328-1398), also known as Zhu Chongba, was born in Zhongli, Haozhou (located in present-day Fengyang County, in north eastern Anhui Province). He came from a poor peasant family and worked as a cowherd and shepherd for a landlord in his youth. When Zhu Yuanzhang was 17 years old, in 1344, a severe drought followed by an epidemic broke out in northern Huainan. As a result, Zhu Yuanzhang's parents and eldest brother fell ill and passed away. In September, the destitute Zhu Yuanzhang entered Huangjue Temple (located in present-day south western Fengyang County, which was later moved to the north of the county and renamed Dalongxing Temple) as a servant monk.

Zhu Yuanzhang served as a servant monk for about 50 days, but due to the heavy impact of the disaster, Huangjue Temple could not collect rent on rice, and many monks left the temple to wander. Zhu Yuanzhang was also sent away and disguised himself as a monk, venturing out to travel. He roamed the Huai-Western region for about four years. During this time, this area witnessed active proliferation of the teachings of Peng Yingyu[24] and the White Lotus. Zhu Yuanzhang was deeply influenced and eventually joined the White Lotus sect. By the end of 1348, he had returned to Huangjue Temple.

In May 1351, Liu Futong, the leader of the White Lotus sect in Yingzhou, incited a rebellion and captured the city. In August, White Lotus followers such as Zhima Li, Peng Da, and Zhao Junyong rose up and seized Xuzhou. White Lotus leaders like Peng Yingyu, Zou Pusheng, and Xu Shouhui also initiated an uprising and took control of Qishui in October. In February of the subsequent year, local landlord and White Lotus follower Guo Zixing aligned with Liu Futong's Red Turban Army rebellion and overran Haozhou, proclaiming himself as the marshal. Given this situation, after receiving a letter from his former cowherd colleague Tang He, who by then was a member of the Red Turban Army, and seeking divination advice through fortune-telling,[25] Zhu Yuanzhang, the future Emperor of the Ming Dynasty, made up his mind to leave Huangjue Temple and join the Red Turban Army.

In the twelfth year of the Yuan Zhi Zheng era (1352 AD), on the first day of the leap month of March, the 25-year-old Zhu Yuanzhang enlisted in Guo Zixing's army as an infantryman. Zhu Yuanzhang had received a few months of education at a private school when he was younger, which endowed him with some literacy. His intelligence and courage in battle allowed him to quickly ascend through the ranks in Guo Zixing's army. He initially served as Guo Zixing's bodyguard, then married Guo Zixing's adopted daughter Lady Ma, thereby becoming his son-in-law. Subsequently, after recruiting soldiers in his hometown, Zhu Yuanzhang was promoted to general, and with Guo Zixing's consent, he led his own forces to expand their territory.

In his military campaigns, Zhu Yuanzhang achieved considerable success. In 1353, he briefly captured Yuanzhou, followed by a takeover of Chuzhou. In

1355, he conquered Hezhou and was designated by Guo Zixing as the supreme commander. In March of that same year, Guo Zixing died. In May, the King of Light Junior appointed Guo Tianxu, Guo Zixing's son, as the Grand Marshal and Zhu Yuanzhang as the Left Deputy Marshal. They adopted the regnal year title "Longfeng" for military declarations. In September, both Guo Tianxu and the Right Deputy Marshal Zhang Tianyou perished in conflict while attacking Jiqing Circuit (now known as Nanjing, Jiangsu). Consequently, Zhu Yuanzhang ascended as the Grand Marshal, assuming command of Guo Zixing's entire military.

In March 1356, Zhu Yuanzhang seized Jiqing Circuit and renamed it Prefecture Yingtian. Using Prefecture Yingtian as his base, Zhu Yuanzhang systematically expanded his dominion to include southern Anhui, southern Jiangsu, northern Jiangsu, and eastern Zhejiang by 1359. He became the preeminent force in the region, solidifying his role as a local warlord.

During this period, Zhu Yuanzhang continued to recognize the Han-Song Longfeng regime as the lawful authority. In 1356, the King of Light Junior named Zhu Yuanzhang as a co-equivalent member of the Council of the Department of Military Affairs and later upgraded him to the role of Chancellor of the State Council for Southern Provinces and other territories. In 1359, Zhu Yuanzhang received further advancement to the post of Left Chancellor of the State Council for Southern Provinces and other regions. In 1361, the King of Light Junior conferred upon Zhu Yuanzhang the title of Duke of Wu. In 1363, he was once again promoted, this time to the position of Right Chancellor of the State Council.

During this period, Zhu Yuanzhang's campaign against the Yuan Dynasty continued under the banner of restoring the "Song" regime. After capturing Wuzhou in 1359, for instance, Zhu Yuanzhang established the Zhejiang Eastern Provincial Government in Prefecture Jinhua. At the entrance of the provincial government, two large yellow flags bore the inscription: "The mountains and rivers once again belong to the land of China, and the sun and moon dawn upon the Great Song Dynasty." In addition, two plaques proclaimed: "The sun and moon in the nine heavens brighten the Yellow Path, and the land and rivers of Song return to their revered state."[26]

In January 1364, Zhu Yuanzhang proclaimed himself the King of Wu. Since 1356, he had made Prefecture Yingtian his stronghold, with the prefecture's name reflecting its location in the Wu region and historical significance as the capital of the Sun Wu state during the Three Kingdoms period. The title "Duke of Wu," bestowed upon Zhu Yuanzhang by the King of Light Junior in 1361, confirmed this association. By 1363, Zhu Yuanzhang had defeated and killed Chen Youliang of the Great Han, leaving Chen Youliang's son besieged in Wuchang. With his other rival, Zhang Shicheng of Pingjiang, contained and no longer a threat, Zhu Yuanzhang declared himself the King of Wu. Despite official documents continuing to bear the dual titles "Imperial Edict of the Emperor, and Decree of the King of Wu," Zhu Yuanzhang had effectively formed an independent bureaucracy, established the State Council, and appointed his eldest son, Zhu Biao, as crown prince.

It is noteworthy that before Zhu Yuanzhang declared himself King of Wu, Zhang Shicheng had already taken the title King of Zhou in March 1356. Yet, in

September 1363, Zhang Shicheng proclaimed himself King of Wu in Pingjiang (now Suzhou, Jiangsu). Despite this, Zhu Yuanzhang maintained the title of King of Wu, signaling his intentions to sever ties with the Longfeng regime and establish his autonomy.

A popular children's ditty at the time went: "Rich man, don't build a tower; poor man, don't build a house; when the Year of the Sheep comes, it will become the state of Wu Family." To resonate with public sentiment expressed by the ditty and its reference to the "State of Wu Family," Zhu Yuanzhang assumed the title of King of Wu.[27]

Moreover, in December 1366, Zhu Yuanzhang executed the King of Light Junior and besieged Zhang Shicheng in 1367 (the Year of Dingwei, corresponding to the Year of the Sheep). To further align with the children's ditty, Zhu Yuanzhang substituted the regnal year title of "Longfeng" with "Wu."

By December of the first year of Wu, Zhang Shicheng of Pingjiang had capitulated and committed suicide, and Fang Guozhen of eastern Zhejiang had been cornered and opted to surrender. Progress was unstoppable as the land and naval forces advanced toward Fujian, and the first-route army was poised to march on Nanping, Guangdong, and Guangxi. The northern expedition had pacified Shandong. Against the backdrop of these victories and with national reconstruction and unification in sight, Ying Tian's civil and military officials submitted a memorial urging Zhu Yuanzhang to ascend the throne. Obliging, Zhu Yuanzhang moved into the newly constructed palace and offered sacrifices to the deities, proclaiming, "The officials counsel a need for a sovereign, urging the adoption of the imperial title. I dare not reject such advice and must inform the heavenly deities. Consequently, on the fourth day of the next lunar year, I shall perform the appropriate rituals on Zhongshan Mountain's sunny slopes to announce my intentions. Should the deities agree, they will manifest themselves under clear and unpolluted skies on the day of sacrifice. If, however, adverse winds and odd phenomena prevail, I will take note."[28] The esteemed astronomer and geographer, Liu Ji (Liu Bowen), had already forecast that the agreed-upon day would indeed bring "clear and pure" conditions, indicating divine endorsement for Zhu Yuanzhang to govern. Therefore, on that day, Zhu Yuanzhang ascended the imperial throne on the southern outskirts of Ying Tian and christened his realm "Da Ming" under the reign title "Hongwu."

In retrospect, Zhu Yuanzhang's choice of "Da Ming" for his country's name is rooted in his formative years. Having entered the monastery at 17 as a novice monk, followed by approximately four years as an itinerant monk and later joining the White Lotus Sect before again donning robes for over three years, Zhu Yuanzhang was deeply influenced by the "Great Amitabha Sutra" and the "The King of Light's Advent" slogan from Han Shantong, as well as the "King of Light Junior" appellation for Han Lin'er. Thus, in naming his country "Da Ming," Zhu Yuanzhang signaled a new era of peace and prosperity analogous to the Western Pure Land prophesied by the White Lotus Sect, as well as a homage to his Buddhist origins.[29] History would remember him as the sole monk to achieve sovereign rule, the embodiment of the Buddhist King of Light.[30]

In conclusion, Zhu Yuanzhang's decision to name the country "Da Ming" can be seen as both clever and effective. The cleverness of the choice lies in its resonance with various groups: the title "Da Ming" aligned with the religious beliefs of the Red Turban Army, which were grounded in White Lotus teachings. For Confucian officials, the name was imbued with historical and philosophical significance, familiar through their scholarly pursuits. Zhu Yuanzhang himself may have chosen this title to honor his Buddhist roots and to embody his ambition of becoming an "enlightened emperor" who rises above worldly afflictions. These interpretations harmonized or, at the very least, were favorably perceived by their respective adherents.

Regarding its effectiveness, the Red Turban Army likely felt vindicated that their founding emperor had not abandoned their shared history. The Confucian officials felt affirmed by the new Dynasty's historical legitimacy, its alignment with the mandate of heaven, and the fulfillment of popular aspirations. As for the populace, they found solace in the promise of a bright and joyful future under the enlightened rule of the "King of Light." This sentiment undoubtedly solidified Zhu Yuanzhang's centralized and authoritative governance, fortifying his family's dominion over the empire.

The Ming Dynasty, characterized by its centralized authority, did enjoy an extended era of prosperity. It was established in January 1368 in the southern region and endured until March 1644, succumbing to a combination of internal and external adversities. The rule of the Ming Dynasty extended even further, until 1661 and beyond, prior to its ultimate demise.[31]

Notes

1 The Veritable Records of Ming Taizu, Volume 29, the day of Yihai of the first lunar month of the first year of Hongwu era.

2 The true completion of the unified enterprise of "Da Ming" would occur later, either in the 15th year of Hongwu era, when Yunnan was pacified, or in the 20th year of Hongwu era, when Liaodong was pacified.

3 The issue of the so-called "Southern Ming" after 1644 is discussed in detail in Chapter 18.

4 In January 1644, Li Zicheng proclaimed himself king and adopted the country name Da Shun, with the era name Yongchang. On the 29th of April, Li Zicheng declared himself emperor. Furthermore, in the early Ming Dynasty, the capital was initially in the city of Taizhou, which was later changed to Nanjing in 1421 and downgraded to a secondary capital. Beijing (formerly known as Prefecture Beiping in 1368, then changed to Prefecture Shuntian in 1403, and established as Beijing) became the capital. Although the official title changed, it was still referred to as Beijing by the general public.

5 In April 1636, Huang Taiji ascended the throne and proclaimed the country as "Da Qing" (Great Qing).

6 Tao Zongyi, Nan Cun Chuo Geng Lu (Records of Tilling Abandoned in the Southern Village), Volume 23, "Zui Tai Ping Xiao Ling"(A Short Lyric of the 'Peaceful' Society).

7 History of the Yuan Dynasty, Chronicle of Emperor Shun

8 Chronicle of Emperor Shun in the *History of the Yuan Dynasty* stated: "In the beginning, Han Shantong's grandfather, a resident of Luancheng, misled the public by burning

incense during the White Lotus Society, and was thus banished to Guangping and Yongnian County." Luancheng was located west of present-day Luancheng County in Hebei province.

9 The following discussion on this issue draws reference from Chen Xuelin's work "A Study on the Distinction Between the National Title and Virtuous Reign of the Song Dynasty," included in his book *Collection of Essays on the History of the Song Dynasty*, published by Dongda Book Company, Taipei, in 1993.

10 According to the record in Volume 3, "Ke Jin Pian," of Ye Ziqi's "Caomu Zi," it is mentioned: "Using the name of Zhao Song, Han Shantong falsely claimed to be the ninth-generation grandson of Emperor Huizong of the Song Dynasty. The fabricated imperial edict stated: 'Conceal the jade seal in the East Sea and recruit elite troops from Japan. From poverty in Jiangnan to wealth in the northern border.'" This was done to incite unrest and turmoil, as Prince Zhao Guang of Song fled to Yashan, and Chancellor Chen Yizhong fled to the Japanese, using this deception to destabilize the nation. At that time, the poor joined the rebellion as if returning home. The court dispatched troops to suppress them, and although they were captured, chaos had already ensued. It is worth noting that the "Prince Zhao Guang" refers to Emperor Zhao Bing of Song. In January of 1276, as the Yuan army approached Lin'an, Prince Zhao Bing was conferred the title of Prince Guang. Additionally, according to Chen Xuelin's work *A Study on the Resettlement of Song Dynasty Refugee Immigrants in Annam and Champa* (included in his book *Collection of Essays on the History of the Song Dynasty*), Chen Yizhong fled to Annam and Champa rather than Japan, and ultimately died in Siam.

11 In Volume 43, "Tian Yin Ji," of He Qiaoyuan's *Mingshan Cang*, it is mentioned: "Liu Guangshi, a native of Bao'an Army (present-day Zhidan

County, Shaanxi Province). In the late Northern Song Dynasty, he participated in suppressing the Fang La Rebellion under the command of Tong Guan. In the early Southern Song Dynasty, he made contributions in resisting the Jin Dynasty and was politically adept at adapting to changing circumstances, thus receiving favored treatment from the court.

12 In Book 14 of Annals of the Tang Dynasty in the *Zizhi Tongjian*, in the 21st year of the Zhenguan era (AD 647), Emperor Taizong of Tang made the statement.

13 For example, in 1283, Huang Hua's uprising in Fujian adopted the reign title of Xiangxing of Emperor Zhao Bing during the Song Dynasty. In 1286, Zhao Heshang in Xichuan proclaimed himself as the Prince of Song in Guangzhou. In 1337, Han Fashi's uprising in Hezhou claimed himself to be the Southern Dynasty's Prince Zhao, and so on. For more details, please refer to Yang Ne and Chen Gaohua, "Compilation of Historical Materials on Peasant Wars in the Yuan Dynasty," Zhonghua Book Company, 1985.

14 It needs to be clarified that among various historical records, Xu Shouhui's regime was referred to as "Tian Wan," which was mistakenly interpreted as having the meaning of "swearing to suppress the Great Yuan." However, this is not historically accurate. The official name of Xu Shouhui's regime was originally "Da Song," and Xu's "Da Song" came earlier than Han Lin'er's "Song" regime. Later, Zhu Yuanzhang, who rose to power in the Longfeng regime (more details below), established the regime name as "Da Ming." Due to the contention for legitimate succession, the recognition of Xu Shouhui's "Da Song" regime was intolerable. Therefore, in the early Ming Dynasty, historians deliberately concealed this fact and, when compiling the "Yuan Shi" and national history, replaced Xu Shouhui's "Da Song" with the fabricated term "Tian Wan." For more details, refer to Yang Ne's "Shi Tian Wan" (published in the "Historical Research" journal, 1978, No. 1), Shi Shuqing's "Bronze Seals of Xu Shouhui's Peasant

Regime at the End of the Yuan Dynasty" (published in the journal of "Cultural Relics," 1972, No. 6), Zhang Cailie's "The Historical Value of the Epitaph of the Xuan Palace" (published in the Journal of Jianghan Forum, 1986, No. 4), and Dai Xuanzhi's "The Anti-Yuan Movement of the White Lotus Religion" (published in the Journal of History at the National Chengchi University, No. 3, Taipei, 1985).

15 In October 1367, Zhu Yuanzhang issued a declaration for the Northern Expedition, detailed in "The Veritable Records of Ming Taizu," Volume 21.

16 Zhi Pan, Fozu Tong Ji (Comprehensive Records of the Buddhas), Volume 48.

17 For more detailed information on the White Lotus Religion during the Yuan Dynasty, refer to Yang Ne's "The White Lotus Religion in the Yuan Dynasty," Collection of Essays on the History of the Yuan Dynasty, compiled by the Yuan History Research Society, Volume 2, Zhonghua Book Company, 1983.

18 Pu Du, Lushan Lianzong Baojian, Volume 2, cited in Yang Ne's compilation *Materials on the White Lotus Religion in the Yuan Dynasty*, Zhonghua Book Company, 1989.

19 Guo Man, Dianshan White Lotus, Collection of the Lushan White Lotus Orthodox Tangu, cited in Yang Ne's compilation *Materials on the White Lotus Religion in the Yuan Dynasty*.

20 Regarding the Pure Land of the Maitreya Pure Land Dharma Gate in Pure Land Buddhism, it refers to the Pure Land where Maitreya resides in the Tusita Heaven. Although the Maitreya Pure Land faith was not as popular as the Amitabha Pure Land faith after the Southern and Northern Dynasties, it has never been completely severed. The image of Maitreya Buddha has always been one of the main Buddha statues worshipped in Buddhist temples. From the Sui Dynasty to the Song Dynasty, there were repeated rebellions using the pretext of "Maitreya's descent."

21 Wu Han, "Ming Jiao and the Great Ming Empire," Journal of Tsinghua University, Vol. 13, No. 1, 1941. This article is included in the selected works of Wu Han's historical studies, Volume 2, published by People's Publishing House in 1986.

22 In Wu Han's book "Ming Jiao and the Great Ming Empire," it is argued that the slogan "Ming Wang Chushi" (the King of Ming is born) and the national title "Da Ming" (Great Ming) originated from the Ming Jiao classic "Da Xiao Ming Wang Chushi Jing" (The Scripture of the Birth of the Senior and Junior King of Light). This scripture was a Manichaean scripture that originated from Persia during the Tang Dynasty. In the 3rd century AD, a Persian named Mani blended Zoroastrianism, Christianity, and Buddhism to create Manichaeism. Since Manichaeism promoted that light would ultimately triumph over darkness, with the highest deity being the Ming Zun (Radiant Lord), and under the Ming Zun, there were various Ming Shi (Radiant Messengers), whose births as Ming Wangs (Radiant Kings) would "enlighten sentient beings and liberate them from suffering." Therefore, in China, Manichaeism was also referred to as Ming Jiao (the Religion of Radiance). Later, Yang Ne wrote "The White Lotus Religion in the Yuan Dynasty," in which he believed that Wu Han's perspective was subjective speculation lacking historical evidence and should be rejected and corrected, proposing the new theory of the White Lotus Religion. This is according to Yang's view.

23 He Qiaoyuan, "Tian Yin Ji" (Record of Celestial Causes), Mingshan Cang, Volume 43.

24 Peng Yingyu was born in Yuanzhou (now Yichun City, Jiangxi Province). He initially became a monk at Cihua Temple on Nanquan Mountain in Yuanzhou and was known as Monk Peng. He was a follower of the White Lotus Religion. In 1338, he and his disciple Zhou Ziwang rebelled against the Yuan Dynasty. Zhou Ziwang declared himself the King of Zhou but was captured and executed, while Peng Yingyu went into hiding in

Huai Xi. While in Huai Xi, Peng Yingyu continued to spread the teachings of the White Lotus Religion, and his influence grew extensively.

25 According to the "Imperial Mausoleum Inscription" written by Zhu Yuanzhang (included in Shen Jiefu's "Compilation of Records" Volume One), during this time, they consulted divination and received the following result: "If you consult divination on escaping or staying, neither is auspicious. It would be better to accept the misfortune and not hinder it," suggesting that neither fleeing nor staying in the temple would bring good fortune, and it might be worth joining the Red Turban Army.

26 Qian Qianyi, "The King of Light Junior of the Song Dynasty," Brief Accounts of the Heroes of the Early Founding of the Country, Volume One, quoting Yu Ben's "Record of the Imperial Ming Dynasty Events."

27 Quan Heng, Records of the Yuan Dynasty, the Five Elements, Geng Shen Waishi (External History of the Geng Shen Ear), Volume One. Due to the existence of two Kings of Wu simultaneously, Zhang Shicheng in Pingjiang was referred to as "Dong Wu" (East Wu) among the common people, while Zhu Yuanzhang in Ying Tian was referred to as "Xi Wu" (West Wu).

28 Ming Taizu Shilu (Veritable Records of the Great Ming Emperor), Volume 28, it records on the day of Jiazi of the twelfth month of the first year of Wu (Zhu Yuanzhang's reign).

29 According to the "Imperial Tomb Inscription" written by Zhu Yuanzhang himself in the eleventh year of the Hongwu era, Zhu Yuanzhang attached great importance to the difficult years before his success and did not mind his Buddhist background at that time.

30 This statement is taken from Yang Ne's work "The White Lotus Sect in the Yuan Dynasty."

31 It is worth emphasizing that even after the demise of the Ming Dynasty, the historical memory surrounding the "Great Ming" did not disappear. In fact, during the early Qing Dynasty, late Qing Dynasty, and the Republic of China era, this historical memory transformed into tangible actions. For example, during the era of the Republic of China, the study of Ming history became a "practical tool," and research on Zheng He's voyages to the West became a popular topic. Numerous works on the Ming Dynasty's resistance against Japanese invasions were also produced. From a deeper cultural psychological perspective, this association with Great Ming is connected to its being the last dynasty of Han in the Chinese history.

He Yiqun, in his article "Great Ming and the 'Fire Virtue' in Chinese History" (Journal of Ming Dynasty History and Culture, 2006, Issue 4), points out that at least from the perspective of the Han nationality, there exists a generational relationship between the Mongol-led Yuan Dynasty and the Han-led dynasties of Zhu Ming and Zhao Song. The reverence for "fire virtue" and the significance of the color red associated with Great Ming had a visible or hidden influence on the history from the downfall of the Ming Dynasty to the early years of the Republic of China. During the early Qing Dynasty, there were movements such as the Hongguang regime of Zhu Youyong in Nanjing, the Longwu regime of Zhu Yujian in Fuzhou, and the Yongli regime of Zhu Youlang in Zhaoqing, all of which used regnal titles with meanings related to the fire virtue, and displayed clear connections to the legitimate imperial lineage of the capital city (present-day Beijing) of the Ming Dynasty. There were also various groups, such as the Restoration Society, composed mainly of Ming loyalists, actively advocating for the restoration of the Ming Dynasty. Secret organizations among the common people, such as the Tiandihui, also had clear aspirations to restore the "Yan Ming" regime. Later on, individuals claiming to be descendants of the Ming imperial family, such as Zhu Liufei, Zhu Yongzuo, Zhu Yigui, Zhu Maoli, Zhu Mingyue, and the like., used the slogan of reviving the Han imperial lineage and reestablishing the Great Ming regime. Towards the end of the Qing Dynasty, the forces advocating for the restoration of Ming became even more diverse. Among them, the Xingzhonghui organization, represented by Sun Yat-sen and the bourgeois revolutionary faction, explicitly proclaimed the goal of "expelling the Manchus, restoring China, establishing a republic, and redistributing land rights." The call to "expel the Manchus and restore China" aligns with Zhu Yuanzhang's call to "drive out the barbarians and restore China" at the end of the Yuan Dynasty as well as the early anti-Qing sentiments. From the perspective of China's traditional historiography, the founding of the Republic of China in 1912 was akin to the restoration of Great Ming. Even the Red Army and the Red Soviet regime, which represented the interests of the masses in the Republic of China era, and later the red flag with five stars of the People's Republic of China, all carry a distinct symbolic meaning.

17 The Great Qing

Turning the Tide

On May 2, 1644, Dorgon, the regent of the Great Qing Empire and the Commanding General, led his troops into the capital of the Ming Dynasty, Beijing (now Beijing Municipality). On September 19, the young emperor of the Great Qing, Fulin, arrived, and on October 1, a grand coronation ceremony was held. Thus, the previously marginal Great Qing officially joined the struggle to become the new ruler since the end of the Ming Dynasty.

Initially, in March 1644, the Emperor of the Ming Dynasty, Zhu Youjian, hanged himself at the Shouhuang Temple in the capital. In April, the King of Dashun, Li Zicheng, declared himself emperor in the capital.[1] In May, the Prince of Fu, Zhu Yousong[2], declared himself emperor in Nanjing (marking the first year of the Hongguang era). Then, in November, the King of Daxi, Zhang Xianzhong, declared himself emperor in Chengdu.[3] At that time, four emperors emerged, each ruling over different parts of the country: the Great Qing controlled the southern part of Inner Mongolia, the north east, and some parts of Hebei; Dashun controlled Shanxi, Gansu, Henan, and some parts of Hebei; Daxi dominated Sichuan; while other regions generally remained loyal to the Ming Dynasty. Comparatively, the Great Qing had an army of about 200,000,[4] the smallest in number, with the core of its forces consisting of around 50,000 Manchu soldiers.

However, history is truly astonishing. It was the Great Qing, with the smallest military force, which achieved incredible feats. In 1645, they vanquished the Hongguang regime and defeated Dashun.[5] In 1646, they conquered Longwu,[6] extinguished the Shaowu[7] regime and defeated Daxi.[8] In 1659, they overthrew the Yongli[9] regime, and in 1664, they extinguished the Dingwu regime.[10] In 1683, they took control of Taiwan.[11] Moreover, in the approximately 20 years following 1644, various armed uprisings against the Qing Dynasty in different regions were successively suppressed. As a result, the empire was unified, and another national government, led by a non-Han ethnic group, was established after the Mongolian "Great Yuan" Dynasty. The last universal ruler of the traditional imperial era in China, the "Great Qing," successfully replaced the "Great Ming," which was once established with the slogan of "driving out the barbarians and restoring China."[12]

DOI: 10.4324/9781003510390-18

17.1 The "Jin" Dynasty of Wisdom: Revering Tradition

On April 19, 1636, in Shengjing (present-day Shenyang, Liaoning Province), Huang Taiji of the Aisin Gioro clan proclaimed himself emperor and established the Qing Dynasty. If we trace back to January 1, 1616, Huang Taiji's father, Nurhaci, had already established a Khanate in Hetuala (present-day Xiaocheng, Xinbin County, Liaoning Province) and adopted the country name "Aisin" (translated as "Jin" in Chinese). His khan title was "Abkai Gurun Be Ujihun Semesi Tehe Ilhaciyeme Han " (meaning "The Wise Khan Bestowed by Heaven to Nurture and Rule Over All Countries"). Nurhaci also created the surname "Aisin Gioro" for his family. In the Jurchen language, "Aisin" means "gold" and "Gioro" means "clan." Thus, the "Jin" Dynasty, ruling over vast territories and millions of subjects, emerged in the north eastern region of the Ming Dynasty.

The establishment of the Jin Dynasty can be traced back to 1583. In that year, Nikan Wailan, the leader of the Suksoo Hudu tribe in Jianzhou, led the Ming army to attack Atai, who led the Right Guard of Jianzhou. Nurhaci's grandfather was Giocangga (a chieftain of the Left Guard in Jianzhou and a Commander for the Great Ming), and his father, Taksi accompanied the army on a campaign. During the chaos of war, Giocangga and Taksi were killed by the Ming army by mistake. In the same year, in May, Nurhaci sent troops to attack his enemy Nikan Wailan, firing the first shot in the establishment of the Jurchen state (later to become the State of Jin, not to be confused with the earlier Jin Dynasty founded by the Jurchens).

The establishment of the State of Jin was closely related to the unification of the various Jurchen tribes. In the early period of the Wanli era (1573-1620) of the Ming Dynasty, the Jurchens were divided into three major tribes: Jianzhou, Haixi, and Donghai (Wild Jurchens), with numerous sub-tribes within each tribe. They frequently fought among themselves, causing chaos and turmoil.[13] Nurhaci, who came from a small tribe in Jianzhou, started his uprising at the age of 25. His father and grandfather had been unjustly killed, and his followers deserted him. He was left with only 13 sets of armor and 30 soldiers.[14] However, after more than 30 years of military campaigns and political alliances, a miracle occurred. The brave and clever Nurhaci managed to surpass all his rivals and achieved the great task of unifying the Jurchen tribes that had been unfinished for hundreds of years. He ascended to the throne as an enlightened Khan and became the great leader of all the Jurchens. At that time, only the Yehe tribe of Haixi Jurchens had not surrendered. They were finally conquered in 1619, leading to the ultimate conquest of all Jurchen tribes. Volume 6 of the *Annals of Manchu* states: "From Donghai to Liaobian, from the north bordering the Mongolian Nen River to the south bordering the Yalu River of Korea, those who speak the same language were all conquered. It was this year that the various tribes were united as one."

In 1616, Nurhaci established the state of the Jin and, two or three years later, minted a seal inscribed with the Manchu phrase[15] "abkai fulingga aisin gurun han i doron," meaning "Seal of the Mandate of Heaven of the Khan of the Golden State." It should be noted that as early as 500 years prior, in 1115, Aguda, the Khitan leader, had founded an independent state also named "Jin." By 1125, this state had defeated the Liao Dynasty, and by 1127, it extinguished the Song Dynasty, marking an unprecedented achievement for the Jurchen people. The Jurchen Jin Dynasty lasted for 119 years. Nurhaci compared himself to his ancestral hero Aguda, and his state can be seen as a revival of the Jurchen Jin Dynasty. In the *Old Archives of Manchu*, there are references to the Jin Dynasty of the 12th and 13th centuries as "our Jin Dynasty" or "our former Jin Dynasty," acknowledging the emperors of the Jurchen Jin Dynasty as predecessors.

Furthermore, "Jin," as a symbol of Jurchen cultural tradition and political identity, was reintroduced by Nurhaci at this time. It was a practical and traditional measure, with significance both internally and externally. Domestically, the name "Jin" signified the political and ethnic unity of the Jurchen people, which was instrumental in uniting and appeasing the conquered Jurchen tribes.[16] Internationally, the reintroduction of the name "Jin" proclaimed Nurhaci's ambition to revitalize his ancestral heritage and establish an independent state, signifying the message to the Ming Dynasty.

On April 13, 1618, Nurhaci initiated a military campaign against the Ming Dynasty, motivated by desires for external expansion and unification. The "Seven Great Hatreds" were cited as the rationale for this decision. They included grievances such as the Ming soldiers killing Nurhaci's father and forefathers, the Ming Dynasty's breach of promise to protect the Yehe Tribe, disputes concerning timber extraction, the Ming Dynasty's support of the Yehe Tribe leading to Nurhaci's betrothed being married to the Mongols, the Ming's prohibition against the Haixi Jurchens (whom the Jianzhou Tribe sought to annex) from harvesting their crops, disrespectful comments made by Ming emissaries towards the Jianzhou Tribe, and the Ming Dynasty's order for Nurhaci to return the Haixi region to its original state. The "Seven Great Hatreds" reflected the significant issues the Jurchens (eventually known as the Manchus) held against the Ming: the mistreatment by the Ming government and the Ming court's resistance to the unification of Jurchen tribes, aimed at maintaining their divided and submissive governance system.[17]

Conflict between the Jin and Ming dynasties led to fluctuating victories. Nevertheless, the Jin Dynasty often had the advantage. In 1619, Jin forces captured Kaiyuan and Tieling, vanquishing the Yehe Tribe. In 1621, they seized Shenyang and Liaoyang, later moving the capital to Liaoyang. By 1622, they had taken Guangning, and in 1625 relocated their capital to Shenyang. Throughout this period, the Ming Dynasty's Liaodong General, Gao Di, ordered the abandonment of cities outside the Shanhaiguan Pass, except for Yuan Chonghuan, who defied the orders and defended Ningyuan City.

In January 1626, Jin forces were unable to capture Ningyuan, and Nurhaci was wounded by artillery fire. On August 11, Nurhaci died at the age of 68, posthumously honored as the "Great Emperor Taizu" of the Qing Dynasty. After a series of power struggles, on September 1, Nurhaci's eighth son, 35-year-old Huang Taiji, ascended to the throne of the Jin Empire. He was titled "Sure han" in Manchu, meaning "Tiancong (wise) Khan" in Han Chinese.[18]

17.2 "The Great Qing" under Emperor Huang Taiji: Assessing the Situation

Emperor Huang Taiji, also known as Abahai, was a visionary leader who sought to usher in a new and prosperous era. After ten years of effort, on April 11, 1636, with the joint counsel and support of Manchu, Han, and Mongol officials and generals, Emperor Huang Taiji held a grand ceremony to proclaim himself emperor. He was endowed with the title "Benevolent and Saintly Emperor of Leniency and Warmth" and established the nation as the "Great Qing," adopting the reign title "Chong De."[19] This marked the formal distinction and equal status between the Emperor of the mighty Great Qing and the Emperor of the waning Ming Dynasty.

One year prior, Emperor Huang Taiji had changed the ethnic designation from "Jurchen" (Jusen or "Zhushen" in Chinese) to "Manchu" (Manju).[20] The introduction of the state name "Great Qing," the reign title "Chong De," and the emperor's title "Benevolent and Saintly Emperor of Leniency and Warmth" are widely recognized as significant indicators of the assimilation of Han Chinese civilization. The significance of the nation's name "Great Qing" will be expounded in the subsequent section. The reign title "Chong De" clearly manifests Confucian influences, while the emperor's title signifies continuity of Han Chinese civilization and the reflection of traditional Confucian ideals and governing principles. Notably, by adopting the state name "Great Qing," Emperor Huang Taiji also deliberately cast aside the moniker "Jin" (of the preceding dynasty), further underscoring the assimilation process.

As previously mentioned, the title "Jin" was influential during Nurhaci's entrepreneurial stage. However, with the dynastic expansion in conquered territories and the incorporation of various ruling ethnic groups, the detriments of the title Jin gradually surfaced. The mounting negative impact even created impediments to Huang Taiji's ambitions. By the time of Huang Taiji's rule, the Jin had evolved into a multi-ethnic empire, comprised of the Jurchens, Mongols, and Han Chinese as the principal ethnic constituents. The name "Jin," evocative of Jurchen resurgence, seemed ethnically restrictive for a nation's title. Moreover, the Ming Dynasty, facing decline, posed the greatest threat and represented Huang Taiji's ultimate aspiration. With its vast territories and sizable population, conquering the Ming would have signified a triumph far surpassing that of the past Jin State, which only held sway over parts of the realm. Compounding this, the distant kinship, and the lapse in civilization, made it implausible to clearly delineate connections between the Jianzhou Jurchens, from whom Nurhaci and Huang Taiji descended, and the Wanyan Jurchens from 500 years earlier. Given the practical political exigencies, Huang Taiji found no compelling reason to perpetuate the use of "Jin" as the state title.

Addressing practical political necessities, Huang Taiji's reign required direct engagement, the subjugation, and even the replacement of the Ming Dynasty, necessitating broad-based support from Han generals, soldiers, officials, and the populace, or at the very least, their passive acquiescence. The title "Jin" for the nation presented a clear impediment in this goal. The Han Chinese were all too familiar with "Jin": in late 1126, the Jin army breached the capital of the Song Dynasty, Kaifeng, and by early 1127, had captured the Song emperor, his empress, many imperial kin, officials, eunuchs, palace maids, craftsmen, and actors. They seized copious ceremonial artifacts, scientific instruments, books, maps, and imperial treasures, inflicting an unparalleled affront and resentment, known as the "Humiliation of Jingkang." The Ming Dynasty also suffered comparable disgrace. In 1449, during the Mongol incursion,[21] the Ming emperor Zhu Qizhen personally led an army of 500,000 into the catastrophic Battle of Tumu (east of modern-day Huailai County, Hebei Province). Tens of thousands perished or were wounded, and Emperor Zhu Qizhen was taken prisoner—This event, the "Tumu Crisis," marked an ignominious chapter in Ming history. Post "Tumu Crisis," Han Chinese racial consciousness hit new zeniths, with acute historical memories and animosity towards Mongols and other foreign groups. Literary works capturing these sentiments were consecrated for the *History of the Song Dynasty*, propagating Han nationalism and exhorting the Han to never forget the "Humiliation of Jingkang " and the cautionary tale of the Mongol obliteration of the Song.[22] Under such circumstances, the State of Jin, the perpetrator of the "Humiliation of Jingkang," was deeply loathed and detested by the people of Han (see Figure 17.1).

During the Nurhaci era of the State of Jin, Ming officials repeatedly lodged complaints via memorials. Nurhaci declared his regime "Later Jin," equating the Ming's decline with the Song's fall and dishonoring the Ming emperor with the use of royal insignia.[23] As power passed to Huang Taiji, the Jin burgeoned in strength

Figure 17.1 The city wall of the earth-based fortress on the Ming Great Wall in Huailai, Hebei in 1907

and breadth. The mere mention of "Jin" agitated the Ming bureaucracy and preyed on the psyche of Han individuals inclined to capitulate to Jin rule.

For political and military needs, Huang Taiji engaged in negotiations with the Ming Dynasty more than ten times. The Ming Dynasty, taking lessons from past experiences with the Song and Jin Dynasties, generally did not respond. In light of this, Huang Taiji repeatedly made his case. In a letter to the Ming general Zu Dashou in 1631, he wrote, "My troops have reached Beijing, and I have earnestly sent letters in the hopes of making peace. However, your country's officials and ministers only take lessons from the Song Dynasty, and no words are sent back to me. Your Ming ruler is not a descendant of the Song Dynasty, and I am not a descendant of the Jin Dynasty either. Each era has its own circumstances."[24]

After inheriting the throne of the State of Jin, Huang Taiji implemented numerous reforms over the span of ten years, leading the state to undergo significant changes. Politically, Huang Taiji strengthened the centralized rule modeled after the Ming Dynasty's political structure, establishing Six Ministries and assuming sole authority. Economically, he changed the policies concerning the Han people, emphasizing "stabilizing the populace" and "prioritizing agriculture" to appease Han officials and civilians and to stabilize and develop agriculture. Culturally, with a well-rounded cultural background, Huang Taiji vigorously promoted educational revitalization and actively absorbed sophisticated Han culture. In terms of military affairs, Huang Taiji's expansion exceeded that of Nurhaci: all sixteen tribes of the outer Mongols had surrendered, Korea lacked the strength to resist, and except for the territories occupied by the Ming army, the entire frontier had become his own. In summary, the "Jin" of 1636 had undergone many significant changes compared to the Jin of the Nurhaci era, and Emperor Huang Taiji of the now-aggressive state of Jin harbored the ambition to challenge the main enemy, the Ming Emperor, in the central plains.[25] Driven by this ambition, he took bold actions that led him to transform from the Emperor of the State of Jin to the Emperor of the Great Qing Dynasty.

The sweeping actions of Huang Taiji had a profound impact on the people of Han. By abandoning the taboo of the title "Jin" and the "Nüzhen" ethnic designation, he, to some extent, alleviated long-standing, deep-rooted ethnic conflicts and lessened the historical memories and resentments of the people of Han. Furthermore, by establishing the national name as "Da Qing" (Great Qing) and adopting a series of related titles, he not only demonstrated the intention to supplant the Ming Dynasty but also urged those who had already pledged loyalty or were considering such a pledge to decisively support this new regime that emerged with a renewed visage.

The fact that this new regime also obtained the "Chuanguo Yuxi" (Imperial Jade Seal passed down through generations, details provided later), which unexpectedly fell into the hands of Huang Taiji, was seen as an auspicious sign of the new ruler's heavenly mandate. It also had an emperor who, based on Han culture, was regarded as the "benevolent, warm, kind, and righteous Emperor." They also established an era name, "Chong De" (Venerating Virtue), which carried a more profound meaning than the Ming Dynasty's "Chong Zhen" (Venerating Auspiciousness), and they built a national name that, in various interpretations, often surpassed and overshadowed the meaning of "Da Ming" (Great Ming).

All these factors could provide reasons for culturally inclined people of Han to pledge loyalty to a non-Han ruling power. Certainly, based on the principle of "loyalty to the emperor," they could sacrifice their lives and shed blood to support the current regime in times of crisis. However, they could also justify their whole-hearted support for the new ruler by claiming to "understand the heavenly mandate" or "recognize the greater situation." Although the "barbarians" were likened to "sealed pigs and wolves," as the saying goes, "According to the *Spring and Autumn Annals* by Confucius, when feudal lords adopted barbarian rituals, they were treated as barbarians; when they advanced into the central plains, they became part of the central plains."[26] This principle is not immutable. Herein lies the genius of traditional Chinese Confucian culture.[27] Huang Taiji, who was not only influenced by this cultural insight but also deeply understood it, had sound reasons for establishing the national title as "Da Qing" based on this understanding.

17.3 Surpassing and Outshining the "Great Ming"

The titles conferred upon Emperor Huang Taiji as the "Kind, Gentle, Benevolent, and Holy Emperor," along with the choice of the reign title "Chong De," are self-explanatory and do not require further explanation. Regarding the late establishment of the first reign title of the Qing Dynasty, " Chong De," its meaning bears similarity to and arguably surpasses the preceding Ming Dynasty's reign title "Chong Zhen" (which began in 1628). A detailed analysis in this regard is not necessary. This raises the question of whether Emperor Huang Taiji's selection of the national title "Great Qing" was a deliberate contrast to Zhu Yuanzhang's 270-year-old national title, the "Great Ming," and whether its significance also exceeded that of "Great Ming."

There is no explicit explanation for the meaning of the national title "Great Qing" in the *Imperial Record of Emperor Wen of Qing Taizong*, nor in contemporary and later literary works of the Ming and Qing periods. However, considering the political, military, cultural, and ethnic circumstances of that time, and the adoption of Han-style honorary titles, reign titles, posthumous titles, and the establishment of Han-style imperial processions, attire, and even Confucian temple worship, it is evident that the choice of the Han-style national title "Great Qing" aligned with Han cultural traditions and the values commonly held by the people of Han. From this perspective, in terms of grandeur and significance, "Great Qing" indeed overshadowed "Great Ming."

Firstly, let's examine the aspect of the Five Elements, which is most obviously identifiable. "Ming" corresponds to the Fire element, and the royal family of the Ming Dynasty, "Zhu" means red, symbolizing the color of fire. Conversely, the word "Qing" and "Manchuria" (the newly designated ethnic name) are associated with the element of Water. This adheres to the Five Elements theory that Water conquers Fire, suggesting an auspicious omen of the Qing Dynasty's triumph over the Ming Dynasty. Furthermore, the original national title "Jin" contravened a major taboo in the Five Elements owing to Fire overcoming Metal. This may have influenced Emperor Huang Taiji to forsake the "Jin" symbol.

Secondly, let's look at the aspect of directional symbolism. Emperor Qianlong of the Qing Dynasty, initially known as Emperor Hongli, composed a poem in the *Imperially Commissioned Investigation into the Origins and History of the Manchus* containing the line, "Tian Zao Huang Qing, Faxiang Da Dong." According to the *Shuowen Jiezi*, "Huang" means great. In the *Explanation of Names: Exegesis on Speech and Language*, "Qing" is linked to the color green or blue, correspondence supported by Ye Dejiong's commentary stating that "green" and "qing" are equivalent. Since green is one of the colors in the Five Colors theory associated with the cardinal directions, representing the East, "Great Qing" symbolizes the eastern direction. Additionally, as the East is considered the foremost cardinal direction, the 'heaven-created' Great Qing is seen to purify and resolve the darkness of the southern Great Ming.

Thirdly, let's analyze the meanings of the characters themselves. From the same line, "Tian Zao Huang Qing," there is a semantic connection between "Tian" (heaven) and "Qing." In Chinese, terms such as "qing tian" (blue sky), "qing miao" (celestial bodies), "qing han" (Milky Way), "qing qiong" (sky), and "qing du" (the celestial emperor's palace) are commonly found. The Manchu people's reverence for "Tian" as the highest existence, their absolute awe in their religious beliefs, and the political ideology that emphasized divine mandate for the nation's protection and prosperity, demonstrate the importance of this connection.[28] While the character "Ming" denotes the sun and the moon individually, the encompassing nature of the heavens includes both celestial bodies. Therefore, "Great Qing," representative of the heavenly, can encompass "Great Ming," with its singular association to the sun and the moon, thereby surpassing it in grandeur.

Fourthly, regarding politics, "Qing" can embody the ruler's elegance and the royal governance ideal seen in terms like "Qing Shi" (a time of peace and prosperity) and "Qing Yan" (a state of tranquility and serenity). Historical usage of "Qing Ming" dates back to ancient times, as noted in the *Book of Rites*: "Therefore, Qing Ming symbolizes the heavens, expansiveness symbolizes the earth, and beginnings and ends symbolize the four seasons." And in the same book: "Qing Ming is within oneself; the spirit and vitality resemble the divine." The Qing Ming Festival, one of the 24 solar terms, places "Qing" before "Ming," giving "Qing" precedence. Likewise, in national titles, "Great Qing" precedes and is placed above "Great Ming." For instance, during the late Ming Dynasty, many editions of the *Guanzi* were published between the Wanli and Chongzhen eras. The section on "Internal Affairs" states, "In observing Great Qing, one looks to Great Ming," and the section on "Mental Philosophies" says, "The mirror of Great Qing reflects that of Great Ming." However, before Emperor Huang Taiji's choice of "Great Qing," the compound term "Ming Qing," with "Ming" preceding "Qing" and placing "Ming" above "Qing," did not exist in historical literature.

Upon the aforementioned indirect speculation, it can be asserted that the reason Huang Taiji chose the state name "Da Qing" within the context of Chinese culture is that the aura and significance of "Da Qing" eclipsed that of "Da Ming."[29]

Moreover, concerning the Jurchen or Manchu people, did they also have considerations regarding "Da Qing"? Research from numerous scholars affirms this. The relevant viewpoints are as follows:

Japanese scholar Ichimura Zensaburo has noted, "The pronunciation of 'Jin' and 'Qing' is somewhat similar in the Beijing dialect. 'Jin' has the upper-level tone of 'Chin,' while 'Qing' has the falling tone of 'Ching.' Natives of Beijing can clearly distinguish between them, but foreigners often mix them up. It was unlikely that the Jurchen could accurately discern the pronunciation of Chinese characters; thus, they altered the state name from 'Jin' to 'Qing' to approximate the sound."[30] Meng Sen further verified this by stating, "Qing is an approximate sound of Jin. There was a substitution to use similar Chinese characters based on pronunciation. ... Among the Manchu, Jin Xihou Liang, author of 'Guangxuan Xiaoji,' also mentioned that 'Qing' approximates 'Jin,' referring to the phrase 'Da Jin Tiancong Nian' inscribed in Chinese characters on the Fuzhen Gate plaque in Shenyang. This illustrates that 'Jin' represents 'Qing,' not 'Manchu.' This assertion is backed by concrete evidence."[31] Additionally, editors Li Xun and Xue Hong of the *Complete History of the Qing Dynasty* have documented and discussed the significance of this theory: "The sound 'Jin' is similar to that of certain Chinese characters, but only the character 'Qing' aptly corresponds with the meaning of the state name. Moreover, the character 'Qing' had never been used in the history of Chinese dynasties before, and whether considering the theory of the Five Elements or other explanations, there is a basis for this. ... The cultural significance of the Qing Dynasty may be less profound than that of the Jin Dynasty, yet it exhibits vast inclusiveness. The Qing Dynasty has no disparity with major dynasties in Chinese history, such as the Han, Tang, Song, Yuan, and Ming, within the Han cultural framework, indicating that the efforts of Nurhaci and Huang Taiji had already aligned with the traditional Chinese cultural system of their time."[32]

Japanese scholar Inoue Kunizumi believes Huang Taiji discarded the old name 'Jin' and chose the new name 'Qing' to create a link between the old and new state names, as is observed: "When selecting a state name, it should have a commonality of representation." The only ancient Chinese legend fulfilling these two crucial criteria is the legend of Shaohao of the Jiuli Tribe. "Shaohao's father was known as Qing, or Zuo Tu Yu Qing. Song Dynasty scholar Luo Mi noted that the Shaohao clan esteemed gold greatly, predominantly featuring the color white. Thus, they were also referred to as the 'Jin Tian Shi' (Gold Celestial Clan). Historically, they have origins traceable to Silla, at the southern tip of Korea, where they were also identified as the descendants of the 'Jin Tian Shi'... Observing the time when Emperor Taizong assumed the throne and officially declared the palatial names, the central palace was 'Qingning Palace,' the eastern 'Guanju,' and the western 'Linzhi.' They also selected ornate names like 'Xiangfeng Tower' and 'Feilong Pavilion' to enhance the royal vista. These gestures almost mirrored Shaohao of the Jin Tian Shi, thereby appropriating the character 'Qing' for naming."[33] Songsumi Matsumura elucidates this by stating, "This not only respects the national identity of the Jurchen without compromising their dignity, but also eases the resentment that the people of Han have harbored against the Jin since the Song Dynasty."[34]

Based on the conclusions of various scholars in Qing history research, each has their own reasoning and complements each other. The change from "Jin" to "Daqing" by Huang Taiji was able to be accepted by people of all ethnicities within the nation, which is reasonable. It can also be pointed out that the various Mongolian tribes who surrendered to Huang Taiji would also support his change from "Jin" to "Daqing."

Firstly, it could avoid embarrassment for both sides. The Jurchens and Mongols have a long history of intermarriage,[35] and during the Ming Dynasty, the Jurchen tribes were once under the rule of the Mongols. Subsequently, Tibetan Buddhism, also known as the Lamaist sect, became a common religious belief for both Mongols and Jurchens. However, tracing back further, the Jurchen Jin Dynasty was annihilated by the Mongols and the Southern Song Dynasty in a joint military action. This historical memory not only made the Jurchen leader Huang Taiji unwilling to use the name "Jin," to avoid causing humiliation to the Mongols, but also brought embarrassment to the Mongol nobles who had already submitted to him. Therefore, in the relationship between the Jurchens and the Mongols, the terms "Jin" and "Jurchen" became inappropriate as national names and ethnic designations, while the Qing Dynasty and the Manchus did not face such a problem.

Secondly, it could bridge the Khanate between both sides. The most significant achievement of the Mongols was the establishment of the Great Mongol Empire under Genghis Khan, while in the Central Plains, it was the inheritance of the position of the Great Khan by the Yuan Dynasty. In December 1634, the Mongolian lama Mörgen brought the sacred golden image known as Mahakala and joined forces with Huang Taiji. Then in August 1635, Huang Taiji obtained the imperial seal of succession from the Mongolian Chahar tribe. Mahakala was a golden Buddha statue cast by the imperial preceptor Bayan for Yuan Emperor Kublai Khan and symbolized the Yuan Emperor and the Mongol Khan. The imperial seal of succession, on the other hand, is a symbol of the legitimate emperor of all of China.[36] In other words, the possession of Mahakala and the imperial seal of succession by Huang Taiji could be seen by the Mongol nobles as powerful evidence that he was qualified to inherit the positions of both the Yuan Emperor and the Mongol Khan. In October of the same year, Huang Taiji changed the name of his tribe to "Manchu," and the following April, he established the dynastic title as the Qing Dynasty. With the establishment of the Qing Dynasty, not only did the various Mongol tribes acknowledge the Qing Emperor as the Emperor of China, but they also recognized Huang Taiji as the inheritor of the Mongol Khanate, following in the footsteps of Genghis Khan.[37]

Thirdly, a win-win situation could be achieved. In terms of the choice of national titles, the Manchu "Da Qing" and the Mongol "Da Yuan" are quite similar, indicating a close kinship. The *Study of the Surnames of the Later Jin Dynasty* by Zhu Xizu pointed out that since the Yuan Dynasty ruled the Central Plains, abstract nouns have been used as the national title for establishing a country. The title "Qing" used by Emperor Taizong of the Qing Dynasty was a conscious imitation, indicating their desire to emulate the Mongols in unifying China and eradicating the colors of foreign domination.[38]

The Mongolian noblemen could accept this "eradication of colors of foreign domination" associated with the national title "Da Qing." Moreover, both "Da Yuan" and "Da Qing" are "beautiful names" with meaningful connotations. "Yuan" signifies the control of heavenly virtues and the benevolent meaning of royal governance, while "Qing" represents heavenly, peaceful, and vast connotations. Therefore, the Mongolian noblemen may even have a favorable impression of the national title "Da Qing."

In conclusion, Emperor Huang Taiji's change from "Jin" to "Da Qing" in 1636 can be seen as the result of various internal and external factors. In terms of internal factors, the title "Jin" was no longer sufficient for planning the future development of the empire and was not conducive to appeasing the Han and Mongolian peoples under its rule. In the context of key external factors, the national title "Da Qing" aligns with the tradition of using "Da Yuan" and "Da Ming" as titles, exerting a stronger presence and significance than "Da Ming." However, Emperor Huang Taiji's transformation from the Khan of Jin to the benevolent Emperor of Da Qing was not a simple change of title; it was an extensive endeavor that drew upon historical and cultural references to serve the present and shape the future. This significant move demonstrated Emperor Huang Taiji's ability to turn passivity into initiative and convert disadvantages into advantages in his confrontation with the Ming Dynasty and his relationship with Mongolia. It also illustrated the meticulous thinking, thoughtful considerations, and ambitious visions of Emperor Huang Taiji and his Manchu, Han, and Mongolian ministers.[39]

On August 9, 1643, the ambitious Emperor Huang Taiji, who had grand visions for his empire, suffered a sudden stroke and passed away at the Qingning Palace in Shengjing at the age of 52. Huang Taiji's achievements are comparable to those of his father, Nurhaci, the founder of the Qing dynasty, who was posthumously honored as the Martial Emperor and later the High Emperor, with the temple name Taizu. Huang Taiji himself was posthumously honored as the Wen Emperor, and his temple name was Taizong.

Of course, Huang Taiji also had regrets. Despite surpassing the Ming dynasty in terms of power and influence, he was unable to completely overcome and surpass them. His dream of entering the Central Plains and relocating the capital to Beijing remained a distant ideal. However, little did Huang Taiji know that just eight months after his passing, with the help of Li Zicheng's peasant army capturing the Ming capital and fueled by the anger of the Ming general Wu Sangui stationed at Shanhaiguan, his half-brother Dorgon led the Qing army—comprised of Manchu, Han, and Mongol forces—to successfully conquer the Ming capital. In less than 15 years, his six-year-old ninth son, Emperor Shunzhi, was seated on the golden throne of the Ming Dynasty. And within four months, with the last Ming emperor fleeing to Myanmar, Emperor Shunzhi formally became the ruler of all under heaven, and the Qing Dynasty was officially established.

The title "Da Qing" was used until the ninth-generation descendant of Huang Taiji, Aisin-Gioro Puyi, who peacefully abdicated the throne on December 25, 1912, marking the end of the Qing Dynasty on the historical stage. Prior to that, on January 1, 1912, in Nanjing, the former capital of the Ming Dynasty, an extraordinary figure, Sun Yat-sen, was inaugurated as the interim President, proclaiming the establishment of the Republic of China.

The departure of the Qing from the historical stage marked the end of autocratic imperial rule and the conclusion of a historical era marked by singular family dynasties and unique reign titles, stretching back to the Xia, Shang, Zhou, Qin, and Han dynasties. With the founding of the Republic of China, a new chapter in the history of national titles commenced, reflecting the image of a modern democratic state in the contemporary sense.[40] Thus, China's history of national titles transitioned from the ancient "dynastic" era to the brand-new "republic" era.

Notes

1 Li Zicheng (1606–1645), born in Mizhi, Shaanxi (now Mizhi County, Shaanxi), came from a peasant background. He started a rebellion in 1629 and declared himself the King of Zhongxing in 1636. In 1643, he proclaimed himself the King of Xinshun, and in January 1644, he declared himself the King of Dashun with the reign title Yongchang. Li Zicheng's forces were the main force in the peasant rebellion at the end of the Ming Dynasty.

2 Zhu Yousong (?-1645), the grandson of Zhu Yijun, Emperor Shenzong (Wanli), was conferred the title of Duke of Fu in 1643.

3 Zhang Xianzhong (1606–1646), born in Liushujian, Shaanxi (now Dong, Dingbian County, Shaanxi), came from a poor background. He started a rebellion in 1630 and declared himself the King of Daxi in 1643. In the peasant rebellion at the end of the Ming Dynasty, Zhang Xianzhong's forces were second only to Li Zicheng in terms of strength.

4 This included the Manchu soldiers, Eight Banners of the Mongols, Eight Banners of the Han army, as well as the armies of the vassal Mongols and Wu Sangui, the Duke of Pingxi of the Ming Dynasty who surrendered to the Qing Dynasty.

5 In the summer of 1645, Li Zicheng was killed by the landlord's armed forces. In the autumn, the remaining forces of Li Zicheng allied with the Ming Dynasty to resist the Qing Dynasty, and stopped using the title Dashun.

6 In the sixth lunar month of 1645, Zhu Yujian, the Prince Tang of the Ming Dynasty, ascended the throne in Fuzhou and changed the reign title to Longwu.

7 In November 1646, Zhu Yujian's younger brother ascended the throne in Guangzhou and changed the reign title to Shaowu.

8 In November 1646, Zhang Xianzhong died in battle against the Qing Dynasty, and his remaining forces later allied with the Ming Dynasty to resist the Qing Dynasty, and stopped using the title Daxi.

9 In November 1646, Zhu Youlang, the Prince Gui of the Ming Dynasty, ascended the throne in Zhaoqing and changed the reign title to Yongli. He later relocated to various southwestern areas. In January 1659, Qing troops entered Kunming, and Emperor Yongli fled to Myanmar. Then, in 1661, Emperor Yongli was captured and killed in Kunming.

10 In 1646, the remaining forces of Li Zicheng and the mountainous peasant army in the Sichuan-Hubei border region formed an alliance and supported Zhu Dian, the Prince Han of the Ming Dynasty, with the reign title Dingwu.

11 In August 1645, Emperor Longwu bestowed the surname "Zheng" and the given name "Chenggong" upon Zheng Sen, a native of Nan'an, Fujian (now Dongfengzhou Town, Nan'an City, Fujian). In 1646, Zheng Chenggong rose up against the Qing Dynasty at sea, using the reign title Longwu. In 1658, Emperor Yongli enfeoffed

Zhu Chenggong as the Marquis of Yanping. In 1662, Zhu Chenggong defeated the Dutch colonial army and took control of Taiwan. In August 1683, Zhu Chenggong's grandson Zhu Kexuan surrendered to the Qing Dynasty, marking the end of the Ming loyalist regime in Taiwan under the legitimate succession of Emperor Yongli. It should be noted that the commonly used name "Zheng Chenggong" today was a deliberate insult from the early Qing Dynasty, referring to him as "cutting the head and appending the tail, adopting the original surname, and receiving a conferred name, called Zheng Chenggong, a rebellious bandit." For further details, please refer to Xie Bilian: "Zheng Chenggong Should Be Called Zhu Chenggong," published by the Tainan City Government, 2004.

12 As of March 1644, when the capital of the Ming Dynasty fell and Emperor Zhu Youjian committed suicide, the widely recognized title of "Great Ming" had already come to an end. From May 1644 until 1664, the remnants of the Ming forces established various regimes, such as the Hongguang regime of the Duke of Fu, the Longwu regime of the Prince Tang, the Lu regime (led by Zhu Yihai), the Shaowu regime of the Prince Tang, the Yongli regime of the Prince Gui, and the Dingwu regime of the Prince Han. In the later period of the Qing Dynasty, these regimes came to be collectively referred to as the "Southern Ming."

13 Annals of Manchu, Volume 1.

14 During his childhood, Nurhaci lost his mother and could not bear the abuse from his stepmother. At the age of 10, he left his family and embarked on a wandering life. He engaged in various jobs such as digging for ginseng, transporting goods over mountains, and enduring hardships of outdoor life. The early hardships shaped Nurhaci into a determined and resilient young man. His extensive interaction with people of Han made him an extraordinary Jurchen who enjoyed reading the *Three Kingdoms* and the *Water Margin*, had broad knowledge, and was adept at strategy.

15 The Jurchen people originally had no written language. In 1599, Nurhaci ordered Jurchen people, including E'erduni, to create a new script based on Mongolian characters and Jurchen phonetics, which became widely used within the region. This script later came to be known as the Old Manchu script.

16 It seems that during the late Yuan Dynasty, there were Han Chinese who rebelled against the Yuan and wanted to restore the Song Dynasty. In 1348, rebellion leaders Lockuonu in Liaodong and Wuyanbaluhan in Liaoyang also referred to themselves as "descendants of the Great Jin" in their propaganda to mobilize the Jurchen people against the Yuan. Detailed information can be found in the *History of the Yuan Dynasty*. In the 18th chapter of the *Complete History of the Qing Dynasty* by Japanese scholar Inoue Kimito, translated by Dan Tao (published by Zhonghua Book Company in 1914), it is pointed out that, "In the early days of the Taizu era, the use of the old name of Jin in Manchuria was to stir up the spirits of the Jurchen people. At the beginning of the founding of the country, the state of Manchuria was divided among various forces. Taizu's intention was focused on unifying these tribes, so he chose a symbolic representation of collective ideology as a means of control. Furthermore, many of the subordinates who served under him were noble Jurchen individuals who regarded Taizu as a reincarnation of Aguda. This was the intention behind it."

17 The Ming Dynasty's rule over the north east was quite strict before the tenth year of Xuande (1435), gradually weakening afterwards and becoming more of a vassalage relationship.

18 Cai Meibiao's "The National Title, Clan Name, and Chronological System Before the Establishment of the Great Qing Dynasty" (Historical Research, 1987, Issue 3) argues

that "Shule Khan" (in Manchu, Shule means intelligent and wise) is not the full title of a Khan, and "Tiancong" should have its origins in the Chinese language.

19 The Imperial Record of Emperor Wen of Qing Taizong, Volume 28, records the events happened on the day Yiyou of the second month of the tenth year of Tiancong.

20 The issue surrounding the clan name is quite complex, and a detailed explanation is not provided here. For further information, you can refer to the book *History and Culture of the Manchu Ethnic Group* edited by Wang Zhonghan, published by the Central University for Nationalities Press in 1996.

21 As is well known, the major external threats to the Ming Dynasty were the "Northern Barbarians" and the "Southern Wokou." "Southern Wokou" referred to the Japanese pirates along the south eastern coast, while the "Northern Barbarians" referred to the Mongol forces in the northern grasslands. The Great Wall of China, stretching for thousands of miles, was constructed by the Ming Dynasty as a defense against Mongol invasions.

22 For a detailed analysis of the arguments and significance surrounding the "State Title" and "Virtuous Rule" of the Song Dynasty, refer to "On the Debate over the Significance of the 'State Title' and 'Virtuous Rule' in the Song Dynasty" by Chen Xuelin, included in the book *Essays on Song History* published by Eastern University Press in 1993, Taipei.

   Furthermore, according to recent research, it is believed that the famous poem "Man Jiang Hong" by Yue Fei during the Southern Song Dynasty, which includes the lines "With great determination, we dine on the flesh of the northern barbarians, with laughter we drink the blood of the Xiongnu," was actually fabricated by Han people during the Ming Dynasty to express their anger.

23 According to Cheng Kaihu's "Illustrated Drafts on Strategies against Liao," volumes 44 and 45, the term "Later Jin" was not originally used as a state title by Nurhaci, the founder of the Later Jin Dynasty, nor was it a later appellation by historians. It was first seen in Korea and then transmitted to the Ming Dynasty. It's possible that Han officials in the Jin dynasty, when drafting official documents, occasionally used the term "Later Jin," but it was not an official name. Lu Zhengheng and Huang Yinong also pointed out in their article "A New Study on the State Titles of the Pre-Qing Period" (Journal of Literature, History, and Philosophy, 2014, Issue 1) that there is still no consensus among scholars regarding the state title of the regime from Nurhaci's reign until the reign of Emperor Taizong. Thanks to the publication and digitization of a large amount of pre-Qing period materials in recent years, a thorough search of relevant Manchu and Han historical materials and artifacts has confirmed that there is no solid evidence to support the use of "Later Jin" as a state title. More than a hundred examples of official usage support the notion that the state title of the pre-Qing period was consistently "Jin."

24 Wang Xianqian, Donghua Chronicles, section 6, the eighth month of the fifth year of Tiancong.

25 In the year 1635, the officials had already submitted a memorial stating: "The Mongols in various regions have all surrendered, and the only enemy we face now is the Ming. However, although the Ming still exists, the state affairs are deteriorating day by day, the army is weak and exhausted, and its downfall is imminent." (Record of Emperor Taizong of the Qing Dynasty, Volume 23, Tiancong Era, June, Yiyu) Furthermore, in 1629 and 1634, the Jurchen troops had also invaded the Ming capital twice, posing a threat to the imperial city.

26 Han Yu, with annotations by Yan Qi, Commentary on Collected Works of Han Changli, Volume 1, "The Original Way."

27 During the transition of dynasties, it often poses a difficult dilemma for ministers, as they struggle to balance loyalty and filial piety. Therefore, those who enter the service of the new dynasty emphasize the concept of "a good bird chooses a tree to roost, a virtuous minister chooses a lord to serve." This emphasizes loyalty over filial piety. On the other hand, those who choose not to serve the new dynasty emphasize the saying "a loyal minister does not serve two lords" and prioritize filial piety over loyalty. Furthermore, if the new dynasty is established by barbarians or foreigners, those who enter the service emphasize the idea of "transforming barbarians into civilized" while those who choose not to serve stress the importance of "defending against barbarians."

A thought-provoking "case study" is the choice made by Wen Tianxiang. According to Liu Jiangsun's "Records of Reading" in the eighth year of the Yuan Dynasty's Dade era (1304), Wen Tianxiang, who was imprisoned in the capital city, wrote a letter to his younger brother Wen Zhang, saying, "I chose to die for loyalty, while you chose to serve with filial piety, and our youngest brother (Wen Zhang) chose to hide ... May our names be praised for thousands of years." In another letter written by Wen Tianxiang in 1281 to his nephew Wen Sheng, while he was imprisoned, he said, "Your father (Wen Zhang) and your uncle (Wen Zhang) have sacrificed themselves to safeguard our family. They have shown both loyalty and filial piety in their actions." (From the *Complete Collection of Works of Wen Tianxiang*, Volume 18.)

28 As for Nurhaci Khan, his seal bears the inscription "Tian Ming" (heavenly mandate), and his title is "Tian Shou" (heavenly bestowment). As for Huang Taiji Khan, his title is "Tian Cong" (heavenly intelligence). The significance of these titles is similar to that of the Han ethnic rulers, who believe that they receive their mandate from heaven. These titles convey the legitimacy of rule and the belief in divine approval among the Manchu people.

29 Dao Yejunshan, translated by Dan Tao, in the 18th chapter of "The Complete History of the Qing Dynasty," states: "In general, they have already employed Han people and gradually assimilated Han culture through the advancement of various knowledge. They came to the realization that using 'Jin' or 'Houjin' as the national name is too simplistic, so they decided to inherit the titles of previous dynasties. However, this interpretation may be criticized for its lack of depth." This provides a reasonable explanation for why Huang Taiji abandoned the national name of 'Jin' based on the framework of Han culture.

30 Shichiro Ichimura's "Study on the National Title of the Qing Dynasty" was included in the first volume of the "Academic Report of the East Asian Association Investigative Department," published in 1909.

31 Meng Sen's "Lectures on Ming and Qing History," Part Four, Chapter 1, Section 2, published by Zhonghua Book Company in 1981.

32 Edited by Li Xun and Xue Hong, "The Complete History of the Qing Dynasty," volume one, Chapter 5, published by Liaoning People's Publishing House in 1991.

33 Dao Yejunshan, translated by Dan Tao: Chapter 18 of "The Complete History of the Qing Dynasty."

34 Matsuura Jun: "A Study on the National Title of the Qing Dynasty," included in the compilation "Collected Papers of the International Academic Conference on Qing History," published by Liaoning People's Publishing House in 1990.

35 During the time of Nurhaci, Mongolian women from the Khorchin tribe were taken as concubines. His sons, Daishan, Manggultai, and Degelie, also married women from the Zhalute tribe of Mongolia. Huang Taiji himself had several Mongolian consorts.

36 From the "Tiancong Jiunian Archives" (Tianjin Ancient Books Publishing House, 1987): "This seal has been passed down as a treasure of the imperial lineage through

the ages, later seized by the Mongol Yuan Dynasty." And there are reports from the surrendering generals of the Ming Dynasty, such as Kong Youde, who said: "This treasure is extraordinary, passed down from the Han Dynasty, already over two thousand years old! It has been acquired by the Khan alone, as he loves the people like his own children and follows the will of heaven. Thus, the heavens bestowed upon him the supreme authority, thousands of miles away, ignoring all obstacles, bringing blessings to the world without a doubt! Not only myself, but the people from all over are rejoicing. The unification of the world, just like Yao and Shun, is happening again today." Geng Zhongming, another surrendering general and commander, also reported: "The seal is the most precious treasure in the hands of the emperor, who rules over the nation. ... The Khan must quickly achieve great accomplishments to fulfill the expectations of his subjects."

37 Jin Qicong: "Examining the Literary Policies of Huang Taiji from the Perspective of Manchu Clan Names," included in Wang Zhonghan's compilation: "History and Culture of the Manchu Ethnicity."

38 Zhu Xizu: "A Study on the Clan Names of the Later Jin Dynasty," included in the "Journal of the Institute of History and Philology, Academia Sinica, Compilation Series," Volume One, 1933.

39 The use of the national title "Da Qing" can be seen as a culmination of the traditional Chinese dynastic titles, as it reflects the idea of the later rulers surpassing the previous ones. The national title "Da Qing" played a visible or subtle role in the transformation of the Qing Dynasty from a regional power in north east China to a unified empire in China.

40 Of course, if we only consider the national title, the period from 1851 to 1864 saw the establishment of the "Taiping Heavenly Kingdom" by Hong Xiuquan, which combined the Chinese ideal of "Taiping" (Great Peace) with Western religious ideals. However, the title of "Taiping Heavenly Kingdom" did not become a universally recognized national title. For more information on the establishment and meaning of the national title "Taiping Heavenly Kingdom," you can refer to Luo Ergang's "When and Where was the Taiping Heavenly Kingdom Established," included in his book "Collection of Taiping Heavenly Kingdom Historical Studies," published by Sanlian Bookstore in 1981, and Jian Youwen's "A Comprehensive Study of the System of the Taiping Heavenly Kingdom," Volume One, published by Jian's Progressive Bookstore, Hong Kong, in 1958.

18 The Republic of China

A New Era of National Titles

On January 1, 1912, Sun Yat-sen assumed the position of Provisional President in Nanjing and announced the establishment of the Republic of China. The year 1912 marked the first year of the Republic of China. After 38 years, on April 23, 1949, the Chinese People's Liberation Army occupied Nanjing, the capital of the Republic of China, and on December 8, the "Central Government" of the Republic of China relocated to Taiwan Province. Since then, the nature of the "Republic of China" in Taiwan has become that of a unique local authority. As for the People's Republic of China, it became the sole legitimate government of China, marked by the First Plenary Session of the Chinese People's Political Consultative Conference held from September 21 to September 30, 1949.

In terms of national titles, both the "Republic of China" and the "People's Republic of China" are related to the term "Zhonghua." Analyzing these two national titles, "Guo" means country, while "Min" and "People's Republic" are modifying elements indicating the nature of the state, and "Zhonghua" functions as the proper noun. The origin and meaning of the term "Zhonghua" will be discussed in detail in Chapter 24 of this book. In this chapter and the following chapters, we will briefly explain the establishment process and related issues of the national titles "Republic of China" and "People's Republic of China."

18.1 "The Legal Tale of Controversy Over the Creation of the Name"

As mentioned at the end of the previous chapter, the national title "Republic of China" marked the transition from the long-standing era of the "Dynasty" to the new era of the "Republic" in Chinese history. In other words, the national title "Republic of China" can be regarded as the beginning of a new era in the history of Chinese national titles. So, how did the name "Republic of China" come about? There are different explanations for this.

In October 1936, Lu Xun (Zhou Shuren) drafted an article titled "A Few Matters Regarding Mr. Taiyan" before his death. In the article, he mentioned, "As for now, the name 'Republic of China' originated from Mr. Taiyan's 'Interpretation of the Republic of China' (initially seen in the 'Minbao' newspaper). It was purely out of great commemoration. However, I'm afraid there aren't many who still know

DOI: 10.4324/9781003510390-19

about this important historical event."[1] This passage is clear, indicating that the national title "Republic of China" originated from Mr. Zhang Binglin (also known as Taiyan) and his "Interpretation of the Republic of China," which was published in the "Minbao" newspaper in 1907. However, what does the term "legal tale" mean? In 1918, Sun Yat-sen wrote in his book *The Strategy of Building a Nation*: "Since the year of the Yiyou (1905), after the defeat in the Sino-French war, I decided to overthrow the Qing Dynasty and establish a Republic ... In the autumn of the year of Yisi (1904), when outstanding individuals from all over the country gathered and established the Revolutionary Alliance in Tokyo, I began to believe that the revolutionary cause could be achieved in my lifetime ... Therefore, I dared to establish the name 'Republic of China' and announced it to the party members, who then returned to their respective provinces to promote the ideology of revolution and disseminate the idea of the Republic of China."[2] This means that before Zhang Binglin published the article "Explanation of the Republic of China" in 1907, Sun Yat-sen had already "established the name 'Republic of China' and announced it to the party members." Moreover, in Sun Yat-sen's speech at the National Youth Federation in Guangzhou on October 21, 1923, he directly stated, "The term 'Republic of China' was originally coined by me."[3]

Therefore, the question of who actually coined the national title "Republic of China"—Zhang Binglin or Sun Yat-sen—undoubtedly becomes a complicated issue, as it involves Zhang Binglin, Sun Yat-sen, and Lu Xun, all of whom are extremely important historical figures.

Another major issue is that it is not an easy question to answer how many regimes claimed to be the "Republic of China" from 1912 to 1949. The Nanjing Provisional Government led by Sun Yat-sen (Temporary Central Government of the Republic of China) was the first government of the Republic of China. Then there were Yuan Shikai's Beijing government, Yunnan Military Government, Sun Yat-sen's Guangdong Military Government, Extraordinary Presidential Mansion, Grand Marshal Headquarters, Guangdong-Wuhan Nationalist Government, Anhui clique led by Duan Qirui, Presidents Li Yuanhong and Xu Shichang, the Beiyang clique led by Feng Guozhang and Cao Kun, Zhang Zuolin's Fengtian Clique Warlord Government with control over land, sea, and air forces, Chiang Chung-cheng's[4] successive governments in Nanjing-Chongqing-Nanjing, Yan Xishan and Feng Yuxiang's Nationalist Government in Beiping, Wang Zhaoming[5] and Hu Hanmin's Guangzhou-based Nationalist Government, and Wang Zhaoming's reestablishment of the Nationalist Government in Nanjing. All these regimes, without exception, were called the "Republic of China." They existed in opposition to each other and claimed themselves to be the "legitimate" or the national central government. They rose and fell in succession, creating a bewildering political landscape.

Understanding the numerous "Republic of China" regimes is indeed a complicated matter and open to interpretation.

18.2 The Main Hall and the Main Peak

In any case, the first regime to be called the "Republic of China" was the one led by Sun Yat-sen, who presided as interim President. Although this regime was short-lived, lasting only three months,[6] its significance was immense and far-reaching. It overthrew the rule of the Qing Dynasty, ended the long-standing monarchy, and established a brand-new bourgeois democratic republic that pursued the ideals of "true republicanism" and the "Three Principles of the People." The origin of the name "Republic of China" also lies in Sun Yat-sen's lifelong struggle for these ideals. The various regimes claiming to be the "Republic of China" and honoring Sun Yat-sen as the "Father of the Nation" further demonstrate the deep connection between Sun Yat-sen and the "Republic of China." Just as a main hall is indispensable to a building, and a main peak amid towering mountains, Sun Yat-sen served as the symbolic main hall and main peak in the establishment of the Republic of China.

Sun Yat-sen[7] (1866–1925), also known as Yixian, was born in Xiangshan, Guangdong (now Zhongshan City, Guangdong). As early as 1885, during the year of the Sino-French War and the failure of the Qing Dynasty, Sun Yat-sen had the determination to overthrow the Qing court and establish a republic. In November 1894, Sun Yat-sen gathered overseas Chinese intellectuals and established the first bourgeois revolutionary group called the "Revive China Society" in Honolulu.[8] The constitution of the Revive China Society declared its purpose as "dedicated to revitalizing China and preserving its national essence," with the alliance pledge stating, "The members of the alliance, from certain provinces and counties, vow to drive away the barbarians, restore China, and establish a government of the people. Anyone with ulterior motives shall be exposed by the divine spirits."[9] Although the call to "drive away the barbarians, restore China" can be traced back to previous movements,[10] the idea of "establishing a government of the people" was a distinctly bourgeois revolutionary language, representing Sun Yat-sen and others' firm political ideal of establishing a federal-style bourgeois democratic republic in China (see Figure 18.1).

A decisive development occurred in 1903. The failure of the "Righteous Harmony" Boxer Movement advocating "support the Qing and exterminate the foreigners," the suppression of the Self-Strengthening Army's "loyalty to the emperor" movement, the invasion of China by the Eight-Nation Alliance in 1900, and the humiliating signing of the Boxer Protocol in 1901 created a context where the Qing government, which had become a tool for imperialist aggression and domination, was beyond redemption. The promotion of the anti-Qing revolution and democratic republicanism spread more widely and gained momentum. In May 1903, the publication of Zou Rong's *The Revolutionary Army* called for revolutionary means to overthrow the Manchu Qing government and establish a nation named "Republic of China." At the end of the book, Zou Rong exclaimed, "Long live the Republic of China. Long live the freedom of the 400 million compatriots of the Republic of China." In addition, in the joint publication of *The Revolutionary Army*, Zhang Binglin's "Refutation of Kang Youwei's Ideas on Revolution criticized Emperor Guangxu of the Qing Dynasty as an ignorant fool and advocated "a united government of the people," stating that "those who unite the people under a government of the people will definitely establish a democracy after the success of the cause."[11] Furthermore, in 1903, the *Alarm Bell for the World* by Chen Tianhua vividly described the deep national crisis and profound sense of

Figure 18.1 Sun Yat-sen's Former Residence in Zhongshan, Guangdong

national doom in popular words and lyrics. Under the pen name of "the majority of descendants of the Yellow Emperor" and edited by "one of the descendants of the Yellow Emperor," the *Soul of the Yellow Emperor* harbored profound resentment towards the Manchus and opposition to the Qing Dynasty. These slogans and propaganda efforts deeply ingrained the ideas of anti-Qing revolution and democratic republicanism in the minds of the 400 million people.

In 1903, Sun Yat-sen developed and finalized his revolutionary program. During the autumn and winter of that year, Sun Yat-sen secretly organized a military school in Japan and reorganized the Revive China Society in Honolulu. The oath used by Sun Yat-sen and his followers was "Expel the Manchu barbarians, restore China, establish a republic, and equally distribute land."[12] The national name "Republic of China" (Zhonghua Minguo) was already emerging. In August 1904, Sun Yat-sen wrote an English manuscript titled "The True Solution to the Chinese Question,"[13] where the English term "National Republic of China" was used for the first time. It stated that only by changing the outdated monarchy of the Manchu Qing government to the "Republic of China" could the Chinese question be truly resolved.

On August 20, 1905, under the leadership of Sun Yat-sen, based on the Revive China Society (Xingzhonghui) and Huaxinghui,[14] and in connection with the Guangfuhui[15] (the Restoration Society), the Chinese Revolutionary Party, also known as the Tongmenghui, was founded in the Akasaka district, Kagurazaka, in Tokyo. It was a revolutionary organization representing the Chinese bourgeoisie and established a nationwide presence. The Tongmenghui adopted a sixteen-word

oath as its guiding principle. In November, the Tongmenghui launched its official mouthpiece, the newspaper "Minbao." In the newspaper's inaugural issue,
Sun Yat-sen further expounded on the sixteen-word principles such as the Three
Principles of Nationalism, Democracy, and People's Livelihood. "Expel the
Manchu barbarians, restore China" pertained to nationalism, aiming to overthrow
the Qing government, deemed a puppet of imperialist powers, and to establish an
independent China. "Establish a republic" pertained to democracy, with the goal of
abolishing the autocratic system and establishing a bourgeois democratic republic.
"Distribute land equally" pertained to the people's livelihood, seeking to address
the land issue and thereby resolving social problems comprehensively.

In the autumn and winter of 1906, the Tongmenghui's "Declaration of the
Military Government" proclaimed, "China belongs to the Chinese; the Chinese
people should determine China's politics. After expelling the Manchu barbarians,
our nation shall be restored. Anyone who behaves akin to Shi Jingtang and Wu
Sangui shall face collective opposition from everyone!" This passage referred to
the restoration of China. Further declarations stated, "Through a revolution by the
common people, a peoples' government shall be established. All citizens shall be
equal and have the right to participate in politics. The President shall be elected
by the citizens. Parliament shall consist of representatives elected by the citizens.
The Constitution of the Republic of China shall be drafted and respected by all.
Any attempt to restore an imperial system shall face collective opposition!"[16] This
articulated the establishment of a republic.

Thus, the nature, method of establishment, and the national name of the
"Republic of China" had been clearly defined at that time.

The foundation of the Chinese Revolutionary Party, the formulation of the
sixteen-word principles, and Sun Yat-sen's exposition on the Three Principles
corresponded with his ideology of the Three Principles of the People. This furnished
clear objectives for the revolutionary bourgeois forces and significantly advanced
the climax of the bourgeois democratic revolution.

Even before the revolution's success, the term "Republic of China," embodying
"by the people, for the people," as well as the notions of "people's sovereignty, governance, and well-being," had already garnered significant traction. On December
2, 1906, Sun Yat-sen officially announced the name "Republic of China" in
Chinese during the first anniversary celebration of "Minbao," reiterating the forth-
coming constitution of the Republic of China.[17] Additionally, in speeches by the
renowned revolutionary and master of national studies, Zhang Binglin, who also
served as editor-in-chief of "Minbao," it was declared, "This revolutionary cause
will not fail; the Republic of China will not fail."[18] Moreover, on July 5, 1907, in
the fifteenth issue of "Minbao," Zhang Binglin published an extensive article titled
"Interpretation of the Republic of China," where he asserted:

The name 'China' differentiates us from other ethnic groups ... When discussing
Han territory, 'China' corresponds to the lands under former Han jurisdiction ...
The nomenclature for various ethnicities is founded on their initial settlements
... The ancestral deities trace back to the western regions, with prefectures Yong

and Liang as their bases ... The Central Plain holds the densest concentration of ethnic groups ... The etymology of 'China' is not racial but rather cultural ... Speaking of ethnicity, it is more accurate to use 'Xia' ... The original Xia people did not have a national title; hence they were called 'Zhu Xia' ... Since Liu Bang's time, ruling the Nine Prefectures, resisting the Xiongnu, and influencing the Western Regions, they spread their culture and teachings far and wide, thus earning the name 'Han Zu' (Han nationality) ... The Han Dynasty was initiated by enfeoffing Hanzhong, in the same region as the River Xia and the same province as Huayang. The common reference to these locations aligns with their historical names. Consequently, 'Hua,' 'Xia,' and 'Han' can be used interchangeably, each bearing its unique significance. 'Han' symbolizes ethnicity, while 'Hua' encompasses the notion of the nation. Hence, the title 'Republic of China' originates.[19]

According to Zhang Binglin's "Interpretation of the Republic of China," it was widely circulated and well-received for its citations of classic texts, passionate tone, and grand scale.[20] Consequently, it became renowned both domestically and internationally, and naturally, it was adopted as the new national title after the success of the revolution, distinguishing it from previous dynastic titles.

However, the realization of the Republic of China could not simply rely on slogans, propaganda, principles, political programs, or ideologies. Overthrowing the imperial system and establishing a republic had to occur through revolutionary violence, given the external threats and internal corruption during the waning years of the Qing Dynasty. Between 1906 and 1911, revolutionary forces of the bourgeoisie, including the Alliance Party and the New Army, initiated over ten heroic and fierce armed uprisings. Although ultimately unsuccessful, these uprisings significantly weakened the Qing government and paved the way for the eventual establishment of the Republic of China.

The Wuchang Uprising began on October 10, 1911,[21] when revolutionary party members within the New Army[22] took swift control of the city overnight. On the evening of October 11th and the early morning of the 12th, the New Army stations in Hankou and Hanyang also joined the rebellion, culminating in the liberation of all three Wuhan towns. The Hubei Military Government was founded on October 11, and immediately it declared "China is to be called the Republic of China," annulled the imperial era name, and issued a declaration demanding the overthrow of the Qing government. On October 12, the revolutionary party members who initiated the uprising invited Sun Yat-sen, who was in the United States at the time, to return and lead the effort.

The Wuchang Uprising galvanized the Tongmenghui members nationwide and various affiliated revolutionary organizations, catalyzing the Xinhai Revolution (in the third year of the Xuantong era, which was called the year of Xinhai). By November 9, a total of 13 provinces, including Hubei, Hunan, Shaanxi, Jiangxi, Shanxi, Yunnan, Zhejiang, Jiangsu, Guizhou, Anhui, Guangxi, Fujian, and Guangdong, had declared their independence, leading to the downfall of the rule of the Qing Dynasty. Sun Yat-sen reached Shanghai on December 25, and on December 29, a conference of delegates from 17 provinces convened at the Dingjiaqiao Jiangsu Consultative Bureau in Nanjing, where Sun Yat-sen was elected the provisional president of the Republic of China. On January 1, 1912, he took the presidential oath at the Governor General's Office of the Two Rivers in Nanjing, officially establishing the country as the "Republic of China."[23]

Following the abdication of Emperor Puyi of the Qing Dynasty on February 12, the first year of the Republic of China, under the edict of Empress Dowager Longyu, the Qing Dynasty officially receded from history. On March 11, Sun Yat-sen proclaimed the "Temporary Provisions of the Republic of China," aimed at restraining Yuan Shikai and having constitutional characteristics. Chapter 1, "General Principles," of the Temporary Provisions stated that "the Republic of China is constituted by the Chinese people;" "the sovereignty of the Republic of China belongs to the entire nation;" "the territory of the Republic of China includes the twenty-two provinces, Inner and Outer Mongolia, Tibet, and Qinghai;" and "the Republic of China is governed through the Senate, the temporary president, the cabinet, and the judiciary." This definition clarified the concept of the "Republic of China." Moreover, the "Declaration of the Temporary President of the Republic of China" stated, "The foundation of the nation lies in the people. Various territories inhabited by Han, Manchu, Mongol, Hui, and Tibetan peoples comprise one country, and these diverse ethnic groups form one nation." In a 1923 speech at the National Youth Association in Guangzhou, Sun Yat-sen outlined, "You are all aware that the Republic of China differs from the 'Chinese Empire.' An empire is ruled by an emperor, whereas a republic is governed by its 400 million people." This comparison highlighted the progressiveness of the national title "Republic of China," emphasizing national unity rather than alignment with a specific familial name.

Drawing upon the historical facts mentioned above, the answer to the question previously posed is as follows: Sun Yat-sen is the proponent of the national title "Republic of China," and Zhang Binglin's "Interpretation of the Republic of China" provides an explanation and analysis of the national title. Thus, Sun Yat-sen is the "creator" of the national title "Republic of China," while Zhang Binglin, through his significant academic contributions, established the national title's historical, geographical, ethnic, and cultural basis. Interestingly, even Lu Xun, a member of the Restoration Society at the time, appeared to lack a clear understanding of these fundamental historical facts concerning this momentous event.

Or, perhaps as suggested in Lu Xun's "On Mr. Tai Yan's Matters," is the statement "the name 'Republic of China' originated from Mr. Zhang's 'Interpretation of the Republic of China'" is a special acknowledgment of Zhang Binglin from Yuhang, Zhejiang, who Lu Xun had previously studied with in Tokyo?

Notes

1 Lu Xun: "On Mr. Tai Yan's Matters," Miscellaneous Writings from the Qie Jie Ting, People's Literature Publishing House, 1973.

2 Sun Yat-sen, "The Strategy of Establishing the Nation" titled "Success Comes to Those Who Have Determination," included in the compiled edition by Sun Yat-sen Research

Office of the History Department of Sun Yat-sen University, Historical Research Office of Guangdong Provincial Academy of Social Sciences, and the Institute of Modern History of the Chinese Academy of Social Sciences: *The Complete Works of Sun Yat-sen*, Volume 6, Zhonghua Book Company, 2011.

3 Sun Yat-sen: "Speech at the National Youth Federation in Guangzhou," The Complete Works of Sun Yat-sen, Volume 8, Zhonghua Book Company, 2011

4 Chiang Chung-cheng, with the courtesy name Jieshi. According to Chinese traditional culture, referring to someone by their "given name" is neutral, neither complementary nor derogatory, while referring to someone by their "courtesy name" is a sign of respect. Therefore, in general, he is referred to as "Chiang Chung-cheng."

5 Wang Zhao-ming, with the courtesy name Jixin, and pen name Jingwei. The name "Jingwei" is derived from the myth of "Jingwei Filling the Sea," symbolizing his steadfast determination to overthrow the Qing government. However, when he later became a traitor collaborating with the enemy, it became highly inappropriate to refer to him as "Wang Jingwei," which was originally associated with a revolutionary spirit.

6 On February 13, 1912, Yuan Shikai telegraphed his approval of the republic. On February 14, Sun Yat-sen submitted his resignation. On February 15, Yuan Shikai was elected as the interim president by the Provisional Senate. On March 10, Yuan Shikai officially took office as the interim president of the Republic of China in Beijing. On April 1, Sun Yat-sen formally stepped down from his position. On April 2, the Provisional Senate resolved to relocate the provisional government to Beijing.

7 Sun Yat-sen, commonly known as "Sun Zhongshan" in modern times. The name "Sun Zhongshan" originated from his alias "Zhongshan Qiao" during his exile in Japan. Prior to using this alias, Sun Yat-sen used names such as "Koya Naga" and "Nakayama Heihachiro" while in Japan. In this case, "Zhongshan" becomes a Japanese surname, and it is one of the larger surnames ranked around the 50th position among approximately 140,000 surnames in Japan. Therefore, based on Sun Yat-sen's identity as a "Chinese" and the principle that one's name follows their preference, it is more appropriate to refer to him as "Sun Wen" rather than "Sun Zhongshan." Then, how did the term "Sun Zhongshan" come about? In 1903, Huang Zhonghuang (Zhang Shizhao) compiled and translated Sun Yat-sen's deeds, speeches, and added comments based on the book *A Dream of Thirty-Three Years* by Miyazaki Torazo from Japan, resulting in the book *Sun Yixian*. Due to Zhang Shizhao's limited knowledge of Japanese at the time, in a section with added comments, he mistakenly combined the true name "Sun Wen" and the alias "Zhongshan Qiao" to form "Sun Zhongshan." When criticized by his friend Wang Kanshu for the overlapping surnames and mixed-up order, Zhang Shizhao had no choice but to admit his mistake. In the 1906 edition, he corrected it to "Sun Yixian." Reference: Bai Ji'an, The Riot at the Lu Shi Naval Academy, The Biography of Zhang Shizhao, Writer's Publishing House, 2004.

8 Honolulu, originally the capital of Hawaii, was annexed by the United States in 1898.

9 "The Charter of the Revive China Society in Honolulu " and "The Pledge of the Revive China Society in Honolulu " are included in *The Complete Works of Sun Yat-sen*, Volume 1, Zhonghua Book Company, 2011.

10 Examples include the slogan "Expelling the barbarians, restoring China," proclaimed by Zhu Yuanzhang during his northern expedition in 1367 at the end of the Yuan Dynasty, and the "Anti-Qing and Restoration of Ming" movement in the early Qing Dynasty.

11 Zhang Binglin, "Refutation of Kang Youwei's Ideas of Revolution," The Complete Works of Zhang Taiyan, Volume 4, Shanghai People's Publishing House, 1985.

12 "The Oath of the Tokyo Military Training Class," The Complete Works of Sun Yat-sen, Volume 1.

13 The English original manuscript of Sun Wen's "The True Solution to the Chinese Question" can be found in Hu Hanmin's compilation: "Reproduced Manuscripts," The Collected Works of the Premier, Volume 4, Shanghai Minzhi Bookstore, 1930.

14 Huaxinghui was established in Changsha in February 1904, with its political manifesto being "Expel the Manchu invaders, revive China."

15 Guangfuhui was established in Shanghai in winter 1904, with its pledge being "Restore the Han ethnicity, reclaim our homeland, devote ourselves to the nation, retire after accomplishing great deeds."

16 "The Revolutionary Strategy of the Chinese Revolutionary Alliance," The Complete Works of Sun Yat-sen, Volume 1.

17 Sun Wen, "Speech at the Celebration of the First Anniversary of the Launch of the Tokyo People's News," The Complete Works of Sun Yat-sen, Volume 1.

18 Zhang Binglin, "Speech at the First Anniversary Celebration of the People's News," included in Zhang Nianchi's compilation, The Complete Works of Zhang Taiyan: Collection of Speeches, Volume 1, Shanghai People's Publishing House, 2015.

19 Zhang Binglin, "The Resolution of the Republic of China," The Complete Works of Zhang Taiyan, Volume 4.

20 It is worth noting that in Zhang Binglin's powerful work "Interpretation of the Republic of China," there is no explicit explanation of the meaning of "Republic" in terms of national or political system. The interpretation of "China" is also somewhat subjective, given the unique context of the overthrow of the Manchu dynasty during the late Qing period, making it somewhat inaccurate.

21 October 10th later became the National Day of the Republic of China.

22 The New Army refers to the modernized army that was reorganized during the late Qing period.

23 Chapter 8: "Ambitions Achieved" from the "Revitalization Strategy for the Founding of a Nation" stated: "On the first day of the first month of the year 1912, I, upon the birth of Christ, assumed office. I then issued a decree to proclaim the official name of the country as the Republic of China, and changed the era name to the First Year of the Republic of China, adopting the Gregorian calendar. Thus, my thirty years of unwavering dedication to the restoration of China and the establishment of a republic finally came to fruition."

References

Chinese Ancient Literature

(arranged in Chinese phonetic order based on the first letter of the title):

"Baihu Tong De Lun" (Evidential Analysis of Debates in the White Tiger Hall) by Ban Gu, published by Shanghai Ancient Books Publishing House in 1990.

"Bao Pu Zi" (Book of the Preservation of Simplicity) by Ge Hong, published by Shanghai Ancient Books Publishing House in 1990.

"Bei Shi" (The History of the Northern Dynasties) by Li Yanshou, published by Zhonghua Book Company in 1974.

"Caomu Zi" (Book of Grass and Trees) by Ye Ziqi, published by Zhonghua Book Company in 1959.

"Cefu Yuangui" (The Imperially Commissioned Encyclopedia of History) compiled by Wang Qinruo and others, published by Zhonghua Book Company in 1960.

"Chaxiang Shi Congchao" (Collected Essays from the Tea Fragrance Room) by Yu Yue, edited by Zhen Fan and others, published by Zhonghua Book Company in 1995.

"Chen Shu" (Book of Chen) by Yao Silian, published by Zhonghua Book Company in 1972.

"Chibei Outan" (Leisurely Talks of the Northern Pond) by Wang Shizhen, edited by Lerei Ren, published by Zhonghua Book Company in 1982.

Chongxiu Qishan Xianzhi (Revised Records of Qishan County), Tian Weijun's repair, Bai Xiuyun's compilation, Chengwen Publishing House, 1976 edition.

"Chouliao Shuohua" (Great Paintings in the Liao Tower) compiled by Cheng Kaihu, from the "The Initial Compilation of Collected Works" edition, published by Xin Wenfeng Publishing Company in Taiwan.

"Chu Ci" (Songs of Chu) by Qu Yuan, Song Yu, and others, annotated and translated by Wu Guangping, published by Yuelu Publishing House in 2001.

"Chuci Jizhu" (Collected Annotations on Songs of Chu) by Qu Yuan, annotated by Zhu Xi, published by Shanghai Ancient Books Publishing House in 1979.

"Chushi Ying Fa Yi Bi Siguo Riji" (Diary of Xue Fucheng's Mission to England, France, Italy and Belgium) by Xue Fucheng, published by Hunan People's Publishing House in 1981.

"Chuxue Ji" (Records of an Amateur) compiled by Xu Jian and others, published by Zhonghua Book Company in 1962.

"Chunqiu Fanlu" (Luxuriant Dew of the Spring and Autumn Annals) by Dong Zhongshu, published by Shanghai Ancient Books Publishing House in 1989.

"Chunqiu Gongyang Zhuan Zhushu" (Annotations and Commentaries on the Gongyang's Commentary to the Spring and Autumn Annals) from the "Annotations and Commentaries on the Thirteen Classics" edition, published by Zhonghua Book Company in 1980.

"Chunqiu Guliang Zhuzhu" (Annotations and Commentaries on the Guliang's Commentary to the Spring and Autumn Annals), "Annotations and Commentaries on the Thirteen Classics" edition, published by Zhonghua Book Company in 1980.

"Chunqiu Mingli Xu" (Preface to the Chronological Records of the Spring and Autumn Period), included in "Weishu Jicheng," compiled by An Juxiang and Nakamura Shozaburo, published by Hebei People's Publishing House in 1994.

"Chunqiu Shili" (Annotation on the Spring and Autumn), by Du Yu of the Western Jin Dynasty, "The Initial Compilation of Collected Works" edition, published by The Commercial Press in 1936.

"Chunqiu Zuozhuan Zhenyi" (The Authentic Interpretation of Zuozhuan of the Spring and Autumn Annals), "Annotations and Commentaries on the Thirteen Classics" edition, published by Zhonghua Book Company in 1980.

"Chunqiu Zuozhuan Zhu" (Annotations on the Zuozhuan of the Spring and Autumn Annals) by Yang Bojun, published by Zhonghua Book Company in 1981.

"Culai Ji" (Collected Works of Cui Cai) by Shi Jie of the Northern Song Dynasty, "The Initial Compilation of Collected Works" edition, published by The Commercial Press in 1936.

"Da Amituo Jing" (The Larger Sutra on Amitāyus Buddha), included in Zhao Puchu's main edition, "Yongle Beicang" Volume 43, published by Thread Binding Books Publishing House in 2005.

"Da Ci'en Si Sanzang Fashi Zhuan" (Biography of the Tripitaka Master of the Great Ci'en Monastery) by Hui Li of the Tang Dynasty, published by Zhonghua Book Company in 1983.

"Da Dai Liji Hui Jiao Jiexie" (Book of Rites by Dai De) by Dai De of the Western Han Dynasty, collated and annotated by Fang Xiangdong, published by Zhonghua Book Company in 2008.

"Da Fangdeng Wuxiang Jing" (Sutra of the Great Possibility of the Equanimity of All Dharmas), included in "Zhonghua Dazangjing" edited by the Editorial Board of the Chinese Tripitaka (Chinese Text Section), Volume 18, published by Zhonghua Book Company in 1986.

"Da Fangguang Fohua Yanyi" (A Commentary on the Mahāprajñāpāramitā Sūtra) by Huiyuan of the Tang Dynasty, published by Zhonghua Book Company in 1991.

"Da Tang Chuangye Qiju Zhu" (Annotations on Daily Life during the Founding of the Tang Dynasty), authored by Wen Daya of the Tang Dynasty, collated and edited by Li Jiping and Li Xihou, published by Shanghai Ancient Books Publishing House in 1983.

"Da Tang Xiyu Ji" (The Great Tang Records on the Western Regions) by Xuanzang of the Tang Dynasty, edited by Zhang Xun, published by Shanghai People's Publishing House in 1977.

"Dayi Juemi Lu" (Records of the Great Righteous Awakening), authored by Aisin Gioro Yinzhen of the Qing Dynasty, included in Shen Yunlong's compilation "Jindai Zhongguo Shiliao Congkan" Volume 36, published by Wenhai Publishing House in Taiwan.

"Daoyi Zhilue Jiaoshi" (Annotated and Revised Brief History of the Barbarians) by Wang Daoyi of the Yuan Dynasty, edited and revised by Su Jiqin, published by Zhonghua Book Company in 1981.

"Dian Youji" (Record of the Trip to Yunnan) by Chen Ding of the Qing Dynasty, "The Initial Compilation of Collected Works" edition, published by The Commercial Press in 1936.

"Dingzheng Zengyi Cailan Yiyuan" (Corrections, Additions, Translations, and Miscellaneous Notes) by Yamamura Saikyo of Japan, published by Qingshi She in 1979.

"Diwang Shiji" (Chronicles of Emperors) by Huangfu Mi of the Wei and Jin Dynasties, "The Initial Compilation of Collected Works" edition, published by The Commercial Press in 1936.

"Dongdu Shilve" (Records of the Eastern Capital) by Wang Cheng of the Southern Song Dynasty, included in "Ershi Wubie Shi," published by Qilu Publishing House in 2000.

"Donghualu" (Compilations of the History of the Qing Dynasty) by Wang Xianqian of the Qing Dynasty, published by Shanghai Ancient Books Publishing House in 2007.

"Dongxiyangkao" (Investigations of the Eastern and Western World) by Zhang Xie of the Ming Dynasty, collated and revised by Xie Fang, published by Zhonghua Book Company in 2000.

"Dongting Ji" (The Collection from Dongting) by Sun Yi of the Ming Dynasty, included in "Beijing Tushuguan Guji Zhenben Congkan" compiled by the Beijing Library's Ancient Books Publishing Editing Group, published by Shumu Wenxian Publishing House in 1998.

"Dushi Fangyu Jiyao" (Essential Principles for Records and Examination of History) by Gu Zuyu of the Qing Dynasty, collated by He Cijun and Shi Hejin, published by Zhonghua Book Company in 2005.

"Dutong Jianlun" (Critique on the Compendium of History) by Wang Fuzhi of the Qing Dynasty, published by Zhonghua Book Company in 1975.

"Erya Yi" (Explanation of Erya), by Luo Yuan of the Southern Song Dynasty, collated and revised by Shi Yunsun, published by Huangshan Publishing House in 1991.

"Erya Yishu" (Annotated Interpretation of Erya), by Hao Yixing of the Qing Dynasty, published by Shanghai Ancient Books Publishing House in 1983.

"Erya Zhushu" (Annotated and Commented Edition of Erya), "Shi San Jing Zhu Shu" edition, published by Zhonghua Book Company in 1980.

"Fanyi Mingyi Ji" (Collections of Translations and Their Meanings) by Fayun of the Southern Song Dynasty, published by Jiangsu Guangling Classics Engraving Society in 1990.

"Fang Yan" (Dialects), authored by Yang Xiong in the Western Han Dynasty, annotated by Guo Pu in the Jin Dynasty, first compiled in "The Compendium of Books and Writings," published by the Commercial Press in 1936.

"Faxian Zhuan" (Biography of Faxian) by Faxian of the Eastern Jin Dynasty, annotated by Zhang Xun, published by Shanghai Ancient Books Publishing House in 1985.

"Fayan" (The Way of the Law) by Yang Xiong of the Western Han Dynasty, published by Zhonghua Book Company in 1985.

"Fengyang Xinshu" (The New Book of Fengyang), edited by Yuan Yixin, Ke Zhonggong, and others, Ming Dynasty, Tianqi Yuan Printing Edition.

"Fozu Tongji Jiaozhu" (Annotated Compilation of Buddhist Ancestors), written by Zhipan in the Southern Song Dynasty, annotated by Shidao Fa, Shanghai Ancient Books Publishing House, 2012 edition.

"Gaoseng Zhuan" (Biographies of Eminent Monks), written by Huijiao in the Liang Dynasty, annotated by Tang Yongtong, compiled by Tang Yixuan, Zhonghua Book Company, 1992 edition.

"Geming Jun" (The Revolutionary Army), written by Zou Rong in the Qing Dynasty, included in Zhang Mei's compilation "Zou Rong Collection," People's Literature Publishing House, 2011 edition.

"Geng Shen Wai Shi" (Extra History of the Geng Shen Year), written by Quan Heng, Ming Dynasty, included in "The Initial Compilation of Collected Works," Commercial Press, 1936 edition.

"Gu Ben Zhu Shu Ji Nian Ji Jiao" (Collected and Annotated Bamboo Annals Compilation), edited and annotated by Wang Guowei, included in "The Collected Works of Wang Guowei," Volume 12, Shanghai Ancient Books Store, 1983 edition.

"Gu Jin Tu Shu Ji Cheng" (Comprehensive Collection of Ancient and Modern Books), compiled by Chen Menglei and others, Zhonghua Book Company, 1934 edition.

"Guo Chu Qun Xiong Shi Lue" (Brief Records of Heroes at the Beginning of the State), written by Qian Qianyi in the Qing Dynasty, Jiangsu Guangling Ancient Books Engraving and Printing Society, 1981 edition.

"Guo Chu Shi Ji" (Events at the Beginning of the State), written by Liu Chen in the Ming Dynasty, Zhonghua Book Company, 1991 edition.

"Guoli Taiwan Daxue Tushuguan Diancang Riben Shu Ji Yingyin · Kankanben · Yuanwei Ben" (Reprint and Textual Research of the Japanese Book Collection in the National Taiwan University Library), authored by Sheren Prince, edited by Fan San and Yamaguchi Masayoshi, translated by Hong Shufen, National Taiwan University Library, 2012 edition.

"Guo Yu" (The Discourses of the States), annotated by Wei Zhao in the Wu Kingdom during the Three Kingdoms period, Shanghai Bookstore Publishing House, 1987 edition.

"Hai Guo Tu Zhi" (Illustrated Gazetteer of Maritime Countries), written by Wei Yuan in the Qing Dynasty, Yue Lu Book Society, 2011 edition.

"Han Changli Wenji Zhushi" (Annotation of Han Changli's Collected Works), written by Han Yu in the Tang Dynasty, annotated by Yan Qi, Sanqin Publishing House, 2004 edition.

"Han Feizi" (Master Han Fei), written by Han Fei in the Warring States period, Shanghai Ancient Books Publishing House, 1989 edition.

"Han Shu" (Book of Han), written by Ban Gu in the Eastern Han Dynasty, annotated by Yan Shigu in the Tang Dynasty, Zhonghua Book Company, 1962 edition.

"Han Shu Di Li Zhi Bu Zhu" (Supplemental Annotations to the Geographical Records in the Book of Han), written by Wu Zhuoxin in the Qing Dynasty, included in the "Er Shi Wu Shi Bu Bian" compilation, Zhonghua Book Company, 1955 edition.

"Hong Fa Da Shi Konghai Quanji" (The Complete Works of Master Hongfa Konghai), Volume 6 "Xing Ling Ji" (Collection of Spiritual Teachings), compiled by the Editorial Committee of the Complete Works of Master Hongfa Konghai, Zhumo Shufang, 1987 edition.

"Hong You Lu" (Record of Vast Guidance), written by Gao Dai in the Ming Dynasty, edited by Sun Zhengrong and Shan Jinheng, Shanghai Ancient Books Publishing House, 1992 edition.

"Hou Han Shu" (Book of Later Han), written by Fan Ye in the Southern Song Dynasty, annotated by Li Xian and others in the Tang Dynasty, Zhonghua Book Company, 1965 edition.

"Hu Lou Bi Tan" (Discussions at the Hu Lou Pavilion), written by Yu Yue in the Qing Dynasty, edited by Cui Gaowei, published in the compilation "Jiu Jiu Xiao Xia Lu," Zhonghua Book Company, 1995 edition.

"Huayang Guo Zhi" (Records of the States South of Mount Hua), written by Chang Qu in the Eastern Jin Dynasty, annotated by Liu Lin, Bashu Book Society, 1984 edition.

"Huayang Tao Yinju Neizhuan" (Internal Biography of Tao Yinju in Huayang), written by Jia Song in the Tang Dynasty, included in the "Guangu Tang Huike Shu" compilation, Guangxu Wuxu Changsha Ye's Xi Garden Reprint.

"Huainanzi" (Book of the Master of Huainan), written by Liu An and others in the Western Han Dynasty, annotated by Gao You in the Eastern Han Dynasty, Shanghai Ancient Books Publishing House, 1989 edition.

"Huang Di Hun" (The Spirits of the Huang Emperor), by the majority of descendants of the Yellow Emperor, Shanghai Dongda Land Book Printing House, 1903 edition.

"Huang Di Nei Jing" (Yellow Emperor's Inner Canon), Heilongjiang People's Publishing House, 2004 edition.

Huáng Zūnxiàn Quánjí, The Complete Works of Huang Zunxian, written by Huang Zunxian in the Qing dynasty, edited by Chen Zheng, published by Zhonghua Publishing House, 2005 edition.

Jiànyán yǐlái Cháoyě Zájì, Miscellaneous Records of the Court and the Field since the Jianyan Era, written by Li Xinchuan in the Southern Song dynasty, edited by Xu Gui, published by Zhonghua Publishing House, 2000 edition.

Jiànyán yǐlái Xìnián Yàolù, Selected Historical Records since the Jianyan Era, written by Li Xinchuan in the Southern Song dynasty, published by Shanghai Ancient Books Publishing House, 1992 edition.

Jiāo Shì Bǐchéng, Jiao's Personal Documentation, written by Jiao Hong in the Ming dynasty, published by Shanghai Ancient Books Publishing House, 1986 edition.

Jìlù Huìbiān, Compilation of Records, edited by Shen Jiefu in the Ming dynasty, reproduced by the Microfilm Center of the National Library of China, 1994 edition.

Jīn Běn Zhúshū Jìnián Shūzhèng, Annotated Edition of The Chronological Records of Bamboo Books Based on Current Texts, edited by Wang Guowei, included in the 12th volume of Wang Guowei's collected works, published by Shanghai Ancient Books Store, 1983 edition.

Jīnshí Suǒ, Index of Inscriptions on Metals and Stones, written by Feng Yunpeng and Feng Yunyuan in the Qing dynasty, published by Shumu Wenxian Publishing House, 1996 edition.

Jīnshí Wénzì Jì, Records of Inscriptions on Metals and Stones, compiled by Gu Yanwu in the Qing dynasty, published by Zhonghua Publishing House, 1991 edition.

Jīnshǐ, History of the Jin Dynasty, written by Tuo Tuo and others in the Yuan dynasty, published by Zhonghua Publishing House, 1975 edition.

Jīn Wén Zuì, Selected Collection of Jin Dynasty Inscriptions, compiled by Zhang Jinwu in the Qing dynasty, published by Zhonghua Publishing House, 1990 edition.

Jìnshū, Book of Jin, written by Fang Xuanling and others in the Tang dynasty, published by Zhonghua Publishing House, 1974 edition.

Jīngyì Shùwén, A Collection of Notes on Classics and Commentaries, written by Wang Yinzhi in the Qing dynasty, published by Jiangsu Ancient Books Publishing House, 1985 edition.

Jǐngshì Zhōng, The Bell of Warning the World, written by Chen Tianhua, included in Liu Qingbo and Peng Guoxing's compilation, revised by Rao Huaimin: "Collected Works of Chen Tianhua," published by Hunan People's Publishing House, 2011 edition.

Jìngzhāi Gǔjīn Tá, Jingzhai's Collection of Ancient and Modern Tantrums, written by Li Zhi in the Yuan dynasty, edited by Liu Dequan, published by Zhonghua Publishing House, 1995 edition.

Jiù Tángshū, Old Book of Tang, written by Liu Xu and others in the Later Jin dynasty, published by Zhonghua Publishing House, 1975 edition.

Jiù Wǔdài Shǐ, Old History of the Five Dynasties, written by Xue Juzheng and others in the Northern Song dynasty, published by Zhonghua Publishing House, 2003 edition.

Kāijuàn Ŏudé, Accidentally Obtained by Reading, written by Lin Chunpu in the Qing dynasty, included in the "Collected Works Compilation Series," published by Xin Wenfeng Publishing Company, Taiwan.

Kāiyuán Shìjiào Lù, Records of the Buddhist Teachings of the Kaiyuan Era, written by Shi Zhisheng in the Tang dynasty, published by Wenyuan Ge Publishing House in the "Complete Library in Four Sections" compilation.

Kǎogǔ Biān, Compilation of Archaeology, written by Cheng Dachang in the Southern Song Dynasty, included in the "Collected Works Compilation Series," published by Zhonghua Publishing House, 1985 edition.

Kùnxué Jìwén, Memoirs of Studying in Difficulties, written by Wang Yinglin in the Southern Song Dynasty, published by Shanghai Ancient Books Publishing House, 2015 edition.

Kuò Dìzhì Jíjiào, Compilation and Collation of Kuodi Zhi, written by Li Tai and others in the Tang dynasty, edited by He Cijun, published by Zhonghua Publishing House, 1980 edition.

Lǎn Zhēnzǐ, Lazy Master, written by Ma Yongqing in the Song Dynasty, included in the "Collected Works Compilation Series," published by Zhonghua Publishing House, 1985 edition.

Lǎo Xué'ān Bǐjì, Notes from the Old Study Hut, written by Lu You in the Southern Song Dynasty, edited by Li Jianxiong and Liu Dequan, published by Zhonghua Publishing House, 1979 edition.

Lǐjì Zhèngyì, Commentary on The Book of Rites, in the edition of the "Annotations and Commentaries on the Thirteen Classics" published by Zhonghua Publishing House, 1980 edition.

Lǐ Fú Kānwù, Errors in Li Fu's Edition, written by Li Fu in the Tang dynasty, published by Wenyuan Ge Publishing House in the "Complete Library in Four Sections" compilation.

Lìmǎdòu Zhōngguó Zhájì, The China Letters of Matteo Ricci, written by Matteo Ricci and translated by He Gaoji, Wang Zunzhong, and Li Shen, published by Zhonghua Publishing House, 1983 edition.

Liángshū, Book of Liang, written by Yao Silian in the Tang Dynasty, published by Zhonghua Publishing House, 1973 edition.

Liáoshǐ, History of the Liao Dynasty, written by Tuo Tuo and others in the Yuan Dynasty, published by Zhonghua Publishing House, 1974 edition.

Liáozhì, Records of the Liao Dynasty, written by Ye Longli in the Southern Song Dynasty, included in the "Collected Works Compilation Series," published by Zhonghua Publishing House, 1985 edition.

Lièzǐ Quányì, Complete Translation of Liezi, written by Lie Yukou in the Warring States period, translated and annotated by Wang Qiangmo, published by Guizhou People's Publishing House, 1993 edition.

Liùcháo Tōngjiàn Bóyì, General Discussion of the History of the Six Dynasties, written by Li Tao in the Southern Song Dynasty, edited by Hu Axiang and Tong Ling, published by Nanjing Publishing House, 2007 edition.

Lù Yóu Jí, Collected Works of Lu You, written by Lu You in the Southern Song Dynasty, published by Zhonghua Publishing House, 1976 edition.

Lu Shi (Complete Library in Four Sections) compiled by Luo Bi from the Southern Song Dynasty, annotated by Luo Ping from the Southern Song Dynasty, Wenyuan Pavilion.

Lun Heng Ji Jie, written by Wang Chong from the Eastern Han Dynasty, collected and explained by Liu Pansui, Guji Press, 1957 edition.

Lun Yu Zhu Shu, from the "Annotations and Commentaries on the Thirteen Classics" edition, Zhonghua Book Company, 1980 edition.

Luo Yang Jia Lan Ji Jiao Zhu, written by Yang Xuanzhi from the Northern Wei Dynasty, annotated by Fan Xiangyong, Shanghai Ancient Books Publishing House, 1978 edition.

Luo Zhong Ji Yi Lu, written by Qin Zaisi from the Northern Song Dynasty, collated from the "Shuo Fu" edition by Tao Zongyi, China Bookstore in Beijing, 1986 edition.

Lv Shi Chun Qiu, published by Shanghai Ancient Books Publishing House, 1989 edition.

Ma Ke Bo Luo Xing Ji, dictated by Marco Polo, transcribed by Rustichello da Pisa, annotated by Francesco Balducci, translated by Feng Chengjun, Zhonghua Book Company, 1954 edition.

Ma Ke Bo Luo You Ji, dictated by Marco Polo, transcribed by Rustichello da Pisa, translated by Manuel Komroff, translated by Chen Kaijun, et al., Fujian Science and Technology Press, 1981 edition.

Man Zhou Shi Lu, Records of the Qing Dynasty, Volume 1, Zhonghua Book Company, 1985 edition.

Mao Shi Zheng Yi, included in the "Annotations and Commentaries on the Thirteen Classics," Zhonghua Book Company, 1980 edition.

Meng Da Bei Lu, written by Zhao Gong from the Southern Song Dynasty, from the "Compilation of the The Initial Compilation of Collected Works," Zhonghua Book Company, 1985 edition.

Meng Gu You Mu Ji, written by Zhang Mu from the Qing Dynasty, supplemented by He Qiutao, included in the "Continuation of the Complete Library of the Four Treasuries," Shanghai Ancient Books Publishing House.

Meng Zi Zhu Shu, included in the "Annotations and Commentaries on the Thirteen Classics," Zhonghua Book Company, 1980 edition.

Ming Shan Cang, written by He Qiaoyuan from the Ming Dynasty, collated and edited by Zhang Dexin, Shang Chuan, Wang Xi, Fujian People's Publishing House, 2010 edition.

Ming Jing Shi Wen Bian, selected and edited by Chen Zilong, et al., Zhonghua Book Company, 1962 edition.

Ming Shi Lu, printed and proofread by the Institute of History and Philology at Academia Sinica, edited by Huang Zhangjian, Zhonghua Book Company, 2016 edition.

Ming Shi, edited by Zhang Tingyu, et al., Zhonghua Book Company, 1974 edition.

Ming Tai Zu Ji, written by Zhu Yuanzhang from the Ming Dynasty, collated by Hu Shi'e, Huangshan Shushe, 1991 edition.

Mo Zi, published by Shanghai Ancient Books Publishing House, 1989 edition.

Nan Cun Chuo Geng Lu, written by Tao Zongyi from the Ming Dynasty, Zhonghua Book Company, 1959 edition.

Nan Hai Ji Gui Nei Fa Chuan Jiao Zhu, written by Shi Yijing from the Tang Dynasty, annotated by Wang Bangwei, Zhonghua Book Company, 1995 edition.

Nan Qi Shu, written by Xiao Zixian from the Liang Dynasty, Zhonghua Book Company, 1972 edition.

Nan Shi, written by Li Yanshou from the Tang Dynasty, Zhonghua Book Company, 1975 edition.

Neng Gai Zhai Man Lu, written by Wu Zeng from the Southern Song Dynasty, Shanghai Ancient Books Publishing House, 1979 edition.

Nian Er Shi Zha Ji, written by Zhao Yi from the Qing Dynasty, China Bookstore, 1987 edition.

Ning Gu Ta Ji Lüe, from the "Continuation of the Complete Library of the Four Treasuries," Shanghai Ancient Books Publishing House.

Pi Ya, written by Lu Dian from the Northern Song Dynasty, annotated by Wang Minhong, Zhejiang University Press, 2008 edition.

Ping Zhou Ke Tan, written by Zhu Yu from the Northern Song Dynasty, edited and annotated by Li Weiguo, Shanghai Ancient Books Publishing House, 1989 edition.

Qi Guo Kao, written by Dong Shuo from the Ming Dynasty, from the "Compilation of the The Initial Compilation of Collected Works," Zhonghua Book Company, 1985 edition.

Qi Xiu Lei Gao (Collection of Manuscripts on the Seven Stuffs) [Ming] Lang Ying, Zhonghua Book Company, 1959 edition.

Qi Dan Guo Zhi (Records of the Khitan Kingdom) [Southern Song] Ye Longli, edited by Jia Jingyan and Lin Ronggui, Shanghai Ancient Books Publishing House, 1985 edition.

Qian Dao Si Ming Tu Jin (Qian Dao's Illustrated Guide to Four Brightness) [Southern Song] Zhang Jin et al., from the "Collection of Song Dynasty and Yuan Dynasty Local Chronicles," Zhonghua Book Company, 1990 edition.

Qian Yan Tang Ji (Collected Works of Qian Yantang) [Qing] Qian Daxin, edited by Lv Youren, Shanghai Ancient Books Publishing House, 1989 edition.

Qin Ding Man Zhou Yuan Liu Kao (Investigation on the Origins of the Manchu Dynasty) [Qing] A Gui and Yu Minzhong, included in Shen Yunlong's compilation: "Collection of Modern Chinese Historical Materials" Volume 14, Wenhai Publishing House, Taiwan.

Qin Guan Ji Bian Nian Jiao Zhu (Chronology and Annotation of Qin Guan's Collected Works), [Northern Song] Qin Guan, annotated by Zhou Xigan, Cheng Zixin, and Zhou Lei, People's Literature Publishing Society, 2001 edition.

Qing Chao Wen Xian Tong Kao (Comprehensive Study of Qing Dynasty Documents) Official Compilation of the Qing Dynasty, Zhejiang Ancient Books Publishing House, 1988 edition.

Qing Hua Da Xue Cang Zhan Guo Zhu Jian (Bamboo Slips of the Warring States Period in the Tsinghua University Collection) Part 1, edited by Li Xueqin, Zhongxi Book House, 2010 edition.

Qing Shi Bie Cai Ji (Selected Collection of Qing Poetry) [Qing] Shen Deqian, Zhonghua Book Company, 1975 edition.

Qing Shi Gao (Draft History of the Qing Dynasty) compiled by Zhao Erxun et al., Zhonghua Book Company, 1976 edition.

Qiu Feng Jia Xian Sheng Shi Xuan (Selected Poetry of Qiu Fengjia) [Qing] Qiu Fengjia, selected and annotated by Li Hongjian, Jinan University Press, 2014 edition.

Qiu Jian Xian Sheng Da Quan Wen Ji (Complete Works of Qiu Jian) [Yuan] Wang Yun, from the "Collection of Four Categories," Shanghai Bookstore.

Quan Jin Shi (Complete Collection of Poetry in the Jin Dynasty) compiled by Xue Ruizhao and Guo Mingzhi, Nankai University Press, 1995 edition.

Quan Ming Shi (Complete Collection of Ming Dynasty Poetry (Volume 1)) compiled by the Committee for the Compilation of Complete Ming Dynasty Poems, Shanghai Ancient Books Publishing House, 1990 edition.

Quan Shang Gu San Dai Qin Han San Guo Liu Chao Wen (Complete Ancient Documents of the Three Dynasties, Qin and Han Dynasties, and Six Dynasties) [Qing] Yan Kejun as editor, Zhonghua Book Company, 1958 edition.

Quan Tang Shi (Complete Collection of Poetry of Tang (Revised and Enlarged Edition)) [Qing] Peng Dingqiu as compiler, edited by the editorial department of Zhonghua Book Company, 1999 edition.

Quan Tang Wen (Complete Collection of Prose of Tang) compiled by Dong Gao et al., Zhonghua Book Company, 1983 edition.

Quan Yuan Wen (Complete Literature of the Yuan Dynasty) edited by Li Xiusheng, Phoenix Publishing House, 2004 edition.

Ri Ben Jiao Yu Shi Lue (Outline of Japanese Educational History), Japan's Ministry of Education, published by Japan's Ministry of Education, 1887 edition.

Ri Ben Kai Zhi Wen Da (Questions and Answers on Knowledge: Elementary School Reader), [Japan] Fujino Nagamasa, Ryoanro, 1874 edition.

Ri Ben Shi Ji (Records of Japanese History) [Japan] Tokugawa Mitsukuni, Anhui People's Publishing House, 2013 edition.

Ri Zhi Lu Ji Shi (Collection and Explanation of Records of Rizhi) [Qing] Gu Yanwu, [Qing] Huang Rucheng as compiler, Qin Kezheng as editor, Yue Lu Publishing, 1994 edition.

Rong Zhai Sui Bi (Random Notes from the Yongzhai Studio) [Southern Song] Hong Mai, edited by Mu Gong, Shanghai Ancient Books Publishing House, 2014 edition.

San Chao Bei Meng Hui Bian (Compilation of the Three Northern Union Meetings), [Southern Song] Xu Mengxin, Shanghai Ancient Books Publishing House, 1987 edition.

San Guo Yan Yi (Romance of the Three Kingdoms) [Ming] Luo Guanzhong, People's Literature Publishing Society, 1973 edition.

San Guo Zhi (Records of the Three Kingdoms) [Western Jin] Chen Shou, [Southern Dynasties] Pei Songzhi as annotator, Zhonghua Book Company, 1982 edition.

Shan Hai Jing (Classic of Mountains and Seas) [Jin] Guo Pu as annotator, [Qing] Hao Yixing as commentator, Shen Haibo as editor, Shanghai Ancient Books Publishing House, 2015 edition.

Shan Lin Guo Bao Ji (Records of the Treasures of Friendly Neighboring Countries) [Japan] Shi Zhoufeng, Oriental Studies Society, 1928 edition.

Shang Kao Xin Lu (Records of Examining Merchants) [Qing] Cui Shu, from the "New Compilation of Collected Books," New Wenfeng Publishing Company, Taiwan.

Shang Shu Da Zhuan (Expositions of the Book of Documents) from the "Initial Compilation of Collected Books," Zhonghua Book Company, 1985 edition.

Shang Shu Jin Gu Wen Zhu Shu (Annotations and Commentaries on the Current and Ancient Texts of the Book of Documents) [Qing] Sun Xingyan as annotator, Chen Kang and Sheng Dongling as editors, Zhonghua Book Company, 1986 edition.

Shang Shu Zheng Yi (Annotations of the Book of Documents) from the "Annotations and Commentaries on the Thirteen Classics," Zhonghua Book Company, 1980 edition.

Sheng Chao Po Xie Ji (Collection of Destroying Evil in the Holy Dynasty) [Ming] Xu Changzhi (editor), Xia Guiqi (compiler), Jiandao Theological Seminary, Hong Kong, 1996 edition.

Sheng Wu Ji (Record of Saint Martial) [Qing] Wei Yuan, Shanghai Ancient Books Publishing House, 1996 edition.

Shi Ben Ba Zhong (Eight Types of Genealogies) [Eastern Han] Song Zhong (annotation), [Qing] Qin Jiamu (compilation), Commercial Press, 1957 edition.

Shi Di Li Kao (Investigation of the Geography of Poetry) [Southern Song] Wang Yinglin, "Collected Works Compilation" edition, Commercial Press, 1936 edition.

Shi Guo Chun Qiu (Annals of the Ten Kingdoms) [Qing] Wu Renchen, Zhonghua Book Company, 2010 edition.

Shi Ji (Records of the Grand Historian) [Western Han] Sima Qian (author), [Southern Dynasty Song] Pei Yuan (collective interpretation), [Tang] Sima Zhen (explanatory notes), [Tang] Zhang Shoujie (correct interpretation), Zhonghua Book Company, 1982 edition.

Shi Ji Zhuan (Commentary on the Collection of Poems) [Southern Song] Zhu Xi (annotator), Shanghai Ancient Books Publishing House, 1980 edition.

Shi Ke Zhai Ji Yan (Records of the Shikezhai Studio) [Qing] Ma Jianzhong, Zhonghua Book Company, 1960 edition.

Shi Lin Yan Yu (Yan's Discourses in the Stone Forest) [Song] Ye Mengde (author), [Southern Song] Yu Wen Shaoyi (editor), Hou Zhongyi (collation), Zhonghua Book Company, 1984 edition.

Shi Liu Guo Chun Qiu (Annals of the Sixteen Kingdoms) [Northern Wei] Cui Hong, "Collected Works Compilation" edition, Commercial Press, 1937 edition.

Shi Ming Shu Zheng Bu (Supplementary Explanations and Evidences to the Shuo Wen Commentary) [Eastern Han] Liu Xi (author), [Qing] Wang Xianqian (explanatory notes), Shanghai Ancient Books Publishing House, 1984 edition.

Shi Qi Shi Shang Que (Critique of the Seventeen Histories) [Qing] Wang Mingsheng (author), Huang Shuhui (editor), Shanghai Bookstore Publishing House, 2005 edition.

Shi Zi (Collected Works of Shizi) [Warring States] Shi Jiao, Shanghai Ancient Books Publishing House, 1989 edition.

Shi Zi Hou (Lion's Roar) [Qing] Chen Tianhua, included in Liu Qingbo and Peng Guoxing's compilation, revised by Rao Huaimin: "Collected Works of Chen Tianhua," Hunan People's Publishing House, 2011 edition.

Shuang Huai Sui Chao (Harvest Notes of the Twin Locust Trees) [Ming] Huang Yu (author), Wei Lianke (collation), Zhonghua Book Company, 1999 edition.

Shui Jin Zhu Shu (Commentary on the Waterways Classic) anonymous author, [Northern Wei] Li Dao Yuan (commentary), Yang Shoujing, Xiong Huizhen (annotation), Duan Xizhong (collation), Chenqiao Yifu Correction, Jiangsu Ancient Books Publishing House, 1989 edition.

Shuo Wen Jie Zi (Explanations and Interpretations of the Chinese Characters) [Eastern Han] Xu Shen (author), [Northern Song] Xu Xuan (revised edition), China Bookstore, 1989 edition.

Shuo Wen Jie Zi Xi Zhuan (Continuation of the Explanations and Interpretations of the Shuo Wen Jie Zi) [Southern Tang] Xu Kai, Zhonghua Book Company, 1987 edition.

Shuo Wen Jie Zi Zhu (Annotated Explanations and Interpretations of the Shuo Wen Jie Zi) [Eastern Han] Xu Shen (author), [Qing] Duan Yucai (commentary), Shanghai Ancient Books Publishing House, 1981 edition.

Shuo Wen Jie Zi Zhu Jian (Annotated Notes on the Explanations and Interpretations of the Shuo Wen Jie Zi) [Qing] Duan Yucai (commentary), [Qing] Xu Hao (notes), Shanghai Ancient Books Publishing House, 1996 edition.

Shuo Wen Tong Xun Ding Sheng (Standard Pronunciations in the Explanations and Interpretations of the Shuo Wen Jie Zi) [Qing] Zhu Junsheng, Zhonghua Book Company, 1984 edition.

Si Ma Wen Gong Wen Ji (Collected Documents of Grand Minister Sima) [Northern Song] Sima Guang, "Collected Works Compilation" edition, Zhonghua Book Company, 1985 edition.

Si Ku Quan Shu Zong Mu (General Catalog of the Complete Library in the Four Branches of Literature) [Qing] Yong Rong et al., Zhonghua Book Company, 1965 edition.

Si Shu Zhang Ju Ji Zhu (Collected Annotations on the Four Classics) [Southern Song] Zhu Xi, Zhonghua Book Company, 2010 edition.

Song Chao Shi Shi Lei Yuan (A Collection of Historical Facts of the Song Dynasty) [Song] Jiang Shaoyu, Shanghai Ancient Books Publishing House, 1981 edition.

Song Da Zhao Ling Ji (Collected Imperial Edicts and Orders of the Song Dynasty) compiled by Sizhi Ancestry, Zhonghua Book Company, 1962 edition.

Song Hui Yao Ji Lu (Compilation of Important Matters of the Song Dynasty) [Qing] Xu Song (compiler), Zhonghua Book Company, 1957 edition.

Song Mo Ji Wen (Records of Pine Forests and Deserts) [Southern Song] Hong Hao, "Continuation of the Collected Works Compilation" edition, Xinwenfeng Publishing Company, Taiwan.

Song Shan Ji (Book of Mountain Song) [Northern Song] Chao Shuozhi, Wen Yuan Ge "Complete Library" edition.

Song Shi (History of the Song Dynasty) [Yuan] Tuo Tuo et al., Zhonghua Book Company, 1977 edition.

Song Shu (Book of the Song), [Liang] Shen Yue, Zhonghua Book Company, 1974 edition.

Sui Shu (Book of Sui) [Tang] Wei Zheng et al., Zhonghua Book Company, 1973 edition.

Tai Ping Huan Yu Ji (Tai Ping Imperial Geographic Gazetteer) [Northern Song] Le Shi (author), Wang Wenchu et al. (proofreading), Zhonghua Book Company, 2007 edition.

Tai Ping Tian Guo Wen Shu Hui Bian (Compilation of Documents of the Taiping Heavenly Kingdom), compiled by the Taiping Heavenly Kingdom History Museum, published by Zhonghua Book Company in 1979.

Tai Ping Yu Lan (Imperial Views of the Taiping Era), compiled by Li Fang and others from the Northern Song Dynasty, published by Zhonghua Book Company in 1960.

Tan Si Tong Ji (Collected Works of Tan Sitong), written by Tan Sitong from the Qing Dynasty, edited by He Zhi, published by Yuelu Book Society in 2012.

Tang Hui Yao (Comprehensive Records of the Tang Dynasty), written by Wang Pu from the Northern Song Dynasty, published by Zhonghua Book Company in 1955.

Tang Lv Shu Yi Jian Jie (Annotations and Explanations of the Tang Legal Code), written by Chang Sun Wuji and others from the Tang Dynasty, with annotations by Liu Junwen, published by Zhonghua Book Company in 1996.

Tang Shi Bie Cai (Selected Tang Poems), written by Shen Deqian from the Qing Dynasty, published by Zhonghua Book Company in 1964.

Tang Tu Xun Meng Tu Hui (Illustrated Guide for Teaching and Educating in Tang Dynasty), authored by Pingzhu Zhuanan from Japan, published in 1719.

Tao Yuan Wen Lu Wai Bian (Additional Compilation of Records from the Tao Garden), written by Wang Tao from the Qing Dynasty, published by Shanghai Bookstore Publishing House in 2002.

Tian Cong Jiu Nian Dang (Documents of the Ninth Year of the Tiancong Era), translated by Guan Jialu, Tong Yonggong, and Guan Zhaohong, published by Tianjin Ancient Books Publishing House in 1987.

Tong Dian (Comprehensive Mirror in Aid of Governance), written by Du You from the Tang Dynasty, edited by Wang Wenjin and others, published by Zhonghua Book Company in 1988.

Tong Jian Di Li Tong Shi (Comprehensive Explanation of Historical Geography), written by Wang Yinglin from the Southern Song Dynasty, based on the "Collected Works of Compendium in the Series" edition, published by Zhonghua Book Company in 1985.

Wang Xiang Qing Bi Ji (Notes by Wang Rangqing), written by Wang Kangnian from the Qing Dynasty, published by Zhonghua Book Company in 2007.

Wei Shu (Book of Wei), written by Wei Shou from the Northern Qi Dynasty, published by Zhonghua Book Company in 1974.

Wen Tian Xiang Quan Ji (Complete Works of Wen Tianxiang), written by Wen Tianxiang from the Southern Song Dynasty, edited by Xiong Fei, Qi Shenqi, and Huang Shunxiang, published by Jiangxi People's Publishing House in 1987.

Wen Xuan (Anthology of Literary Selections), compiled by Xiao Tong from the Liang Dynasty, with annotations by Li Shan from the Tang Dynasty, published by Shanghai Bookstore in 1988.

Wu Dai Hui Yao (Comprehensive Records of the Five Dynasties), written by Wang Pu from the Northern Song Dynasty, published by Shanghai Ancient Books Publishing House in 2006.

Wu Tai Bi Bu (Supplementary Notes from the Black Terrace), written by Wang Yun from the Yuan Dynasty, edited by Wang Xiaoxin, included in the "Three Types of Xiantai Tongji" edition, published by Zhejiang Ancient Books Publishing House in 2002.

Wu Ting Wen Bian (Compilation of Literary Works from the Wuting Studio), written by Chen Tingjing from the Qing Dynasty, included in the "Compilation of Poetry and Literature in the Qing Dynasty" compiled by the Editorial Committee, published by Shanghai Ancient Books Publishing House in 2010.

Wu Xu Bian Fa Dang An Shi Liao (Archives and Historical Materials of the Reform Movement of 1898), compiled by the Ming-Qing Archives Office of the National Archives Administration, published by Zhonghua Book Company in 1958.

Wu Xu Bian Fa Wen Xian Hui Bian (Compilation of Literature on the Reform Movement of 1898), compiled by Yang Jialuo, published by Dingwen Bookstore, Taipei, in 1973.

Wu Li Lun (Treatise on Physics), written by Yang Quan from the Western Jin Dynasty, based on the "Collected Works of Compendium in the Series" edition, published by Zhonghua Book Company in 1985.

Xi La La Ding Zuo Jia Yuan Dong Gu Wen Xian Ji Lu (Compilation of Ancient Documents from Greek and Latin Writers in the Far East), compiled by Godias, translated by Geng Sheng, published by Zhonghua Book Company in 1987.

Xi Luo Duo De Li Shi (Herodotus' Histories: History of the Greco-Persian Wars), written by Herodotus from Greece, translated by Wang Yizhu, published by Commercial Press in 2009.

Xi Meng Hui Yi Shi Mo Ji (Records of the Beginning and End of the Xi Meng Conference), edited by the Xi Meng Royal Reception Office, included in the "Research Library of China's Borderlands First Edition Northern Borderlands" Volume 2, published by Heilongjiang Education Publishing House in 2014.

Xi Yang Fan Guo Zhi (Records of Foreign Countries in the Western Regions), written by Gong Zhen from the Ming Dynasty, annotated by Xiang Da, published by Zhonghua Book Company in 1961.

Xi You Ji (Journey to the West), written by Wu Cheng'en from the Ming Dynasty, published by Zhejiang Ancient Books Publishing House in 2010.

Xian Qin Han Wei Nan Bei Chao Shi (Poetry from the Pre-Qin, Han, Wei, Jin, and Northern and Southern Dynasties), edited by Lu Qinli, published by Zhonghua Book Company in 1983.

Xiao Er Ya Yi Zheng (Explanations and Evidence of the Xiao erya), written by Hu Chenggong from the Qing Dynasty, with annotations by Shi Yunsun, published by Huangshan Book Society in 2011.

Xin Yi Zhai Wen Cun (Collected Works of Xinyi Zhai), written by Zou Hanxun, included in the "Continuation of the Complete Library in Four Sections" edition, published by Shanghai Ancient Books Publishing House.

Xin Bian Dong Ya San Guo Di Zhi (New Compilation of Geography of the Three Kingdoms in East Asia), written by Fuji Tinghua, popularizing accommodations, published in 1900.

Xin Bian Wang Zhong Ji (New Compilation of Wang Zhong's Works), written by Wang Zhong from the Qing Dynasty, edited by Tian Hanyun, published by Guangling Book Society in 2005.

Xin Tang Shu (New Book of Tang), [Northern Song Dynasty] by Ouyang Xiu and Song Qi, Zhonghua Book Company, 1975 edition.

Xin Wu Dai Shi (New History of the Five Dynasties) [Northern Song Dynasty] by Ouyang Xiu, annotated by Xu Wudang, Zhonghua Book Company, 1974 edition.

Xu Bo Wu Zhi (Continuation of the Compendium of Miscellaneous Knowledge) [Southern Song Dynasty] by Li Shi, collated by Li Zhiliang, Bashu Press, 1991 edition.

Xu Fu Ze Quan Ji Di Er Juan (Continuation of the Complete Works of Fuze) by Fuzé Yugi, translated by Iwanami Shoten, 1933 edition.

Xu Han Shu Zhi (Continuation of the Book of Han), [Western Jin Dynasty] by Sima Biao, supplemented by Liu Zhao, included in Fan Ye's "Hou Hanshu," Zhonghua Book Company, 1965 edition.

Xu Zizhi Tongjian (Continuation of the Zizhi Tongjian), by Bi Yuan, Shanghai Ancient Books Publishing House, 1987 edition.

Xu Zizhi Tongjian Changbian (Compilation of the Continuing Chronicle of Zizhi Tongjian), [Southern Song Dynasty] by Li Tao, collated by Shanghai Normal University and Shanghai Teachers College, Zhonghua Book Company, 1985–1986 edition.

Xuelin, [Southern Song Dynasty] by Wang Guangguo, Yuelu Press, 2010 edition.

Xunzi Ji Jie (Collected Expositions of Xunzi), [Warring States Period] by Xun Kuang, annotated by Wang Xianqian, collated by Shen Xiaohuan and Wang Xingxian, Zhonghua Book Company, 1988 edition.

Yantielun Jiaozhu (Annotations of the Discourses on Salt and Iron), [Western Han Dynasty] by Huan Kuan, annotated by Wang Liqi, Tianjin Ancient Books Publishing House, 1983 edition.

Yang Du Ji (Works of Yang Du), by Yang Du, edited by Liu Qingbo, Hunan People's Publishing House, 2008 edition.

Yelv Chucai Xiyoulu Zuben Jiaozhu (Yelu Chucai's Annotated Travelogue of the West), annotated by Yao Congwu, included in the compilation "Yao Congwu's Collected Works (Volume 7): Liao, Jin, and Yuan Dynasty Essays," Zhongzhong Book House, Taipei, 1982 edition.

Ye Ji, [Ming Dynasty] by Zhu Yunming, included in the "The Initial Compilation of Collected Works–First Compilation," Zhonghua Book Company, 1985 edition.

Yizhou Shu Jixun Jiaoshi (The Annotated and Collated Collection of the Lost Zhou Documents), [Qing Dynasty] by Zhu Youzeng, The Commercial Press, 1937 edition.

Yongzhuang Xiaopin (Resurging Vignettes), [Ming Dynasty] by Zhu Guozhen, Zhonghua Book Company, 1959 edition.

Yuandai Bailianjiao Ziliao Huibian (Compilation of Historical Materials on the White Lotus Sect during the Yuan Dynasty), compiled by Yang Ne, Zhonghua Book Company, 1989 edition.

Yuandai Nongmin Zhanzheng Shiliao Huibian (Compilation of Historical Documents on Peasant Uprisings during the Yuan Dynasty), compiled by Yang Ne and Chen Gaohua, Zhonghua Book Company, 1985 edition.

Yuanfeng Jiuyu Zhi (The Treatise on the Nine Regions during the Yuanfeng Era), [Northern Song Dynasty] by Wang Cun, collated by Wei Songsan and Wang Wenchu, Zhonghua Book Company, 1984 edition.

Yuanhe Junxian Tuzhi (Gazetteer of Yuanhe Prefectures and Counties), [Tang Dynasty] by Li Jifu, collated by He Cijun, Zhonghua Book Company, 1983 edition.

Yuanhe Xingzuan (The Genealogical Compilation of Surnames during the Yuanhe Era), [Tang Dynasty] compiled by Lin Bao, collated by Cen Zhongmian, organized by Yu Xianhao and Tao Min, Zhonghua Book Company, 1994 edition.

Yuanshi (The History of the Yuan Dynasty), [Ming Dynasty] by Song Lian, Zhonghua Book Company, 1976 edition.

Yuanshi Yiwen Zhengbu (The Supplement of Translated Texts and Supporting Evidence for the History of the Yuan Dynasty), by Hong Jun, revised by Na Ke, Wenqiutang Bookstore, 1902 edition.

Yuanwen Lei (The Literary Category of the Yuan Dynasty), [Yuan Dynasty] compiled by Su Tianjue, The Commercial Press, 1936 edition.

Yu Di Guangji (The Extensive Records of Geography), [Northern Song Dynasty] by Ouyang Min, annotated by Li Yongxian and Wang Xiaohong, Sichuan University Press, 2003 edition.

Yugong Zhuizhi (The Precise Offerings of Yu the Great), [Qing Dynasty] by Hu Wei, collated by Zou Yilin, Shanghai Ancient Books Publishing House, 2006 edition.

Yuhai (The Jade Sea), [Southern Song Dynasty] by Wang Yinglin, Jiangsu Ancient Books Publishing House, Shanghai Bookstore, 1987 edition.

Yunei Huntong Micai (The Secret Strategies for Unity in the Cosmos), by Sato Nobuyuki, included in the "Complete Works of Japanese National Treasures, Volume 19," Japanese National Treasures Publishing Council, 1917 edition.

Yupian Zhiyin (The Precise Pronunciations of the Jade Chapters), [Southern Dynasties Liang and Chen] by Gu Yewang, included in the "Completing the Collection of Books–First Compilation," Zhonghua Book Company, 1985 edition.

Yun Yan Guoyan Lu (A Chronicle of Passing Moments), [Southern Song Dynasty] by Zhou Mi, included in the "Completing the Collection of Books–First Compilation," Zhonghua Book Company, 1985 edition.

Zetang Ji (Collected Works of Ze Tang) [Southern Song Dynasty] Jia Xuanweng, Wen Yuan Ge "Siku Quanshu" edition.

Zhan Guo Ce (Strategies of the Warring States) [Western Han Dynasty] Liu Xiangjilu, Shanghai Ancient Books Publishing House, 1985 edition.

Zhanguo Jinian (Chronicles of the Warring States) [Qing Dynasty] Lin Chunpu, "Xu Xiu Siku Quanshu" edition, Shanghai Ancient Literature Publishing House.

Zhanran Jushi Wenji (Collected Works of Zhān Rán) [Jin Meng] Yelv Chucan, Shangwu Yinshuguan, 1937 edition.

Zhina Lishi (History of China) [Japan] Qianqiao Xiaoyi, Toyama Room, 1891 edition.

Zhifang Waiji Jiaoshi (Annotated Edition of Zhifang Biography) [Italy] Ai Rulüe, Xie Fang's annotation, Zhonghua Book Company, 1996 edition.

Zhinang Quanji (Complete Works of Wisdom) [Ming Dynasty] Feng Menglong, Luan Baoqun, and Lü Zongli's annotations, Zhonghua Book Company, 2007 edition.

Zhongdeng Xin Dili (Intermediate New Geography) [Japan] Ota Hoichiro, Hachio Shudian, 1894 edition.

Zhong Shuo (Remarks of Wenzhong Zi) [Sui Dynasty] Wang Tong, Zhejiang Ancient Books Publishing House, 1998 edition.

Zhongxi Jiaotong Shiliao Huibian (Compilation of Historical Materials on China's Western Communications) Zhang Xinglang's annotations, Zhu Jieqin's editing, Zhonghua Book Company, 2003 edition.

Zhouji Bianlue (Brief Compilation of Zhou Dynasty) [Qing Dynasty] Huang Shisan, Cheng Jihong's editing, Phoenix Publishing House, 2008 edition.

Zhou Li (Rites of Zhou) "Annotations and Commentaries on the Thirteen Classics" edition, Zhonghua Book Company, 1980 edition.

Zhou Shu (Book of Zhou) [Tang Dynasty] Linghu Defen, Zhonghua Book Company, 1971 edition.

Zhouyi Jijie (Collected Interpretations of the Book of Changes) [Qing Dynasty] Sun Xingyan, Chengdu Ancient Literature Bookstore, 1988 edition.

Zhouyi Zhengyi (Collected Expositions of the Book of Changes) "Shisanjing Zhu Shu" edition, Zhonghua Book Company, 1980 edition.

Zhuzi Wenji (Collected Works of Zhu Zi) [Southern Song Dynasty] Zhu Xi's compilation, Zhonghua Book Company, 1985 edition.

Zhuzi Yulei (Classified Sayings of Zhu Zi) [Southern Song Dynasty] Li Jingde's compilation, Zhonghua Book Company, 1986 edition.

Zhuzhai Ji (Collected Works of Zhusai) [Yuan Dynasty] Wang Mian, Xiling Seal Society Publishing House, 2011 edition.

Zhuangzi Jijie (Interpretations of Zhuangzi) [Warring States Period] Zhuang Zhou's compilation, [Qing] Wang Xianqian's annotations, Zhonghua Book Company, 1954 edition.

Zhuotang Wenhua (Conversations in Zhuotang) [Japan] Saito Masayoshi, included in Wang Shuizhao's compilation: "Historical Conversations of the Past Dynasties, Volume Ten," Fudan University Press, 2007 edition.

Zizhi Tongjian (Comprehensive Mirror for Aid in Government) [Northern Song Dynasty] Sima Guang's compilation, [Yuan Dynasty] Hu Sansheng's annotations, Zhonghua Book Company, 1956 edition.

Zizhi Tongjian Waiji (Records of Comprehensive Mirror for Aid in Government) [Northern Song Dynasty] Liu Shu, Shanghai Ancient Literature Publishing House, 1987 edition.

Chinese Modern Literature

Ataka, M. (1988). *Studies on the Ancient History of the Khitan*. (F. Xing, Trans.). Inner Mongolia: Inner Mongolia People's Publishing House.

Bai, J. (2004). *Biography of Zhang Shizhao*. Beijing: Writers Publishing House.

Beijing Foreign Language Institute Russian Department Linguistics Research Group. (1959). *Language in the Works of Classic Marxist Writers*. Beijing: The Commercial Press.

Bertho, H. (1933). *A Comparative Study of India and Guangdong*. (C. Feng, Trans.). Beijing: The Commercial Press.

Burnouf, B. (1982). *The Silk Road*. (S. Geng, Trans.). Urumqi: Xinjiang People's Publishing House.

Cen, J. (1986). *History of Totem Art*. Beijing: Xuelin Publishing House.

Cen, Z. (1982). *History of Sui and Tang Dynasties*. Beijing: Zhonghua Book Company.

Central Compilation and Translation Bureau of the CPC Central Committee. (1955). *Constitution of the People's Republic of China*. Beijing: Zhonghua Book Company.

Central Literature Research Office of the CPC Central Committee. (1996). *Collected Poems of Mao Zedong*. Beijing: Central Literature Publishing House.

Chang, J. (1999). *Selected Works of Yu Dafu Diaries*. Qinghai: Qinghai People's Publishing House.

Chen, D. (1936). *Ancient Names of Countries*. Beijing: The Commercial Press.

Chen, D. (2000). *Old Stories of National History*. Beijing: Zhonghua Book Company.

Chen, S. (1986). *Draft of Khitan Political History*. Beijing: People's Publishing House.

Chen, Y. (1977). *Selected Poems of Chen Yi*. Beijing: People's Literature Publishing House.

Chen, Y. (1982). *Essay on the Political History of the Tang Dynasty*. Shanghai: Shanghai Ancient Books Publishing House.

Chen, Z. (1986). *Talks on the Origins of Words*. Guangxi: Guangxi People's Publishing House.

Chen, Z. (2002). *Brief History of Vietnam*. Hanoi: Xiangang Publishing House.

Deng, S. (1983). *Exploration of Historical Sites in Bashu*. Chengdu: Sichuan People's Publishing House.

Ding, F. (1984). *Great Dictionary of Buddhism*. Beijing: Cultural Relics Publishing House.

Engels. (1972). Dialectics of Nature. In *Selected Works of Marx, Engels, Lenin, and Stalin* (Vol. 3). Beijing: People's Publishing House.

Fan, H., & Liu, Z. (2008). *Studies on Vietnamese Language and Culture*. Beijing: Ethnic Publishing House.

Fan, W. (1955). *Concise History of China* (Revised Edition). Beijing: People's Publishing House.

Fei, Z., & Lai, X. (1992). *China: Tradition and Change*. (C. Chen et al., Trans.). Nanjing: Jiangsu People's Publishing House.

Feng, C. (1980). *Place Names in Western Regions*. Beijing: Zhonghua Book Company.

Fu, P. (2012). *The Book of Changes and Life*. Beijing: Dongfang Publishing House.

Gao, M. (1980). *Anthology of Ancient Scripts*. Beijing: Zhonghua Book Company.

Gao, S., & Shao, J. (1991). *Emperors of Jinling in Ten Dynasties*. Beijing: People's University Press.

Gao, W., & Cai, Z. (1979). *Genealogy of the Mongols*. Beijing: Chinese Academy of Social Sciences Press.

Ge, J. (1989). *Under Heaven–Unification, Division, and Chinese Politics*. Changchun: Jilin Education Press.

Gu, J. (1996). *A Brief History of Academic Studies in the Han Dynasty*. Shanghai: Oriental Publishing House.

Gu, J. (1996). Politics and History in the Theory of the Five Virtues. In *Collected Essays on Ancient History* by Gu Jiegang (Vol. 3). Beijing: Zhonghua Book Company.

Gu, J., & Shi, N. (1938). *A History of Territorial Changes in China*. Beijing: The Commercial Press.

Guo, M. (1983). Compilation of Divinatory Inscriptions. In *Complete Works of Guo Moruo: Archaeology* (Vol. 2). Beijing: Science Press.

Guo, M. (1984). Age of Slavery. In *Complete Works of Guo Moruo: History* (Vol. 3). Beijing: People's Publishing House.

Hakunakokichi. (1934). *Research on the Donghu Ethnic Group*. (Z. Fang, Trans.). Shanghai: The Commercial Press.

Han, Z. (1981). *Historical and Geographical Studies of the South China Sea Islands*. Beijing: Zhonghua Book Company.

He, G. (1992). *History of the Xia Dynasty*. Jiangxi: Jiangxi Education Press.

He, X. (1986). *The Origins of the Gods—Ancient Chinese Mythology and History*. Beijing: Sanlian Bookstore.

Hong, C. (1982). *Selected Readings in Chinese Linguistics*. Nanjing: Jiangsu People's Publishing House.

Hu, A. (1991). *Introduction to Onomastics*. Nanjing: Unpublished Manuscript of Nanjing University.

Hu, A. (1996). *A Brief Overview of Military Geography in Chinese History*. Hohai University Press.

Hu, A. (2000). *Research on the Territory and Political Divisions of the Six Dynasties*. Xi'an: Xi'an Map Publishing House.

Hu, A. (2013). *Properly Naming China: Hu Axiang on National Names*. Beijing: Zhonghua Book Company.

Hu, A. (2013). *Titles and Medieval Chinese Geography*. Beijing: Sanlian Bookstore.

Hu, A. (2014). *Getting Engrossed in History: The Inexhaustible Tales of Chinese History*. Beijing: People's Publishing House.

Hu, A., & Peng, A. (2004). *The Great Geographic Discoveries of China*. Jinan: Shandong Pictorial Publishing House.

Hu, A., & Shen, Z. (2015). *Stories of Chinese Titles and Appellations*. Jinan: Shandong Pictorial Publishing House.

Hu, G. (1995). *Territory and Political Divisions in Chinese History*. Shenyang: Liaoning Ancient Books Publishing House.

Hu, S. (1984). *A Lengthy Compilation of the Chronological Biography of Hu Shi*. Lianjing Publishing Company, Taipei.

Hua, L. (1999). *Origins and Development of Chinese Toponymy*. Changsha: Hunan People's Publishing House.

Inoue, K. (1914). *Complete History of the Qing Dynasty*. Beijing: Zhonghua Book Company.

Institute of Archaeology, Chinese Academy of Sciences. (1965). *Compilation of Oracle Bone Inscriptions*. Beijing: Zhonghua Book Company.

Jia, J. (1990). *Summary of Ethnic History and Culture*. Changchun: Jilin Education Press.

Jian, Y. (1958). *A Comprehensive Study on the Institutions of the Taiping Heavenly Kingdom*. Jian Shi Meng Jin Bookstore, Hong Kong.

Jiang, Y. (1990). *History of Chinese Nationalities*. Beijing: Ethnic Publishing House.

Jin, Q. (1984). *Dictionary of Jurchen Texts*. Beijing: Cultural Relics Publishing House.

Jin, Y. (1941). *General History of North east China*. Sendai: Tohoku University.

Lei, H. (1998). *Modern Vietnamese Chinese Dictionary*. Beijing: Foreign Language Teaching and Research Press.

Li, C. (2001). *Examination of Chinese Reign Titles throughout History*. Beijing: Zhonghua Book Company.

Li, X., & Xue, H. (1991). *Complete History of the Qing Dynasty*. Shenyang: Liaoning People's Publishing House.

Li, Z. (1954). *Ancient Chinese Social History* (Vol. 1). Taipei: Chinese Culture Publishing Committee.

Lian, H. (2005). *Notes from an Elegant Hall*. Nanning: Guangxi People's Publishing House.

Lin, H. (1936). *History of Chinese Nationalities*. Beijing: The Commercial Press.

Lin, J. (1981). *Draft of Qin History*. Shanghai: Shanghai People's Publishing House.

Liu, S., Guo, J., & Hao, L. (2005). *Weather of the Great Tang: The China Story from 581 to 763*. Shanghai: Shanghai Literature and Art Publishing House.

Liu, Y. (1988). *History of Chinese Culture*. Beijing: China Encyclopedia Publishing House.

Liu, Y. (2016). *Talking about the Silk Road*. Hefei: Anhui People's Publishing House.

Lu, H. (2016). *Names and Titles throughout the History of Nanjing*. Nanjing: Nanjing Press.

Lu, X. (2014). *Morning Flowers, Evening Tunes*. Beijing: People's Literature Publishing House.

Luo, Z. (1927). *An Annotated Study of Updated Yin and Xia Clan Inscriptions*. Dongfang Academy.

Lv, S. (1941). *PreQin History*. Beijing: Kaiming Bookstore.

Lv, S. (1982). *Reading Notes on History by Lv Simian*. Shanghai: Shanghai Ancient Books Publishing House.

Lv, S. (1987). *History of Chinese Nationalities*. Beijing: China Encyclopedia Publishing House.

Mahmud, K., & Zhong, Y. (Trans.). (2002). *Comprehensive Dictionary of the Turkic Language*. Beijing: Ethnic Publishing House.

Meng, G. (Ed.). (2009). *Integrated Historical Geography, Vol. of History*. Beijing: Higher Education Press.

Meng, S. (1981). *Lecture Notes on the Ming and Qing Dynasties* (Vol. 2). Beijing: Zhonghua Book Company.

Nishino, Y. (1980). *The History of Sino Japanese Cultural Exchange*. Beijing: Commercial Press.

Peng, B. (1988). *An InDepth Study of Commercial History*. Chongqing: Chongqing Press.

Perfet, A. (1995). *Stagnant Empire: The Collision of Two Worlds*. (G. Wang et al., Trans.). Beijing: Sanlian Bookstore.

Peter, B. (2001). *Civilization: The Transformation of Tang and Song Thoughts*. (N. Liu, Trans.). Nanjing: Jiangsu People's Publishing House.

Qi, Z. (2009). *2000 Essential Historical Knowledge*. Nanjing: Jiangsu People's Publishing House.

Qian, M. (1935). Chronological Biography of Liu Xiang and His Son. In *Selected Writings of Ancient History by Gu Jiegang* (Vol. 5). Pushe.

Qian, M. (1984). *Study of Place Names in the Records of the Grand Historian*. Taipei: Sanmin Book Company.

Qian, Z. (1979). *Compilation of Guan Zhuo* (Vol. 4). Beijing: Zhonghua Book Company.

Rong, G. (1959). *Compilation of Inscriptions on Gold*. Beijing: Science Press.

Senate Compilation. (1912). *Provisional Constitution of the Republic of China*. Beijing: Senate.

Shao, X., & Zhou, D. (Eds.). (1983). *Dictionary of Foreign Toponymic Etymology*. Shanghai: Shanghai Dictionary Publishing House.

Shen, F. (1985). *History of Cultural Exchange between China and the West*. Shanghai: Shanghai People's Publishing House.

Shen, Q. (1983). *Chronology of Major Events in Chinese History* (Ancient History Volume). Shanghai: Shanghai Dictionary Publishing House.

Shi, A. (2014). *The Invention of Dragons in China: Dragon Politics and Chinese Image from the 16th to 20th Century*. Beijing: Sanlian Bookstore.

Shu, F. (1984). *Draft of the History of Liao*. Wuhan: Hubei People's Publishing House.

Shu, Y. (1991). *Chronicles of the Founding of the Nation*. Beijing: China Overseas Chinese Publishing House.

Sun, D., & Li, R. (1997). *History of Chinese Toponymy*. Beijing: China Environmental Science Press.

Sun, M. (1987). *Draft of Xia and Shang History*. Beijing: Cultural Relics Publishing House.

Sun, W. (2011). Strategy for Establishing a Nation. In *Complete Works of Sun Yatsen* (Vol. 6). Beijing: Zhonghua Book Company.

Sun, Y. (1981). *Selected Works of Sun Yatsen*. Beijing: People's Publishing House.

Tan, Q. (Ed.). (1982). *Historical Atlas of China* (Vol. 1). Beijing: Map Publishing Company.

Tang, L. (1981). *Introduction to Ancient Sinology* (Revised Edition), (Vol. 1). Jinan: Qilu Press.

Tang, S. (1992). *Mysterious Culture of China*. Nanjing: Hohai University Press.

Tanigawa, M. (2004). *Formation History of the Sui and Tang Empires*. Shanghai: Shanghai Ancient Books Publishing House.

Tao, M. (1985). *Outline of the Five Dynasties*. Beijing: People's Publishing House.

Tian, C., & An, Z. (Eds.). (1993). *History of the Qin and Han Dynasties*. Beijing: People's Publishing House.

Tojitani, M. (1939). *Reality of Mainland China*. Tokyo: Tomiyama House.

Tong, E. (1979). *Ancient Bashu*. Chengdu: Sichuan People's Publishing House.

Tong, S. (1946). *Brief History of China's Territory Evolution*. Beijing: Kaiming Bookstore.

Tsujihara, Y. (2004). *Viewing History through Place Names*. Taipei: World Tide Limited.

Tsujino, H. (1981). *Discussion on the History of Chinese Students Studying Abroad*. First House.

Tsujino, H. (1983). *A History of Chinese People Studying in Japan*. Beijing: Sanlian Bookstore.

Wan, S. (Ed.). (1987). *Lectures on Wei, Jin, Southern and Northern Dynasties by Chen Yinke*. Huangshan: Huangshan Book Company.

Wang, X. (1979). *Candles as Seen in Ancient Characters*. Jinan: Qilu Press.

Wang, Y. (1984). *Exploration of Oracle Bone Inscriptions in Western Zhou*. Beijing: China Social Sciences Press.

Wang, Z. (1980). *Geographical Records of the Northern Zhou Dynasty*. Beijing: Zhonghua Book Company.

Wang, Z. (1996). *History and Culture of the Manchu*. Beijing: Central University for Nationalities Press.

Wang, Z. (1997). *Cultural Excavation of Records of the Grand Historian*. Wuhan: Hubei People's Publishing House.

Wei, L. (1986). *Draft of the History of the KaraKhitan Khanate*. Urumqi: Xinjiang People's Publishing House.

Wen, Y. (1956). *Mythology and Poetry*. Beijing: Zhonghua Book Company.

Wen, Y. (1982). New Interpretations of the Lament for Departure in Classical Chinese Literature. In *Complete Works of Wen Yiduo* (Vol. 2). Beijing: Sanlian Bookstore.

Wu, T. (1983). *Draft of the History of the Western Xia Dynasty*. Chengdu: Sichuan People's Publishing House.

Xia, S. (2000). *Report on the Xia-Shang-Zhou Chronology Project, 19962000*. Beijing: World Book Publishing Company (Beijing).

Xia, Y. (1946). *Fascist Bacteria*. Beijing: Kaiming Bookstore.

Xia, Z. (1979). *Cihai*. Shanghai: Shanghai Lexicographical Publishing House.

Xia, Z. (Ed.). (1999). *Cihai* (Color Edition). Shanghai: Shanghai Lexicographical Publishing House.

Xia, Z. (2014). *Ancient Chinese History*. Shanghai: Shanghai People's Publishing House.

Xiang, D. (1957). *Chang'an in the Tang Dynasty and Western Region Civilization*. Beijing: Sanlian Bookstore.

Xie, B. (2004). *Zheng Chenggong Should be Called Zhu Chenggong*. Tainan: Tainan City Government Press.

Xin, J. (1991). *China's View of the World*. Beijing: Xuelin Publishing House.

Xinhua Bookstore Editorial Department. (1949). *Carry the Revolution through to the End*: New Year's Speech 1949. Xinhua Bookstore.

Xinhua Bookstore Editorial Department. (1949). *Important Documents of the First National Congress of the Chinese People's Political Consultative Conference*. Xinhua Bookstore.

Yang, J., Shi, G., Yu, T. (Eds.). (1984). *The Rising of the Five Star Red Flag: The Birth Chronicles and Selected Materials of the Chinese People's Political Consultative Conference*. Beijing: Historical and Literary Sources Press.

Yang, R. (2010). *The Sick Man, Yellow Peril, and Sleeping Lion: The Imagination of the Chinese Image in the "Western" Perspective and the Discourse of the Modern Chinese Nationality*. Taipei: National Chengchi University Press.

Yang, S. (1954). *JI Wei Ju Elementary School Description Forest*. Chinese Academy of Sciences.

Yang, Y. (2009). *Full Function Dictionary of Modern Chinese for Students* (Illustrated Edition). Jiangxi Education Press.

Yang, Z., Li, G., Wang, N., Ma, B. (1989). *Nanjing*. Beijing: China Architecture Press.

Ye, Y. (1934). *Precompilation and Interpretation of Oracle Inscriptions at the Yin Ruins*. Shanghai: Da Dong Bookstore.

Yu, S. (1979). *Forest of Oracle Bone Inscriptions*. Beijing: Zhonghua Book Company.

Yuan, K. (1985). *Dictionary of Chinese Myths and Legends*. Shanghai: Shanghai Lexicographical Publishing House.

Yuer, K., Coudie, R. (Revised), Zhang, X. (Trans.). (2008). *Records of Eastern Lands: Records of Ancient China from the Perspective of the West*. Beijing: Zhonghua Book Company.

Zeng, Z., & Jiang, Z. (1957). *Report on the Excavation of the Two Mausoleums of the Southern Tang Dynasty*. Beijing: Cultural Relics Publishing House.

Zhang, M. (Ed.). (2007/2012). *Modern Japanese People's Travelogues in China* (Series). Beijing: Zhonghua Book Company.

Zhang, S. (2004). *Collection of Works by Qing Dynasty Scholars (Additional Edition)*. Wuhan: Central China Normal University Press.

Zheng, B., & Gao, G. (Eds.). (2008). *Centennial Illustrations of Dunhuang Mogao Grottoes*. Lanzhou: Gansu People's Publishing House.

Zheng, J. (1988). *Preliminary Exploration of Xia History*. Zhengzhou: Zhongzhou Ancient Books Publishing House.

Zheng, W. (1999). *Analysis and Interpretation of Lunheng*. Chengdu: Bashu Press.

Zhou, F. (1951). *Zero Explanation of Seal Script*. Historical Language Research Institute Publication, No. 34.

Zhou, Z., & You, R. (1986). *Dialects and Chinese Culture*. Shanghai: Shanghai People's Publishing House.

Zhou, Z. (1987). *Geographic Divisions of the Western Han Dynasty*. Beijing: People's Publishing House.

Index

Note: Page numbers in *italic* refers to Figures.

agriculture: "Qin" (秦) as 'forage grass/
dense-growing grain,' 46–49, *48–49,*
51; Qi as ancestor of Zhou people (Zhou
Houji) and, 32, 34–41, *37–38*
ancestral lineage, 117, 142, 145–146, 157,
169; "Shang" origins and meanings and,
23; agriculture and Qi (启) as ancestor
of Zhou people, 32, 36–40, *37–38,* 41;
Emperors' Lineage, 129, 170, 224; Liu
Bei and lineage of Han Dynasty, 94–96;
Qi as ancestor of Zhou people (Zhou
Houji), 32, 36–37, *37,* 38, *38,* 41; Qi (契)
as son of Emperor Ku, 23, 36, 170–171;
Qin Dynasty and Boyi ancestry, 47,
51–52; Tang and Tao Tang clan and, 120,
126, 149, 151; Tao Tang clan and, 130

barbarians, 40, 44, 79, 103, 106, 205;
Chinese as 'Xia' to, 6; Confucius
on, 211; Sun Yat-sen's expulsion of,
223–225
beautiful name mandate, 80, 82, 84–85
beginning, "Yuan" (元) as, 184
Benji (biographic sketches of emperors),
19–20, 23
big, "Yuan" (元) as, 184–185
Book of Changes, 160, 183–185
Book of Documents, 20, 27, 129, 172
Book of Han (Ban Gu), 6, 115, 127,
133; China as "Xia" in, 6, 14; on Han
Dynasty, 58, 63, 66–67, 91, 96; on Jin
Dynasty, 103; on Qin Dynasty, 51–52,
59; on Song Dynasty, 171, 185; on Sui
Dynasty, 115; on Tang Dynasty, 127,
129, 133; on Xin Dynasty, 76–78, 83–84
Book of Jin, 107, 126

Book of Shu, 94, 96, 98
Book of Songs, 34–35, 37, 40, 128, 172;
"Yin"/"Shang," 20–21, 23; on horses in
Qin culture, 52; on Qi as Emperor Ku's
son, 170
Book of Sui, 114–116
Book of Wei, 96, 116, 127
Book of Wu, 96
Book of Zhou, 59, 114–116, 127, 172
Bu Zhu (son of Qi (弃)), 32–33, 38
Buddhism, 116; "King of Light Jr." ("Xiao
Mingwang"), 192–199; Empress Wu
Zhao and, 147–149, *150;* Zhu Yuanzhang
as "King of Light," 195, 199–200

Cao Cao, 92; establishment of by Three
Kingdoms and, 91–92; establishment
of Wei Dynasty and, 91–92, 95, 102;
prophecy and naming of Wei and, 92–93;
Shu *vs.* Han Dynasty titles, 94–95
Cao Pi: establishment of Wei Dynasty and,
91–92, 94–95, 102; Shu *vs.* Han
Dynasty titles, 94–95, 97; Wu Dynasty
and, 98
cattail, "Qin" (秦) as, 48
Central Plains Dynasties, 2–3, 226;
dynastic titles in, 166; reunification of,
165
Chen Sheng Uprising, 59–60
Chen Shou, 96, 98. *See also Records of the
Three Kingdoms* (Chen Shou)
Chen Yinke, 126, *126,* 148
China: as 'Han,' 71; as "Jin," 99; as "Xia,"
6, 14; as "Zhong Guo," 6; "Zhou" as
original name of, 44; alternate names
for, 114

China, People's Republic of: *vs.* "Republic of China," 221, 227; founding of, 216; Zhonghua as term for, 221, 224

China, Republic of: "Interpretation of the Republic of China" (Zhang Binglin) and, 225–227; *vs.* "People's Republic of China," 221, 227; "Republic of China" regime of Sun Yat-sen, 222–223; establishment of, 2, 216, 221; name origin, 221–222, 225–227; numerous competing regimes of (1912-1949), 222; Zhonghua as term for, 221, 224

Chinese characters. plasticity of, 118

Chinese Revolutionary Party (Tongmenghui), 224–225

"Chong De" (Venerating Virtue, reign title), 208, 210–211

"Chuanguo Yuxi" (Imperial Jade Seal), 93, 95, 210

cicada (Xia "夏"), 26; theory of Xia as, 2, 5–12, *10, 12,* 15–16

civil service system, Song Dynasty and, 166

Confucius and Confucianism, 20, 149, 151; "Chong De" reign title and, 208; "Yin" and, 28; on barbarians, 211; Confucian classics, 46; Dong Zhongshu and, 80–81, 85, 133; Five Virtues theory, 81–82, 172; on grandeur of Emperor Yao, 130; on women in governance, 148; in Xin Dynasty, 80–81, 83, 85, 133

connotations in national titles, 23, 27, 119, 156, 184, 215; of "Sui," 116; of "Xia," 12, 14–16, 28

Continuation of the Book of Han (Liu Zhao), 91

corruption, Yuan Dynasty and, 189–190

coups, non-violent of Xin Dynasty, 77

criticism of Dynastic predecessors, 120

Da Ming" ("Great Brightness"), Ming Dynasty as, 189, 195–196, 199–200, 211

Da Wenkou culture, 26

"Da Yuan" (Great Yuan), 182

"da" (大, great/greatness), 6, 15, 68, 185

"Divine Emperor of the Holy Mother" (Empress Wu Zhao), 141, 146–148

Dong Zhongshu, 80–81, 85, 133

Earth Virtue of Tang, 132–133

Eastern (Later) Han Dynasty, 68, 85, 93, 95, 173; establishment of, 58. *See also* Han Dynasty

Eastern Jin Dynasty (Sixteen Kingdoms), 154, 165, 193; historical overview, 110–112; national titles of, 154. *See also* Jin Dynasty; Sima family, Jin Dynasty and

Eastern Zhou, 32, 44, 54

Emperor Bing, 166. *See also* Song Dynasty

Emperor Gaozu (Liu Bang), 59, 64, 66, 87, 95, 125, 134–135, *136,* 157, 160, 162. *See also* Han Dynasty

Emperor Guangwu (Liu Xiu), 77, 87, 95, 157. *See also* Han Dynasty

Emperor Huang Taiji, 208; "Chong De" (Venerating Virtue) reign title, 208, 210–211; death of, 215. *See also* Qing Dynasty

Emperor Ku, 25, 129; consorts of, 36, 175; Qi as son of, 23, 36, 170–171

Emperor of Sui, 113–115

Emperor Qi, 8–9, 12

Emperor Shen Yao (Tang Dynasty, Li Yuan), 133–136, *135–136,* 141

Emperor Shi (Later Jin, Shi Jingtang), 156

Emperor Shizong of Zhou, 167

Emperor Shizu (Li Bing), 125, 185

Emperor Shun of Yuan, 23, 50–52, 124, 189–191, 194. *See also* Yuan Dynasty

Emperor Toghon Temür, 178

Emperor Wen of Sui (Sima Zhao), 92, 102–103, 114, 116–117, 147, 211

Emperor Wu of Han, 46, 80

Emperor Wu of Jin, 110

Emperor Wu of Song, 160

Emperor Xian of Han (Liu Xie), 91–94, 102. *See also* Han Dynasty

Emperor Xianzong (Liu Zhang), 157

Emperor Xuanzong of Tang, 133, 141

Emperor Yang of Sui, 124, 128, 131, 134

Emperor Yao, 128, 133; "Yao" 尧 and, 129; appointment of Li Yuan as Ambassador of Pacification by, 131–132; legends of, 129–134, *131. See also* Tang Dynasty

Emperor Zhao Kuangyin: as founder of Song Dynasty, 20, 154

Emperor Zhao of Han, *97,* 133. *See also* Lui Bei

Emperor Zhu Qizhen, 209

Empress Wu Zhao, 141, 150; as "Divine Emperor of the Holy Mother," 141, 146–148; Buddhism and, 147–149, *150*

Fei Zi, horse raising of Qin Dynasty and, 45, 49–53

"feng" (凤, Phoenix), 24–25
Five Dynasties, 3, 168; beginning of,
  154; end of, 165; *History of the Five
  Dynasties,* 154, 157, 161–162, 167, 172;
  succession of, 155–157
Five Elements theory, 211–213
Five Virtues theory, 81–82, 172

Genghis Khan, 184, 214; Great Mongol
  Empire and, 178–181, *179. See also*
  Monghol Khanate; Yuan Dynasty
geographic names, 64–66, 115, 127; China
  as "Xia" and, 6, 13–14; Han Dynasty
  and, 66–71, *69–70*; Jin Dynasty and, 103,
  106, 156; Qin Dynasty and, 45, 47; Song
  Dynasty and, 168–169; Sui Dynasty
  and, 115; Tang Dynasty and, 127–128,
  130, 133; Xia Dynasty and, 13–14; Xin
  Dynasty and, 77–78
grain, "Qin" (秦) as, 46–49, *48–49,* 51
"Great Court", 183, 185. *See also* Monghol
  Khanate
Great Mongol Empire (Yeke Mobgghol
  Ulus), 178–181, *179,* 183, 185; evolution
  of title of, 182
Great Mongol State, 182–183. *See also*
  Monghol Khanate
great, "Yuan" (元) as, 184–185
great/greatness (大, "da"), 6, 15, 68, 185
greatness, Xia "夏" as, 14–15
Gugong Danfu, 35–36, 38, 40–41
Guo Wei, 157, 162, 165

Han Chinese, 2, 71; "Humiliation of
  Jingkang" and, 208–209; "Interpretation
  of the Republic of China" (Zhang
  Binglin) and, 225–227; Han assimilation
  during Qing Dynasty, 208–211, 213–215;
  Han-based naming conventions of
  Monghol Khanate, 185; Song Dynasty
  and, 193; under Yuan Dynasty, 192
Han Dynasty, 3, *97,* 133, 154, 156, 226;
  'Tianhan' (Heavenly Han) as Milky Way
  and, 63–64, 68, *70,* 70–71; 'Tianhan'
  and origin of title of, 59, 63–64, *65*;
  "Hanzhong" and Han river and, 66–71,
  69–70; after fall of Wang Dang/Xin
  Dynasty, 85–86; conclusions on, 70–71;
  Eastern (Later) Han Dynasty, 58, 68,
  85, 87, 93, 173; fall of and Cao family
  replacement, 91–95, 99, 102; historical
  overview, 58–64; inappropriateness of Shu
  Dynasty name for, 96–98, 133; Liu Bang

(King of Han) and, 58–64, 95, 157; Liu
  Bei and lineage and restoration of, 94–99;
  as name for China, 71; profound historical
  influence of, 71; restoration of post-Xin
  under Liu Xiu, 85–87, 91; small seal script
  of, 68, 70. *See also Book of Han* (Ban Gu);
  Western (Former) Han Dynasty
Han Lin'er , as "King of Light Jr."
  ("Xiao Mingwang"), 192–199
Han river, 66–68, *69–70,* 95; "Han Jing Fu"
  (poem, Cai Yong) on, 68–69
Han Shantong, 190–191, 194–195, 199
"Hanzhong": Hanzhong" and Han river
  and, 66–71, *69–70*; establishment of
  Hanzhong Prefecture, 66; origin of name,
  66–68
History of the Five Dynasties, 154, 157,
  161–162, 167, 172
History of the Northern Dynasties,
  114–116, 126
horse raising/breeding, Qin Dynasty and,
  45, 49–53
Hu Sanxing, 20

imperial sovereignty, 1
"Interpretation of the Republic of China"
  (Zhang Binglin), 225–227

Ji Fa, 32, 40–41
Ji Wang Temple, *38*
Jin Dynasty, 3, 96, 99, 154, 156, 165;
  "Humiliation of Jingkang" (invasion
  of Song Dynasty), 209; "Sanjin" (the
  Three Jins) and, 106; conflict with Ming
  Dynasty, 207–210; establishment of, 206;
  establishment of Jurchen Jin Dynasty,
  206–207; fall of, 110; name origin of,
  102–103, 106, 108, 156, 208; Nanyang
  and, 105–106; in Pre-Qin Period,
  103–106, *105*; as prophecy fulfillment,
  108; Sima family and, 102–108, 110; Wei-
  Jin transition and, 102, 106–107. *See also*
  Eastern Jin Dynasty (Sixteen Kingdoms)
Jurchen, 213–214; "Da Qing" national
  title and, 214–215; to "Manchu," 208;
  establishment of Jurchen Jin Dynasty,
  206–207

King Nan of Zhou, 32, 44–45
"King of Light Jr." ("Xiao Mingwang"),
  192–199
Kublai Khan: national title of Yuan Dynasty
  and, 183–185. *See also* Monghol Khanate

Sun Yat-sen, 215, 221–222; "Republic of China" name origin and, 222, 224–227; "Republic of China" regime of, 222–224; residence of, *224*
sustenance, cultivating, 34–35

Taiwan, 221
Tang Dynasty, 3, 21, 26, 154–156, 168; "Tang" as ancient country name, 127–128; "Tang" as expansiveness and moral grandeur of Emperor Yao, 130–131; "Tang" territory and, 130; Empress Wu Zhao as "Divine Emperor of the Holy Mother," 141, 146–148; establishment of, 119, 124, 128; fabricated ancestral/geographical origin of Li family and, 125–127; legend of Emperor Yao of Taotang Clan and, 129–134, *131*; Li Hu and posthumous title of Duke of Tang and, 124–125, 127–128, 130; Li Yuan and Earth Virtue of Tang/color yellow and, 132–133; Li Yuan appointment as Ambassador of Pacification by Yao and, 131–132; Li Yuan as Emperor Shen Yao, 133–136, *135–136*, 141; Li Yuan founding of, 125, 128, 131–132, 141, 154; name origin and influence, 124–125, 127, 130, 133, 155; Sui-Tang transition, 123–124, 131–132; use of "Sui" 随 by, 120; women in governance and Buddhist symbolism and, 148–149; Wu Zhao's change to Zhou/Li Zhi reinstatement to Tang, 141–146, *144*, 148, 150–151
Taoism, 116. *See also Book of Changes*
Taotang Clan, 129–134, *131. See also* Tang Dynasty
Ten Kingdoms, 3, 154, 168; division of, 157–162
Three Kingdoms, 3, 23, 96; end of, 99; establishment of, 91–92; *Records of the Three Kingdoms* (Chen Shou), 94, 96–98. *See also* Shu Dynasty (Three Kingdoms); Wei Dynasty (Three Kingdoms); Wu Dynasty (Three Kingdoms)
"Three Principles of the People", 223, 225
"Tianhan" (Heavenly Han): "Hanzhong" and Han river and, *70*, 70–71; as Milky Way, 63–64, 68, *70*, 70–71; origin of as title of Han Dynasty, 59, 63–64, *65*
totem worship, 8–10, 12, 23–26, 37

vassal states, "Qin" as, 45, 49–53

Wang Mang: "New" Emperor and Xin Dynasty name origin, 84–85; "new" policies of, 82–83, 86; "new" titles and naming conventions of, 83–84; "receiving of Mandate anew" political context and, 80–82, 85–86; fall of, 85–86; political ascent of and Xin Dynasty name origin, 76–80, 85; *vs.* Zhou Gong, 79. *See also* Xin Dynasty
warlords, 110, 123, 134, 155, 222; anti-Yuan campaign of, 192–193, 198; during Tang Dynasty, 168
Wei Dynasty (Three Kingdoms), 97–98; Cao family establishment of, 91–95, 102; end of, 99; establishment of Three Kingdoms and, 91–92; naming of, 92–93; Wei-Jin transition and, 102, 106–107
West, "Xia" as representing, 13–14
Western (Former) Han Dynasty, 87, 95; "receiving of Mandate anew" political context and, 80–82; Confucianism in, 80–82; Xin Dynasty in history of, 76–77, 87. *See also* Han Dynasty
White Lotus Sect: prophecy of, 190, 199; Pure Land Buddhist Tradition and, 193–194, 199; Red Turban Rebellion and, 193
women in governance, Confucius/Buddhism on, 148–149
Wu Dynasty (Three Kingdoms), 97–98; Cao Pi's bestowing of Kingship on Sun Quan and, 98–99; end of, 99; establishment of Three Kingdoms and, 91–92
Wu Shiyue (father of Wu Zhao), 141–142, 144–146
Wu Zhao, 141–146, *144*, 148, 150–151
Wuchang Uprising, 226

Xia Dynasty, 4, 15–16, 36; "Xia (夏)" as cicada, 2, 5–12, *10, 12*, 15–16, 26; "Xia (夏)" as elegance/greatness, 14–15; "Xia (夏)" as representing West directional, 13–14; end of, 19; estimated framework for, 4–5; geographical location of, 13–14; theories on origin/meaning of, 5
Xiang Yu, 70–71; bestowing of King of Han on Liu Bang, 58–64, 66, 71; defeat of, 58; geographic names of kingdoms established by, 64–66
Xin Dynasty: "new" policies/titles/naming conventions and, 82–84, 86; "Xin" (新, new) name origin, 77–80, 82, 84–86; fall of, 85–86; as first example of non-violent

coup, 77; historical overview, 76–80,
  85–87; semantic *vs.* geographic origin of
  name, 77–78. *See also* Wang Mang
Xu Shen, 46–47. *See also Shuowen Jiezi*
  (Xu Shen)

Yang Jian, 113; replacement of "Sui" 隋
  with "Sui" 隋 by, 114–120
Yellow Emperor, 1, 9, 129, 170, 224; Earth
  Element and, 82
Yellow River, 190
Yellow Turban Rebellion, 91
Yin Dynasty, 65; "Shang" (商) and "Yin"
  (殷) and, 19–23, 26–28, *28*
Yuan Dynasty, 3, 20; "Da Yuan" (Great
  Yuan) as official title of, 178, 185;
  "Yuan" (元) as "the head/leader" and
  "beginning," 184; "Yuan" (元) as "great/
  big," 184–185; anti-Yuan Movement
  and, 191–195, 198; corruption and
  inequalities in, 189–191; end of, 178,
  186, 189, 191; establishment of, 178;
  ethnic classification of, 192; evolution
  of Mongol Khanate titles and, 182–183;
  interpretation of national title of,
  183–186; Mongols as founders of, 178;
  non-Han ethnic groups and, 189; White
  Lotus Sect in, 194. *See also* Monghol
  Khanate

zeitgeist, national titles as mirroring,
  15–16
Zhang Binglin, "Republic of China" name
  origin and, 221–222
Zhao Hongyin, 20, 170–176, *172*
Zhao Kuangyin, 166; as Commander of
  Imperial Army, 167–169; as founder of

Song Dynasty, 20, 154, 165–168, *168*;
  Song national title and, *168*, 168–169
"Zhong Guo", China as, 6, 8
"Zhonghua", "Republic of China" /
  "People's Republic of China" and, 221,
  224
Zhou Dynasty, 3, 108, 128; "Zhou" (周)
  as clan/state name to title of dynasty,
  35–41, *38*; agriculture and, 34–41,
  37–38; *Annals of Zhou,* 33, 35–36, 44,
  104; Eastern Zhou Dynasty, 32, 44, 54;
  Empress Wu Zhao as "Divine Emperor
  of the Holy Mother," 141, 146–148; four
  periods of pre-Zhou history, 32–33; Later
  Zhou Dynasty, 3, 154, 157, 162, 167,
  169, 174; migration to Qixia Plain as
  beginning of, 33, 38–41; overthrowing
  of by Qin Dynasty, 32, 41, 44–45;
  overthrowing of Shang Dynasty by, 36,
  40–41; usurpation of Later Zhou by Zhao
  Kuangyin, 154, 167
Zhou Gong, 104; *vs.* Wang Mang, 78–80
"Zhou, later". *See* Later Zhou Dynasty
Zhu Wen, establishment of Liang Dynasty
  by, 151, 154–155
Zhu Yuanzhang (King of Wu): as "King of
  Light," 195, 199–200; establishment of
  "Da Ming" by, 189, 196–200. *See also*
  Ming Dynasty
Zizhi Tongjian-Han Ji, 76–78, 154;
  "Chronicle of Jin" of, 102; *Annals of
  Later Jin,* 156; *Annals of Later Zhou,*
  157; *Annals of Sui,* 116; *Annals of Tang,*
  124, 132, 146; *Annals of Wei,* 92
Zu Zhuan, 13–14, 20, 26, 129, 170–171
"Zui Taiping Xiaoling" (folk song, A Short
  Lyric of the Peaceful Society), 189–190